NIETZSCHE

Edited by
JOHN RICHARDSON
and
BRIAN LEITER

OXFORD
UNIVERSITY PRESS

OXFORD

UNIVERSITY PRESS

Great Clarendon Street, Oxford OX2 6DP

Oxford University Press is a department of the University of Oxford.
It furthers the University's objective of excellence in research, scholarship,
and education by publishing worldwide in

Oxford New York

Athens Auckland Bangkok Bogotá Buenos Aires Cape Town
Chennai Dar es Salaam Delhi Florence Hong Kong Istanbul Karachi
Kolkata Kuala Lumpur Madrid Melbourne Mexico City Mumbai Nairobi
Paris São Paulo Shanghai Singapore Taipei Tokyo Toronto Warsaw

with associated companies in Berlin Ibadan

Published in the United States
by Oxford University Press Inc., New York

Introduction and selection © Oxford University Press, 2001

First published 2001

British Library Cataloguing in Publication Data

Data available

Library of Congress Cataloging in Publication Data

Data available

ISBN 0-19-875270-9

1 3 5 7 9 10 8 6 4 2

Typeset in Times
by RefineCatch Limited, Bungay, Suffolk
Printed in Great Britain by
TJ International Ltd., Padstow, Cornwall

CONTENTS

A NOTE ON REFERENCES TO NIETZSCHE'S WORKS

We have standardized references to Nietzsche's works according to the following system. We cite by Nietzsche's section numbers, for example BGE 22. Where the book is divided into chapters or parts with separately numbered sections, we cite these by an intermediate roman numeral, for example GM I. 1. (Where one of our papers writes out the title of one of these chapters, we often retain it; for example TI, 'Skirmishes of an Untimely Man', 19.) *Ecce Homo*'s third chapter contains parts (with separately numbered sections) on most of Nietzsche's prior books; we cite these using the abbreviations for those books, for example EH III, BT 1. *Human, All Too Human* includes the works Nietzsche previously published as *Mixed Opinions and Maxims* and *The Wanderer and his Shadow*; we cite these as HH II and HH III.

Here are the abbreviations for Nietzsche's books:

A | *The Antichrist*
BGE | *Beyond Good and Evil*
BT | *The Birth of Tragedy*
CW | *The Case of Wagner*
D | *Daybreak*
EH | *Ecce Homo*
GM | *On the Genealogy of Morals*
GS | *The Gay Science*
HH | *Human, All Too Human*
NCW | *Nietzsche contra Wagner*
TI | *Twilight of the Idols*
UM | *Untimely Meditations*
Z | *Thus Spoke Zarathustra.*

We also cite by section number references to the posthumous selection from Nietzsche's notebooks:

WP | *The Will to Power.*

We use these abbreviations for Nietzsche's early, unpublished essays:

PTAG | 'Philosophy in the Tragic Age of the Greeks'
TL | 'On Truth and Lies in a Non-Moral Sense'.

We have let the papers retain their own systems for referring to German-language editions of Nietzsche's notebooks. The main editions in use are:

KGW   *Werke. Kritische Gesamtausgabe*, ed. Giorgio Colli and Mazzino
       Montinari (Berlin: Walter de Gruyter, 1967–).
KSA   *Sämtliche Werke. Kritische Studienausgabe in 15 Bänden*, ed.
       Giorgio Colli and Mazzino Montinari (Berlin: Walter de Gruyter,
       1967–77).

INTRODUCTION

JOHN RICHARDSON

Nietzsche anticipated chairs devoted to the study of his *Zarathustra*.[1] But could he have anticipated an Oxford Readings in Philosophy volume on his thought? And if he had, would he have welcomed it?

There is an air of anomaly in such a volume on Nietzsche—a way the medium and message seem to clash. Or, perhaps, it's the way both 'sides', Nietzsche and the (certain kind of) scholarly method that the Oxford Readings in Philosophy embody, seem to have reasons *against* being brought together. Each has grounds for dissatisfaction with the other—or so I think it is commonly seen and felt. I begin by looking quickly at some of the grounds for such hesitations. By first duly recognizing these factors, but then rebutting them, we can pose more clearly the main issues we face in Nietzsche. So what are these seeming incompatibilities?

On Nietzsche's side, there is his apparent scorn for many of the elements of this series' method—most broadly, for any '*scholarly*' account of him. He attacks scholars, and seems to renounce many of the virtues or practices I think we associate with good scholarship. Indeed, these include basic virtues we associate not just with scholarship but with philosophy—conceptual clarity, for example. And by renouncing these virtues—I think many now feel—he renders his writings adverse and unsuited to our study.

Consider, to begin with, his diagnosis and critique of 'scholars' (*Gelehrten*) in part 6 of *Beyond Good and Evil*. He here has a broad target: the practitioners of academic disciplines generally, the 'Wissenschaften' or sciences in an extended sense. He attacks in particular the effort by some of these[2] to play the role of genuine philosophers—to use science to do philosophy's job. They 'call themselves "philosophers of reality" or "positivists" . . . [but are] at best scholars and specialists themselves . . . all of them

---

[1] EH III. 1: 'Some day one will need institutions in which one lives and teaches as I understand living and teaching; perhaps one will then even set up professorial chairs for interpretation of Zarathustra.'

[2] Leiter argues (p. 308) that he especially means certain German materialists (physicians, physiologists, chemists), such as Büchner.

beaten, and *brought back* under the hegemony of science, after having once willed *more* of themselves without having had the right to this "more" and its responsibilities' (BGE 204). They lack what's needed for accomplishing the philosopher's true work, of 'creating values'; this requires a very different kind of thinking than scholars or scientists can manage (BGE 211, 213).[3]

Conceiving himself as such a philosopher, Nietzsche seems to renounce not only the scholars' virtues, but even the philosophical virtues that would suit him for scholarly study.[4] I should say more precisely what these virtues are, that he seems to reject and frustrate. I'll mention four—traits that we would like to bring to our study of him, or that we would need him to possess, to make such study worth while (these often coincide). Nietzsche seems to oppose each one. Several of these virtues are given special weight in the kind of philosophy (and philosophical scholarship) now commonly called '*analytic*', so Nietzsche's critique may seem especially applicable there.

A first thing such study would want to do is to say what Nietzsche 'means' by his main philosophical concepts and claims. A first scholarly virtue we would want to practise towards him is clarity about these concepts and claims: to give something like a definition for his main concepts, and to formulate his claims explicitly and precisely out of those concepts. But Nietzsche is famously resistant to having his 'meanings' pinned down in this way. Indeed, he seems to have arguments that this whole enterprise is misguided.

This effort at conceptual clarity is perhaps greatest, and perhaps most characteristic, in the case of analytic scholarship. Consider for a moment the form it takes there. It is not, of course, that the very business of analytic philosophy is 'conceptual analysis'.[5] Still, it is a characteristic move of this method to begin any investigation (or defence) of a claim by asking (or saying) 'what it means' by the key terms in which it is stated. It 'takes apart' these meanings, and then in turn the claim itself in terms of them.[6] These

---

[3] EH III, UM 3: 'I set my concept "philosopher" miles apart from a concept that includes even a Kant, not to mention from the academic "ruminants" and other professors of philosophy.' UM III. 7: 'A scholar can never become a philosopher; for Kant himself was not capable of it.' See also BGE 6, which allows scientific scholars a kind of objectivity philosophers must lack. Leiter (pp. 246–7) remarks that Nietzsche's conception of the philosopher as culture critic may make analytic philosophers uncomfortable.

[4] Z II. 16 ('On Scholars'): 'I have moved from the house of the scholars and I even banged the door behind me. . . . I am not, like them, trained to pursue knowledge as if it were nut-cracking.' (This is Zarathustra speaking.)

[5] Many are persuaded by Quine that there can be no genuine analyses—truths by virtue of meanings alone. And many more would deny that such analyses are the ultimate aim or product of philosophy. 'Analytic' is, if heard in these ways, a misleading label for the practice.

[6] It presents the claim as a statement (often set off from the text and labelled) clearly structuring these clarified concepts. And it tries to do the same at the level of arguments, carefully decomposing these into the premises and steps they comprise.

familiar moves of 'analysis' are important devices by which those who practise this method pursue the clarity and precision they prize. But, of course, philosophers through history have also pursued such clarity, and have been 'analytic' in this sense.[7] And so too have scholars of philosophers.

What, however, does Nietzsche say about analysis? HH I.2: 'All philosophers have the common failing, that they start out from humans of the present, and mean to reach their goal through an analysis (*Analyse*) of them.' Philosophers have been occupied with analysing the concepts, values, and practises common *now*: they either ignore altogether how these have 'become', or they tell a self-flattering story that depicts them as the 'goal' of a progressive development. So the project of analysis expresses a lack of *historical sense*, which is the 'inherited failing' of philosophers.[8] Such analysis can't reach the kind of meaning our concepts and values have. When we see how these have evolved, we see that this evolution has crystallized layers of meaning into them that can only be uncovered by genealogy, a retrospective diagnosis of how they came to be. So it is, for example, with the concept and practice of 'punishment', as Nietzsche famously develops this point in GM II. 13: its complex history has the result that this notion is 'hard to analyse and . . . completely *undefinable*'.[9]

It seems that Nietzsche would apply this point not just to the social concept and practice of punishment, but to philosophers' concepts as well. Here too meaning isn't settled by the individual's choices and intentions, but by the psychological and even social sources of the individual use.[10] Nietzsche denies that philosophers have been any more in control of their concepts, or more able to constrain them to an analysable simplicity; their own meanings aren't transparent to them.[11] And it is tempting to connect these points with what may seem like Nietzsche's own lack of interest in conceptual precision

---

[7] Hence the view that 'analytic' philosophy is not really a genre within philosophy, but is just *good* philosophy, by standards intrinsic to the discipline itself. An analogous kind of 'analysis' also seems characteristic of science.

[8] HH I. 2 again; also TI III. 1, WP 408.

[9] The point occurs elsewhere, e.g. at KSA 11. 40 [54] (1885). (For *Nachlass* notes not included in *The Will to Power* I give the location in the *Kritische Studienausgabe* (KSA): volume number, followed by notebook number, followed by note number in square brackets. I also include the date of the note in parentheses, which allows it to be located in the *Kritische Gesamtausgabe* (KGW) as well.) See Geuss (p. 332): 'Although the "meaning" imposed at any time by a successful will may in some sense be superseded by a later "meaning" (imposed by a later will), the original meaning will in general not go out of existence altogether but will remain embedded in at least a modified form'; also (p. 333).

[10] CW, Epilogue: 'all of us have in our bodies, without knowing, without willing, values, words, formulas, moralities of *opposite* descent' (he means of both master and slave values).

[11] WP 409: '[philosophers] have trusted concepts just as unconditionally as they mistrusted the senses: they have not considered that concepts and words are our inheritance from times, when heads were very dim and modest.'

or clarity. He doesn't even try to control his concepts in that way—to mean them in precise senses, and build ideas carefully from them. So how could we hope to analyse or explicate his concepts as our scholarly method wishes?

A second thing philosophical scholars will want from Nietzsche is *argument*—to say how he justifies his claims, what reasons he gives us for accepting what he says. If this scholarship is to have philosophical interest, these arguments will need to be compelling or plausible enough to evoke arguments of our own. But here again Nietzsche gives critiques and diagnoses that call in question his allegiance to the method—it may seem to be method itself—of reaching one's positions by lines of reasoning, and thereby justifying them to others.

Here he seems to think that philosophers, the genuine ones, have had it right: they don't follow such argumentative paths in finding their truths.[12] He makes Socrates the main culprit in an excess or overstressing of argument within philosophy: Socrates' development of eristic is a symptom of decadence.[13] Arguments are usually ineffective; they, and the opinions they purport to determine, are both just symptoms of certain deeper causes.[14] And as for those persuaded by arguments: a reverence for them betrays one's need to follow or obey.[15] Nietzsche even attacks logic itself as a pragmatic device resting upon certain false premises.[16] Once again, this whole critique of argument may seem especially at odds with analytic interests, but really poses a much broader threat to philosophical and scholarly method generally.

Again it is tempting to think that this critique affects his own practice. He sometimes purports to disdain and renounce argument himself.[17] He seems to embrace self-contradiction, and not to feel bound to follow logical rules. He proclaims that his own views issue out of him organically, not as the endpoints of research and reasoning.[18] Or he claims that they issue in bursts of inspiration that seem likewise irrational.[19] And when he

---

[12] He offers a romantic image of them as leaping from idea to idea as from peak to peak—not labouring up to their conclusions with reasons and inferences: PTAG 3.

[13] TI II. 4: 'Socrates' decadence is suggested . . . by the hypertrophy of the logical'; TI II. 6: 'One chooses dialectic only when one has no other means.' Also BT 13; HH II. 295; EH I. 1.

[14] GS 39: 'Opinions, with all proofs, refutations, and the whole intellectual masquerade, are merely symptoms of the change in [general] taste . . . '.

[15] TI II. 10 says that Socrates made reason his tyrant, to prevent his appetites' being so. See also BGE 213.

[16] See e.g. WP 512, 516.

[17] Zarathustra says (Z II. 17): 'I do not belong to those, whom one may ask about their why. | . . . It was long ago that I experienced the reasons (*Gründe*) for my opinions. | Would I not have to be a keg of memory if I wanted to have my reasons with me?' Nietzsche renounces an interest in 'refuting' positions or ideals: GM, Preface, 4; EH, Preface, 3; EH III, HH 1.

[18] See again GS 39.

[19] See e.g. EH III, Z 3.

tries to persuade us to these views, arguments—at least of the kind we expect from philosophers—can seem rare or absent. So he can look like an enemy of argument, not someone we could hope to engage in any current debates.

A third problem emerges when it comes to *evaluating* whatever claims and arguments we can find in Nietzsche. For here he seems to offend yet another of our virtues: our solidarity with (natural) *science*. Again, this allegiance seems especially strong in analytic practice, but surely is widely common in those engaging Nietzsche as 'philosophical scholars'. In assessing philosophical claims, most will enforce the minimal condition that for a position to be viable it must be consistent with scientific findings. Indeed, the naturalistic movement now dominant in analytic practice carries this a step further: philosophical answers must be not just consistent with scientific knowledge, but extracted or derived from it.[20]

Yet it often seems that Nietzsche applies no such condition—but instead quite a contrary one: philosophy must *detach* from science. He fights against what he sees as a prevailing tendency to assimilate philosophy to science, and warns against thinking the latter could take the place of the former.[21] His true philosophers even detach, it seems, from science's project of truth, since he often insists that they are creators, not discoverers.[22] So what allegiance to science could he himself have? This may seem to explain the apparent implausibility of some of his most famous ideas (will to power and the eternal recurrence, for a start).

There is a fourth basic virtue Nietzsche seems to oppose. Our own scholarly and philosophical practice allies itself with science in a further way: it adopts parts of the scientists' method or practice into its own 'discipline'. In particular, it tries to build a quasi-scientific *community* that makes overall progress by the specialized contributions of many interacting members. The 'analytic' strategy itself, of breaking problems into parts, encourages apportioning them to specialists, whose micro-progresses can then be accumulated by the community. I think this emulation of science is an important part of this analytic method's self-conception—a reason it feels able to make philosophical progress, pushing forward the level of argumentative clarity and comprehensiveness. But once again this is a trait and virtue of philosophers and scholars much more broadly.

---

[20] This is what Leiter calls 'results continuity' in his account of naturalism (p. 302).

[21] See again BGE 204; also BGE 211, WP 422.

[22] WP 972 says there are *both* kinds of philosophers; among the 'legislating' kind, some (e.g. Plato) 'deliberately blindfolded themselves' against recognizing their own creative act. Later, in BGE 211, those (e.g. Kant) who merely formulate existing values are demoted to the status of 'philosophical labourers'; for 'genuine philosophers', by contrast, 'their "knowing" is *creating*, their creating is a legislation, their will to truth is—*will to power*'.

And it stands in obvious contrast with Nietzsche's stress on the virtue of *solitude*.[23] He preaches (and practised) removal of oneself from such communities.[24] Being attracted into them is a symptom of the 'herd instinct'—of *needing* to find one's views from and in relation to others. Nietzsche also deplores the effects of this communal practice on individuals: it works precisely by forcing individuals into specialized niches that deprive them of the scope needed for philosophy.[25] Philosophers can't be thinking *together* with others this way—one more thing that distinguishes them from scientists and scholars.

In these several ways, Nietzsche seems to discourage a studious interest in him—opposing and belittling all the scholarly virtues we would practise on him, as well as the philosophical virtues we think would license that study, stressing their discontinuity with and inferiority to (what *he* thinks) the philosophical virtues themselves. He seems *not to want* his ideas to be handled this way, and to repel, with insults, those who would approach him so.[26] Are there any other philosophers who mock the eye that would study them? I think scholars analysing other philosophers face no such conflict between their own enterprise and the practice and values of the subject they study. Nietzsche seems to stand quite apart here.

These various campaigns Nietzsche fights, and what they suggest about his own intellectual practice have led many to doubt his suitability for scholarly (or analytic) study. He might *not* be a 'philosopher'—much less a good one—in the sense of the method or practice the Oxford Readings in Philosophy embody. If he dismisses logic and argument, can he really offer the right sort of materials for that method to work upon? If he denies that concepts are definable, and forsakes the effort to use them precisely and consistently, what kind of clarity about his thought could we hope for? In rejecting him, the series can, as it were, return Nietzsche's insults in

[23] See e.g. D, Preface, 2; EH III, Z 6.

[24] Compare the critique of the state of academic philosophy in UM III. 8. The only 'community' Nietzsche seems willing to count himself in is the line of great philosophers—the others all dead.

[25] TI VIII. 3 complains against 'the *despiritualizing* influence of our current [German] science-industry . . . The hard helotism to which the tremendous range of our sciences condemns every [scholar]'. GS 366: 'Almost always with the book of a scholar there is something oppressive, oppressed; the "specialist" emerges somewhere—his zeal, his seriousness, his fury, his over-estimation of the nook in which he sits and spins.' See WP 597.

[26] Z II. 16 (Zarathustra, again): 'so far I have been heard least well by the most scholarly. . . . I live *over* their heads with my thoughts.' GS 373: 'It follows from the laws of rank-order that scholars, insofar as they belong to the spiritual middle class, can never catch sight of the really *great* problems and question marks.' UM III. 8: 'for the genius . . . this rummaging about in the countless perverse opinions of others is about the most repulsive and unwelcome business imaginable'. EH II. 8: 'The scholar gives his whole strength . . . in the critique of what's already thought,—he himself no longer thinks.' See also UM III. 7; BGE 137; GS 366.

kind: wouldn't it have to lower its standards to accommodate such an inappropriate subject? These doubts are reinforced by some striking features of the secondary literature about Nietzsche, which has a quite different flavour and character from the writing on philosophers like Aristotle or Descartes. It is, for a start, remarkable for its sheer volume—which of course expresses the breadth of Nietzsche's appeal, the very wide and diverse audience for books about him. The popular and democratic nature of this appeal (so contrary to his insistence that he is addressing only the very 'few'), as well as his special reach to young people, have the consequence that most writing about him proceeds at an elementary level. This skewing is also reflected within philosophy departments' curricula. I wager that Nietzsche is much less taught at the graduate than at the undergraduate level, and at the latter, less in advanced than in introductory courses. There is a widespread sense that he appeals to a crude and impatient taste that will not survive a rigorous training in the field.

So it is partly on account of this skewed audience that the literature on Nietzsche is so mixed or uneven, both in interpretative style and in quality. But of course it is also because of all those aspersions Nietzsche throws against the scholarly virtues, and the very different model he himself sets for those attending to him. The way he is always deriding scholars and their values has been partly responsible, I think, for the extremely uneven scholarly standards of the writing on him. He is constantly inviting or tempting his readers out of scholarly ways of treating him. And, predictably, those most inclined to that way of analysing philosophers' concepts and arguments will tend not to judge him a viable subject for their work.

They have an additional reason to deny him in the company he keeps. Post-modernists and deconstructionists have rushed in where analytic philosophers have hesitated to step. They have claimed Nietzsche for their own—as an ancestor who laid the groundwork for their own philosophical methods, and who can only be adequately treated by those methods. They deny that analytic or scholarly handling can get at the kinds of truths Nietzsche has or intends.[27]

However, I think there are answers to all of these challenges. Turning to

---

[27] See Paul de Man's account (*Allegories of Reading: Figural Language in Rousseau, Nietzsche, Rilke, and Proust* (New Haven: Yale University Press, 1979), 98) of how one gets Nietzsche's meaning only out of the interplay between his 'metalinguistic statements about the rhetorical nature of language and . . . a rhetorical praxis that puts these statements in question'; he illustrates this 'deconstructive' approach in his surrounding reading of BT. See the analyses and critiques of de Man's reading of Nietzsche in M. Clark, 'Deconstructing *The Birth of Tragedy*', *International Studies in Philosophy*, 19/2 (1987), 67–75, and H. Staten, *Nietzsche's Voices* (Ithaca: Cornell University Press, 1990).

them now, we see that there are much stronger affinities between Nietzsche and our own, philosophical-scholarly practice than tend to appear at first. These affinities are more than enough to legitimize an exact and argumentative attention to him. And although they don't annul or obliterate all the differences I have just reviewed, they give them quite a different aspect or significance: rather than ruling out such study of him, they pose some of the most interesting problems that study must address.

Starting again on Nietzsche's side, there is a way in which his business is precisely to *clarify concepts*—but in that historical or evolutionary way we have seen he requires. So the passage above, from GM II. 13, said that punishment is 'hard to analyse and . . . completely *undefinable*': the analysis is hard (not impossible) *because* it can't be a definition—something that 'determines' a single meaning for the concept, in the way that 'present intentions' might be thought to do.[28] (So the usual way of arriving at definitions is by introspecting 'what we mean', or else evoking it by present intuitions on hypothetical cases.) Analysis is harder because it must be historical, and must reach out to the social and even species levels at which meanings are constituted. But 'analysis'—clarifying concepts—is still what needs to be done; Nietzsche doesn't limit *it* to its conventional form, but lets it grow into the new role he has for it. So we often find him proposing some task of 'analysis', or attacking analyses by others.[29] Analysis now requires *genealogy*, of the meanings layered into our words and practices by their histories.

Not only does Nietzsche promote a task of analysis, he also accepts the challenge to mean his terms precisely, in senses that *he* determines. He may appear to use terms casually and inconsistently. But, in fact, he thinks he uses them with a clarity others can't match. He claims this precisely by virtue of his insight into their genealogy, their social and historical sources and meanings. As the first to recognize what (for example) 'moral' means, by that extended genealogy of it, he can then use that and related terms with a new

---

[28] GM II. 13: 'Today it is impossible to say determinately why one is really punished: all concepts in which a whole process is semiotically held together evade definition; only what has no history is definable.' KSA 11. 40 [54] (1885): 'The *intentionality* of the action is not decisive in morality (it belongs to the short-sighted *individualistic* tendency). "End" and "means" are only symptomatic, in relation to the whole kind out of which we grow, in itself many-meaninged and nearly ungraspable.'

[29] KSA 8. 2 [107] (1877): 'The error of nearly every philosophy is a lack of knowledge of humans, an inaccurate psychological analysis.' Nietzsche is especially interested in finding an 'analysis' of the truth-drive (e.g. KSA 7. 29 [4] (1873)). BGE 186 says that philosophers (the example is Schopenhauer) have really been engaged in 'the opposite of an examination, analysis (*Zerlegung*), doubting, vivisection of this [moral] faith'; they have simply taken it for granted. Geuss, in Ch. 12, says that Nietzsche offers not a 'definition' of Christianity, but an ' "analysis" of the contingent synthesis of "meaning" . . . [it] . . . represents' (p. 333).

'transparency'. He is the first person to know what he means.[30] And, in fact, Nietzsche is insistent that he *has* meanings, which he is afraid his audience may miss.[31] This confidence in his ability to control his meanings gives us optimism that there are determinate meanings and claims for our own analyses of him.

Similarly, he cares much more for *argument* than his many critiques suggest.[32] His books are obviously full of arguments, though usually in non-standard forms. Here too we should see those critiques as intended not to renounce argument, but to amend it in form. He means to shift the *kind* of argument we need and should want. Given that the meanings of our words and practices lie in that history—in the social and psychological purposes they have served, that explain why we have them—the way to argue over meaning is to examine those sources (and not one's introspective intuitions on cases[33]). So the arguments Nietzsche quite characteristically gives are precisely those genealogies: social and psychological diagnoses *why* some belief or value is accepted. These arguments bear on the belief or value from a different angle than usual. But they have an argumentative structure, and a logic, that are suited to be analysed: here again method can work.

Nietzsche's relations with *science* are also much more friendly than they sometimes seem. He shares with analytic philosophy a strong naturalizing impulse—an effort to see through the mystifications of religion and metaphysics and to treat all aspects of the human with a scientific eye.[34] He intends that genealogical analysis to be a naturalistic or scientific account of human values and practices. He thinks this is precisely the domain in which science has so far been least effective, since these practices have so promoted a *false* analysis of themselves, which scientists have had a hard time throwing

---

[30] WP 409: 'What dawns on philosophers at last: they must no longer accept concepts as a gift ... they are, after all, the inheritance of our furthest, stupidest as well as shrewdest ancestors. . . . What is needed above all is an absolute skepticism against all inherited concepts.'

[31] He often explicitly offers definitions for concepts (e.g. TI IX. 43; A 10; EH III. 5), or speaks of 'my concept of . . . ' (e.g. TI IX. 38, 44). He often expresses the worry that he is not being understood (e.g. EH IV. 7).

[32] GS 348 praises Jews for making Europe think more logically, and for '*cleanlier*' intellectual habits'.

[33] Our intuitions about 'what we mean' carry very little weight, since they are generally designed to cast those beliefs and practices in a flattering light—designed, that is, by the same factors that sustain the practices themselves: the social and psychological roles they have been selected to play (and which must be extracted by genealogy). See BGE 295 on how Dionysus rejects our 'lovely solemn pomp- and virtue-names'.

[34] See e.g. GS 7, 109; BGE 230; A 14; EH III, HH 3. Note Zarathustra's defence of science in Z IV, 'On Science'. See B. Leiter, 'Nietzsche's Respect for Natural Science', *Times Literary Supplement*, 4983 (2 Oct. 1998), 30–1, on Nietzsche's naturalism. It is also clear that Nietzsche does not give up on truth; he claims indeed to be the most truthful person so far (see EH IV. 1).

off.[35] Even those who most seem and claim to have given a naturalistic account of these values and practices, the Darwinists, have really been in thrall to those values, and have merely reworked that false self-analysis. So Spencer, Nietzsche thinks, is really just an apologist for the conventional morality: he fabricates an evolutionary story depicting this morality as the goal of an inevitable progress.[36] Nietzsche claims to tackle these sensitive topics in a more fully scientific spirit than these scientists themselves have done.

And as for his contempt for scholars and their *communal* and incremental approach to knowledge, this is certainly consistent with his also appreciating their use, even their necessity. This appreciation is perhaps most evident in the Remark appended to GM I, which calls for the scientific and academic study of the evolution of moral concepts, through institution of a 'series of academic prize-essays'. Even if there is some jest in this note, Nietzsche elsewhere shows himself eager to set going a communal research project into values.[37] He also welcomes scholarly attention to himself.[38] And he even acknowledges his need for this scholarly outlook and practice *in himself*, as a tool for the larger work he claims for himself of creating values. The philosopher needs to assimilate and embody the strengths of these other types (scientist, scholar, genealogist), just as Nietzsche uses his original philological training, and the self-education in science he later lays over it.[39] In order to get to that work of making new values, one needs to go through genealogy—analysing the social and psychological sources of current values.

For all of these reasons Nietzsche is far more suited to our analytic and scholarly interests than at first appears. And, indeed, this approach has shown itself increasingly interested in Nietzsche—able to find profit in engaging with him. My impression is that he is more often introduced sympathetically and informedly into treatments of 'the issues themselves'. Together with this, the level of philosophical scholarship on him is quickly

[35] BGE 23: 'All psychology so far has remained stuck in moral prejudices and fears: it has not ventured into the depths.'

[36] WP 253: the omnipotence of faith in morality 'betrays itself in [the way] even the basic conditions of life are falsely interpreted for the benefit of morality: despite knowledge of the animal world and plant world. "Self-preservation": the Darwinian perspective for reconciliation of altruistic and egoistic principles'. Also WP 243 and 685.

[37] See esp. GS 7; also BGE 186, GM, Preface, 7, GS 345. There are many other places where he gives a positive though subordinate role to scholars; e.g. GM III. 23: 'the last thing I want is to spoil the pleasure these honest workers take in their craft: for I rejoice at their work'. Also BGE 39. See how A 59 blames Christianity for cheating Europe of the 'scholarly culture' already achieved by the Greeks and Romans.

[38] D, Preface, 5: 'My patient friends, this book desires for itself only perfect readers and philologists: *learn* to read me well!' Also GM, Preface, 8 and EH III. 5; compare GS 102. See n. 1 above.

[39] See BGE 211; GS 382. And again EH III, HH 3.

rising, by strengthening all four of the features I have mentioned. We see an ongoing increase in rigour, and in the extent to which discussion of his handling of topics is informed by acquaintance with current philosophical treatments of them. We also find an improving level of acquaintance with Nietzsche's texts (though perhaps still less commonly with the European secondary literature on him).

This improvement has been abetted by rapidly improving resources for scholarship, in the form of improved access to Nietzsche's works. For a start, we now have an array of new English translations of his books, good enough to compete with the Kaufmann(–Hollingdale) ones, which for so long were the only serious options. Still more important has been the economical and high-quality edition of Nietzsche's writings in German, the *Kritische Studienausgabe*, together with its more comprehensive parent, the *Kritische Gesamtausgabe*, both edited by Colli and Montinari and published by de Gruyter. These editions offer Nietzsche's *Nachlass* in something like the original state and order of the notebooks in which he recorded these thoughts, permitting much better scholarly attention to it. Moreover, this edition is now available on CD-ROM and in some academic contexts even on line—an invaluable scholarly resource allowing searches through his corpus for words or phrases. Such access will surely become standard for scholarly study of Nietzsche. Moreover, this Colli–Montinari edition will eventually become available to English readers in the Stanford University Press edition, edited by Bernd Magnus. This will make Nietzsche's (mature) *Nachlass* available to English readers for the first time, in something like the form in which he left it, rather than in the pastiche non-book *The Will to Power*.

The present volume will, it is hoped, do service in this same cause. It tries to gather together some of the best and most influential treatments of Nietzsche that have advanced this philosophical-scholarly discussion of him over the last twenty or so years. It tries to cover, with these selections, the main topics that have occupied such interpreters. All of the papers have been previously published, with the exception of Chapter 3, written for this volume by Peter Poellner.

For purposes of unity and coherence it largely excludes treatments within different interpretative genres. Familiarly, Nietzsche has appealed to audiences outside philosophy, and to audiences with very different notions of philosophy than our own. He has evoked from those audiences a literature that forgoes, for the most part, allegiance to scholarly or argumentative virtues—or else interprets those virtues very differently. He has been treated, in short, in the many different interpretative fashions that are commonly lumped together as 'Continental'. It cannot and need not be disputed that

Nietzsche *also* has affinities with their rather different projects and interests in him. And those approaches have borne fruits of use and even importance for scholarly readings of him. Several of the contributors to this volume acknowledge debts to that 'Continental' literature—to the readings by Heidegger, Foucault, and Deleuze, for example. As a sample of these other styles of approach, this volume includes Foucault's important essay on genealogy. One can gauge from it both the uses of this other literature and its differences from the tone that otherwise prevails.

In the rest of this Introduction, I survey the main topics these collected articles address. In the usual way, I introduce and summarize the articles by locating them as positions in a landscape of problems. I also take the liberty of sometimes filling out that landscape with certain further positions not represented in the articles but helpful, I think, in pulling the issues together. Throughout, I work with an eye on the same broad question I have been weighing so far, of Nietzsche's availability to philosophical-scholarly treatment. For even after we decide that he merits such treatment, we still face problems in seeing how to proceed with it. These problems arise all across the range of the main topics that need to be addressed in Nietzsche. We must tackle these problems in order to see just *how* our method can engage with him.

Before turning to the main issues, let me mention and set aside two background and technical problems. One of these arises in the interpretation of most philosophers, whereas the other is of unusual importance in Nietzsche's case.

The first is the issue of Nietzsche's philosophical development—the shifts in his views over his roughly twenty years of philosophical activity. What are the changes, and how significant are they? It is most common to distinguish three 'phases' of Nietzsche's writing: the quasi-Schopenhauerian one in *The Birth of Tragedy* and *Untimely Meditations* (written in 1869–76), the positivist and sceptical phase in *Human, All Too Human* and *Daybreak* (1876–81), and the mature views in the works from *The Gay Science* onwards (1881–8). There have been other schemas for Nietzsche's changes or stages.[40] However, none of these changes may go very deep. Nietzsche himself tries (especially in the new prefaces written in 1886 for the earlier works, and in *Ecce Homo*) to mark these differences, but he also insists on the ultimate unity and coherence of his works. He and others have remarked how even the Schopenhauerianism of his first books is already qualified and undermined (at times

---

[40] Clark has defended a quite different account of Nietzsche's philosophical development in M. Clark, *Nietzsche on Truth and Philosophy* (Cambridge: Cambridge University Press, 1990) and 'On Knowledge, Truth, and Value: Nietzsche's Debt to Schopenhauer and the Development of his Empiricism', in C. Janaway (ed.), *Willing and Nothingness: Schopenhauer as Nietzsche's Educator* (Oxford: Oxford University Press, 1998).

even without Nietzsche himself yet quite aware of it).[41] This problem of his changing viewpoint is bound up in the more general problem of his perspectivism, which I discuss below. Apart from this connection, I don't think the problem of development arises any differently for Nietzsche than for many other philosophers.[42]

The second question concerns Nietzsche's *Nachlass*, i.e. his notebooks.[43] Of course, other philosophers have left notes and drafts, which scholars reach into; but in Nietzsche's case their use is unusually controversial. Why this is so is a complicated matter, beginning with a historical point: it was Nietzsche's sister, with her abhorrent axes to grind, who first made use of this material, excerpting a small and perhaps unrepresentative sample as *The Will to Power*. So, on the one hand, she turned some of these notes into a 'book' that came to be treated almost interchangeably with his genuine books. This was carried a step further by Heidegger, who famously claimed that this *Nachlass* material is *more* reliable and illuminating of Nietzsche's views than the books. And, on the other hand, in backlash to this abuse, many have taken use of the notebooks to be thoroughly discredited and suspect. It is argued that Nietzsche takes positions in the notebooks that he thought better of, positions that are either not present in his published books, or at least less common and less central there. Foremost among these positions is the ontology or metaphysics of will to power; I come back to this below.

Let us turn now to the main issues themselves. In introducing and organizing them, I think it is helpful to divide them into those that concern the 'content' of Nietzsche's writing and those that concern its 'tone' or 'force'. Part of Nietzsche's point is to erode or reconfigure the distinction between these,[44] but we best get at that point by beginning with this familiar division.

[1] Let us start with the question of Nietzsche's 'tone'. Perhaps what is most immediately striking about him is *how he writes* (not what he says). His books are so unlike other philosophical texts as to seem to belong to (or constitute) a different genre. We could put the point in different ways: he

---

[41] See BT, 'Attempt at a Self-Criticism', 6; EH III, BT 1–2; and EH III, UM 3. De Man, *Allegories of Reading*, puts great stress on the self-subverting (self-deconstructing) character of BT.

[42] There is a subordinate problem peculiar to Nietzsche: should we disregard his very last works, or at least read them differently, in the light of his coming madness? Should we, for example, discount the still more blaring hyperbole typical of *The Antichrist* and *Ecce Homo*?

[43] On this topic, see B. Magnus, 'The Use and Abuse of *The Will to Power*', in R. Solomon and K. Higgins (eds.), *Reading Nietzsche* (New York: Oxford University Press, 1988) and R. Schacht, 'Nietzsche as Colleague', *International Studies in Philosophy*, 22/2 (1990), 59–66.

[44] So A. Nehamas, *Nietzsche: Life as Literature* (Cambridge, Mass.: Harvard University Press, 1985), 39.

writes (as if) from an unusual persona; he performs a different kind of 'speech act' than other philosophers do. So a first challenge, before we can understand any of his particular views or positions, is to determine how he means what he says.

Because this matter is presupposed by all those particular matters of 'content', each of the papers included in this volume must at least touch on it. In attributing some view to Nietzsche, each needs to give evidence by citing what he says; but this evidence can only be employed on the basis of decisions about how he means it. With most other philosophers this question of tone doesn't arise, because they all alike adopt the same persona, purporting to perform the speech act of a rational truth-seeker conveying truths to other such seekers. So their tone seems obvious, as well as completely 'transparent' onto the content they assert. Nietzsche sometimes speaks in this vein, but often does not. Indeed, as Nehamas has developed, it is not just that he has a different tone, but that he has *many* tones or styles.[45] He exhibits a 'stylistic pluralism' that further complicates our problem: to reach his claims, we must learn to distinguish and interpret these 'multifarious' styles.

Our common and central interest in all these styles is their relation to that traditional philosophical speech act of conveying rational truths. Is Nietzsche's 'tone' that of someone who is telling us the truth? It is only if he still, sometimes and to some extent, performs this speech act that there would be a philosophical content, 'something he says', at all. And so we try to recognize this speech act and content 'through' those styles—how Nietzsche is still 'saying something' in them. But those styles are not transparent onto any such content in the way the conventional philosophical style seems to be.[46] This might lead us to suspect that his point in adopting these styles is to *renounce* that speech act altogether—to cut himself loose from the business of 'saying how things are', and commit himself to quite different goals than stating truths.

One tempting response to this problem is to focus on those works or passages in which Nietzsche's style looks most like the standard philosophical one: where he *does* seem to advance positions, and to give

---

[45] Ibid. 18. He mentions, among others, the styles of BT ('depend[ing] on the form of a scholarly treatise', UM ('essays in a most classical sense'), and BGE ('a monologue [exhibiting] a definite and striking personality').

[46] Some will, no doubt, suspect that this opaqueness is deliberate, and that Nietzsche is aware his views won't survive exposure in clear light. When we strip off the style, is there really much content left? Don't his ideas get most of their appeal from the strikingness with which he offers them, and look thin and implausible when that glittering surface is removed? When we turn to his 'content', one challenge will be to answer these doubts.

arguments for them. We might ignore (at first) the contexts where his tone is notably different, as in *Thus Spoke Zarathustra*, his poetry, or even (as a diatribe) *The Antichrist*. By focusing on the more soberly discursive passages, we could hope to identify a 'content' of positions and arguments, from which we might come back to those more florid works, to read them as gestures presupposing that content. I think it is this strategy that attracts many people to the notebooks, where Nietzsche's writing has much less stylistic overlay and tends to give plainer statements of positions and arguments. But the scarcity of this fact-arguing idiom in his books themselves counts against giving it this kind of priority.[47]

This problem about Nietzsche's styles is confirmed and given shape by many of the 'methodological' remarks he makes—above all those having to do with *truth* and *perspectivism*. His critiques of truth, and the 'perspectivism' he famously proclaims, are our most direct evidence in interpreting his many tones and styles. They suggest that he has principled reasons for avoiding that usual idiom or speech act, of stating and arguing rational truths. These topics are addressed in the papers by Gemes, Clark, and Poellner (Chapters 1–3), which are therefore the ones most relevant to this general problem of tone.

Nietzsche's critique of truth has been much discussed. Sometimes he gives arguments against its value, other times against its very existence or possibility, advancing what I shall call a 'truth-nihilism' or a *no-truth theory*.[48] Our main question is whether he himself still cares about, and aims at, truth—whether he offers what he says as (intended to be, trying to be) 'true'. Given his various critical remarks, the question presses itself on us. It is reinforced by what he says that he (or 'the philosopher') does do. As we have seen, he says that the philosopher's primary task is to create values, not to discover truths. And the philosopher writes in order to propagate those values in the audience, which need not be by reasons or arguments.[49]

This forces us back into doubts addressed above. Since we won't, I think, concur in so detaching philosophy from truth, Nietzsche's depictions of philosophy really give us grounds for doubting that he is a philosopher in

---

[47] So I don't think we should follow Heidegger in treating the *Nachlass* as where Nietzsche's views are most forthright and perspicuous—the time when he really says, as it were to himself, what he thinks, whereas all his writerly styles are 'masks' he puts on for some audience. We can't, for a start, be so sure that even in his notebooks ('by himself') Nietzsche doesn't speak always within some adopted persona. But more importantly, it is surely in his books that we get 'the real Nietzsche'—even if we do need to read it *through* (by taking account of) those styles and masks. For the notebooks clearly serve his books, and Nietzsche culls from the former to give the latter as his best.

[48] See e.g. GS 265; WP 539, 616.

[49] On value-creating, see n. 22 above. In EH III. 4 he says that his many styles are designed to communicate 'an inner tension of pathos'.

our sense. Indeed, if he doesn't intend his claims to be true (i.e. to be as true as possible—if he doesn't aim them at truth), why should we take them seriously? And if he neither offers nor has any reasons (rational grounds) why we should take on his views ourselves, shouldn't we rather mistrust his exhortations to us? His writerly strategies now appear to be mere propaganda for his values and other inventions.

This would, in particular, deflate and vitiate the kind of arguments we have seen that Nietzsche characteristically employs—his genealogies. When he diagnoses Christianity, for example, he attributes it to certain historical and psychological sources, such as resentment and bad conscience. Can he really dispense with the claim that these diagnoses are true? When he attacks Christianity for its inhibiting and spoiling effects on exceptional individuals, can he dispense with his claim that it *does have* these effects? Without these truth-claims about Christianity's sources and effects, I think Nietzsche's account and assessment of it would lose their title to our attention.

Not only does this disengagement from truth seem to take away our grounds for interest in what he says, it also seems to land Nietzsche in deep self-contradiction and paradox. Analytic readers have often raised this issue, posing it as the question whether Nietzsche's critique of truth, or else his perspectivism (which we should bring in now too), is self-refuting.[50] These two paradoxes can be posed as questions: How could it be true, that there is no truth? And how could the perspectivism *not* be just a perspective? These questions bring out how both the truth-nihilism and the perspectivism seem to undermine themselves: if either is true, then it is false.

Since the no-truth view (as well as the unqualified perspectivism) would undermine Nietzsche's claims to our attention, and even land him in incoherence, we have reason to reinterpret the point of his critique of truth. Perhaps the critique aims to deny and disavow not truth altogether, but only a certain conception of truth, or certain reasons for wanting it. So it is not truth per se, but only a notion of truth, or a motivation towards it, that is the target. There have been many versions of this general strategy of ameliorating (and rendering coherent) Nietzsche's attacks on truth, by defining and restricting their target.

Gemes ('Nietzsche's Critique of Truth', Chapter 1) gives one main version. He argues that Nietzsche's critique is not meant to rule out truth (or claims to truth), which he agrees would be paradoxical. But nor is it meant to revise the notion of truth by advancing a new truth-theory. Instead, Gemes argues, Nietzsche 'is not interested in the notion of truth per se' (p. 56), nor in the business of saying what it is. Rather, he is interested in 'the

---

[50] Clark, *Nietzsche on Truth and Philosophy*, 3–4, puts it well.

role that the concept and rhetoric of truth has played within various cultures' (p. 41), and in whether people have been helped or hurt by the project of truth.[51] Aiming at truth—adopting the project of matching one's views to reality—betrays an effort to escape the responsibility of authoring those views oneself. Moreover, even the possession of truth can be harmful, since illusions are necessary for life. So (on Gemes's account) Nietzsche's attack bears mainly on the *value* of truth—but of truth as we want it. He has no theory about what truth itself is, and offers no arguments about it, nor against it. This makes him exempt from the self-refuting paradoxes.

We may call this the *no truth-theory* reading of Nietzsche (by contrast with the 'no-truth theory' reading of him). First we should set aside one kind of reason for denying such a theory to Nietzsche: that he gives no sustained treatment of the topic, that his views must be pieced together from scattered contexts, and that when they are they seem a diverse and even divergent (contradictory) lot. This is, of course, the state of affairs for *many* of Nietzsche's topics. He seems not to offer us anything as coherent as a 'theory' on most topics we notice, but only passing and disjointed reflections. This is just another aspect of the very problem we have been dealing with—whether he still aims at truth.

But this is not, I think, Gemes's ground for denying that Nietzsche has a truth-theory. Instead he refers to Nietzsche's repeated effort to shift attention from the topics (like truth) philosophers have always addressed, to psychological and social diagnoses why or how those topics have been raised and treated as they have been. Gemes refers, that is, to Nietzsche's persistent 'subjectivizing' of the existing questions—his asking about the asking of them. So if he has theories, it might seem he has only the theories involved in those psychosocial diagnoses. He is not interested in, and takes no positions on, those philosophical issues themselves. Since he takes no positions on truth, Gemes argues, he never denies or rules it out, and is not subject to self-refutation.

Others, however, have doubted that Nietzsche can avoid taking positions about truth. How can he, when his own teachings involve or depend on truth-claims—when it is, after all, a certain kind of *insight* that he flaunts and vaunts to us, in demanding our attention and interest? How can he coherently sustain this claim to be more knowing than we—which is surely a strong ingredient in most of those many tones he adopts—without some sense of how *his* known truth escapes the criticisms he directs against

---

[51] Geuss concurs (p. 329): 'see him not as trying to propound his own variant theory of truth, but as formulating a new question "How and why does the will-to-truth come about?"'

'truth'?[52] Mustn't we suppose that the sense in which he means his views true, reflects the critiques he makes of truth's possibility and value—that he means them in a way that somehow avoids or survives those critiques? Such questions have led other readers to the second main strategy for saving Nietzsche from self-refutation: by distinguishing the kind of truth he attacks from the kind he purports to have.

In this effort to state Nietzsche's positive sense of his truth, all those criticisms of truth are principal data. It would seem a surprising blindness and lack of self-awareness in Nietzsche if he did *not* adjust his own practice (his 'tone') to his criticisms in this way. Since those attacks are against certain 'aspects' of truth, or certain motives for wanting it, we can use them as information 'in negative' about the kind of truth he favours. There have been various accounts of what Nietzsche's new kind of truth might be.

Danto gave early expression to one option, arguing that Nietzsche advances a 'pragmatist theory of truth'.[53] However, I think by now this reading has been convincingly rebutted.[54] Nietzsche constantly *judges* truth by pragmatic standards, finding it harmful in various ways; so he can't *define* truth pragmatically. There are, however, other accounts of what this revised notion of truth might be.

The obvious and most promising candidate for a Nietzschean notion of truth is '*perspectival truth*', which joins together truth and what had seemed the main objection to it. The challenge, of course, is to specify how these apparent incompatibles *can* be conjoined—especially in the light of Nietzsche's occasional suggestions that they can't.[55] What kind of truth can it be if it is (just) perspectival? The perspectivism holds, in brief, that all views and claims are perspectives. But what are perspectives, and what does their perspectivity entail? What kind of truth does it rule out, and what kind does it allow? In reconciling these seeming incompatibles, we must try to do justice to both, and not sacrifice either truth or perspectivism to the other.

We also need to avoid what is a common practice here, of shoving the two together and opportunistically stressing whichever is more useful at the moment. This happens in a common way of proceeding with Nietzsche: one reads his views straight—as meant to be true—up to the point where one

---

[52] Including, we should notice, the critique of truth's value. For doesn't Nietzsche think that *his* truths—such as his insights into Christianity's motives and effects, his diagnosis of our historical and social situation—are of surpassing value and importance?

[53] A. Danto, *Nietzsche as Philosopher* (New York: MacMillan, 1965), e.g. 80. He acknowledges that Nietzsche's language often reflects a correspondence theory of truth, which Nietzsche couldn't clearly detach himself from.

[54] See e.g. Geuss's paper (pp. 327–8). Also Nehamas, *Nietzsche*, 52 ff.

[55] e.g. WP 540, which argues from 'many eyes' to 'many truths' to 'no truth'; see also WP 616. It should be noted that Nietzsche uses the expression 'perspectival truth' only twice, in WP 563 and 565, and that in the latter 'truths' is in scare quotes.

arrives at something one cannot stomach (for example, his attack on pity, or his views on women), when this point is passed off as self-avowedly 'just his perspective'. Indeed, Nietzsche makes this move himself, at this very point; in BGE 231: ' . . . I shall perhaps be permitted . . . to express a few truths about "woman as such": assuming that one knows now beforehand how very much these are after all only—*my* truths'. If *all* of his truths are perspectival, there seems nothing to justify the different way *these* are here being offered to us.

The papers by Clark and Poellner give conflicting—though also related—accounts of this perspectival truth. What they have in common is their beginning with a Kantian, or rather a neo-Kantian model for Nietzsche's view. They read perspectival truth as basically like the 'phenomenal' (or empirical or internal) truth in Kant, with the exception that the very notion of the 'noumenal', things-in-themselves, is ruled out as incoherent (which I shall take to be the principal neo-Kantian revision). This has the effect of validating our empirical knowledge by expunging any reality it could never reach. So both Clark and Poellner chiefly read Nietzsche's perspectivism as an anti-sceptical idea. Its effect is to show truth not more difficult than we had thought, but more feasible. In this they contrast with the way the perspectivism is more commonly read—as damaging our claims to know.

Clark ('The Development of Nietzsche's Later Position on Truth', Chapter 2) argues that this neo-Kantianism is Nietzsche's mature position, represented in his last six books (after *Beyond Good and Evil*). She recounts his evolution towards it, from the early views in *On Truth and Lie in an Extra-Moral Sense* (the essay draft that has been so important to deconstructionists), where he held a 'falsification theory', rejecting science and common sense as inevitably false. The crucial turning point, on Clark's account, is Nietzsche's recognition (first achieved in *The Gay Science*) that a thing-in-itself is inconceivable and impossible.[56] Without any such noumenal reality for our empirical knowledge to fall short of, there is no longer any reason to count that knowledge false. And in those last works, Clark claims, Nietzsche does not say that science, causation, logic, or mathematics is false; those works 'exhibit a uniform and unambiguous respect for facts, the senses, and science' (p. 67).

Although Clark does not treat Nietzsche's perspectivism in the chapter included here, in the one that follows it in her book[57] she reads it to make this

---

[56] It should be noted that Clark revises this chronology in 'On Knowledge, Truth, and Value', now dating Nietzsche's embrace of the possibility of empirical truths back to *Human All Too Human*; she also somewhat restates Nietzsche's motive for the turn.

[57] 'Perspectivism', ch. 5 in Clark, *Nietzsche on Truth and Philosophy*. The passages quoted in the text are on pp. 128, 132, 134.

very point: it is 'a metaphorical expression of Nietzsche's neo-Kantian position on truth that is designed to help us overcome the falsification thesis'; it 'invites us to think of what things are in themselves as the cognitive equivalent of . . . what they would look like from nowhere'. Hence 'perspectivism excludes only something contradictory', and to say that a view is a perspective is *not* to imply that it distorts, or is false. Clark (influenced by Putnam) reads the thing-in-itself as a (would-be) reality independent not just of our capacities, but of our cognitive interests. So when Nietzsche rules out the thing-in-itself, he is denying that 'what would satisfy our best standards of rational acceptability might still be false'. Science is true, to the extent and degree that it satisfies those cognitive interests.

Poellner ('Perspectival Truth', Chapter 3) in some ways treats Nietzsche still more faithfully to that neo-Kantian model. He attributes to Nietzsche the principle of essential representation dependence (ERD), that (spatio-temporal) objects must have characteristics 'that mark them out as represented' (p. 91). So he finds in Nietzsche something like Kant's claim that space, time, and the categories are all ways we require objects to be, ways we 'construct' them. It is easy to see how Nietzsche could have received these views through Schopenhauer. Poellner thinks Nietzsche grounds this claim of ERD in an 'empiricist conception of thought' (p. 92), together with an argument that we cannot conceive of (imagine) any object not qualified by characteristics marking it as represented.

Poellner also attributes to Nietzsche a principle of essential interest dependence (EID), that our concept of objective reality limits it to what is 'relevantly related to our actual dominant concerns' (p. 106). Here Poellner gives a different account of the 'interests' that Nietzsche claims our (phenomenal) reality is determined by. Clark thinks it is our *hypothetical cognitive* interests that dictate the limits of Nietzsche's reality: reality cannot exceed what our ideal knower (as projected by those 'standards of rational acceptability') could discover. Poellner objects (p. 96 n. 20) that this doesn't limit reality enough (as it were): if Nietzsche were excluding (as an incoherent thing-in-itself) *only* something eluding that ideal knower, he would not be denying what anyone (not even Kant[58]) would affirm. This would drain Nietzsche's view not just of its radical intent, but of philosophical interest altogether. But instead, Poellner argues, Nietzsche ties reality not to hypothetical cognitive interests, but to our *strongest actual* interests, which will usually *not* be cognitive (p. 107).

Poellner here identifies an important way in which Nietzsche's 'perspectivism' goes beyond Kant's 'phenomenalism'—a way itself prepared in

---

[58] Inasmuch as Kant conceives of an 'intuitive intellect' with access to the thing-in-itself.

Schopenhauer. Nietzsche looks for the subtle and concealed ways certain practical interests shape our theories and dictate the kind of reality they can reveal. So he shifts attention from the structure of our cognition itself—its structuring by certain a priori intuitions and concepts, which Kant had stressed—to certain external forces or motives that typically control cognition. Above all, these motives are our interests in survival and in power. Nietzsche's diagnoses of the 'perspectivity' of our theories, including our scientific theories, show how they are shaped by those external interests.[59] He often puts this as their subjection to (and expression of) some 'will to power'.

Poellner's insistence on the role of interest gives Nietzsche a more sceptical edge than he has in the purer neo-Kantian reading.[60] But there is room, I think, for a position that gives still more weight to this sceptical aspect. In the spirit of 'mapping the available options', I shall sketch this more sceptical reading of perspectival truth. It brings out an aspect of Nietzsche's overall tone that will be important when we turn to consider his content, his ideas themselves.

Although Nietzsche does indeed use his perspectivism (the inevitability of perspectivity) to validate our empirical knowledge—by *in*validating the noumenal standard it would fail—surely his *usual* use of it is quite different. His usual aim and effect, on those innumerable occasions when he 'uncovers' the perspectivity of some claim, is to *undermine* that claim.[61] When he analyses perspectives, in his omnipresent diagnoses, the effect is generally to reduce their epistemic standing: those holding these views *don't* know, in the way they think they do. Rather than validating these particular views, the pervasive and cumulative effect of Nietzsche's analyses is: by seeing how interests other than truth have shaped our views, we feel their claims to truth eroded or discredited. A more sceptical reading of perspectival truth would put more weight on this critical and undermining aspect of perspectivity; it

---

[59] This difference is not contradicted by Kant's admission of practical and aesthetic a prioris—ways we must think of reality, for the sake of being able to will and feel about it as we require. For Kant stresses that these other a prioris are *not constitutive* of reality, and don't enter into our determinative theories about it; only the forms of intuition and categories play a constitutive role.

[60] Kant's dominant aim is to *justify* science by showing it underwritten by certain universal and necessary a prioris: space, time, and the categories. Within these, we can get the truth about phenomena, which is all we can know. And the neo-Kantians make this justification more complete, by ruling out as incoherent any 'noumena' that would transcend these constraints.

[61] Notice that on the *only* occasion when Nietzsche uses the term 'perspectivism' (*Perspektivismus*) in his books, it has this undermining point: GS 354: 'This is the genuine phenomenalism and perspectivism, as *I* understand them: the nature of *animal consciousness* brings with it, that the world of which we can become conscious is only a surface- and sign-world . . . '. (The word's only appearances in the *Nachlass* are KSA 12. 7 [21] (1886–7), WP 481 and 636, which see.) Note also the upshot of GS 374. But I mainly have in mind not such programmatic statements, but Nietzsche's many 'local' exposures of perspectives. He more often speaks of 'perspectival illusion' than of perspectival truth; see n. 55 above.

faces the challenge of fitting this together with perspectivism's positive role (stressed by Clark) of justifying science and allowing truth.

One way to preserve both sceptical and positive lessons would be to treat Nietzsche's sceptical move—always diagnosing and deflating perspectives— as precisely his method for truth. Or at least, it is his method for truth about *us*, in our meanings and perspectives. Understanding us is always a matter of seeing the *limits* to our perspectives, their 'partiality', the ways in which they are incomplete and therefore (in a very extended sense) unjust. So the diagnostic move, exposing this partiality, is the crucial move in the kind of knowing Nietzsche is most interested in.[62]

On this reading, Nietzsche draws a different lesson from our perspectivity than I think the neo-Kantian reading suggests. The lesson is not, as it were, to accept and put up with our perspectivity, on the ground that there is no noumenal reality it falls short of. Nor are we just to be reconciled to the inevitable role of our interests, including non-cognitive interests, in dictating our views. Here a certain shift from Kant is key: by making our views the expressions of particular and contingent 'interests', rather than of Kant's universal and necessary 'conditions of the possibility' of human experience, Nietzsche leaves room for overcoming these constraints—in their particular instances, though not overall.

So, this last reading argues, Nietzsche's lesson from perspectivism is not to comfort himself that such constraints are inevitable, and to learn to live with the ones he has. Instead, his ideal person (and ideal philosopher) is someone who works ceaselessly to lay bare the particular ways these interests have shaped or dictated theories and values. And this is Nietzsche's own unrelenting effort in all of his books.[63] So while his perspectivism assigns us to perspectivity, the lesson is not to embrace it, but to intensify our efforts against it, from within it. We are, as it were, to *sculpt* this perspectivity—by cutting much of it away.

I'll return to these points below, in relation to three main issues about Nietzsche's content: his immoralism, his notion of freedom, and his method of genealogy. I'll try to show that this sceptical aspect of his perspectivism can help us to understand and connect those three main ideas. The method for knowing perspectives by diagnosing them will get developed as Nietzsche's 'genealogy', and the particular way it undermines Christianity

---

[62] HH I, Preface, 6: 'You shall learn to grasp the perspectival in every valuation—the displacement, distortion and seeming teleology of horizons and all that belongs to the perspectival.' EH IV. 1: 'I was the first to *discover* the truth, by being the first to experience lies as lies.'

[63] A 54: 'great spirits are skeptics. Zarathustra is a skeptic. Strength, *freedom* through force and hyperforce of spirit, *proves* itself by skepticism.' On Nietzsche's own practice, cf. e.g. HH I, Preface, 1 ('I myself do not believe that anyone has ever looked into the world with an equally deep suspicion').

and our prevailing values will clarify the force of his 'immoralism'. And this act of baring perspectives by critical diagnoses will be (one way of reading) his ideal of 'freedom'.

To sum up these several options on Nietzsche's 'tone': The general problem they address is how his attacks on truth can be reconciled with his own need to claim some truths for himself. One option, represented by Gemes, is to read him as making no claims about truth itself, being interested only in our attitudes about it. The other main option, represented by Clark and Poellner, and the sceptical variant I have sketched, is to allow that he attacks truth—but only a certain kind of truth, different from the perspectival truth he claims. The challenge is then to say precisely how perspectivism alters truth—to specify this in a way that both does justice to the radical, undermining effect Nietzsche thinks the perspectivism has, but that also lets him aim his own views at a kind of truth with the weight he wants those views to have.

[2] When we turn to Nietzsche's 'content', i.e. what he says, it looks hard, initially, to find philosophical 'grip' in his most familar ideas. Can any of them be taken seriously? When we line up the best known of Nietzsche's 'teachings', they look a rather implausible lot, especially as we think of subjecting them to analytic scrutiny. The death of God, the overman, will to power, eternal return, the master and slave moralities, the Apollonian and Dionysian art-drives—these are the views most associated with him in the common awareness. But none of them looks to survive that scrutiny, or to constitute a plausible move in any live debate.

Once again we must bear in mind the option sketched by Gemes, of denying that Nietzsche really means these as 'philosophical doctrines', in answer to the problems of his predecessors. Perhaps he instead intends certain psychological or sociological insights, about the attitudes or perspectives in which these views are held. When he examines other philosophers' beliefs, it is often as psychic or social phenomena, and not in their contents' match with reality. Maybe some of his own pronouncements have that status too, and he offers them not as true, but as healthy or strengthening. Perhaps he is really depicting and commending to us the type of person who would hold these views.

In treating each of those familiar teachings, it is crucial to keep this issue in mind. Even if, as I think, there is in each of them always *some* truth-claim lurking in or behind the idea, none of them is just simply and transparently such a claim. All of them are subjectivized in one way or another, i.e. stated in some different tone from that of an objective truth-claim. In each case, the key to Nietzsche's point is to catch this tone—to analyse the particular speech act he performs in offering it.

The teaching that most obviously wears its subjectivist nature on its sleeve is the '*death of God*'. Although stated as a claim about the entity theology treats, it is (almost) never read so, but instead as stating a social and historical point about a decay of faith in God, along with the morality and metaphysics associated with that faith. This use of a seemingly objective statement (about some *x*) to make a subjective point (about *views about x*) is a clearest case of a strategy Nietzsche deploys very commonly, though often much more subtly (what makes the use unsubtle here is that Nietzsche so clearly disbelieves in the *x*). We should note, however, that there is still a truth-claim being made here—about those views about God. It is meant to be true that a certain overall social-historical shift is in process, and Nietzsche offers further hypotheses about why (e.g. that the Christian values undermine themselves).[64]

The issue of subjectivity arises a bit differently in the teaching of '*eternal recurrence*'. This idea is often read as making a 'cosmological' claim: reality—the universe—repeats itself endlessly in vast cycles identical down to the smallest detail. But although Nietzsche does (especially in his notebooks) try out arguments for this cosmological claim, many recent interpreters have thought that his real point is something else, and that the key to the idea is *not* to read it straight. Familiarly, Nietzsche mainly employs it as a thought experiment, as a test or challenge: *are* you the kind of person who can welcome the thought of your life, and the world in general, repeating down to the smallest details? *try to be* such a person! And, it is now often thought, this use as a test or challenge does not depend on the cosmological claim being true—which is fortunate for Nietzsche, since he has no good arguments for it.

Nehamas ('The Eternal Recurrence', Chapter 4[65]) argues convincingly against the cosmological claim. Although Nietzsche sometimes slips into making it, the use he mainly has for the idea of eternal recurrence doesn't depend on it, and may even be at odds with it.[66] However, Nehamas does not detach the psychological use of that idea from the making of any claim whatsoever: it still rests on a (purported) truth. This approach has the great advantage that it gives Nietzsche a *justification* for his psychological challenge to us. There must be some correlation between the thought

---

[64] There is still this truth-claim, *unless* Nietzsche's point is inflected and disguised still further, and he says that there *is* (and must be) this decay in faith, only as a way of inducing or encouraging it. I shall return to this strategy of reading Nietzsche to 'value but not assert' below.

[65] Revised as 'This Life—Your Eternal Life', ch. 5 in Nehamas, *Nietzsche*.

[66] Nehamas repeats (p. 126) Soll's argument that since psychological continuity is required for concern with self, and there is no such continuity with our past or future lives, we should be indifferent about them—which is of course not an attitude Nietzsche associates with eternal recurrence.

experiment and the way we and the world really are—for why else would it push us 'in the right direction'? If it is not strictly true that all my life will recur, this must still reflect some *other* truth about my life for that test to be apposite.

Nehamas thinks Nietzsche does root the test in a 'metaphysical' truth—but one that is hypothetical, not categorical. He states it as, 'If my life were to recur, it would recur in exactly identical fashion,' (p. 127), along with its generalization, 'If anything in the world recurred (including an individual life, or even a moment of it), then everything in the world would recur in exactly identical fashion' (p. 129). Nehamas thinks Nietzsche bases this claim on his doctrine that 'a thing is the sum of its effects'—such that all our actions are essential to us. And the lesson for us is to strive towards 'a life so organized and coherent that if anything in it were changed, everything in it would fall apart' (p. 134). By giving life such unity, we would be able to affirm it as it (metaphysically) is, i.e. with all its actions essential to it.[67] Nehamas goes on to develop this lesson with his well-known analogy to literary characters: we are to give our lives the kind of unity such characters' lives possess.

These questions of 'tone' and truth-claim arise for another of Nietzsche's best-known teachings, the *'will to power'*. As with the eternal recurrence, many have found this idea implausible, understood as a straightforward, factual claim. When Nietzsche presents it as an ontology—claiming that 'the world' or 'everything' is will to power—it seems a laughable piece of animism. And when, more commonly, he restricts it to 'life', or even just to humans (which is, of course, where he mostly applies it), he still claims for it a pervasive or basic role, either in biology or in psychology, which it cannot plausibly bear. He still seems to be saying that *all* of our drives or motives are ultimately wills to power. Foot, reading him so, takes his psychology to be spoiled by its use of this 'underlying principle'; Nietzsche is a 'victim of the delusion of having seen things whole' (p. 220).

Clark ('Nietzsche's Doctrines of the Will to Power', Chapter 5[68]) argues that the notion can only be useful if it is *not* universal, but stands in contrast with drives or motives to other things. But, she thinks, this is just how Nietzsche means it, really. Willing power is one kind of drive among others, and his real point is precisely to *value* or *commend* this kind (as 'the most life-affirming drive'), in contrast with others. When he *does* sometimes state it as an ontology or (univeral) psychology, this is a 'self-conscious

---

[67] ' . . . to lead an ideal life is to understand what that self is which is already there and to live according to that understanding' (p. 138).

[68] Revised as 'The Will to Power', ch. 7 of Clark, *Nietzsche on Truth and Philosophy*.

myth' (p. 139) intended to glorify that motive—to promote its value for us. Nietzsche is not, however, trying to deceive us in this valuative use of (seeming) factual claims: we are meant to understand that he is myth-making, since he leaves us clues that this is so.[69] It is important that, for Clark, even this valuative point still involves or depends on Nietzsche's making certain truth-claims; for example, that it is true that the sense of power is needed for the affirmation of life (see p. 148, including n. 30). So even here the tone is not utterly divorced from asserting or positing; Nietzsche is never *just* valuing.

By contrast my own piece ('Nietzsche's Power Ontology', Chapter 6[70]) tries to read this teaching straight—as a 'power ontology'. I try first to give conceptual specificity to 'will to power', and then to show it as indeed Nietzsche's general view of reality, providing the schema and terminology within which his other main views are framed. So the idea of will to power is bound into, and not detachable from, his perspectivism, his insistence on becoming, his distinction of the basic types master, slave, and overman, and his valuative standards of strength, activeness, and health. I try to show how, by beginning with that ontological schema, all those other familiar ideas of Nietzsche's can be clarified (given more precise senses) and shown to fit together into an overall philosophical 'system'—despite Nietzsche's well-known aspersions against system. I argue that he offers this central 'power ontology' not as an a priori truth, but as a hypothesis to be judged by how well it—along with all the rest of his philosophy, as organized by it—fits and clarifies our lives and experience.[71]

Another of Nietzsche's best-known ideas is his distinction between the '*Apollonian*' and '*Dionysian*' types. This doctrine has a different status from the others we shall consider, since Nietzsche's principal statements of it date from the very beginning of his philosophical career, in *The Birth of Tragedy*. This book, in its outlook and issues, stands somewhat apart from the others and merits treatment on its own. Schacht's paper ('Making Life Worth Living: Nietzsche on Art in *The Birth of Tragedy*', Chapter 7) examines the book's famous analysis of 'tragic art' as fusing those Apollonian and Dionysian 'art impulses' (drives).

We have been noticing how Nietzsche's ideas are subjectivized, yet still

---

[69] Clark justifies this especially by her careful readings of two important sections in BGE, 22 and 36.

[70] Extracted from ch. 1 of J. Richardson, *Nietzsche's System* (New York: Oxford University Press, 1996).

[71] In J. Richardson, 'Nietzsche contra Darwin', *Philosophy and Phenomenology Research* (forthcoming) I develop a more 'naturalistic' account of will to power by stressing the Darwinian aspect to Nietzsche's thinking.

bear truth-claims. Here the interesting question is how far this is true of that tragic art itself, under his analysis.[72] Given the strong Schopenhauerian elements in BT, it might have seemed that Dionysian art 'gives us truth', by exposing the reality of a pointless, chaotic struggle (Schopenhauer's 'world as will'). But Schacht argues persuasively that Nietzsche treats *both* Apollonian and Dionysian art as working by 'illusions', by falsifying reality—the former doing so by 'images', the latter by 'symbols' (pp. 195–6). Nietzsche treats *all* art as 'transfiguring', breaking with Schopenhauer's 'cognitivist' aesthetics (p. 192).

Nevertheless, Schacht agrees that Dionysian art 'expresses the reality of nature in a way enabling us to overcome our abhorrence of it' (p. 198), and that tragic art gives us 'a way of apprehending this reality that enables us to come to terms with it' (p. 204). So even if art does not *give* truth, it is still, in its highest forms, an adjunct to it—something that lets us live with the truth. And Nietzsche's theory of art is still dependent on certain truth-claims: his account of art as illusion depends on a theory about the reality that illusion helps us to live with. So again we find that Nietzsche's subjectivizing move still bottoms out in truth-claims.

Together with the 'overman', these four (death of God, eternal recurrence, will to power, Apollonian–Dionysian) are probably Nietzsche's most famous ideas. But in the rest of this Introduction I shall focus on three others that in fact occupy much more of his attention—and are also more instructive about his relations with our analytic practice. They can be formulated in the terms 'immoralism', 'freedom', and 'genealogy'. They stand in this relation: the first gives Nietzsche's critique of prevailing values, the second (one statement of) the new value he proposes, and the third the method for thinking that connects the critique with the new ideal. They are the topics of our remaining papers. So Foot and Leiter (in Chapters 8 and 9) analyse and assess his attack on morality, Nehamas and Leiter (in Chapters 10 and 11) his notion of freedom, and Geuss and Foucault (in Chapters 12 and 13) his genealogical method.

[*a*] Nietzsche's critique of Christianity, and (more generally) of the ethics or morality of pity and altruism, is arguably the idea most important to him—the idea that increasingly *became* most important to him. We may call it, as Nietzsche himself often does, his '*immoralism*'.[73] As his vehemence

---

[72] This question is interesting partly for how it may bear on Nietzsche's own tone. It may be tempting to treat sectors of his thought as intended artistically, as a kind of myth-making. We have seen how Clark so treats the 'doctrine' of will to power. So the relation between art and truth may be important for how we treat Nietzsche's own 'views'.

[73] Or rather, he often identifies himself as an 'immoralist', e.g. BGE 32, 246; HH I, Preface, 1; D, Preface, 4; TI I. 36, V. 3, 6; EH III, UM 2; EH IV. 6.

escalated in his last year, it became his crusade. So the tone of *The Antichrist* betrays a loss of balance, of the willingness to see the positive even here, a trait he had earlier prized in himself. His last letters suggest how deeply he felt himself in this role. But this attack is also an important theme in his work from very early on.[74]

This immoralism is also, I think, the idea it is hardest for us to treat sympathetically in Nietzsche. However compelling he may be on other topics, however much we may admire and be swayed by his writings, we are likely, virtually all of us, to find his immoralism, and the social or political consequences he seems to draw from it, grossly unacceptable. There are, of course, some parts or adjuncts of his attack that many might embrace, for example against the metaphysics and theology used to justify morality, and the 'other-worldly' incentive often given for it. But Nietzsche considers these falsehoods ('holy lies') less disturbing than the values they support. His attacks on pity, altruism, egalitarianism, and democracy strike much more deeply, at preferences we probably feel ourselves immovable in.[75] And what could ever shift us into *his* views, when they strike us not just as immoral, but as ugly and distasteful as well?[76] We inevitably associate them with some of the worst episodes in recent history. His views here seem so out of bounds that we may wonder why or whether they haven't corrupted all the rest of what he says. He seems so wise otherwise—but his going so wrong here, in his values, may make us more cautious elsewhere too.

Distaste or discomfort with Nietzsche's values made them, for a while, less favourite topics for interpreters, whether analytic or otherwise. The paper by Foot ('Nietzsche: The Revaluation of Values', Chapter 8) was an influential 'legitimizer' of Anglo-American attention to Nietzsche's values. It treats his critique of morality as deserving serious attention, and issues an indirect rebuke to analytic philosophers for their neglect of it: 'by and large he has

---

[74] EH III, D 1 identifies *Daybreak* as the book with which 'my campaign against morality begins'.

[75] A 2: 'The weak and the failures shall perish: first principle of *our* love of man. And one should even help them to it.' GS 377: 'we are not at all "liberal", we do not work for "progress", ... [the song about] "equal rights", "a free society", "no more masters and no servants" does not attract us!—we hold it by no means desirable that a realm of justice and concord should be established on earth'. EH I. 4: '*pity* is only called a virtue by decadents'.

[76] Consider, for example, his well-known remarks about women, or his many favourable (though still ambiguous) remarks about 'slavery' (GS 377: 'we think about the necessity for new orders, also for a new slavery—for every strengthening and elevation of the type "human" also involves a new kind of enslavement'; also BGE 44, 188, 239, 242, 257). Or WP 862: 'The annihilation of the decaying races. Annihilation of Europe. ... The annihilation of suffrage universal: i.e. the system through which the lowest natures prescribe themselves as laws for the higher.' Such values lack even aesthetic appeal for us, and fail the test he so often employs, of judging 'by smell'.

neither been accepted nor refuted, and this seems a remarkable fact'
(p. 210).[77]

Foot finds the root of Nietzsche's critique of morality in a quasi-aesthetic
valuation of 'strong and exceptional individuals'. This need not be a matter
for argument: she can imagine such values prevailing simply through people
coming to care more about these individuals than about morality (p. 216).
But she also thinks that Nietzsche defends his position with certain factual
assertions—about the effects of pity on pitier and pitied, for example—and
that here he can be argued against: 'he has got to be *right* about the effect of
teaching pity and justice—that it merely hides the *ressentiment* of the weak
while it does injury to the strong' (p. 220). Foot disputes his credentials for
making these claims: despite Nietzsche's psychological acuity, he doesn't
seem to have 'great knowledge of life and of the human heart' (p. 220).[78]
And she thinks these claims have, in fact, been discredited by current events:
'How could one see the present dangers that the world is in as showing that
there is too much pity and too little egoism around?' (p. 220). Foot concludes
by speculating that Nietzsche himself might have changed his views in the
light of these events.

Leiter ('Nietzsche and the Morality Critics', Chapter 9) shares some main
lines of Foot's approach, but gives a more developed analysis and critique of
Nietzsche's position. He brings the attack on morality ('morality in the
pejorative sense'[79]) into sharper focus, by comparing it with the critique of
moral theory offered by several contemporary philosophers, in particular
Bernard Williams. These 'Morality Critics' reject the overridingness of
moral demands in so far as they interfere with the good life (p. 230).
Nietzsche differs from them, Leiter argues, in disputing not the (any) moral
theory itself, but its pervasive cultural effects—which are due partly to the
way it is held. Even if the theory itself is revised (e.g. by removing the claim
to overridingness), it would continue to have a pernicious effect on the 'highest'. Leiter (like Foot) takes this to be Nietzsche's main complaint against
morality—the damage it does to exceptional individuals. It harms them by

[77] In Philippa Foot, 'Nietzsche's Immoralism' (*New York Review of Books*, 38 (13 June 1991);
repr. in R. Schacht (ed.), *Nietzsche, Genealogy, Morality: Essays on Nietzsche's 'On the Genealogy
of Morals'* (Berkeley: University of California Press, 1994)), she asks: 'Why do so many contemporary moral philosophers, particularly of the Anglo-American analytic school, ignore
Nietzsche's attack on morality and just go on as if this extraordinary event in the history of
thought had never occurred?' Leiter concludes his paper (p. 254): 'it does remain striking that
more than one hundred years after Nietzsche cast down his challenge to morality, the topic still
remains largely unexplored'.

[78] As we have seen, she takes as evidence for this, his claim that the 'underlying principle of
human behavior was the will to power' (p. 220).

[79] See his fuller account of this in B. Leiter, 'Morality in the Pejorative Sense: On the Logic of
Nietzsche's Critique of Morality', *British Journal for the History of Philosophy*, 3 (1995), 113–45.

preaching as virtues traits (e.g. altruism) that are really useless or even inimical to their pursuit of 'human excellence', and by condemning as vices traits
(e.g. self-love) that are really useful for it (p. 237).

When it comes to assessing Nietzsche's immoralism, Leiter reaches more
positive conclusions than Foot. He agrees with her that these values can only
be criticized by examining their factual premises. But he finds a subtler and
more defensible value-stance, relying on premises some[80] of which are much
more plausible than the ones Foot finds. For example, Leiter denies that
Nietzsche's immoralism opposes the *practice* of altruism, just the *ideology* of
it, which is most likely to be taken seriously by just those whom it would
most damage (p. 250). Leiter thinks that Nietzsche poses important and
difficult questions about the practical effects of morality—beyond the
content of the moral theory itself: it *might really be* that this practice is
damaging to 'creative excellence'.

The recognition that some of Nietzsche's factual premises might survive
makes it more pressing to address the difference in his root values themselves. Disputing those factual claims can only reach to what we might call
his 'applied values'—the consequences he draws from those facts, together
with certain primary, underived values. But, I think we must suspect,
Nietzsche cannot be brought back to us (into morality) just by correcting his
facts; a deeper disagreement will survive all such updatings. It lies in something both Foot and Leiter stress: Nietzsche puts overriding value on the
'highest individuals', and not, as I suppose we do, on 'overall well-being'.
Let me briefly elaborate.

This difference contains two points. Nietzsche differs, first of all, in his
conception of how the 'higher' or 'better' persons are to be identified: not at
all by being more moral or compassionate or unselfish, for example. I return
to this first point below. But he also differs in the kind of overriding value he
accords these highest: their importance so transcends that of the 'lower',
that it justifies the use and sacrifice of (even great numbers of) the latter on
their behalf.[81] So he differs not just in his criterion for rating persons or lives,
but also in how that rating is 'scaled': changes at the top count far more than
those at the bottom.[82] This difference in scaling—the way Nietzsche's values

---

[80] Other premises Leiter rejects: that it is really morality that is responsible for our 'culture of
mediocrity' (rather than economic and other material factors), and that it is morality (rather than
precisely the lack of it) that is most to blame for hindering human flourishing (pp. 248–9).

[81] BGE 258; WP 859.

[82] Either (*a*) Nietzsche judges states of affairs *not* with regard to 'overall good' (summed over all
persons involved), but only with regard to 'good of the highest', or (*b*) he does care about overall
good, but weighs the good of the highest far more heavily than we do, in calculating overall good.
Or both: sometimes he says that the weak or sick don't count at all, sometimes just that they count
for little.

are 'maximax'—may be just as important as the difference in his criterion for the 'best' persons. It, and not the latter, is the real root of the elitism in his values.

How can we respond to these differences in Nietzsche's primary values? Should we accept that our disagreement cannot be addressed by reasons or arguments—since we have reached down under all those factual premises—but is simply a matter for a choice? Sometimes it seems that Nietzsche himself thinks precisely this, acknowledging that his values are 'just his perspective', and inviting us to create different values of our own. This is, as I have mentioned, a popular way of responding to the disturbing and affronting parts of Nietzsche's values: to deny that he makes any rational or argumentative claim on us with his values. If Nietzsche is an anti-realist about values as, for example, Clark and Leiter argue,[83] it seems we can legitimately ignore his own values as 'just his', or can pick out any parts of them that might suit our own taste. So the tone of his values would make it unnecessary, and indeed impossible, to argue with their (basic) content.

However, there is also room for a more 'realist' reading of Nietzsche's values, which it is helpful to sketch. That anti-realist reading faces a problem or challenge: it stands in tension with the great assurance with which Nietzsche asserts his values. Even as he allows that they belong to his perspective, he seems exceptionally sure that his perspective is 'higher' than (say) Christianity's, or his contemporaries'. Would he really be content to allow that his ranking of persons is just his perspective, with no real argument against Christians' opposite ranking? This prompts us to consider what arguments for his values he could have.

I think the strongest option for this more realist reading is to take Nietzsche to ground his values in his psychology. This fits with the way his rankings are all tied in with diagnoses of different human types. He thinks he *sees* that these human types, and their values, stand in a certain 'rank-order'—and that if we don't see it too, it is because of limits in our own insight.[84] Were we, in particular, able to 'see into' persons as he does, and understand them by their impulses, healthy and sick, and were we also able to 'look down' on all these comprehended types, by virtue of having passed

---

[83] Clark, 'On Knowledge, Truth, and Value'; B. Leiter, 'Nietzsche's Metaethics: Against the Privilege Readings', *European Journal of Philosophy*, 8 (2000), 277–97.

[84] HH I, Preface, 6: 'you should see the problem of *rank-order*, and how power and right and comprehensiveness of perspective grow into the heights together'. I think it is very hard to read him as allowing that rank-order is itself relative to perspectives, such that every perspective, with equal legitimacy, ranks in its own way.

through them, then we would rank persons as he does.[85] I shall return to this argument below.

[*b*] Let us look more closely at Nietzsche's conception of the 'highest' persons—the ideal he tries to set up in the place of those prevailing Christian and altruistic values. Who are those 'exceptional individuals' to whom he gives such disproportionate status? Nietzsche insists (whether or not this is 'just his perspective') that some people are better than others, *simpliciter* or overall—not just better at some things or in some respects, but in a privileged or synoptic way. There is some primary criterion for ranking persons, who stand (in an image he often uses) on rungs in the 'ladder' of human types.

What is the vertical dimension along which the ladder runs? What determines an individual's height? The readiest way to state Nietzsche's criterion for his rankings of persons is that the highest are distinguished by their *strength*.[86] But this leaves us almost as large a challenge, to specify what he means by 'strength'.[87] One thing seems clear enough—that Nietzsche has in mind a *spiritual* kind of strength, not muscle-power. He values a kind of strength exercised in one's intellectual, artistic, and emotional activities, not in athletics, and not simply in virtue of economic, political, or military control. But what is spiritual strength?

One reading that has been especially prominent in the literature is that the kind of strength Nietzsche means is that involved in '*freedom*'. This reading emphasizes what we might call an 'existentialist' theme in Nietzsche—his suggestion that a 'self' is something each of us needs to create for him/ herself, and that only in or by this *self-creation* are we 'free'. He thinks great strength is required for this self-creation, and that by it one rises, as it were, to a different level or kind of strength.[88] This account of Nietzsche's ideal renders it much more attractive than does his vocabulary of 'power' and 'strength'. It has been a favourite focus of attempts to state Nietzsche's positive values appealingly.

Probably the most influential such reading of Nietzsche has been the

---

[85] EH IV. 6: 'Nobody yet has felt *Christian* morality to be *beneath* him: that requires a height, a view of distances, a hitherto quite unheard-of psychological depth and profundity.' EH III, BT 2: 'Whoever does not merely comprehend the word "Dionysian" but comprehends *himself* in the word "Dionysian" needs no refutation of Plato or Christianity or Schopenhauer—he *smells the decay*.'

[86] See e.g. A 2; WP 674 and 710. WP 858: 'What decides rank is the quantum of power that you are; the rest is cowardice.'

[87] In Richardson, *Nietzsche's System*, ch. 3, I try to develop this criterion, as a consequence of the background 'power ontology'.

[88] See how GS 347 treats freedom as a proof of strength. Also A 54. See how GM II. 2 describes the new kind of strength of the 'sovereign individual'.

paper by Nehamas ('How One Becomes What One Is', Chapter 10[89]). He takes as his guiding puzzle the question how to interpret Nietzsche's recurring reference to 'becoming what one is'—given that the readings that first suggest themselves all run afoul of other things he says. It can't, in particular, be a matter of actualizing some pre-existing self or essence, since Nietzsche denies there is any such thing. Because 'a thing is the sum of its effects' (the doctrine Nehamas associates with will to power), we consist, each of us, simply in the sum of what we do—our actions, including mental ones (p. 258). However, these actions stand in conflict: 'Our thoughts contradict one another and contrast with our desires, which are themselves inconsistent and are belied, in turn, by our actions' (p. 265). Since we are no more than the sum of these acts, each of us lacks unity, and can achieve it only by bringing those mental acts into coherence with one another. Nehamas thinks Nietzsche sets this to us as our task.

What is it that pursues such unity? It is not the self-as-subject, since (again) there is none. Instead it is one's 'dominant traits', which experience conflicts among themselves, as well as with lesser traits. They have (on Nehamas's account) three options in dealing with such conflicts (p. 268). A first is dishonesty: the dominant traits ignore the existence of competitors. A second is akrasia: the dominant traits fail to control the others, so that the individual acts on whatever drive is uppermost. But Nietzsche favours a third: the dominant traits work to 'incorporate' the others, in the process changing both themselves and the others, 'integrating' them with one another. So, Nehamas says, to become who one is is 'to identify oneself with all of one's actions . . . In the ideal case, it is also to fit all this into a *coherent* whole . . . it is to give style to one's character' (p. 275). Nehamas famously compares this unity with that belonging to literary characters, suggesting that Nietzsche tries to achieve it in the 'character' he creates in his works. He also argues that the test of this integration and unity is so to welcome all one's traits and actions as to be able to embrace the thought of eternal recurrence—which connects this paper with Nehamas's other.

However, such existentialist readings of Nietzsche face challenges or problems. How can he believe in freedom when he persistently denies freedom of the will, condemning the very notion as contradictory? And how can he believe in self-creation when he thinks each of us is irrevocably constituted as a person of a certain type, without the capacity for self-transformation that philosophies and religions have credited us with (the better to blame us, in Nietzsche's view)? Leiter ('The Paradox of Fatalism and Self-Creation in Nietzsche', Chapter 11) assembles these contrary points into a critique of the

---

[89] Revised as ch. 6 of Nehamas, *Nietzsche*.

common reading of Nietzsche as 'the philosopher of self-creation'—a reading he attributes to Nehamas, along with Jaspers and Rorty. Against it Leiter reads Nietzsche as a fatalist who thinks that the *causa sui* is incoherent, and that consciousness (including our conscious 'choice') is epiphenomenal, and not really able to determine what we do. Instead, our behaviour is caused by type-facts about us, i.e. by the 'kind' of person each of us unalterably is, in virtue of his/her 'psycho-physical constitution' (p. 294).

Leiter thinks that Nietzsche's fatalism has been often overlooked, as part of a more general neglect of his *naturalism*. He elaborates this important aspect of Nietzsche's thinking, showing how he came by it from his early absorption in the German materialists, from whom he learned to think of persons as 'essentially natural, bodily organisms, organisms for whom free will was an illusion' (p. 311). Superimposed upon this, on Leiter's analysis, was Schopenhauer's view that we have an 'unalterable character' that determines our actions (p. 312). Together they lead Nietzsche to the conclusion that 'The trajectory of a person's life ... follows a necessary course, one determined by the constitutive type-facts, in interaction with the environment and circumstances' (p. 299).

Yet Nietzsche's fatalism still needs to be reconciled with those passages in which he does still talk about self-creation. This is the 'paradox' Leiter chiefly addresses. He answers it by arguing that Nietzsche means something unusual by 'self-creation'—something that not only abandons the 'Autonomy Condition' it normally entails (p. 317), but even dispenses with any (conscious) 'self' (p. 318). What does the creating is not a free or conscious agent, but certain drives in the struggling mix of drives that constitute the person. Now since Nehamas allows this, and makes it part of his own analysis (pp. 263, 271), the line of disagreement between him and Leiter is subtler than had seemed. This is the more so given that Leiter's own account of Nietzsche's ideal also stresses both 'creativity' and the Dionysian attitude that wills to eternally repeat one's life.[90] So it is perhaps a matter less of a different ideal than of describing this ideal of freedom and creativity in ways that fully accommodate Nietzsche's fatalism.

I think Leiter is right that this fatalism shifts the sense of Nietzsche's notions of freedom and creation in ways we almost invariably lose sight of—

---

[90] These are the two factors Leiter mentions in Ch. 9 (pp. 234–5) as distinguishing the 'higher types'; they are the topics of Nehamas's two papers. There remains a gap between Leiter's criterion of 'creativity' and Nehamas's of 'self-creativity' as accounts of Nietzsche's ideal. It might be thought, against Nehamas, that Nietzsche's ideal persons aren't all as *self*-focused as the latter makes them—that Nietzsche values just as much the ability to create in materials outside oneself, to shape art works, or laws and societies, for example. On the other hand, Leiter himself takes a step in Nehamas's direction, when he agrees (p. 316) that a kind of 'self-creating' is involved in 'creating values'—since this seems so much to be, for Nietzsche, the best creating of all.

and that tend to be forgotten in existentialist readings of him. This fatalism has radical consequences not just for what that ideal is, but for the way it is offered to us. Nietzsche does not think of his ideal as democratically available to all: most people (nearly all people?) are barred from ever achieving it by their irrevocable types. Nor does he even think that everybody should *try* to achieve it. He advocates different values for different individuals, precisely because they have such limited capacities for changing themselves. And this shifts—as we can put it once more—the tone in which he offers his values.

We prima facie presume that he offers these just as other philosophers do, addressing them to our conscious reason in the expectation of persuading it that *this* is how we should strive to be. But if Nietzsche thinks our consciousness is ineffective and our character fixed, it seems we need some different account of his writerly intentions—of the kind of impact on us he wants his ideal and values to have.[91] Indeed, this opens up a new question, whether *we* belong to his proper audience at all: our eagerness, even our ability to understand him, are no longer enough to qualify us, much less our humanness alone. This strikes at a basic conception we have of our relation to a philosopher—the kind of 'discourse' or 'speech act' taking place between us.

Nevertheless, even if Nietzsche means to affect his audience—whoever they are—mainly somehow 'beneath' the level of their conscious reason, still it seems unavoidable that he *also* means to affect how they think, and that this change is crucial in turning them towards his ideal. Indeed, a certain kind of understanding is a precondition for that ideal, or even constitutive of it: we become free by and in (a certain) insight. Both Leiter and Nehamas recognize that self-creation depends on understanding, despite all of Nietzsche's doubts against consciousness and the self. For Leiter, it is understanding *scientifically* 'the patterns of value-inputs and action-outputs' (p. 316) for the (type of) psychophysical system each of us is; this knowledge lets one 'create oneself', one's actions, by informedly changing one's values. For Nehamas, freedom lies in integrating (and so welcoming the eternal recurrence of) everything about oneself—which depends on insight into all these parts of one's life (all one's 'doings').[92]

On both of these readings, understanding serves our freedom by identifying what we are and can't help but be—which we then affirm, and live in the

---

[91] TI II. 11: 'It is a self-deception on the part of philosophers and moralists, that they step out of decadence by waging war against it. Stepping out [of it] is beyond their strength . . . they *change* the expression [of decadence], they don't get rid of it.'

[92] Also, it is the metaphysical insight into our identity with the sum of our actions, that sets us this goal to begin with. Perhaps Nehamas means both points at (p. 138): 'Nietzsche seems to think that to lead an ideal life is to understand what that self is which is already there and to live according to that understanding.'

light of. This is surely a main part of Nietzsche's point. But once again I think there is also room for a reading that gives a more negative and critical role to this understanding. I shall quickly sketch this, as allied to the more sceptical reading of his 'perspectival truth' given earlier.

On this view, understanding serves freedom not just by identifying what in ourselves we need to accept and integrate, but also, more pertinently, by revealing what we *can* overcome—revealing it in a way that even amounts to overcoming it.[93] This is how Nietzsche's immoralism makes him free: the revelation of the sources and purposes of Christianity and morality frees him from those ways his values had been determined. That insight gives him, as we saw near the beginning, the ability to give his words (like 'ought') his own meanings, rather than retaining unreflectively the meanings embedded by genealogy. This explains his incessant diagnosing of our culture's perspectives and values: the wealth of these insights serves to distance and so free him, in detail, from having his beliefs and values determined those ways. By these many acts of insight he rises above those various meanings and values; the insight accomplishes his 'revaluation of values'. So the method of diagnosis, genealogy, is bound up in his ideal.[94] By it, he thinks he wins a freedom surpassing all his contemporaries'.

[c] This brings us, in the end, to Nietzsche's psychology, which is probably the main source (apart from the flourish of his style) of his immediate and broad appeal. It is the basis of his claim to 'know something *more*' than the rest of us.[95] This psychology shows enormous subtlety and plasticity. But what is most important, I think, is to see its role in Nietzsche's overall revaluative project—and its relation to the freedom he prizes.

For reasons we saw back at the start, this psychology must become *genealogy*: it needs to uncover layers of meaning deposited historically into our concepts and values; this is required for a proper analysis of those values. The papers by Geuss and Foucault interpret this genealogy in very different styles, and to somewhat different effects. I shall focus on one chief difference, connected with the above debate between positive and negative readings of Nietzschean truth and freedom. Here the issue is whether genealogy *devalues* what it studies.

Geuss ('Nietzsche and Genealogy', Chapter 12) clarifies Nietzsche's genealogical method by developing its contrast with (the giving of) a

---

[93] GS 335: 'Your understanding *of the manner in which moral judgments have originated* would spoil these grand words [duty and conscience] for you.' EH IV. 8: 'Whoever uncovers morality has also uncovered the disvalue of all values in which one believes or has believed.'

[94] So too perhaps Foucault, who speaks of critical history's 'liberation of man by presenting him with other origins than those in which he prefers to see himself' (p. 358).

[95] EH II. 1. EH IV. 6: 'There was no psychology at all before me.' See also EH III. 5's opening.

pedigree: the latter purports to support the value of some x, by tracing its unbroken descent from some single origin, the source of its value (p. 324). Geuss argues that Nietzsche reverses each element in this analysis, so that he is very far from being (as Habermas thinks) 'a conscious archaizer' like Heidegger. Geuss illustrates the method by offering a map of Nietzsche's genealogy of Christianity, showing how a certain abiding 'form of life' (including habits, feelings, perceptions) gets repeatedly reinterpreted by different 'wills', each imposing a new meaning upon it (p. 329). Genealogy uncovers these strands of meaning, imposed by these various wills, each of whose contributions can be displayed as 'a branching node of a genealogical tree'—of which Geuss gives a diagram (p. 334).

Given that genealogy does not, like a pedigree, justify the value of its x, the question arises whether Nietzsche thinks that it does the reverse, that it lowers or refutes the x's value. Geuss points out that Nietzsche 'asserts very clearly' that insight into history can have no 'direct bearing' on a practice's value—though it *can* undermine beliefs about its source that those who engage in the practice need to sustain themselves in it (p. 338). So the genealogy shows Christianity involved in various lies, but Geuss argues that this is only objectionable from a Christian point of view, not the genealogist's. Nietzsche's genealogies do not directly justify his own values (will and life). However, his ability to give better histories than alternative values shows the strength and vitality of his viewpoint (and 'he judges things by the vitality they exhibit'; p. 340).

Foucault's influential paper on genealogy ('Nietzsche, Genealogy, History', Chapter 13) is couched in a distinctly different style than Geuss's. There is, however, significant overlap in their accounts of Nietzsche's method.[96] The main difference in content, I think, is that Foucault depicts genealogy as a more deeply critical and undermining method; he puts this succinctly: 'knowledge is not made for understanding, it is made for cutting' (p. 351). Foucault says that with genealogy, traditional history becomes 'effective (*wirkliche*) history'. This studies what lies closest to us—our own values and practices—but in such a way as to put it at a distance. It undermines our own pretensions to unity, our confidence in being justified in all we do and value, for it shows that 'truth and being does not lie at the root of what we know and what we are, but the exteriority of accidents' (p. 346). So genealogy introduces discontinuity into us, depriving the self of its reassuring stability.

Foucault thus stresses the critical and destructive side of genealogy. It

---

[96] For example, both proceed by distinguishing genealogy from a more reverential search for 'origins' (Foucault) or 'pedigrees' (Geuss).

expresses the 'will to truth', which (he thinks) Nietzsche diagnoses as a malicious and destructive tendency. In genealogy, this will turns against the subject who enacts it, which leads to the 'unavoidable sacrifice of the subject of knowledge' (p. 358). Foucault appears to think that Nietzsche either welcomes this outcome or considers it inevitable—that he reverses his earlier (in *Untimely Meditations*) rejection of critical history because it sacrificed 'life' to truth. Foucault thinks that his later view favours 'risking the destruction of the subject who seeks knowledge in the endless deployment of the will to knowledge' (p. 359). So he finds in Nietzsche the opposite of what Nehamas does: the project not of unifying the self, but of tearing it apart.

This carries to one extreme what I have been calling the 'negative' reading of genealogy (and the allied readings of truth and freedom sketched earlier). It shows what a thoroughly critical and deconstructing upshot Nietzsche can be read to have. But perhaps it goes too far. It seems contradicted by Nietzsche's own insistence that despite all his critiques and underminings, his ultimate stance is to affirm and 'say yes'.[97] I want to conclude by sketching how the negative approach (to truth, freedom, and genealogy) can still be accommodated under that ultimate affirmation. This subordinates Nietzsche's diagnostic–destructive aspect to his validative–creative, giving genealogy's critical work a more positive point than Foucault seems to do.

The position is obvious by now: it puts together the pieces above. It is by and in Nietzsche's critical and undermining work that his truth and freedom are won. His perspectival truth is a truth through and about perspectives; it is grasped in the sceptical move of *diagnosing* perspectives. This is what (a part of) science must become, to understand our human views and values. The kind of understanding suited to this subject matter consists precisely in 'seeing through' those viewpoints: seeing at once both *as* they see, and *why*, in such a way that we learn something about them that they do not. We see as the perspective does, but also better than it does, and so advance up the ladder of perspectives.

This cognitive advance is also Nietzsche's freedom. To the extent that one turns this scrutiny on oneself and diagnoses the cultural viewpoints, values, or habits that one's life is woven from, one achieves a 'freedom from' those sources. Or, to put the point in closer contrast with Foucault: that work of 'cutting into' the self with undermining diagnoses is still Nietzsche's method for a self-constructive project. Indeed, Nietzsche thinks it makes a kind of

---

[97] EH IV. 1: 'I contradict as has never been contradicted and yet am the opposite of a no-saying spirit.'

self never possible before: an individual who is for the first time 'responsible' for his/her values and behaviour.[98]

I began with the common suspicion that Nietzsche's writings are so different in tone, and so thin in argumentative content, as neither to permit nor merit a philosophical-scholarly handling. I hope, in the meantime, to have sketched an interesting landscape of positions and problems, well suited for such handling. The papers themselves do much more of this work. But if Nietzsche is successful with us, he will not just engage our philosophical-scholarly practice, but alter it. These connected points about his immoralism, freedom, and genealogy indicate, I think, the sorts of change he would hope to induce in that practice, to let it serve the kind of truth (and freedom) he most values.[99]

---

[98] GM II. 2 speaks of 'the autonomous, super-ethical (*übersittliche*) individual (for "autonomous" and "ethical" exclude one another)'. HH I, Preface, 3 speaks of the 'will to self-determination, to evaluating on one's own account, this will to *free* will'. TI IX. 38: 'For what is freedom! That one has the will to self-responsibility.'

[99] I am most grateful to my co-editor, Brian Leiter, for extensive comments, sharp yet patient, to earlier drafts of this Introduction. He has helped me to improve main lines in my presentation, especially in its beginning—though I know I have still not met all of his reservations. I also thank Ken Gemes for very penetrating comments that likewise helped me to see the way better at some key points.

NIETZSCHE'S CRITIQUE OF TRUTH

KEN GEMES

1. INTRODUCTION

In several places Nietzsche calls into question the value of truth: "The false-ness of a judgment is for us not necessarily an objection to a judgment" (BGE 4).[1] At some places he disdains the desire for truth: "No, this bad taste, this will to truth, to 'truth at any price,' this youthful madness in the love of truth—have lost their charm for us" (GS, Preface to the Second Edition, 4). At other places Nietzsche questions the very existence of truth:[2] "There exists neither 'spirit,' nor reason, nor thinking, nor consciousness, nor soul, nor will, nor truth" (WP 480). Indeed, he even claims that he does not use truth and reason to convince but rather seeks to "seduce" his readers through extreme rhetoric:

A powerful seduction fights on our behalf, the most powerful that there has ever been—the seduction of truth—"Truth"? Who has forced this word on me? But I repudiate it; but I disdain this proud word: no, we do not need even this: we shall conquer and come to power even without truth. The spell that fights on our behalf, the eye of Venus that charms and blinds even our opponents, is *the magic of the extreme*, the seduction that everything extreme exercises: we immoralists—we are the most extreme. (WP 749)

To deny the existence of truth is *prima facie* paradoxical. Such denials invite the question "Is it true that there is no truth?" To answer 'Yes' is to claim there is at least one truth, namely that there is no truth. To answer 'No' is to deny that there is no truth and hence to commit oneself to the claim that there is some truth.

From Ken Gemes, "Nietzsche's Critique of Truth," *Philosophy & Phenomenological Research*, 52 (1992), 47–65.

[1] [Editors' note.] Citations from Nietzsche's works have been adjusted to the system explained in the Note on References to Nietzsche's Works above. In addition, this paper uses the abbreviation SW, followed by volume and page number, to refer to: *Sämtliche Werke in Zwölf Bänden*, ed. Alfred Bäumler (Stuttgart: Alfred Kröner Verlag, 1965).

[2] This denial of the existence of truth can not be dismissed as mere hyperbole since it is repeated consistently. For instance, WP 540, 616, 625 and 804, and EH II. 10.

To admit that one seeks influence not through truth but through seduction is to invite dismissal as a mere rhetorician.

What then are we to make of Nietzsche's various pronouncements about truth? The simple answer is, I believe, that Nietzsche is ultimately not interested in (theories of) truth. This is not to say that Nietzsche is not acutely concerned with the role that the concept and rhetoric of truth has played within various cultures. By the same token an interest in the role the concept of witches played in 17th century English culture need not betoken any interest or belief in witches. Yet whether or not Nietzsche is ultimately interested in truth he has *prima facie* made some paradoxical claims about truth. In the following I attempt an interpretation of his various pronouncements about truth which I hope will remove that initial air of paradox. In so doing I hope to provide a general framework for Nietzsche interpretation.

Before beginning I should briefly digress to say a few words about an alternative, cognitivist approach taken, for instance most recently, by John Wilcox and Richard Schacht.[3] According to this approach Nietzsche's contradictory remarks about truth can, to some degree, be reconciled by distinguishing various concepts of truth. Following Kant, or more recently, Putnam, we might distinguish the claim that our various theories are true of the transcendental world (Kant's world of noumena, what Putnam derisively labels "THE WORLD") from the claim that they are true of the world of appearances, the empirical world, the world as we experience it.[4] The world of noumena is meant to exist independently of our experience of it, to be unconditioned by our categories. The empirical world is a world conditioned/made possible by prior categorization. We might thus seek to reconcile Nietzsche's various pronouncements about truth by claiming that his skeptical comments about truth concern the notion of transcendental truth, as in, "true to the world of noumena," while his own claims are taken as being true of the conditioned world of appearances. Such an interpretation, heavily reliant on the many Kantian elements found mainly in the notes of the *Nachlass*, can, I suppose, be made to jibe with much of Nietzsche's text. One problem with this interpretation is that it makes Nietzsche appear less interesting and original than he is. It gives us a Nietzsche who is merely rehashing familiar Kantian themes, minus the rigor of Kant's exposition. Of course Nietzsche, at times, and unlike Kant,

---

[3] Cf. John Wilcox, *Truth and Value in Nietzsche* (Washington: University Press of America, 1982), esp. chs. II, III, and IV; and Richard Schacht, *Nietzsche* (London: Routledge & Kegan Paul, 1985), esp. ch. 2.

[4] For Putnam's recasting of the Kantian distinction between empirical and transcendental realism in terms of internal and metaphysical realism, cf. the last chapter of his *Meaning and the Moral Sciences* (London: Routledge & Kegan Paul, 1978).

takes a fairly sceptical line on the very notion of a noumenal world, a world of things-in-themselves, and denies the Kantian claim that certain categories are both a priori and inevitable. But these are moves long familiar from Hegel and other post-Kantians. A second problem with this interpretation is that it involves a certain insensitivity to the context of much of Nietzsche's writings on truth. It fails to consider against whom Nietzsche's various works were aimed. In Nietzsche's published works his analyses of the notion of truth usually serve expressly polemical purposes. To treat Nietzsche as developing a philosophical account of the notion of truth is, to some degree, to ignore his expressly rhetorical intent of using his audience's received notions of truth in order to subvert their wider Weltanschauung. But more of this soon. For the moment suffice it to say that while I believe that the Kantian problematic was indeed an influence behind many of Nietzsche's pronouncements on truth, I will not here pursue this line because it has already received a thorough exposition in the works of the authors previously cited. In the following I will rather concentrate on the rhetorical function of Nietzsche's various apparently paradoxical pronouncements about truth, arguing that when seen in the light of their polemical intent they lose a good deal of the air of paradox.

2. WILL TO TRUTH AS A WILL TO IMPOTENCE

In Nietzsche's *The Gay Science* (125) the story is told of a madman who rushes into a marketplace crying incessantly "I seek God! I seek God." His audience, being atheists, mock him asking "Did he lose his way?" etc. To this the madman replies "We have killed him. You and I." He then proceeds to ask a series of startling questions, "How could we drink up the sea? Who gave us the sponge to wipe away the entire horizon? What were we doing when we unchained this earth from its sun?" And later he asks "How shall we comfort ourselves, the murderers of all murderers?" and "What festivals of atonement, what sacred games shall we have to invent? Is not the greatness of the deed too great for us? Must we not become Gods simply to appear worthy of it?" Then looking at his audience who stare at him in astonished silence he proclaims "I have come too early ... This tremendous event is still on its way ... the light of stars requires time; deeds though done, still require time to be seen and heard. This deed is still more distant from them than the most distant stars—*and yet they have done it themselves.*"

When the madman claims that this tremendous event is still on its way, etc., he is claiming that even the atheists do not appreciate the meaning of "the death of God." For God here is not merely the metaphysical underpinning of the Christian cosmology. He is the very notion of a basis, an external authority, on which opinions are founded—the very notion of a horizon against which everything can be seen and judged. Thus it is that the madman suggests that we must become gods to be worthy of our deed. That is to say that we must become our own authorities, our own basis.

According to Nietzsche, a primary function of the invocation of God is the provision of a means of escaping responsibility. For the Christian the world, including himself, is a product of the will of God. Truth, reality, is founded in God for the world is God's word. Typically atheists, having rejected God as the basis of all values and belief, supply a new basis. For instance, positivists take experience to be the ultimate justifier of our beliefs. Utilitarians and Socialists take the *summum bonum* as the grounding for all actions. Nietzsche rejects these new gods as further attempts to evade responsibility for one's beliefs and actions. The mechanics of evasion are simple. In response to the question "Why do you think suicide is wrong?" the Christian answers, "Because the Bible says so!" In response to the question "Why is punishment of criminals justified?" the utilitarian answers, "Because it promotes the *summum bonum*." In response to the question "Why do you believe in the existence of everyday physical objects?" the positivist answers "On the authority of sensory experience." In each case what is being denied is the effect of the individual will. In effect the interlocutor is saying, I do not believe this because I choose to, because this kind of belief suits me (cf. section 4 below), I believe this because that is how things are and hence I cannot choose otherwise *and neither can you.* According to Nietzsche, the invocation of God, the *summum bonum*, the senses, are merely vehicles of escape. Indeed the very notion of truth must be added to the list. Who does not claim to believe what he believes because it is the truth? Not because he wishes to believe but because that is how things are even though he might wish them to be otherwise. As Nietzsche observes, "One positively wants to repudiate one's own authority and assign it to circumstances" (WP 422). To become God is, in part, to forgo the balm of deferred responsibility.

This resignation of responsibility does not merely provide comfort. It is an indispensable rhetorical device in the subjugation of others. How much less convincing it is to say "Do so because I wish you to do it," than to command "Do it because it is God's Will!" How much less convincing to say "Believe because I will you to believe" rather than "You must believe because it is the truth, because that's the way the world is." Thus Nietzsche claims, "Faith is always most desired, most pressingly needed, where there is a lack of will . . . that is to say, the less a person knows how to command, the more urgent is his desire for that which commands, and commands stemly,—a God, prince, caste, physician, father confessor, dogma, or party conscience" (GS 347).

Here then we have one of the motivations for Nietzsche's attack on truth: The notion of truth is used to escape responsibility for one's actions and beliefs and is employed as a means of coercing uniformity of belief. This is not to say that Nietzsche was against all coercion. Rather, one might say, he was against the coercion of all. This theme is dealt with in detail in section 5 below.

This is not to suggest that Nietzsche has a voluntaristic conception of belief, à la Sartre. Nietzsche, as a naturalist, takes all our beliefs to be thoroughly conditioned. The point is that given our beliefs we can choose to make them our own, that is even accepting that they are conditioned by various causal factors, we can choose to take responsibility for accepting them. This is part of what Nietzsche refers to as "becoming what you are." And is this choosing to become what you are also not a matter of causal conditioning? Emphatically so; it is precisely this fact that motivates Nietzsche's effort, for Nietzsche's writings are themselves another part of the earthly causal order, and as such, may well influence many of his readers to take responsibility for their beliefs rather than deferring to some presumed higher authorities.[5]

3. BEING VS. BECOMING, DESCRIPTION VS. PRESCRIPTION

Together with the traditional notion of truth comes the notion of beliefs as reports on an antecedently existing reality. According to this realist notion of truth, a belief is true if it adequately reflects reality, if it describes things the way they are. On this model the ideal believer is a disinterested, passive entity who is merely reflecting the antecedently existing order, an order that is not of his making and hence an order for which he is not responsible. The ideal believer is one who extricates himself from worldly involvement in order to achieve an objective perspective, a God's view. In its extreme form, as developed by Plato, this ideal believer transcends the illusory world of appearance to achieve true knowledge of the unchanging eternal forms. For Nietzsche, Christianity and Platonism are equivalent in their rejection of

---

[5] This paragraph owes much to conversations with Mark Migotti. For more on Nietzsche's notion of becoming what you are, cf. Alexander Nehamas's "'How One Becomes What One Is'" (Ch. 10 in this volume).

this world, the world of appearance, the world of becoming, in favor of an alleged higher order, an alleged world of being.

For Nietzsche, believing is not some privileged activity by which we transcend the apparent world to achieve a God-like harmony with the real order of eternal truths. As a naturalist he sees belief as another human activity, another tool for survival, for manipulating the world to suit "our interests." In believing we are not reporting how the world is; rather, we are prescribing a way of looking at the world, a means for furthering a particular form of life. To bring others to share one's views is not to bring them into harmony with the pre-existing order; it is to create the very order one is allegedly describing: "Will to truth is a making firm, a making true durable, an abolition of the false character of things, a reinterpretation of it into beings. 'Truth' is therefore not something there, that might be found or discovered—but something that must be created and that gives a name to a process" (WP 552).

While truth is always created rather than discovered, by pretending otherwise man escapes the responsibility of authorship and paves the way for the passive acceptance of received views. Real philosophers, according to Nietzsche, explicitly take up the task of creation: "*Genuine philosophers, however, are commanders and legislators:* they say, '*thus* it *shall* be'. . . . Their 'knowing' is *creating*, their creation is a legislation, their will to truth is— *will to power*" (BGE 211). While Nietzsche says that all will to truth is a will to power, in the case of his "genuine philosophers" it is a will to power that recognizes itself as such. In the case of others, for instance, Christians, it is, according to Nietzsche, a will that does not recognize itself as a will to power, preferring to hide itself with a pretense of disinterested, passive objectivity.

Here then is a second strand in Nietzsche's critique of truth: Taking something as true is exhibiting a will to create or to maintain prior creations though it is usually deceptively presented as an attempt to describe independent antecedently existing phenomena. This is not to say that Nietzsche is against all forms of deception. Indeed we shall soon see that he regards deception as an inevitable part of life.

4. WHY NOT UNTRUTH RATHER THAN TRUTH?

In *Beyond Good and Evil*, among other places, Nietzsche raises the question of the value of truth:

For all the value that the true, the truthful, the selfless may deserve, it would be possible that a higher and more fundamental value for life might have to be ascribed to deception, selfishness and lust. (BGE 2)

The falseness of a judgment is for us not necessarily an objection to a judgment; in this respect our new language may sound strangest. The question is to what extent it is life preserving, species-preserving, perhaps even species cultivating. (BGE 4)

What we need to note here is the separating of the pragmatic question of the usefulness of a judgment from the question of its truth value. Philosophers have tended to assume that the fact that a judgment is in the long run useful in helping us order and predict our experience and/or increasing our survival prospects is strong evidence that the judgment is true. Yet Nietzsche rejects this alleged link: "a belief, however necessary it may be for the preservation of a species, has nothing to do with truth" (WP 487).

In this light Nietzsche's rejection of the importance of truth is not so startling. After all, who but an ascetic fanatic would choose to have true but perhaps life-destroying beliefs over false but life-enhancing beliefs?[6] Nietzsche, like many modern philosophers of science,[7] claims there is no clear connection between truth and various pragmatic virtues. Once we separate the question of pragmatic virtues from the question of truth the property of truth loses its importance. Indeed, if pragmatic virtues are no guide to truth it would seem that truth is unobtainable—for how could we ever recognize it—and hence doubly unworthy of our interest.

Nietzsche uses this divorce to raise another serious question totally ignored by modern philosophers from Kant to later-day scientific realists: Why value the pragmatic features we do in fact (explicitly or implicitly) value? For instance, in theory choice certain pragmatic features—conservatism, simplicity, generality—are said to be valued because they are indicators of truth. Yet if, as Nietzsche maintains, this is not so, this opens up the possibility of favoring alternative pragmatic features. The Christian perspective, the socialist perspective, might be useful for furthering particular kinds of life, a particular type of man. Yet, asks Nietzsche, is that the type of life we wish to promote? This theme will be pursued in section 7 below.

Nietzsche is not merely a sceptic who questions the link between utility and truth. In fact he positively suggests that utility and truth are inversely linked: "Truth is the kind of error without which a certain species of life could not live. The value for life is ultimately decisive" (WP 493). By "Truth" Nietzsche here presumably means that which is taken to be true. Thus he is

---

[6] Actually, this seems to have been a possibility taken rather seriously by the early Nietzsche of *The Birth of Tragedy*.

[7] For instance, cf. Bas van Fraassen, *The Scientific Image* (Oxford: Clarendon Press, 1980), 4, 87, 88, and 90.

here saying that what we take to be true, that is, that which is "species" preserving, is a kind of error. Yet in what sense is that which is taken to be true an error? Is it an error in the realist sense of being an inaccurate description of the facts? Such an interpretation seems ruled out by Nietzsche's rejection of the notion of facts: "facts are precisely what there is not, only interpretations" (WP 481). The clue to this problem is to be found in Nietzsche's contention that all judgments involve life preserving simplifications; "The entire apparatus of knowledge is an apparatus for abstraction and simplification—directed not at knowledge but at taking possession of things" (WP 503). Through such simplifications we create a manageable world. But in so doing we must, at least at the moment of making the judgment, ignore alternative simplifications that would result in other worlds. And usually we insist that all opposing views are false.

Here then is a third strand in Nietzsche's critique of truth: By overestimating the importance of truth we fail to recognize the primary dynamic importance of ideas as vehicles for promoting and stultifying various forms of life.

5. NIETZSCHE'S WAR ON THE UNCONDITIONAL

If we follow Nietzsche in regarding beliefs and values as adaptive equipment, we should acknowledge that like all such equipment they may in changing circumstances lose their beneficial effects. The utility of beliefs and values will vary over both people and times.

An idea that may be suitable for one type of person may at the same time be stultifying for another: "What serves the higher type of man as nourishment or delectation must also be the poison for a very different and inferior type. The virtues of the common man might signify vices and weakness in a philosopher" (BGE 30). This is the basis of Nietzsche's vehement rejection of what he calls "the worst of tastes the taste for the unconditional" (BGE 31). It is this tendency towards the unconditional, towards the notion that what is good for one is good for all, that Nietzsche identifies as the heart of all moralities (cf., for instance, BGE 198, A 9). Nietzsche is wary of the unconditional because it serves to make one standard, usually the mediocre standard of the herd, fit all.

If we agree that an idea that is useful for some individuals might be stultifying for others we will, by the same token, allow that an idea that at one time proves useful for an individual might at another time be stultifying for that same individual. This claim is well exemplified by Nietzsche's attitude towards his own ideas. He does not treat his ideas as permanent positions reached at the end of painstaking and comprehensive inquires. Rather he treats them as experiments and temporary expedients:[8]

For me they were steps, I have climbed upon them—therefore I had to pass over them. But they thought I wanted to settle down on them . . . (TI I. 42)

They ["our accidental positions"] serve us as hostels for the night, which a wanderer needs and accepts—we beware of settling down. (WP 132)

At times we see certain solutions of problems that inspire faith in *us*; some call them henceforth *their* "convictions." Later—we see them only as steps to self knowledge, signposts to the problem we *are* . . . (BGE 231)

Nietzsche rejects the notion of unconditional truth, the notion that if an idea is true for one it is true for everyone at all times.

Yet there are texts that apparently belie this claim. For instance in *The Will to Power* we read: "we demand that the herd morality be held sacred *unconditionally*" (132—emphasis mine). We should also note that an overly strident rejection of the unconditional can quickly lead to paradox: To claim that *everyone* (at all times) should reject the notion of unconditional truth is to make an unconditional statement. Hence if we truly accept it then we must reject it. Indeed Nietzsche demonstrates a shrewd awareness of the paradoxical nature of an unconditional rejection of the unconditional when he writes: "Every morality is, as opposed to *laisser aller*, a bit of tyranny against 'nature'; also against reason; but this in itself is no objection, as long as we do not have some other morality which permits us to decree that every kind of tyranny and unreason is impermissible" (BGE 188). Presumably Nietzsche the amoralist does not have such an alternative morality, for inasmuch as the term "morality" has a pejorative sense for Nietzsche it is to be understood as referring to such universal prescriptions. Nietzsche is quite content that *certain people*, for instance "tame Christians," accept the notion of unconditional truth. Now consider again the passage from *The Will to Power* quoted above: Though Nietzsche demands that the herd morality be held sacred unconditionally he does not demand that *everyone* hold it sacred unconditionally. Presumably he does not himself hold it sacred and clearly he does not intend his "free spirits" to subscribe to herd morality. What Nietzsche is demanding is that members of the herd hold herd morality to be sacred unconditionally. Thus he says "The ideas of the herd should rule in the herd—but not reach out beyond it" (WP 287). The unconditional, absolutist morality of the herd provides herd members with a perspective

---

[8] This raises the question of how Nietzsche wishes his (ideal) audience to receive his views. After all, if he sees his various claims as merely temporary steps, it would be somewhat incongruous for him to desire that his audience be wholly and permanently convinced of the truth of those claims. This question is addressed at the end of section 6 below.

whereby they can tolerate their lives and in so doing makes them manageable. The notion that there is universal right and wrong is intrinsic to the Christian faith. That faith was necessary for certain great individuals to arise (including, presumably, Nietzsche himself) and is for certain weak wills still a necessary condition of existence.

Nietzsche's rejection of the unconditional is itself a conditional rejection. He wants those who are capable of greater life and who are hampered by the notion of unconditional truth to dispense with that notion, to no longer feel its constraints. Yet he is happy that lesser mortals should remain with their unconditional truths. Thus it is that he does not reject Christianity *in toto*:

To ordinary human beings, finally—the vast majority who exist for service and the general advantage, and may exist only for that—religion gives an inestimable contentment with their situation and type. . . . Perhaps nothing in Christianity and Buddhism is as venerable as their art of teaching even the lowest how to place themselves through piety in an illusory higher order and thus to maintain their contentment with the real order, in which their life is hard enough—and precisely this hardness is necessary. (BGE 61)

Thus it is that he says:

What I fight against: that an exceptional type should make war on the rule—instead of grasping that the continued existence of the rule is the precondition for the value of the exception. (WP 894)

Nietzsche's rejection of the unconditional is not based on the belief that everything unconditional is false. Nor is it based on the belief that everything unconditional represents a self-deception, a refusal to acknowledge the possibility of alternative interpretations. According to Nietzsche self-deception is an inevitable part of life. Nietzsche's primary complaint against the unconditional is that it serves to promote the interests of average men, the herd, over the development of great individuals.

More generally when Nietzsche rails against the unconditional, metaphysics, truth, we would do well to realize that his is not an unconditional rejection. For instance, against the Heideggerian claim that Nietzsche sought to end all metaphysics we might say that Nietzsche merely desired that *particular* metaphysical notions, for instance the Christian cosmology, be abandoned.[9] More accurately, he desired that they be abandoned by certain types of people. But this is not to say that Nietzsche desired to be permanently rid of *all* metaphysics. Certainly Nietzsche sees every metaphysics as a deception, a lie. Yet, as noted above, Nietzsche does not claim that falsity, self deception, are vices to be avoided at all cost (cf. also GS

---

[9] Cf. M. Heidegger, *Nietzsche: The Will to Power as Art* (New York: Harper & Row, 1971), esp. ch. 1: "Nietzsche as Metaphysical Thinker," 3–6.

344). Indeed, since he claims "untruth is a condition of life" (BGE 4) and maintains that he is the one truly life-affirming spirit, he is, in some sense, committed to affirming the false, that is, in the very act of speaking he is involved in promoting a perspective that promotes his ideal kind of life at the price of thereby suppressing other, *possibly* equally, valid perspectives. As Nietzsche himself so dramatically puts it, "Enough, I am still alive; and life has not been devised by morality: it wants deception, it lives on deception" (HH, Preface, 1). For Nietzsche the desire to escape illusion is a desire to escape life. It is no more than a return to the ascetic ideal (cf. GM III. 25). It is typical of members of the priestly caste and their successors, the professional scholars, to regard the inevitability of error as a tragedy. Nietzsche is not committed to the elimination of all metaphysics, to the elimination of "error qua error." What he does desire is that certain metaphysical notions, certain errors that retard individuals, not be universally adhered to.

6. NIETZSCHE'S VALUES

In his rejection of dogma and the unconditional Nietzsche is a would-be liberator. Yet what sets him so far apart from many of his modern democratic counterparts is that he seeks to liberate only those few he regards as fit for liberation—presumably those who are capable of arising above the herd and becoming truly "free spirits." Nietzsche does not reject ideas because he regards them as false. Thus he says of Christian morality "it is not error as error that horrifies me at this sight" (EH IV. 7). Nietzsche rejects certain interpretations because of their stultifying effects. Thus he says: "The whole absurd residue of Christian fable, conceptual cobweb spinning and theology does not concern us, it could be a thousand times more absurd and we would not lift a finger against it. . . . What is it we combat in Christianity? That it wants to break the strong" (WP 252). Similarly, in *The Antichrist* Nietzsche, after putting the rhetorical question "Is there any difference whatever between a lie and a conviction?" (A 55), tells us: "Ultimately the point is to what *end* a lie is told. That 'holy' ends are lacking in Christianity is *my* objection to its means. Only *bad* ends: the poisoning, slandering, denying of life, contempt for the body, the denigration and self-violation of man through the concept of sin—*consequently* its means too are bad" (A 56—emphasis Nietzsche's). Nietzsche's attack on Christianity is based on the fact that it enfeebles strong wills, not that it is false. Thus after characterizing the popular notion of God as "a crime against life" Nietzsche, with typical hyperbole, exclaims "If this God of the Christians were proved to us to exist we should know even less how to believe in him" (A 47). That Christianity enfeebles is not a point of logic but a psychological observation. It is possible that Christianity could serve to help certain individuals achieve a great destiny; indeed it has so served. Yet in the modern era this is rarely the case. Rather it functions more to retard greatness in certain individuals who but for religious influence might have been thoroughly remarkable.[10] For Nietzsche Christianity has in this sense outlived its time. Part of Nietzsche's project is to combat this stultifying effect. In the *Genealogy of Morals* he places Christianity as a merely historical phenomenon arising from the exigencies of particular circumstances. In so doing he allows his readers a perspective from which the dictates of the Christian world view will no longer appear as eternal imperatives. Nietzsche, we might say, seeks to historicize Christianity in order to overcome it.

And what of those for whom Christianity is the highest form of life possible? First, such individuals are unlikely to be among Nietzsche's readers. Second, they are not particularly likely to be affected by his writings. And finally, Nietzsche is not concerned with catering to what he takes to be mediocre forms of life.

Nietzsche not only refuses to reject ideas simply because he takes them to be false. He questions the very enterprise of seeking truth: "Reverence for truth is already the consequence of an illusion . . . one should value more than truth the force that forms, simplifies, shapes, invents" (WP 602). For Nietzsche truth and falsity are simply not the issues. What he is concerned about is "cultivating the plant man": "A doctrine is needed powerful enough to work as a breeding agent" (WP 862).

This talk of cultivating the plant man and of breeding agents does not give a very clear picture of what Nietzsche does value. Clearly he values the cultivation of great individuals over the happiness of what he disparagingly calls "the herd" (cf., for example, WP 766, BGE 126, 258). But what is a great individual and how is one to become one? Nietzsche is occasionally willing to cite examples, with Goethe and Napoleon figuring predominantly, but gives no general recipe. Yet, as Alexander Nehamas points out in his recent *Nietzsche: Life as Literature*[11] this reticence is hardly surprising. There is neither an informative general characterization of individual greatness nor a recipe for achieving it. Anything that could be captured by such a general characterization would hardly be uniquely individual. Rather than describing such an individual Nietzsche, through his writings, exemplifies one. This individual is not an example to be followed but an end in itself. Yet hopefully

---

[10] One of Nietzsche's favorite, though highly implausible examples of such retardation is the case of Pascal. I say implausible because it seems to me that the very fact that Pascal took Christianity so seriously is the root of his extraordinary thought.

[11] (Cambridge, Mass.: Harvard University Press, 1985); cf. pp. 229–35.

such an end might provoke other beings to become ends in themselves rather than mere herd animals.

Nietzsche did not seek pale imitators but bold innovators and experimenters. Thus his repeated claim that his words are intended only for select ears (for instance, cf. EH, Preface, 3). His own work was not intended to provide a body of truths to be built upon through further research. Thus he tells us

I mistrust all systematizers and avoid them. The will to a system is a lack of integrity. (TI I. 26)

I am not narrow enough for a system—not even my own system. (SW X. 378—translation mine)

More appropriately his work was intended as a tool for liberation. As for the liberated it is up to them to create their own individuality. Thus Zarathustra's fatal words:

This—is now *my* way: where is yours? (Z III, "On the Spirit of Gravity," 2)

7. NIETZSCHE'S LANGUAGE

A lot has been made and said of Nietzsche's language and often in the way of apologia by those who would seek to reclaim Nietzsche to the scholarly fold. On this view Nietzsche's language is to be seen as an unfortunate excess. Against this trend Nehamas[12] suggests that Nietzsche's eccentric style, or, more accurately, Nietzsche eccentric styles, serve an expressly ideological purpose: They highlight the fact that Nietzsche's views are exactly that, *his views*, one perspective among many competing alternatives.[13] As Nehamas points out, it would be both self-defeating and boring for Nietzsche to continually preface all his contentions with disclaimers such as "the following is merely my view." Instead Nietzsche alerted his readers to this fact by his use of various writing styles which, by their very literary nature, serve to constantly bring before the reader the fact that he is hearing one man's voice. Where others use a self-effacing measured scholarly style, implicitly suggesting that theirs is the voice of a universal reason, Nietzsche uses loud, bombastic self-advertising tropes.

I believe Nehamas provides a useful corrective to those interpretations which treat Nietzsche's rhetoric as a mere character flaw to be excused. Yet,

---

[12] Nehemas, *Nietzsche: Life as Literature*, ch. 1.

[13] This is not to claim that all perspectives are equally worthy. Nietzsche is only claiming that no perspective is to be unconditionally preferred over all others.

as Nehamas says, while his analysis does explain why Nietzsche uses a multiplicity of styles and why he uses such writerly styles and tropes, it does not explain why he uses the particular styles and tropes he does employ. In the rest of this section I examine a few of his most prevalent metaphors and attempt to show how they augment the general interpretation I have been developing.

When we turn to Nietzsche's language we find two types of metaphors particularly striking and pervasive, namely, martial and organic metaphors. Repeatedly, where others talk of arguing against and refuting ideas, Nietzsche talks of making war on and annihilating ideas. In *Ecce Homo* Nietzsche talks of "overthrowing idols" (EH, Preface, 2) and tells us that he conceives of his kind of philosopher "as a terrible explosive" (EH III, UM 3). Continuing this use of martial metaphors he talks of his "campaign against morality" (EH III, D 1) and of Zarathustra's, and implicitly his, virtue of shooting well with arrows (EH IV. 3). In *Twilight of the Idols*, subtitled "How to Philosophize with a *Hammer*" (emphasis mine) he tells us "This little book is a declaration of war" (TI, Preface). In the same place he disparages dialectics as "the last ditch *weapon* in the hands of those who have no other weapon left" (TI II. 6; emphasis Nietzsche's). In *The Antichrist* he repeatedly makes declarations of war (A 9, 13).

Of his organic metaphors amongst the most sustained is his continual talk of poisons, infections, antidotes and healing. Thus he talks of Wagner as an "antitoxin against everything German" (EH II. 6) and of *Human, All Too Human* putting to an end "all my infections with 'higher swindle', 'idealism'" (EH III, HH 5). In *The Gay Science* he tells us: "Every philosophy, every art may be regarded as a healing and helping appliance in the service of growing and struggling life: that always presupposes suffering and sufferers" (GS 370). In *Twilight of the Idols* he exclaims "The doctrine of equality! . . . But there exists no more poisonous poison" (TI IX. 98) and characterizes Thucydides as a "cure for all Platonism" (TI X. 2). In *The Antichrist* he describes "the theological blood" in philosophy as a "poison" that "extends much further than one thinks" (A 8). In *Beyond Good and Evil* he says: "What serves the higher type of men as nourishment or delectation must also be poison for a very different and inferior type" (BGE 30).

Amongst his favorite metaphors perhaps the most vivid are the forensic where he combines the martial and the organic. A case in point is his repeated characterizing of his kind of philosophy as a knife wielding surgery promoting health through the dissecting and cutting out of stultifying ideas (cf. BGE 210, 211, and A 7). Thus he says, "I do not refute ideals, I merely put on gloves before them" (EH, Preface, 3).

These various metaphors serve a number of interconnected purposes. They help emphasize that Nietzsche is not interested in the scholarly world of measured reasoning aimed at eternal truths. Rather he wishes to affect and promote earthly life. Characteristically, philosophers have taken the mind and reason, the world of the intellect, to be separate from the body and other earthly encumbrances. By characterizing beliefs as weapons aimed at achieving various effects, as poisons capable of destroying life, Nietzsche is providing a language which allows us to refer to the mental without implicitly accepting that it is divorced from the physical. These dynamic metaphors emphasize Nietzsche's characterization of ideas as tools aimed at specific effects as opposed to the traditional picture of ideas as disinterested replicas of an alleged pre-existing order. The intellect, according to Nietzsche, is not a bridge to the heaven of objectivity and Godliness but merely another factor in the earthly causal order. Through his use of organic and martial metaphors Nietzsche promotes his emphasis of becoming over being.

From this perspective we can appreciate his use of crude physiological metaphors. A case in point is his repeated claim that bad cooking and inadequate nutrition are the root of much that is wrong with European man (cf. EH II. 1, BGE 234). Otherwise sympathetic critics have expressed embarrassments about these apparently crude physiological speculations. Yet such critics, besides lacking a Nietzschean sense of humor, fail to realize the polemical intent of these claims. They are not primarily intended to represent Nietzsche's sincere beliefs about the effects of food. Rather they are intended to undermine the Christian and Platonist dualistic conception of man. Where a Christian or Platonist ascribes man's ills to his possessing the wrong representations of reality, to a fault in his spiritual world, the naturalist Nietzsche locates the problem in his least spiritual organ: the stomach. Nietzsche's comments are not simply funny; they help to subvert the Platonic Christian conception of the spirit as being the prime mover in our world.

In *Ecce Homo* (II. 10) Nietzsche himself offers the same justification for his insistence on the importance of physiological considerations:

One will ask me why on earth I've been relating all these small things which are generally considered matters of indifference: I only harm myself, the more so if I am destined to present great tasks. Answer: these small things—nutrition, place, climate recreation, the whole casuistry of selfishness—are inconceivably more important than everything one has taken to be important so far.... What mankind has so far considered seriously have not even been realities but mere imaginings—more strictly lies promoted by the bad instincts of sick natures that were harmful in the most profound sense—all these concepts, "God," "soul," "virtue," "sin," "beyond," "truth," "eternal life."

There is indeed much much more that needs to be said about Nietzsche's use of organic metaphors but this is not the appropriate place.[14]

8. NIETZSCHE'S TRUTH

Above I claimed that Nietzsche uses ideas as weapons. He uses ideas not as means of describing but as tools for affecting change. As a philosopher he aims to be a legislator concerned with a world of becoming rather than a scholar cataloging a presumed world of being (cf. BGE 211, WP 972). This reading helps explain both his use of certain metaphors and his tendency to champion certain somewhat bizarre claims. Indeed, though I will not here argue the point, I believe that Nietzsche's doctrines of the eternal recurrence and the will to power are best interpreted, not as metaphysical postulates, but as devices aimed at combating certain received interpretations. For instance, part of the rhetorical force of the eternal recurrence is directed at Christianity with its pious rejection of this world in favor of the heavenly world to come. The eternal recurrence claims that this world is the eternal world. To minds fed on the importance of eternity and the irrelevance of earthly life what better way to emphasize the importance of earthly life than to claim that it in fact is the eternal life?[15] As for the oft-mentioned weirdness of the eternal recurrence as a metaphysical postulate, it could not be that hard to swallow for minds that had already been fed a steady diet of the metaphysical preposterous, the Trinity, transubstantiation, the Virgin Birth, and the like. That Nietzsche proposes the eternal recurrence not as a new metaphysical truth, but as a device for destroying old stultifying life forms (the Christian world-view) and making way for the new is suggested by notes 417 and 462 of *The Will to Power* where he exclaims

[14] What I am alluding to here is the much discussed and deeply vexing question of Nietzsche's responsibility for the subsequent use of his texts by his sister and yet more sinister elements. Against those who would defend Nietzsche by invoking the traditional distinction between author's intent and a work's causal effects Derrida, in his *The Ear of the Other* (New York: Schocken Books, 1985), has appropriately raised a typically Nietzschean suspicion of this distinction. Those who take seriously the Nietzschean slogan "a thing is the sum of its effects" will concur with Derrida's observation that "[t]here is nothing absolutely contingent about the fact that the only political regimen to have *effectively* brandished his name as a major and official banner was Nazi." In fact I believe the real question of Nietzsche's culpability is best addressed in terms of his responsibility for fostering a set of metaphors, in particular, and most dangerously, the metaphor of degeneration. Nietzsche's complicity rests not in what he said but in his very language itself.
[15] Of course Christians do see this earthly life as being important in the sense that what one does in it will determine one's position in the life to come. But this is merely an instrumental value. The Christians do not see this earthly life as intrinsically valuable in itself.

We have to be destroyers. . . . To the paralyzing sense of general disintegration and incompleteness I opposed the eternal recurrence.

In place of "metaphysics" and religion, the theory of the eternal recurrence (this as a means of breeding and selection).

It is also salutary to keep in mind here Nietzsche's admonition that

An educator should never say what he thinks himself, but only what he thinks of a thing in relation to the requirements of those he educates. (WP 980)

Nevertheless conceding these rhetorical motives we may return to Nietzsche's various pronouncements on truth and ask what then are we to make of them. In particular what are we to make of Nietzsche's claim that truth does not exist? What is Nietzsche's theory of truth? So far I have claimed that Nietzsche attacks the notion of truth in order to attack other related notions that he sees as "non life enhancing." Note it is not being claimed that Nietzsche sees these other notions, for instance Christian other-worldliness, as necessarily damaging to life. His is merely a historical contingent assessment. It is not universal over time, nor indeed is it even universal over all people of a given time. At the particular historical point of time where Nietzsche finds himself he sees certain notions as being life threatening for certain types of individuals. His interventions are aimed at allaying that threat. But then does he not at least regard the claim that Christian otherworldliness is life destroying for certain individuals as being true? To answer "Yes" is to subscribe to the picture of Nietzsche as being to committed to the notion of truth after all. To answer "No" is to deny the interpretation we have been arguing for.

At the beginning of this paper I proposed an analogy between an historian's approach to the notion of witches and Nietzsche's approach to the notion of truth. It was claimed that an interest in the role witch talk plays in various cultures need not betoken interest or belief in witches, and by the same token Nietzsche's interest in the rhetoric of truth need not betoken any interest in the notion of truth. We should now recognize the limits of this analogy. Clearly the historian can study the role of witch talk, giving its causes and effects, while positively disbelieving in witches. This position bears no suggestion of paradox. Yet to claim that Nietzsche is interested in the role of the rhetoric of truth while positively disbelieving in truth is to engage paradox. It would leave us with a picture of Nietzsche according to which he is making various claims about the causes and effects of that rhetoric while at the same time believing that those claims are not true. But note, we have never claimed that Nietzsche disbelieves in truth, only that he is not interested in the notion of truth per se. On this interpretation Nietzsche has nothing to say on the notion of truth itself. At least, he has no definition of truth. Primarily, he attacks the notion of truth as a means of attacking other (contingently, that is, historically) allied notions. He attacks these other notions because of their contingent life-destroying capabilities.

But then why not simply circumvent all this talk of truth and directly attack the notions that are doing the damage? The problem is that of how to press such a direct attack. It would be totally ineffective for Nietzsche to attack, say Christianity or utilitarianism, by claiming that each of these has castrating effects, that it inhibits the development of individuals worthy *by Nietzsche's lights*. The problem of course is that the Christian, the utilitarian, are not concerned with the production of individuals that are interesting by Nietzsche's lights. If "castration" is the price one must pay to reach the world of the blessed our Christian will happily pay the price. While Nietzsche objects to the very ends of Christianity and utilitarianism he realizes he cannot simply proceed by attacking those ends. So even though it is ultimately the ends he objects to, he proceeds obliquely by attacking the worldviews that give rise to those ends.[16]

9. NIETZSCHE AS PRAGMATIST

In this essay I have characterized Nietzsche as somewhat of a pragmatist. This is not to say that he is advancing what has become known as a pragmatist theory of truth—truth as the useful, truth as what is good in the way of belief, etc. Nietzsche is not offering any theory of truth. Nietzsche is a pragmatist in that he is concerned with ideas and perspectives as tools to various ends. He is not concerned with viewing them as would-be mirrors of nature's essence.

This may tempt some to dismiss Nietzsche as a *mere* pragmatist: Might we not simply regard Nietzsche as a brilliant rhetorician who is indeed capable of influencing individuals, but who is ultimately irrelevant to those concerned with truth? Such a response would be too hasty in ignoring Nietzsche's critique of truth. Especially since that critique is based on an assumption common to nearly all post-Kantian philosophy, namely, that our views are not the result of direct contact with an independent reality but are crucially tempered by our own subjective constitutions and interests. For naturalists, especially, Nietzsche raises important questions. Thus suppose we follow Nietzsche in seeing our various perspectives as tools for promoting various forms of life rather than as increasing accurate steps

---

[16] This section owes much to conversations with Rüdiger Bittner.

towards the objective truth. In that case must we not face Nietzsche's momentous question of deciding which kinds of life we wish to promote?[17]

[17] Thanks are due to Rüdiger Bittner, Randall Havas, Mark Migotti, and Alexander Nehamas for comments on earlier drafts.

2

THE DEVELOPMENT OF NIETZSCHE'S LATER POSITION ON TRUTH

MAUDEMARIE CLARK

This chapter provides evidence that Nietzsche's later works overcome the denial of truth in 'On Truth and Lies in a Non-Moral Sense' (TL). In these works, Nietzsche was able to adopt unambiguously the neo-Kantian position of TL—the rejection of transcendent or metaphysical truth as a contradiction in terms—because he rejected as contradictory the very idea of a thing-in-itself. He thereby lost all basis for denying truth, or for its equivalent, the thesis that human knowledge falsifies reality. I will offer this reasoning as the best explanation for the absence of the falsification thesis in Nietzsche's last six books. Although Nietzsche himself initially failed to appreciate this implication of his neo-Kantian position, there is evidence that he later recognized this failure, and my interpretation offers a way of explaining why it occurred.

1. THE REJECTION OF THE THING-IN-ITSELF

Human, All Too Human (1878) already differs significantly from TL. The latter's denial of truth shared with BT the aim of devaluing the truths accessible through science and common sense and establishing the cognitive superiority of art. Nietzsche completely repudiates this aim in HH. He now regards it as the mark of a higher culture to value "the little unpretentious truths" won by strict or scientific method more highly than "the beautifying and brilliant errors" of metaphysical and artistic ages (HH 3).

HH may seem to take a position very similar to TL's devaluation of human truths. It explicitly equates the "world as representation"—the world of perception and common sense—with "the world as error" (HH 19). At one point (last line of HH 19), the reason even seems to be TL's reason for

From Maudemarie Clark, "The Development of Nietzsche's Later Position on Truth," in her *Nietzsche on Truth and Philosophy* (Cambridge: Cambridge University Press, 1990), 95–125. The paper includes references to other chapters and sections of *Nietzsche on Truth and Philosophy*.

denying truth: that the world as representation does not correspond to the thing-in-itself. More often, however, a quite different reason operates. HH considers the world of common sense erroneous because it fails to correspond to the world disclosed by science (HH 10).

In contrast to TL, HH considers the thing-in-itself of little interest. The "strongest interest in the purely theoretical problem of the 'thing-in-itself' and the 'appearance' will cease," predicts Nietzsche, once the origins of religion, art, and morality can be explained without recourse to metaphysics (HH 10). He bases this prediction on the following account of the origin of the distinction in question. The world became "colorful, frightful, profound, and soulful" because human beings projected into it their own "moral, aesthetic, and religious pretensions," as well as their fears, passions, and mistaken conceptions. "That which we now call the world is the result of a host of errors and fantasies which have gradually arisen and grown entwined with one another" and which "are now inherited by us as the accumulated treasure of the entire past." When human beings began to reflect, they were unable to find in the world what they had projected into it. This led to the distinction between two worlds, the thing-in-itself and the world of appearance (HH 16). Unable to find evidence of moral motivation in the world as it appears to us, for instance, they posited moral motivation in the world (or the self) as it is in itself. Nietzsche therefore proposes that naturalistic explanations for the so-called higher human activities would render the thing-in-itself theoretically superfluous. He attempts to provide such explanations by practicing "historical philosophy which is no longer to be thought of as separate from the natural sciences" (HH 1). He argues, for instance, that there are no morally motivated actions, but only egoistic actions mistakenly believed to be unegoistic.[1] Using the same approach to other "higher" activities throughout HH, Nietzsche argues that these activities are not what they seem, but only "human, all-too-human." He also gives a historical account of why they would have seemed more than human.

"Strict science is able to liberate us from this world of representation only slightly," Nietzsche writes, because

it cannot break the force of primitive habits of feeling: but it can gradually elucidate the history of the rise of the world as representation—and, at least for a moment, lift us beyond the whole process. Perhaps we will then recognize that the thing-in-itself is worth a Homeric laugh: that it seemed so much, indeed everything, and is actually empty, namely, empty of meaning. (HH 16)

---

[1] I argue for this interpretation of HH's critique of morality in the first chapter of my dissertation "Nietzsche's Attack on Morality." This interpretation is based in large part on a comparison of HH and D. Among the passages from HH that support it are HH 133 and 138, as compared, for instance, to D 9 and 103.

We must conclude therefore that HH represents a change from the position of TL. Nietzsche still believes that most of our beliefs are false. But he can now explain how he knows they are false, namely, that they are incompatible with what we learn through "strict science." Thus, Nietzsche apparently believes that science, especially in its "greatest triumph"—his own "history of the origins of thought" (HH 16)—gives access to truth, even though he does not claim that such truths correspond to the thing-in-itself. This is just what we would expect if he resolved the difficulties in the argument of TL by unambiguously accepting the neo-Kantian position he articulated in that essay: that the whole idea of correspondence to things-in-themselves (i.e., of transcendent truth) is a contradiction in terms.

However, Nietzsche does not reach that point in HH. Instead he adopts TL's agnostic position regarding transcendent truth. "It is true that there might be a metaphysical world; the absolute possibility of it can hardly be disputed. We view all things through the human head and cannot cut this head off; though the question remains, what of the world would still be there if it had been cut off" (HH 9). A metaphysical world, on Nietzsche's account, is a *"second real world"* (HH 5), one that differs radically from the empirical world, and therefore, given HH's rejection of metaphysical or *a priori* knowledge, from any world human beings can know. To believe in a metaphysical world is to believe that our best empirical theory is not merely false, but radically false.

I interpret the metaphysical in these terms because Nietzsche claims that the metaphysical conception of the world differs widely from what can be disclosed empirically (HH 10) and that knowledge of the metaphysical world would be "the most useless of all knowledge: more useless even than knowledge of the chemical components of water must be to the sailor in danger of shipwreck" (HH 9). Since HH does not assume that scientific knowledge has direct practical value, the point of this remark is that the metaphysical world does not connect up in any way with the kind of knowledge accessible to human beings. It is not as if we could get to the metaphysical world from where we are by a process of internal criticism, or by developing better theories. Even acquiring information that is in principle inaccessible to human beings would not suffice to give access to a metaphysical world, for such information might be very helpful to us, that is, might help us solve our cognitive problems. HH 9 implies that metaphysics—knowledge of the metaphysical world—would not provide answers that we could find cognitively useful. I formulate this point as the claim that for Nietzsche the metaphysical world differs *radically* from the empirical.

Nietzsche's understanding of a metaphysical world is closely related to the second way of conceptualizing the thing-in-itself discussed in Chapter 2. To believe in the thing-in-itself, on this account, is to believe that truth and reality are independent not only of our capacities, but also of our cognitive interests, in the sense that what would satisfy our best standards of rational acceptability might still be false. As I use the phrase "radically" above, to believe in the thing-in-itself is to believe that our best theory *might* be not only false, but radically false, that the truth *might* differ radically from what can be manifest to us. To believe in a metaphysical world, in contrast, is to believe that our best theory (which would be an empirical theory, given Nietzsche's view in HH) *is* radically false, that truth *does* differ from what would satisfy our cognitive interests.

Belief in a metaphysical world therefore presupposes belief in the existence or conceivability of the thing-in-itself but is not identical to it. There is a metaphysical world only if truth differs radically from what human beings can know (empirically), whereas the world is a thing-in-itself if (as far as we can tell from our concept of truth) its true nature *might* differ radically from the best human theory of it. HH's claim that there *might* be a metaphysical world therefore amounts to the claim that there *is* a thing-in-itself, that is, that the world's true nature is independent of (but not necessarily different from) the best human theory.

This way of construing the difference between the thing-in-itself and the metaphysical world allows for the possibility of a metaphysical realism, an understanding of truth as correspondence to the thing-in-itself, that affirms the ability of empirical science to give us truth. Such realism would insist that the truth could have differed from what satisfies our cognitive interests, but in fact does not, due to the goodness of God (Descartes) or the contingent requirements of the evolutionary process (contemporary scientific realism).

HH's position on the metaphysical world is equivalent to TL's agnosticism regarding truth. We cannot rule out the possibility that the truth differs radically from our best theory, but we cannot know whether or not it does. This means that we cannot know whether or not our truths correspond to things-in-themselves or possess metaphysical truth. HH's position therefore remains incompatible with the neo-Kantian rejection of metaphysical truth. However, the agnosticism of HH shows a marked change of emphasis. In TL, Nietzsche resorted momentarily to agnosticism when he recognized an objection to his much greater temptation to affirm a metaphysical world (to insist that truth does indeed differ from what can be disclosed empirically). In HH, on the other hand, his agnosticism fights what would otherwise be his tendency to discard the whole idea of a metaphysical world. He cannot yet discard it because he has not yet found a way to deny the conceivability of the thing-in-itself.

By the time he writes *Beyond Good and Evil* (1886), Nietzsche evidently thinks he has found a way. The following passage explicitly rejects the conceivability of the thing-in-itself. "That 'immediate certainty,' as well as 'absolute knowledge' and the 'thing-in-itself,' involve a *contradicto in adjecto*, I shall repeat a hundred times; we really ought to free ourselves from the seduction of words!" (BGE 16). The remainder of this passage explains Nietzsche's criticism of the idea of "immediate certainty." It does not make obvious why the very idea of the thing-in-itself involves a contradiction in terms. The best explanation I can find in the published works belongs to *The Gay Science* (1882). In GS 54, Nietzsche repeats the claim of HH, that the appearance of things to human beings is determined by what we have inherited from our "human and animal past, indeed [from] the whole primal age and the past of all sentient being" (GS 54). However, he no longer stresses the erroneous character of this apparent world. Instead, he writes: "What is 'appearance' for me now? Certainly not the opposite of some essence: what could I say about any essence except to name the attributes of its appearance! Certainly not a mask that one could place on an unknown X or remove from it!" (GS 54). In TL, Nietzsche wrote of the "mysterious X of the thing-in-itself" and equated it with "the essence of things." The passage above evidently denies that we have any way of conceiving of such an essence. Nietzsche offers the same argument against the thing-in-itself discussed in Chapter 2, that we have no way of conceiving of a thing's essence except in terms of its appearance. If we can conceive of what something is only in terms of its possible appearances, we have no way of conceiving of it as it is in itself.

This argument is effective against the thing-in-itself only if we conceptualize the latter in the first and most obviously objectionable way discussed in Chapter 2, that is, if the thing-in-itself is independent of (possibly different from) how it could appear to any possible knower. If we can think of a thing's essence only in terms of its possible appearances, we cannot think of its essence as independent of these appearances. But this seems compatible with understanding its essence as independent of its possible appearances to human beings, thus insisting on the possibility of a metaphysical world.

I nevertheless believe that the argument of GS 54 gives Nietzsche all he needs to reject the positions of both TL and HH. TL is the more obvious case because it explicitly makes the thing-in-itself into an unknowable essence, forever concealed from view by the thing's appearances. Given TL's representational view of knowledge, this essence must be independent of its appearances not only to human beings, but to any possible knower. Because the object known is always a representation, the thing itself is always hidden by the representation, and its essence may differ from it. This Nietzsche explicitly rejects when he claims that we can think of a thing's essence only in terms of its possible appearances.

HH, on the other hand, does not so clearly commit Nietzsche to an essence that is independent of all possible appearances. In refusing to rule out a metaphysical world, it insists only that truth or essence might differ radically from its possible appearances to human beings. Further, the reason Nietzsche gives for this claim seems convincing: "We view all these through the human head and cannot cut this head off: though the question remains, what of the world would still be there if it had been cut off" (HH 9). Because we only know things as they appear to us, we obviously cannot know what they would be like if we could remove from their appearance what our way of knowing contributes. How, then, could we possibly know that reality and truth do not differ radically from how things appear to us?

From the viewpoint of GS and later works, the problem with this argument—in particular, with the question as to "what of the world would still be there if [the human head] had been cut off"—is that it presupposes that a thing's essence is independent of all its possible appearances. It suggests that if we could only subtract the contribution our mode of knowing makes to a thing's appearance, we would know what it really is, what it is in itself. But there are two ways to understand "what it really is." The most obvious is "what it is independently of how it appears." In this case, the argument of HH 9 presupposes what GS 54 rejects: the possibility of an essence that differs from all of the thing's appearances. To avoid interpreting HH 9 in these terms, we would have to take its final question to mean that, for all we can know, there might be a better or more adequate way of knowing things than the ways available to human beings. But HH 9 does not seem concerned with other ways of knowing. It suggests a comparison not of human with other ways of knowing, but of a thing's appearance to humans with what it is apart from our way of knowing it. And even if "what it is apart from our way of knowing it" does mean "what it is in relation to a better way of knowing," Nietzsche's argument could not establish the conclusion he wants—that there might be a metaphysical world—unless it presupposes that the thing's essence is independent of its appearances to all knowers. For we must ask what would make the other way of knowing "better." If we say that its results correspond more closely to what the thing really is, we imply that the thing's essence is independent of all of its appearances. To avoid this implication, we would have to say that the other way of knowing is superior because it would, if we could only have it, satisfy our standards of rational acceptability or cognitive interests (other than truth) better than does our own way. In this case, however, we would be talking not about a metaphysical world, but about another world of appearance. As I have argued earlier in this section, HH 9 denies that belief in a metaphysical world would be cognitively useful to us. Its truth or superiority to the empirical world clearly cannot depend on its ability to satisfy our cognitive interests (other than truth).

Therefore, HH's commitment to the thing-in-itself in the apparently innocuous sense—that reality and truth differ radically from their appearance to human beings—actually relies on the more obviously objectionable idea of the thing-in-itself, on the assumption that reality might differ from any of its possible appearances. Nietzsche's argument against the latter in GS 54 is therefore effective against both senses of the thing-in-itself, and therefore against HH's claim that there might be a metaphysical world (see section 4 for more on this issue).

Because he thus repudiates the thing-in-itself as a contradiction in terms, Nietzsche should be able to adopt fully and unambiguously the neo-Kantian position of TL. His position should be that our beliefs do fail to correspond to things-in-themselves, but that, since the whole idea of such things is a contradiction in terms, we cannot consider our knowledge limited or devalued by this "failure." This would leave no basis for understanding truth as correspondence to the thing-in-itself or for judging the truth of our beliefs in terms of such correspondence. Nietzsche would therefore lose the basis for TL's denial of truth and should admit that many of our beliefs are true. The question is whether Nietzsche himself drew this conclusion from his denial of the thing-in-itself. The following sections of this chapter offer evidence that he did.

2. TRUTH AND SCIENCE IN NIETZSCHE'S LATER WORKS

The most important evidence that Nietzsche drew the correct conclusion from BGE's rejection of the thing-in-itself is his remarkably changed view of truth thereafter. In the six books that follow BGE, there is no evidence of Nietzsche's earlier denial of truth: no claim that the human world is a falsification, no claim that science, logic, or mathematics falsify reality.

GS and BGE do retain TL's claim that truths are illusions. GS insists that only art allows us to bear "the realization of the general untruth and mendaciousness (*Verlogenheit*) that is now given us through science—the realization that delusion and error are conditions of human knowledge and sensation" (GS 107). BGE suggests that the human world is a "fiction" (BGE 34), and that at its best, science keeps us in a "suitably falsified world" (BGE 24). In both works, logic itself appears as a source of error (BGE 4;

GS 111). In apparent contrast to HH, Nietzsche now counts as falsifications not merely common sense views, but also scientific ones. Although he no longer counts falsity as an objection to a view (BGE 4), his conclusion otherwise seems identical to TL's.

In works after BGE, we find a completely different view. These works begin with *On the Genealogy of Morals* (1887), the first section of which claims that "such truths do exist"—"plain, harsh, ugly, repellent, unchristian, immoral" truths (GM I. 1). Nowhere does this work qualify its initial claim, suggest that such truths are illusions, or that they are not really true. GM does give powerful expression to Nietzsche's perspectivism, and to his claim that the belief in truth expresses the ascetic ideal. I argue in the next two chapters that these positions affirm rather than deny the existence of truth and actually constitute a critique of Nietzsche's earlier denial of truth. If we prescind for the moment from these two controversial Nietzschean positions, it becomes difficult to find in Nietzsche's final six books any remnant of TL's denial of truth or to avoid the conclusion that his view of truth has changed radically.

Twilight of the Idols and *The Antichrist* make this change most evident. In these books, Nietzsche no longer claims that science falsifies reality. Instead, he celebrates science as "the wisdom of the world" (i.e., of "this" world), which Paul wanted to make something shameful (A 47), and presents science as the great liberator from the falsifications perpetuated by religion and metaphysics, which were invented to exploit and prolong any natural tendency to error that may be found among human beings. In contrast to the suggestion in BGE and GS that causality falsifies, he identifies science with "the sound conception of cause and effect," and claims that the concepts of guilt and punishment—"*lies* through and through"—were invented "*against* science, *against* the emancipation of man from the priest to destroy man's causal sense: they are an attempt to assassinate cause and effect" (A 49). An even more striking account of what Christianity destroyed comes ten sections later:

The whole labor of the ancient world *in vain*: I have no word to express my feelings about something so tremendous. . . . Wherefore Greeks? Wherefore Romans?

All the presuppositions for a scholarly culture, all the scientific methods, were already there; the great, the incomparable art of reading well had already been established—that presupposition for the tradition of culture, for the unity of science, natural science, allied with mathematics and mechanics, was well along on the best way—the *sense for facts*, the last and most valuable sense, had its schools and tradition of centuries. (A 59)

The theologian, on the other hand, shows an

incapacity for philology. What is here meant by philology is, in a very broad sense, the art of reading well—of reading facts without falsifying them by interpretation, without losing caution, patience, delicacy, in the desire to understand. Philology as *ephexis* in interpretation . . . The manner in which a theologian, in Berlin as in Rome, interprets a verse of Scripture or an event—for instance, a victory of the armies of the fatherland in the higher light of the Psalms of David—is always so audacious that it makes a philologist climb the walls. (A 52)

In contrast to his earlier claims that "delusion and error are conditions of human knowledge and sensation" and that mathematics and logic falsify reality (GS 107–11), Nietzsche takes the following position:

And what magnificent instruments of observation we possess in our senses! . . . Today we possess science precisely to the extent that we have decided to *accept* the testimony of the senses—to the extent to which we sharpen them further, arm them, and have learned to think them through. The rest is miscarriage and not-yet-science—in other words, metaphysics, theology, psychology, epistemology—or formal science, a doctrine of signs, such as logic and that applied logic which is called mathematics. In them reality is not encountered at all, not even as a problem—no more than the value of such a sign-convention as logic. (TI III. 3)

Because he treats logic and mathematics as formal sciences that make no claims about reality, Nietzsche must surely abandon his earlier claim that they falsify reality. He also rejects as "miscarriage" doctrines which can get off the ground only on the assumption (shared by Plato, Descartes, Schopenhauer, and the early Nietzsche, among others) that the senses deceive us, that they tell us only about "appearance," and not reality. He evidently calls metaphysics and theology "miscarriage" because they cannot be done on an empirical basis, and psychology and epistemology "not-yet-science" because they are not yet done on such a basis, that is, one that respects the relevance of sense testimony.

These passages from TI and A contain no hint of the view that human truths, science, logic, mathematics, or causality falsify reality. Instead, they exhibit a uniform and unambiguous respect for facts, the senses, and science. I find nothing in Nietzsche's final six works that contradicts them. TI's analysis of how the "True World" became a fable might be presented as a counterexample. Section 3 argues that it supports my interpretation. The only other plausible counterexample—prescinding again from Nietzsche's perspectivism and his claim that truth expresses the ascetic ideal—is TI's claim that "the lie of unity, the lie of thinghood, the lie of substance" involve "falsification of the testimony of the senses" (TI III. 2). Wilcox includes this passage (the only one he cites from works after BGE) in his list of those that give evidence of Nietzsche's belief that concepts falsify reality.[2] I will argue

[2] J. T. Wilcox, *Truth and Value in Nietzsche* (Ann Arbor: University of Michigan Press, 1974), 133.

against his interpretation to help show that Nietzsche does not claim that knowledge falsifies in his last six works.

If the quoted line meant that the application of any concept of a thing, and any notion of permanence or unity, involve lies or falsification, it would imply that knowledge inevitably falsifies. In works after BT, Nietzsche denies the existence of nonconceptual knowledge. But concepts always involve unity, and some level of permanence. One cannot know something as a desk, a book, or an electron if one merely apprehends a "chaos of sensation." However, there is no reason to think that Nietzsche regards as inevitable the lies or falsification he discusses in this passage. He explains that "'reason' is the cause of our falsification of the testimony of the senses" (TI III. 2). Because he places it in quotation marks, Nietzsche evidently does not use "reason" to refer to a faculty he believes human beings possess. He evidently refers instead to the interpretation of our faculty for reasoning by those with whom he disagrees, to the interpretation of reason as a nonnatural faculty (as belonging to human beings only insofar as they participate in a world other than the natural or animal world), and as capable of knowledge of reality uncontaminated by connection to the senses. In that case, "reason" means "pure reason," the faculty of *a priori* knowledge. Nietzsche denies the existence of such a faculty, which is equivalent to rejecting non-natural inter-pretations of our reasoning abilities. Chapter 6 will argue that Nietzsche also analyzes such interpretations as expressions of an ideal he rejects, the ascetic ideal. But if only this nonexistent faculty (this wrong and ascetic interpret-ation of reason) forces us to falsify the testimony of the senses, this falsifica-tion is not inevitable. It is forced upon us only by the dispensable assumption that such a faculty exists, by the interpretation of reason as a non-natural faculty.

Nietzsche suggests how this works when he identifies "reason" with "faith in grammar," and "the presuppositions of reason" with "the basic presuppositions of the metaphysics of language" (TI III. 5). This might imply the inevitability of falsification if "faith in grammar" were a matter of following, or believing that one ought to follow, grammatical rules. But it would be completely implausible to equate such faith with "reason" (i.e., a belief in pure reason). Nietzsche's claim is much more plausible if he is suggesting instead (as he seems to be, most obviously in TI III. 5) that philosophers were able to believe in "reason," that is, in their capacity for *a priori* knowledge, because they assumed that grammar reflected the structure of reality. This means that philosophers believed they had nonem-pirical access to reality and a basis for rejecting the relevance of sense testi-mony because they were reading (misreading, on Nietzsche's account) the structure of reality off of the structure of language. Whereas the senses show "becoming, passing away, and change" (TI III. 2), the subject-predicate structure of our language(s) led them to assume an underlying substrate for change, something that does not itself change, but which is the subject of properties which do change. The latter is the concept of a thing or substance that Nietzsche holds responsible for "falsifying the testimony of the senses."

We therefore have no reason to suppose that TI presents our ordinary concept of a thing as a "lie." A thing in this ordinary sense remains the "same thing" when we can attribute to it spatio-temporal continuity under the same concept, even though the thing itself will have changed in the process. It seems highly implausible that "everything empirical plainly contradicted" the assumption that this concept of a thing has application. But that is precisely what Nietzsche says about the concepts or categories of reason he calls "lies" and "errors" (TI III. 2–5). To avoid attributing to Nietzsche such an implausible position, we can take the concept of a thing he calls a "lie" to be the metaphysical concept of a substance, the concept of an unchanging substrate that underlies all change.

That Nietzsche understood the metaphysical concept of substance as an unchanging substrate is clear from the following passage of HH.

Fundamental Questions of Metaphysics.—When one day the history of the genesis of thought comes to be written, the following sentence by a distinguished logician will also stand revealed in a new light: "The primary universal law of the knowing subject consists in the inner necessity of recognizing every object in itself as being in its own essence something identical with itself, thus self-existent and at bottom always the same and unchanging, in short as a substance." (HH 18)

HH insists that this belief in "unconditioned substances and identical things is a primary, ancient error committed by everything organic," and that we have inherited it from "the period of the lower organisms" (HH 18). In both HH and GS, Nietzsche considers this belief in self-identical, unchanging things or substances a purely intellectual error, caused by a failure to notice changes in things (HH 18; GS 111). The TI passage offers an alternative explanation of the same belief. Rather than a purely intellectual error, Nietzsche now finds its ultimate source in philosophers' "hatred of the very idea of becoming" (TI III. 1). This fits with Nietzsche's new view, articulated in BGE 6, that philosophers have always employed understanding "and misunderstanding" as a "mere instrument" (see Chapters 6 and 7 for more on this). Philosophers' hatred of becoming prejudiced them in favor of being, and inclined them to consider being and becoming mutually exclusive. "Whatever has being does not become; whatever becomes does not have being" (TI III. 1). To defend their prejudice in the face of empirical evidence that everything changes, they claimed that the senses—"which are also so immoral otherwise" (TI III. 1)—deceive us about reality, making it appear to involve becoming. To render this plausible, they had to claim that nonempirical access to reality showed them that reality excludes becoming. They therefore had to interpret reason as "reason," a faculty of *a priori* knowledge. But they also needed something to make this plausible, and they found it, Nietzsche suggests, in "faith in grammar," the tendency to suppose that the structure of language gives us knowledge of the world (cf. HH 11). If the subject-predicate structure of language reflects the nature of the world, it can seem plausible, for instance, that all change involves an underlying substrate, something that does not itself change. Because the senses showed no such thing, philosophers could then seem to have a nonempirical mode of access to reality and a reason to reject the relevance of sense testimony.

If this interpretation is correct, the concepts Nietzsche calls "lies" are quite dispensable. They show up not in common sense beliefs or the sciences, but rather in the *a priori* philosophical disciplines Nietzsche rejects as "miscarriage" (TI II. 3). Of course, nonphilosophers also make use of the concepts in question, particularly in the case of the ego or soul and God, but Nietzsche certainly thinks we can and should dispense with these concepts. (When he denies that we need get rid of the "soul" in BGE 12, he specifically rejects the idea of the soul as an unchanging substrate). His final six books do nothing to suggest that these "concepts of reason" need be involved in either the common sense picture of the world of relatively enduring middle-sized objects or the scientific world-view.

Nietzsche's last six books therefore provide no evidence of his commitment to the falsification thesis, no reason to deny his commitment to the possibility of truth in science, nor to the truth of his own theories. Given his earlier works, this seems remarkable and in need of explanation. I find the most plausible explanation to be that Nietzsche abandoned the falsification thesis because he realized that his account of the thing-in-itself as a contradiction in terms deprived him of any basis for it. It constitutes a major objection to this explanation, however—and is probably the main reason other commentators have not seen Nietzsche's development in the way I propose—that Nietzsche maintains his denial of truth in the very works in which he rejects the thing-in-itself. If he abandons his denial of truth because he recognizes its dependence on the thing-in-itself, why does he continue to insist that science, logic, mathematics, and causality falsify reality in GS and BGE, the works in which he rejects the thing-in-itself as a contradiction in terms? My next section provides evidence that it took Nietzsche some time to realize that his denial of truth depended on the assumption of a thing-in-itself.

3. THE ERROR OF THE "TRUE WORLD"

Nietzsche includes "How the 'True World' Finally Became a Fable" in *Twilight of the Idols*, one of his last books. If we equate the "true world" with truth, this story provides strong evidence that he continued to regard truths as illusions (fictions, or fables). I will argue that we have reason to interpret it instead as evidence that Nietzsche abandoned his denial of truth in his last works because of its dependence on the thing-in-itself. It also provides evidence of Nietzsche's realization that he initially failed to draw the correct conclusion from his rejection of the thing-in-itself.

Subtitled "The History of an Error," Nietzsche's story contains six stages, six different sets of beliefs concerning the "true" world. In each case, the "true" world is contrasted with "this" world, the merely apparent or illusory world. Nietzsche makes this clear just before he presents his history.

First Proposition. The reasons for which "this" world has been characterized as "apparent" are the very reasons which indicate its reality; any other kind of reality is absolutely indemonstrable.

Second Proposition. The criteria which have been bestowed on the "true being" of things are the criteria of non-being, of *naught*; the "true world" has been constructed out of contradiction to the actual world (TI III. 6).

To believe in a "true world" is to believe that "true being" belongs to a world other than "this" world, which one therefore regards as merely apparent or illusory (*scheinbar*). But which world is "this" world? Which world has been regarded as illusory? We cannot distinguish it from the "true" world by equating "this" world with the one accessible to human beings, because stage 1 of Nietzsche's history makes the "true world" knowable by at least some humans. "This" world seems instead to be the empirical world, the world to which we grant "true being" if we accept the testimony of the senses instead of insisting that they deceive us. It is therefore appropriate that Nietzsche's history of the "true world" follows the part of TI on "'Reason' in Philosophy" (TI III. 1–5)—discussed in section 2 above—which praises the senses, insists that the senses "do not lie," and claims that we possess knowledge only to the extent that we accept the testimony of the senses (the rest is "miscarriage and not-yet-science").

The "true world" may be knowable, then, but not empirically. The "true world" of TI is equivalent to the metaphysical world of HH. If knowable, it is so only by *a priori* methods. We can therefore interpret Nietzsche's claim that any other reality is "absolutely indemonstrable" as a reiteration of the previous section's rejection of *a priori* knowledge and insistence that all knowledge (except for formal science) is empirically based, that is, based on accepting the relevance of sense testimony. Notice, however, that Nietzsche does not claim that the empirical world is the only world. It is the only *demonstrable* world. Nietzsche therefore leaves open the possibility that reality might differ from our best empirical theory. That he completely denies the existence of a "true" world, as I will discuss, means that this passage gives added support to my earlier interpretation (Chapter 4, section 1) of the "metaphysical world" (now the "true world"). It shows that if in fact truth and reality do differ from what our best empirical theory says they are, Nietzsche would not consider this a reason to say that there is a "true" or metaphysical world. This means that a "true" world must be independent not only of our capacities, but also of our interests or standards of rational acceptability. In accord with my earlier formulation, a metaphysical world must differ *radically* from the empirical world.

Platonism, Christianity, and Kantianism occupy the first three stages of Nietzsche's history. "True being" is ascribed to the world of forms, the Kingdom of God, and the thing-in-itself.[3]

1. The true world—attainable for the sage, the pious, the virtuous. He lives in it; he is it.
(The oldest form of the idea, relatively sensible, simple, and persuasive. Circumlocution for the sentence, "I, Plato, *am* the truth.")
2. The true world—unattainable for now, but promised for the sage, the pious, the virtuous ("for the sinner who repents").
(Progress of the idea: it becomes more subtle, insidious, incomprehensible—*it becomes female*, it becomes Christian.)
3. The true world—unattainable, indemonstrable, unpromisable; but the very thought of it—a consolation, an obligation, an imperative.
(At bottom, the old sun, but seen through mist and skepticism. The idea has become elusive, pale, Nordic, Königsbergian.)

Nietzsche leaves no doubt about the occupants of these three stages. At his most oblique, he calls the third stage "Königsbergian" rather than Kantian. It is otherwise with the final three stages.

4. The true world—unattainable? At any rate, unattained. And being unattained, also unknown. Consequently, not consoling, redeeming, or obligating: how could something unknown obligate us?
(Gray morning. The first yawn of reason. The cockcrow of positivism.)
5. The "true world"—an idea which is no longer good for anything, not even obligating—an idea which has become useless and superfluous—*consequently*, a refuted idea: let us abolish it!

---

[3] True being is actually ascribed to the thing-in-itself in all but the sixth stage, as I have construed these terms. The Kantian stage is distinguished from the others not by its commitment to the thing-in-itself, but by the attempt to establish the nature of the thing-in-itself on the basis of practical (moral) reasoning.

(Bright day; breakfast, return of *bon sens* and cheerfulness; Plato's embarrassed blush; pandemonium of all free spirits.)

6. The true world we have abolished. What world remains? The apparent world perhaps? But no! *With the true world we have also abolished the apparent one.*

(Noon; moment of the briefest shadow; end of the longest error; high point of humanity; INCIPIT ZARATHUSTRA.)

No one denies that Nietzsche places his own philosophy in stage 6. The relationship of his philosophy to the other two stages seems less clear. Magnus finds Nietzsche's philosophy only in stage 6, whereas Heidegger interprets stage 5 as "the beginning of Nietzsche's own way in philosophy" and Wilcox claims that elements from periods in Nietzsche's own development are found in all three of the final stages.[4]

Wilcox's view seems the most plausible. That each of the final three stages represents a stage of Nietzsche's own thinking fits best with the obvious break between the first and the second half of the list in terms of the explicitness of Nietzsche's allusions (and probably, with his estimate of his own importance). Magnus, who takes Comte as the major representative of stage 4, notes that Nietzsche's reference to positivism here is "uncharacteristically gentle."[5] This is understandable if Nietzsche has in mind not Comte, but his own early work. Stage 4 matches my account of HH, usually regarded as the beginning of Nietzsche's positivistic period: Nietzsche argues that the true or metaphysical world has no function to play, but does not deny its existence (HH 9). The occupant of stage 4 argues that the true world plays no cognitive, and therefore, no practical role, but does not deny its existence. The latter point seems clear from the absence of quotation marks in stage 4; the true world has not yet become the "so-called 'true' world." Stage 4 still considers it possible that "true being" belongs to a world that differs radically from the empirical world.

Stage 5, on the other hand, fits my account of GS and BGE. Not content to exhibit its superfluousness, the occupants of stage 5 abolish the "true" world. This means that they deny its existence. Quotation marks around "true world" are now appropriate. The world whose existence stage 5 denies is not one to which it ascribes "true being," and it therefore becomes the "so-called 'true' world," a world to which others have ascribed "true being." This is precisely Nietzsche's position in GS and BGE. As I have argued, these works reject HH's claim that there might be a true or metaphysical world on the grounds that we have no way of conceiving of such a world. Even

---

[4] B. Magnus, *Nietzsche's Existential Imperative* (Bloomington: Indiana University Press, 1978), 135–40; M. Heidegger, *Nietzsche*, 2 vols. (Pfullingen: Neske, 1961), i. 239; Wilcox, *Truth and Value in Nietzsche*, 123.

[5] *Nietzsche's Existential Imperative*, 136.

granting its possibility requires us to presuppose that the world is a thing-in-itself in the most obviously objectionable sense, that is, that its essence is independent of its possible appearances. We lack not only knowledge of such a world, but also any noncontradictory way of conceiving of it. That this is Nietzsche's position explains why he claims, on the page before his history of the "true" world, that "to invent fables about a world 'other' than this one has no meaning at all, unless an instinct of slander, detraction, and suspicion against life has gained the upper hand in us; in that case, we avenge ourselves against life with a phantasmagoria of 'another,' a 'better' life" (TI III. 6). Because it is based on a contradictory concept, the belief in a "true world" can have no cognitive basis or significance. Nietzsche therefore looks for some other explanation as to why philosophers have been inclined to believe in such a world and finds it in the need for revenge against life (see Chapters 6 and 7). For Nietzsche and other occupants of stage 5, the "true world" is the nonexistent and inconceivable world others erroneously regard as possessing true being.

Why, then, is not stage 5 the "end of the longest error"? What defines the further stage for which Nietzsche reserves this honor? Stage 6 involves a realization evidently absent from stage 5: that *with the true world we have abolished the apparent one.* I interpret this as the realization that denying the "true" world destroys all basis for characterizing the remaining world as merely apparent or illusory. The absence of this realization means that stage 5 denies the existence of the "true" world, but continues to regard the empirical world as merely apparent or illusory. The empirical world is regarded as illusory, for instance, if one insists that empirical science cannot give us truth, or that human truths are really illusions. As I have argued, we find such claims in GS and BGE coupled with a denial of a metaphysical world. Therefore, Nietzsche would include GS and BGE in stage 5. If this is correct, Nietzsche must have overcome the denial of truth found in these works.

Stage 6 brings the realization that we can consider the empirical world illusory only if we ascribe "true being" to another world. Stage 5 does not bring to an end the "longest error" because its devaluation of "this" world makes sense only if it ascribes "true being" to another world. Only stage 6 completely overcomes the "true world." With the complete denial of the "true" world, however, all basis is lost for regarding the empirical world or the results of empirical investigation as illusory.

To deny the true world is not to deny truth. Instead, stage 6 overcomes Nietzsche's denial of truth. In TL, GS, and BGE, Nietzsche's characterization of truths as illusions or fictions amounts to calling the empirical world, the world accessible through common sense and science, illusory or fictitious. His history of the "true" world indicates that he gives up ascribing reality to any world other than the empirical world (stage 5), *and* that he recognizes that this requires him to relinquish his claim that the empirical world is illusory (stage 6). That he puts the logical consequences of stage 5 in a separate stage gives strong evidence that Nietzsche later recognized his initial failure to appreciate the consequences of denying the thing-in-itself, which means that he himself went through a period in which he denied the thing-in-itself, but continued to characterize the empirical world as mere appearance or illusion. This fits perfectly my description of GS and BGE. His "History of an Error" is therefore a major piece of evidence for my account of Nietzsche's development and for my claim that he overcomes his denial of truth, present from TL through BGE, in his final works.

In fact, I think he had substantially overcome his denial of truth already in his two previous books, Z and BGE. Although I have so far placed BGE in stage 5, I think it largely belongs to stage 6 (my discussion of it in Chapter 7 will confirm this), but that it still retains some formulations from stage 5 (e.g., BGE 4 and BGE 25). As the passage on the "True World" makes clear, because Nietzsche places *Zarathustra* in stage 6, we must presume that he would place all his later works, including BGE, in stage 6. My interpretation can explain this in the following way. By the time he wrote *Zarathustra*, Nietzsche had pretty much overcome the ascetic ideal (and certainly recognized the need to overcome it), which had provided the motivation for his earlier view that truths are illusions (see Chapter 6). The spirit of Z and later works therefore belongs to stage 6. But it is hardly surprising that a few of the formulations would be holdovers from stage 5, especially in BGE where Nietzsche is in the midst of formulating reasons for the necessity of moving to stage 6 (e.g., BGE 15).

Given the importance of my interpretation of stage 6 as evidence for my overall interpretation, I now consider other interpretations. The only alternative to my interpretation of what it means to abolish the "apparent world"—to deny all basis for considering the empirical world merely apparent or illusory—would be that it means to abolish that world itself, the world that has been regarded as illusory. Magnus gives plausibility to this alternative when he interprets stage 6 as reducing this world to "an aimless becoming in which all ultimate distinctions between veridical and delusory disappear."[6] Magnus believes that for Nietzsche the denial of the "true" world deprives the human world of its highest values (in effect, the distinctions that have made it a world), and therefore brings with it the great danger of passive nihilism. I agree with Magnus that Nietzsche believes something

---

[6] Ibid. 137.

like this (see Chapter 8). However, I find no textual basis for interpreting what he says about stage 6 in these terms.

Nietzsche's history of the "true world" follows a section devoted to denouncing philosophers' devaluation of the senses and empirical knowledge that culminates in the claims that any reality other than that of the empirical world is "absolutely indemonstrable" and that the "true" world is "constructed out of contradiction to the actual world" and has "no meaning at all" (no cognitive significance) except as an expression of revenge (TI III. 6). The issue in this section concerns whether the empirical world or some other is the object of "true" knowledge, and hence possesses "true being." Because we can plausibly interpret stage 6 in terms of these concerns, in such a way that it makes a fairly obvious but important point, there is no textual basis for interpreting it in terms of the otherwise important issues Magnus introduces.

Even if one agrees that abolishing the true world means denying that the empirical world is merely apparent, one might still reject my account of the relation between Nietzsche's final two stages. Heidegger's influential interpretation does just that. Although the apparent world is abolished, he writes, "the sensuous world is the 'apparent world' only according to the interpretation of Platonism."[7] Heidegger thus seems to see in stage 6 a rejection of the Platonic claim that the sensuous or empirical world is merely apparent or illusory. However, Heidegger denies that this leaves the sensuous world as the only one. He takes the addition of a sixth stage as evidence of Nietzsche's belief that he "must advance beyond himself and the simple abolition of the supersensuous (*Übersinnlichen*)."[8]

Stage 5 retains Platonism, Heidegger claims, despite its rejection of the "true" world. I agree with this. It retains Platonism in the sense that it still needs a "true" or metaphysical world, one that differs radically from the empirical world, as a basis for considering the latter illusory. Heidegger gives a different account. He claims that stage 5 retains Platonism because it retains "the vacant niche of the higher world and the blueprint of an above and below." Heidegger takes the addition of stage 6 as evidence of Nietzsche's view that to free ourselves from Platonism we need "neither abolition of the sensuous nor abolition of the nonsensuous (*Nichtsinnlichen*)."[9] We need instead a new "ordering structure" that does not merely reverse the old structural order, "now revering the sensuous and scorning the nonsensuous." Heidegger expresses some doubts, however, concerning whether Nietzsche himself saw his way clear to such a structure.[10]

---

[7] *Nietzsche*, 242.   [8] Ibid. 240.   [9] Ibid. 242.   [10] Ibid.

In fact, it seems clear that Nietzsche did not, given his claims on the page that precedes his story of the "true" world. He claims that as far as we can know, the world that has been considered "apparent," the sensuous or empirical world, is the only world: "any other kind of reality is absolutely indemonstrable." He also insists that the "true world" has been "constructed out of contradiction to the actual world" and "has no meaning at all," no cognitive significance, except as an expression of revenge against life. It is therefore difficult to understand how abolishing the "true" world could introduce the danger of retaining Platonism's "blueprint" of a higher and a lower world. To abolish the "true" world is to say that as far as we can know, there is only one world. It is not to say that what we know through nonempirical means has lower ontological reality than what is known empirically; it is to deny that there is any nonempirical, that is, *a priori*, knowledge of the world. It further denies that we have any noncontradictory conception of the thing-in-itself, and therefore any reason to search for *a priori* modes of knowledge that might allow knowledge of the thing-in-itself. Heidegger's interpretation gets much of its plausibility from his failure to make clear exactly what the supersensuous or nonsensuous world is, and his slide from the "supersensuous world" to the "supersensuous world of spirit."[11] If the nonsensuous world is the world accessible to *a priori* or nonsensuous knowledge, Heidegger gives us no reason to doubt that Nietzsche flatly denies its existence. Of course, Nietzsche is not telling us to revere the senses and renounce spiritual concerns (art and philosophy, for instance). But Heidegger gives us no basis for interpreting his history of the "true" world in terms of this issue. None of the surrounding text suggests that the abolition of the "true" world means scorning spiritual concerns in favor of sensuous ones. The obvious interpretation is that it means denying that we have any conception of a transcendent or metaphysical world, a world that differs radically from the empirical world and would therefore be accessible only to *a priori* knowledge. The addition of stage 6 is fully understandable (and in accord with Nietzsche's claims about the "true" world previously described) as an expression of the realization that one who denies the existence of the "true" world may erroneously continue to regard the remaining world as illusory, the truths about it as "fictions." My next section provides further evidence that Nietzsche did exactly this in GS and BGE by explaining how he got caught in stage 5, denying the "true" world but requiring it for his devaluation of the empirical world.

[11] Ibid.

4. REPRESENTATIONALISM IN NIETZSCHE'S
LATER WORKS

Nietzsche's history of the "true" world, I have argued, indicates that his falsification thesis and denial of truth depended on acceptance of the thing-in-itself. He should therefore have abandoned them in GS and BGE when he rejected the thing-in-itself. His continued insistence in these works that knowledge falsifies suggests that his denial of truth had some other basis than his early belief in the thing-in-itself.

Nietzsche himself certainly denied its dependence on the thing-in-itself. Explaining perspectivism in GS as the claim that "all becoming conscious involves a great and thorough corruption, falsification, reduction to super-ficialities, and generalization," he denies that his falsification thesis has any-thing to do with "the opposition of 'thing-in-itself' and appearance; for we do not 'know' nearly enough to be entitled to any such distinction" (GS 354).

I will argue that he was wrong about this, that the falsification thesis commits him to a "true" world, which makes sense only on the assumption that reality is something in itself. But his falsification thesis and denial of truth had a deeper source than his commitment to the thing-in-itself, in the representational model of knowledge he inherited from Schopenhauer. I have already argued (in Chapter 3) that TL's denial of truth rests on the assumption that there is a thing-in-itself and that this assumption depends crucially on Nietzsche's representationalism. I will now argue that we find the same view of knowledge in later works. This will help to explain both Nietzsche's continued denial of truth in GS and BGE and his failure to recognize that this denial committed him to a "true" world.

Consider, again, GS 54, which rejects the conceivability of the thing-in-itself.

I have discovered for myself that the human and animal past, indeed the whole primal age and past of all sentient being continues in me to invent, to love, to hate, to infer. I suddenly woke up in the midst of this dream, but only to the consciousness that I am dreaming and that I must go on dreaming lest I perish—as a somnambulist must go on dreaming lest he fall. What is "appearance" for me now? Certainly not the opposite of some essence: what could I say about any essence except to name the attributes of its appearance! Certainly not a mask that one could place on an unknown X or remove from it! (GS 54)

I have interpreted the last three sentences of this passage as a claim that we can conceive of a thing's essence only in terms of its appearance (see section 1). The preceding sentences evidently formulate the conclusion Nietzsche draws from this denial of the thing-in-itself, namely, that life is a dream.

This seems a clear expression of subjective idealism. As the dream exists only for the dreamer, the world exists only for the knower. The world has no existence of its own. Why does Nietzsche hold such a position? And why does he think it follows from his denial of the thing-in-itself? Nietzsche's representationalism provides an answer to these questions.

The passage indicates that Nietzsche has not abandoned the representational view of knowledge he assumed in both BT and TL. If life is a dream, the objects of consciousness exist only as representations; they have no existence except in relation to the knower/dreamer. In that case, Nietzsche has only two options: Either there are independently existing things which cannot be direct objects of knowledge or only representations exist. The first option commits him to the thing-in-itself; the second amounts to subjective idealism.

In the former case, the world is always hidden from the knower by the representation. Its essence is therefore independent of what can be known of it. Only an *a priori* argument that the representation corresponds to the object behind it could show it to be knowable. Once Nietzsche denied that there are nonempirical modes of access to the world (i.e., after BT), representationalism left him with a choice between Kant's unknowable thing-in-itself and the Berkeleyan idealism Schopenhauer had adopted with respect to the empirical world. In TL, I have argued, Nietzsche rejected Schopenhauer's view that we have no idea of empirical objects except as representations. Contrary to Schopenhauer, he apparently believed that perception causes us to adopt beliefs about independently existing objects. But his acceptance of Schopenhauer's claim that the object perceived is only a representation forced him to treat any independently existing thing as an unknowable thing-in-itself. Because the thing itself (the independently existing thing) remains hidden from us by our representation of it, we can only conceive of its nature as an unknown and unknowable X, as what would be there if we could only cut our head off. The passage quoted from GS 54 rejects the conceivability of such a hidden essence. This rejection of a thing-in-itself can be made compatible with representationalism only by embracing idealism. If we can only know representations and have no way of conceiving of something hidden by or behind the representation, then we have no conception of anything possessing independent existence. This reasoning explains Nietzsche's conclusion in GS 54, that life is a dream.[12]

---

[12] It is surprising that Nietzsche would present this essentially Schopenhauerian position as "wonderful and new" (GS 54) at this late date—when he had been fighting Schopenhauer's influence for many years. We can explain this by recognizing that Schopenhauer's position involves an inconsistent affirmation of the thing-in-itself that Nietzsche here discards and that this involves a new way of fighting Schopenhauer. He fought Schopenhauer at first by insisting on the

It does not yet explain how representationalism could provide a basis for denying truth given Nietzsche's rejection of the thing-in-itself. In conjunction with this rejection, representationalism would seem to work against the falsification thesis. In TL, the thesis made sense because Nietzsche claimed that our representations fail to correspond to the thing-in-itself. But if there are only representations, to what could they fail to correspond? What is left to be falsified? When Nietzsche claims in GS and BG that logic and science falsify reality, what does he believe they falsify?

The most plausible answer[13] seems to be that knowledge falsifies the "chaos of sensations." Although the most direct evidence for this answer comes from the *Nachlass*, a similar account is found in GS. In GS 354, Nietzsche claims that we think continually without knowing it, but that only the worst and most superficial part of this thinking enters consciousness. Consciousness develops, he claims, "*under the pressure of the need for communication*," and therefore "the world of which we can become conscious is only a surface- and sign-world, a world that is made common and meaner," and which involves "thorough corruption, falsification, reduction to superficialities and generalization" (GS 354). In WP 569, he makes a similar point: our psychological perspective is determined by the need for communication, which requires something "firm, simplified, capable of precision." Nietzsche concludes from this that "the material of the senses [must be] adapted by the understanding, reduced to rough outlines, made similar, subsumed under related matters. Thus the fuzziness and chaos of sense impressions are, as it were, logicized" (WP 569). He then adds that "the antithesis of this phenomenal world is not 'the true world,' but the formless unformulable world of the chaos of sensations—*another kind* of phenomenal world, a kind of 'unknowable' for us."

In its reference to the "chaos of sensations," Nietzsche's unpublished notes make explicit what is required to make sense of the published passage. The latter asserts the following connection between consciousness and communication (and therefore language): "the emergence of our sense impressions into our own consciousness, the ability to fix them and, as it were, exhibit them externally, increased proportionately with the need to communicate them to *others* by means of signs" (GS 354). When Nietzsche then concludes that consciousness involves corruption and "falsification," the most natural interpretation is that consciousness falsifies precisely sense

unknowability of the thing-in-itself (e.g., in TL and HH). GS 54 reverses this. It seems to accept the argument for idealism—for the claim that the world is my representation—from the first two pages of Schopenhauer's major work, but, in opposition to Schopenhauer, insists that the argument rules out the conceivability of the thing-in-itself.

[13] Wilcox, *Truth and Value in Nietzsche*, 133; Heidegger, *Nietzsche*, i. 551 ff.

impressions, which can enter consciousness only in communicable, or "logicized" (universal), and therefore falsified, form.

This interpretation fits nicely with the fact that the specific features of knowledge GS and BGE pick out as falsifying reality are ones Kant construed as *a priori:* mathematics, logic, and the concepts of substance and causality. In these works, Nietzsche seems to accept a naturalized version of Kant's theory of knowledge. He agrees with Kant's denial that the form or structural features of our representations derive from experience, but explains these features naturalistically, in terms of their contribution to the survival of the species (e.g., BGE 4, 11 suggest this). Nietzsche treats the *a priori* features of our representations as the result of an inherited program in terms of which the human brain structures the data of sensation. In this, he follows Schopenhauer and Lange, but adds from evolutionary theory the idea that the program developed over the very long course of human history in terms of what aided survival. This helps explain why he continued to maintain the falsification thesis in GS and BGE. If the data of sensation constitute reality, the *a priori* features the brain's organization imposes on sensations falsify reality, making it appear to have features it does not actually possess.

Given this view, judgments about the desk upon which I am writing involve not only the selection and simplification of sense data, which must be "reduced to rough outlines, made similar, subsumed under related matters" (WP 569), but also the falsification involved in the assumption of an enduring thing and bearer of properties. That we judge such a thing to be present must result from the organization imposed on sensation, since it is nowhere to be found, as Schopenhauer and Hume both argued, in the sense impressions themselves.

The reasoning just outlined explains why GS treats as a falsification the common sense idea of an enduring thing or substance. In TI, I have argued, Nietzsche counts as a falsification only the metaphysical notion of a substance, the idea of a thing that does not change (see section 2). I made a large point of this precisely because GS and BGE seem to regard as a falsification even the ordinary idea of an enduring thing. In GS 110, for example, Nietzsche counts among "erroneous articles of faith" that "there are enduring things; that there are equal things; that there are things, substances, bodies." Nietzsche's belief that there are no enduring things helps explain why he believes that logic and mathematics falsify reality (BGE 4), for he believes that mathematical and logical truths presuppose the existence of substances (GS 111), presumably as possessors of properties, and things to be counted and measured. That logic and math could not have been developed in the absence of a notion of enduring things seems plausible. No such plausibility attaches to the idea that they required the idea of an unchangeable thing. It is not surprising, therefore, that Nietzsche reduces his critique of substance to the critique of an unchanging substrate at the point that he abandons his claim that logic and math falsify reality (see analysis of TI III in section 2).

The most basic assumption underlying Nietzsche's claim that the idea of an enduring thing falsifies reality is his identification of reality with the chaos of sensation. But why would Nietzsche identify reality with the chaos of sensation? His representationalism provides an answer. If only representations exist, it could seem plausible to identify reality with whatever part of the representations we do not "make up." The naturalized Kantian understanding of representations makes sensations the only given aspect, the only thing not made up by our minds. But how could Nietzsche know that reality is constituted by the chaos of sensations, if he claims that the latter is "unknowable by us" (WP 569)? Nietzsche evidently means that it is unknowable by us from a first-person perspective. We can never become aware directly of this chaos of sensations that must be falsified to enter consciousness, but we can nevertheless have knowledge of it on the basis of what Nietzsche considered an empirical theory of knowledge. In GS 354, he explicitly appeals to "physiology and the history of animals" for the theory that leads him to regard consciousness as a corrupter and falsifier. Schopenhauer had already claimed that empirical investigations show that we construct the world by imposing *a priori* forms on the matter of sensation (see Chapter 3 for some relevant passages), and Lange's *History of Materialism* would have added more evidence to this effect. It would therefore seem to Nietzsche that he had the backing of empirical theory for his insistence that the empirical world is illusory or a "fiction."

This explains how he found himself in what he later analyzed as stage 5 of the history of the "true" world, denying the existence of a "true" world, yet insisting on the illusory character of the empirical world. He thought he could regard the empirical world as illusory without belief in a "true" world because he denied that the chaos of sensations is a "true" world (WP 569). It is not a true or metaphysical world because we have knowledge of it by empirical means. If this were the case, no commitment to a thing-in-itself would be involved.

But there is a major problem with this way of justifying Nietzsche's falsification thesis, as he seems to have realized when he writes that "to study physiology with a clear conscience, one must insist that the sense organs are *not* phenomena in the sense of idealistic philosophy; as such they could not be causes" (BGE 15). That is, one cannot consistently give an empirical (i.e., physiological) account of the role of sensations in knowledge, and yet reduce to arrangements of sense data the sense organs presupposed by that account.

> What? And others even say that the external world is the work of our organs? But then our body, as a part of this external world would be the work of our organs! But then our organs themselves would be—the work of our organs! It seems to me that this is a complete *reductio ad absurdum*, assuming that the concept of a *causa sui* is something fundamentally absurd. Consequently, the external world is *not* the work of our organs—? (BGE 15)

This passage shows Nietzsche's realization that for the purposes of giving an empirical account of human knowledge, he must presuppose the existence of real, independently existing, things: brains, sense organs, the bodies to which they belong, and the bodies with which they interact. It follows that empirical accounts cannot provide a basis for equating reality with the chaos of sensations, since they must presuppose that sense organs and bodies are real.[14] Nietzsche therefore has no empirical basis for his claim that the *a priori* aspects of knowledge falsify reality, nor any basis for denying that the chaos of sensations is just another "true" world insofar as it is equated with reality.

In TI, Nietzsche clearly links his abolition of a "true" world to a rejection of *a priori* knowledge. To deny the existence of a metaphysical or "true" world, I have argued, is to deny that our best empirical theories can be radically false. In that case, we have no need for *a priori* knowledge, but only for better empirical theories. On the other hand, empirical theories cannot give us knowledge of a "true" world, but only of the empirical one. As I have reconstructed it, Nietzsche did not recognize the chaos of sensations as a "true" world, because he believed he based its identification with reality on an empirical theory. He did not realize (until he formulated the argument BGE 15) that his empirical theory presupposed the existence of independently existing things. He therefore believed he could draw from an empirical theory conclusions that would follow only from an *a priori* theory about the thing-in-itself. Only an *a priori* account of the construction of the world from sensations could ground his equation of reality with sensations, and thereby his falsification thesis. But if it is accessible only to an *a priori* account, Nietzsche must count the world of sensations as a "true" world.

---

[14] I take the final question of the passage to be an invitation to recognize that we need not therefore deny that our interpretations of the world depend on something about us, for example, the type and range of our sense organs. But as my next chapter argues, Nietzsche's mature perspectivism denies that the "subjective" character of such interpretations gives us reason to deny their truth. See A. Nehamas, "Who are 'the Philosophers of the future'? A Reading of *Beyond Good and Evil*," in R. Solomon and K. Higgins, *Reading Nietzsche* (Oxford: Oxford University Press, 1988), 47–9, for a different reading of this passage.

Contrary to his own claim, then, the account he gives in GS and BGE of the empirical world as merely apparent or illusory does presuppose the existence of a "true" or metaphysical world.

Nietzsche's representationalism plays the ultimate culprit in this tale. It is responsible for his continued denial of truth in GS and BGE and his failure to recognize that this denial required the positing of a "true" world. As I have argued, representationalism made idealism necessary once Nietzsche rejected the thing-in-itself, and that, in conjunction with his naturalized Kantian theory of knowledge, made the equation of reality with the chaos of sensations seem reasonable. This, in turn, seemed to provide a basis for considering illusory the nonchaotic world of which we have knowledge without committing him to a belief in a "true" world. But this position is vulnerable to the *reductio* Nietzsche himself explained in BGE 15.

Nietzsche needed a way out. The way out suggested by both BGE 15 and the interpretation I have offered is to reject representationalism. BGE 15 implies that Nietzsche cannot "study physiology with a good conscience," that is, base his account of knowledge on an empirical theory, unless he recognizes that the senses are not mere representations. Unless he wants to embrace an independently existing object hidden from knowledge by the representations—and thus be back with the thing-in-itself—he must therefore reject representationalism. This, I shall argue in the next chapter, is accomplished by Nietzsche's mature perspectivism.

3

PERSPECTIVAL TRUTH

PETER POELLNER

1. INTRODUCTION

One of Nietzsche's most influential ideas, finding great resonance also in recent decades, is his perspectivism. In various respects about which I shall seek to gain greater clarity here, what Nietzsche has to say under this heading has been seen as in accord with the concerns of contemporary anti-realist or pragmatist philosophers and as anticipating their claims. Indeed, it has even been said that 'there is scarcely anything in any of these [contemporary] arguments against the possibility of absolute representations that cannot be found somewhere, in some form, in Nietzsche.'[1] On this reading, a version of which I shall develop in Sections 2 and 3 of this paper, what Nietzsche's perspectivism centrally involves is the rejection of a certain construal of our epistemic practices as ideally engaging with and mapping reality, or parts or structural features of it, as these are *anyway*, independently of any *point of view*. In contrast to this, Nietzsche is said to maintain that all non-formal or non-conceptual truth is perspectival—hence there is no absolute material truth about the actual world. Many of his utterances suggest or indeed explicitly state some such claim. The caveat should, however, immediately be added that these utterances conflict with others, occasionally even within the same note or passage, which in some cases seem to deny not only the possibility of absolute truth, but of truth *tout court*. While I shall not pursue in detail here this (to my mind unrewarding) apparent line of thinking in Nietzsche, I shall address the important question of the significance of there being some conflicting assertions on this topic in his work at the end of the paper.[2]

---

[1] A. W. Moore, *Points of View* (Oxford: Clarendon Press, 1997), 103.

[2] Brian Leiter has shown clearly how those popular interpretations of Nietzsche which privilege remarks by him that on a literal interpretation seem to negate the possibility of truth altogether not only entangle him in insuperable self-referential paradoxes, but are also in conflict with the great majority of his own utterances and concerns. Leiter makes a powerful case—both textually and philosophically—for abandoning such self-stultifying interpretations. See Brian Leiter, 'Perspectivism in Nietzsche's *Genealogy of Morals*', in Richard Schacht (ed.), *Nietzsche, Genealogy, Morality* (Berkeley: University of California Press, 1994).

It is not difficult to find statements denying the possibility of absolute truth about the world in the notebooks of the 1880s:[3]

appearance as I understand it is the genuine and sole reality of things—that to which all existing predicates apply and which is relatively best described by means of all, that is also by contradictory predicates . . . So I do not oppose 'appearance' to 'reality' but, on the contrary, regard appearance as the reality which resists any transmutation into an imaginary 'true world' . . . (KGW VII. 3. 40. 53)

The perspective therefore decides the character of the 'appearance'! As if a world would still remain over after one deducted the perspective! By doing that one would deduct relativity! (WP 567)[4]

The 'reality of things', that which all our representations of particulars are about, is said to be essentially apparent (*Schein*), while appearances in turn are claimed to be essentially perspectival. Thus, the reason why there is '*only* a perspectival "knowing"' (GM III. 12) is, according to these notebook passages, that the object of knowledge—the world—is itself perspectival. It is the perspectival character of reality which requires any true representations of its essential characteristics to be perspectival. In order to assess this idea and indeed properly to grasp its import we first of all need to get clearer about what the term 'perspectival' means here. Since it is used, in the much quoted passage from *On the Genealogy of Morals* (GM III. 12), as qualifying representations, and since this is also its most common use in contemporary discussions, we initially need to ask: what is a perspectival representation?

We should distinguish perspectival representations from those whose contents turn out, on reflection, to be essentially relative to a specific cognitive equipment, or to be constituted by their aptness to elicit specific cognitive responses from knowers of certain types. For example, the Lockean secondary qualities such as colour are plausibly understood as knower-relative or response-dependent in this sense. For something to be scarlet is, arguably, for

---

[3] I shall make free use of Nietzsche's notebook material, some of which is collected in *The Will to Power*. Most of his reflections on epistemological and metaphysical issues are contained in the notebooks, while the relatively scarce remarks on these topics in the published works tend to be much more condensed and often highly elliptical or allusive. The main reason for this public reticence is arguably Nietzsche's central concern to emancipate philosophical discussion from a paradigm in which epistemological and metaphysical questions are seen as of primary or even exclusive importance (see Sect. 4 below). The philosophical justification for the use of the *Nachlass* clearly should not rest on Nietzsche's own final judgement on it—even were it available—but on its intrinsic philosophical value, and this can only be established through a detailed and informed engagement with it.

[4] The same point is made in BGE 34, GS 54, WP 556, 560, 569. But see GS 374 for a more tentative formulation. Translations from Nietzsche's works are my own, except those from WP, which are by R. J. Hollingdale and W. Kaufmann. *Nachlass* fragments not in WP will be quoted from G. Colli and M. Montinari (eds.), *Kritische Gesamtausgabe* (KGW), by division, volume, notebook, and fragment number, in this order.

it to be such as to look scarlet to beings with the relevant cognitive apparatus—that in fact possessed by standard human perceivers as they actually are—in certain substantively specified conditions of observation. The best philosophical account of secondary qualities like scarlet may be one which construes them as constitutively response-dependent in this sense. The general idea is that in order to characterize them adequately we need to make reference to the possible cognitive responses of subjects of some kind or other. When Nietzsche speaks in one passage of 'this perspectival world, this world for the eye, tongue, and ear' (WP 602), he might be thought to be using 'perspectival' in just this sense, and the claim that the truth about the world is essentially perspectival would then need to be understood as asserting the non-detachability of our true representations of the world from the concepts of (some) secondary qualities. While a few of Nietzsche's remarks may perhaps, with some stretching, be fitted into this Berkeleian mould (e.g. WP 563–4), this is clearly not his main point. One reason for this may be that secondary qualities are not *manifestly* knower-relative. They do not, so to speak, wear their response-dependence on their sleeves, but rather standardly appear to us as non-dispositional, intrinsic features of things. Nothing about the appearance of scarlet marks it out as essentially perceiver-relative or for that matter as a dispositional property. Its essential perceiver-relativity is a feature of it which we attribute to it, if we do, as a result of theoretical reflection and, in many cases, as a result of a certain metaphysics (for example, one according to which secondary qualities as they appear cannot be thought of as causes). When Nietzsche speaks of the perspectivalness of representations or, more often, of 'knowledge', his examples and analogies are usually rather different, and mostly of two kinds:

1. the manifestly perspectival character of spatial, especially visual, perception;
2. the perspectival nature of what he variously calls interests, valuations, or (affective) concerns.

In one of the main statements of this idea in the published works both of these aspects are present:

Let us guard . . . better from now on against that dangerous old conceptual fiction which assumed a 'pure, will-less, painless, atemporal subject of knowledge', let us guard against the snares of such contradictory concepts as 'pure reason', 'absolute spirituality', 'knowledge in itself'; here one is always asked to think of an eye that is inconceivable, an eye that is supposed to have no direction at all, where the active and interpreting forces through which alone seeing becomes a seeing of something are supposed to be suspended or lacking . . . There is *only* a perspectival seeing, *only* a perspectival 'knowing'; and the *more* affects we allow to have their say on a matter, the *more* eyes, different eyes we know how to use for the same thing, the more comprehensive will be our 'concept' of the thing, our 'objectivity'. (GM III. 12)

In the following section I shall focus on the sense of 'perspective' in which the word applies to visual perception, although the import of Nietzsche's argument is clearly not restricted to this specific sensory modality. The conclusion of this argument will be seen to be that actual spatio-temporal objects without characteristics marking them as represented are impossible (the thesis of essential representation-dependence, ERD). The evaluative component of perspectivism, referred to in (2) above, will be addressed in Section 3. It will turn out to comprise three conceptual theses: (1) all representations are dependent on interests; (2) affectivity and the experience of volitional agency are conditions of the possibility of a self–world distinction; (3) what can count as objectively real for us is essentially related, in a manner to be explained, to our actual dominant interests or concerns (the thesis of essential interest-dependence, EID). The plausibility of thesis (3) will be seen to depend on the argument discussed in Section 2, while theses (1) and (2) are entirely independent of this. In Section 4, an alternative, metaphysically indifferen't, reading of perspectivism will be presented which is in principle compatible with the anti-realist interpretation developed in Sections 2 and 3, and which has affinities with elements of both the pragmatist and phenomenological traditions.[5]

2. THE ESSENTIAL PERSPECTIVALNESS OF SPATIAL OBJECTS

To say that visual perception is essentially perspectival or from a point of view means in part that, necessarily, its objects are arranged in a gestalt around the point of origin of the visual field. The space of visual perception is thus an oriented or 'egocentric' one.[6] Things show up in visual perception in ways which might adequately be expressed, for example, as 'about three feet away', 'sloping gently into the background to the right', 'behind and

---

[5] The positions attributed to Nietzsche here can be found in the *Nachlass* from (at least) 1881 until 1888, i.e. the final year of Nietzsche's philosophical activity. In the published works of the 1880s only the claims discussed in Sect. 4 and theses (1–2) of Sect. 3 are fairly unambiguously stated (in HH 9 and TI IV, and GM III. 12, respectively). There is also some evidence in the published works for ERD (GS 54; BGE 16, 34). But these published statements are somewhat vague and general, and thus allow for a rather broad range of interpretations if read in isolation from the more specific formulations in the pertinent fragments of the notebooks.

[6] See Gareth Evans, *The Varieties of Reference* (Oxford: Oxford University Press, 1982), 151–2. The term 'egocentric' should not be taken to imply that the representing *subject* figures itself necessarily among the contents of the perceptual state.

partly covered by the tree in the middle of the foreground', 'on top of the shelf over *there*', 'moving slowly towards me', 'rising more steeply in *this* direction', 'flat over here', and so forth. Such locutions and many others carrying a reference to the point of origin of a visual field[7] attempt to express that aspect of the contents of visual perception which is its perspectivalness. A *purely perspectival* content is one in which there is no explicit relativization to one particular point of view *among others*, e.g. 'The Matterhorn is straight ahead', while a *partly perspectival* content is one which presupposes a point of view (and thus purely perspectival contents), but the latter is relativized, i.e. represented as itself occupying a position on a (relatively) more objective map, e.g. 'The Matterhorn is straight ahead from where Jones is currently standing, relative to his axis of vision'. A *non-perspectival* or *absolute* spatial representation would be one whose content contained no egocentric components at all. Now one way of drawing the distinction between perspectival and absolute representations would be this: absolute representations—if there are any—are simply additive in the sense that all true absolute representations are compatible with each other and can in principle be recognized to be so without needing to deploy a different type or level of representation. By contrast, pure perspectival representations can be true but incompatible. For example, the assertions 'The Matterhorn is straight ahead' and 'The Matterhorn is on the extreme left' can both be true, but they are incompatible unless relativized to different times or different synchronic points of view (and thus no longer purely perspectival).[8] While this way of making the distinction draws attention to one mark of difference, one may feel that it does not so much explain it as stand itself in need of explanation.[9] A promising explanatory approach would seem to be this. An absolute representation of some spatial state of affairs would have to be one in which the manner of representation does not ineliminably qualify the object represented. Since an absolute representation would have to represent the object as being from *no* point of view, it obviously would have to represent it as, precisely, not implying any point of view on it. Hence the object would have to be characterized as independent of any aspect of its being represented. But what is distinctive of purely perspectival representations as illustrated earlier is that the manner of representation explicitly qualifies the

---

[7] The reference is often implicit, i.e. the point of origin (or zero point of orientation) is often not itself thematically represented.

[8] Moore, *Points of View*, 9–14.

[9] As Nietzsche remarks: 'To reduce something unfamiliar to something already familiar, to lose the feeling of strangeness—this is what *counts* as *explaining* for our sensibility' (KGW VIII. 3. 34. 246).

entire object of representation.[10] It is because the objects themselves here are
transparently qualified *as* represented that we can come to understand, once
we attain a more detached or comprehensive perspective in which there is
room for the idea of *different* points of view, how each of these representations may be true and thus not really be incompatible while appearing to be
so when merely confronted with each other.[11] For example, we easily understand why two perceptual contents A and B can both be true, although
incompatible if entertained at the same time from the same point of view,
as soon as we grant that A and B are presenting their respective objects *as
represented objects*. If two thoughts A and B present their objects as
representation-*independent*, then it is mysterious how they could both be
incompatible and jointly true, but the mystery disappears as soon as we
assume that their objects are given as represented. A prior grasp, however
inexplicit or undeveloped, of what a representation and a point of view is
would thus seem to be needed to make sense of the claim that perspectival
representations are non-additive. This leaves us with the suggestion that a
representation's being (purely) perspectival is most clearly understood by us
as involving the idea that some aspect of the *mode* of representation here
qualifies *what* is being represented—the object or referent of the representation. To say, then, that 'all truth about the world is perspectival' would on
this construal amount to the claim that, necessarily, all true thoughts
(beliefs, etc.) about the world represent it *as* represented. This is, in fact,
precisely the form in which Nietzsche casts the question when pondering
whether 'the perspectival is of the essence':

Basic question: whether the *perspectival* is of the *essence*? Rather than just being a
form of viewing it, a relation between different beings? Are the various forces in
relation such that this relation is bound up with a perceptual aspect (*Wahrnehmungs-
Optik*)? (KGW VIII. 1. 5. 12)

What is here and in GS 374 phrased as a question is emphatically asserted in
other notes:

The question 'what is that?' is an imposition of sense from some other point of view.
'Essence', the 'essential nature', is something perspectival and already presupposes a
multiplicity ... In short: the essence of a thing is only a *belief* about the 'thing'. Or
rather: 'it is considered' is the real 'it is', the sole 'this is'. (WP 556; cf. WP 567)

---

[10] A manner or mode of presentation (MP) in the logically primary sense is of course not itself
an object, neither a particular (real) nor an abstract (ideal) one. It is rather an aspect (or better, a
'moment') of a state of representing. It is only secondarily or derivatively that MPs can become
objects of thought. This happens, for example, in the thought expressed by 'I believe that *Nietzsche
is the author of Thus Spoke Zarathustra*'. Here the italicised clause refers to an MP (or sense),
which has thus been modified into an object of thought. The idea that senses in their primary
manifestations are objects is a central deficiency of Frege's philosophy of intentionality.
[11] Cf. John Richardson, *Nietzsche's System* (New York: Oxford University Press, 1996), 279.

Perhaps Nietzsche's thought is phrased most concisely in a formulation from another notebook which, while written somewhat earlier (1881), corresponds closely to many later remarks and can thus plausibly be read as making the same point:

> To think away the subject—that is to represent the world without a subject: is a contradiction: to represent without representation. (KGW V. 1. 10. D82; see WP 560 for a later formulation)

Let us first attempt to get clear about the position that is rejected in this remark as incoherent. We may call it *strong realism*: there are some entities, including some particulars, whose existence and properties do not in any way depend on the existence of knowing subjects and their representations of them. They, or their essential characteristics, are not constituted by or otherwise non-contingently dependent on our or any other subjects' beliefs, concepts, or theories. Let us call them, therefore, *absolute objects*. It is such absolute objects which absolute representations seek to represent. The impossibility of absolute truth is thus introduced by Nietzsche as a consequence of the impossibility ('contradiction') of absolute objects—objects as putatively conceived by strong realism. We may notice here a general feature of Nietzsche's reflections on this topic. If we examine the actual arguments he himself adduces, we find that they tend not to be based on claims about the logical, second-order concept of truth, but on views about certain fundamental ontological (first-order) concepts, in particular *object*, *subject*, and *essence*.[12] This constitutes an important difference from many contemporary anti-realisms. Implicit in this Nietzschean approach is the not unreasonable assumption that our grip on such first-level concepts, while still far from unproblematic due to their abstract, formal character, is nevertheless stronger and more reliable than our corresponding 'intuitions' about the yet further removed second-order logical or semantic concepts. Minimally, then, we may take Nietzsche to be claiming in the remarks quoted above that

(ERD)   it is incoherent to suppose that there are or could be actual, particular (spatio-temporal) objects ('things') without characteristics that mark them out as represented.

This thesis of *essential representation-dependence* (ERD) is the first half of Nietzsche's perspectivism. The last remark quoted (KGW V. 1. 10. D82) and WP 560 actually go further. According to these passages, we cannot 'think away' the *subject* when thinking of or perceiving an object. Now, it would be

---

[12] I therefore largely concur with one sense of Ken Gemes's observation that 'Nietzsche has nothing to say on the notion of truth itself' ('Nietzsche's Critique of Truth', Ch. 1 in this volume, p. 56.) While Gemes is perhaps overstating the point, it is true that there is indeed no sustained analysis of the concept of truth in Nietzsche's later writings.

manifestly implausible to argue that in any representation of an object the representing subject is co-represented. Clearly there can be (for example) conscious perceptions of objects without any *self*-consciousness on the part of the perceiver. Similarly, when (say) visualizing a scene, one can visualize it without representing either oneself or any other subject from whose point of view the scene is visualized. The subject need not be part of what is visualized in visualizing the scene.[13] It is rather more plausible as well as more fruitful to take Nietzsche's point here to be that every representation of an object implies a subject while not necessarily co-representing it. Why this should be so and exactly what it means is a question I should like to defer until I have explicated the second main component of Nietzsche's perspectivism (Section 3). For the moment I shall adopt a minimal reading of the passages under discussion, articulated in ERD.

Why should one accept ERD? One of Nietzsche's own formulations prima facie invites a comparison with Berkeley's notorious argument that it is 'a contradiction to talk of conceiving a thing which is unconceived' since 'the tree or house . . . which you think of' as 'existing by itself, independent of . . . any mind whatsoever' is after all 'conceived by you'.[14] If this argument were sound, it would entail rather more than Berkeley wanted, namely that no one can conceive of a thing which he has never thought of. As Brentano and many critics since have pointed out, the basic flaw of Berkeley's reasoning here lies in the absence of a distinction between the *act* of conceiving, the *object* conceived, and the object *as* conceived.[15] If, then, Nietzsche's thinking behind ERD is different, what is it? It relies ultimately on a certain conception of what it is to think of—to represent or conceive of—a particular. Nietzsche has a strong and unwavering commitment to a broadly empiricist conception of thought which implies that the contents of (at least) all non-logical, object-referring[16] terms are dependent, either immediately or indirectly, on a sensory or quasi-sensory acquaintance with particulars. He often remarks that our ability to 'understand' either is or depends upon an ability to reduce or to derive the items to be understood from something with which we are familiar or acquainted (*bekannt*) (e.g. GS 355; KGW VIII. 1. 5. 10). The most direct evidence that the cognitive relation in

---

[13] Bernard Williams, 'Imagination and the Self', in his *Problems of the Self* (Cambridge: Cambridge University Press, 1973), 34–7. Williams also makes the further clearly correct point that in visualizing something one need not visualize it *as seen*, i.e. as actually perceived, rather than, for example, as imagined.

[14] George Berkeley, *Three Dialogues between Hylas and Philonous*, in his *Philosophical Works*, ed. M. R. Ayers (London: Dent, 1993), 190.

[15] Franz Brentano, *Psychology from an Empirical Standpoint* (London: Routledge, 1973), 93.

[16] 'Object' is here used in a broad sense covering particulars (including property exemplifications) and abstract or ideal objects, if there are any.

question is to be interpreted along broadly empiricist lines as involving an experiential acquaintance with particulars can be found in Nietzsche's remarks on causal explanations and the explanatory paradigm of Newtonian science. Here he characterizes the covering law model of explanation, at least at the basic level, as 'descriptive', and expresses scepticism concerning our 'comprehension' of the events subsumed under mathematical, functional laws (e.g. GS 112; WP 624). Adequate comprehension, he claims, would require an acquaintance with the causal powers involved, with the 'compulsion' (WP 664) which we believe to bring about or necessitate a given effect. Yet, according to some notes, we have no such comprehension because we lack a relevant 'experience' (*Erfahrung*) whose content could legitimately be attributed, even if only by analogy, to processes in the external world (ibid.).[17] Elsewhere he continues this line of thought, observing that the term 'force' remains an 'empty word' if we cannot 'imagine' the 'quality' it purportedly refers to (WP 621; also WP 660, 689). For Nietzsche, then, the intelligibility of (at least) non-logical verbal signs ultimately derives either from experiences of particulars to which they apply, or their meanings must be analysable into components for which this is the case, or else what the sign is about must be 'imaginable'. I take him to mean by the latter expression that, for any intelligible object-referring symbol, it must at least be possible to envisage an instantiation of what is expressed by it by way of (possibly remote) material analogy with items of which we can be aware through sensory or quasi-sensory 'experience'.

Thus when Nietzsche says that 'to represent [an object] without representation' is a 'contradiction' we can plausibly interpret this as the claim that it is impossible to conceive of—to imagine—an object that is not conceived of as qualified by characteristics which mark it as a represented object, hence as a perspectival object. But an object we cannot conceive, so we may extrapolate from his remarks on force, is no more than an empty word. This need not imply that all genuine representing or understanding has to be of a disengaged or contemplative kind. There is no reason why Nietzsche should deny that certain signs or marks which bear no relevant resemblance to the objects conceived (e.g. a linguistic inscription), and which function simply to effect certain practical, behavioural adjustments to one's environment, may also (granted certain further conditions) count as ways of representing aspects of that environment. This should be uncontroversial at least for those cases where the behaviour prompted is not entirely devoid of

---

[17] It should be emphasized that these 'sceptical' notes concerning our adequate comprehension of causality are contradicted by other passages (e.g. WP 689). This is one of the central areas of ambiguity in Nietzsche's later thought. Cf. my *Nietzsche and Metaphysics* (Oxford: Clarendon Press, 1995), 36–46.

phenomenal awareness of the environment.[18] However, Nietzsche would certainly have to deny that a complex consisting of (say) a sign-stimulus and resultant behavioural adjustment devoid of *any* relevant awareness can count as an adequate conception of what the signs are about—adequate, that is, for the purpose of considering questions at a highly theoretical level about the ontological status or structure of objecthood as such.

It is still unclear, however, why it is that in an adequate conception of an object the mode of conception should essentially qualify the object conceived. The answer to this must presumably be sought in the close relation that obtains between *imagining* and *perceiving*. (Remember Nietzsche's formulation, in KGW VIII. 1. 5. 12, of the perspectivist thesis in terms of an essential 'perceptual' relativity adhering to any object of representation.) While imagining an object is not necessarily imagining it as perceived, what it has in common with perceiving is that it includes components which are egocentric or perspectival in the sense elucidated earlier. For example, when I visually imagine the Matterhorn, I imagine it as from some point of view or as from a succession of such points. (I may represent it, say, as one would see it from an aeroplane circling around it.) This characteristic is obviously not restricted to the modality of vision. When one represents an abstract sculpture in a tactile mode, its contours will be presented as quasi-resistances to a tactile approach from a certain direction and angle, or successively from a series of such. Thus in both the as-if-visual and the as-if-tactile cases of envisaging the exemplification of certain properties, what is envisaged will be given as having various egocentric (perspectival) features, such as 'curving away to the right', 'jutting out in *this* direction from the horizontal plane', etc. But can't these perspectival features of the representation be discounted or abstracted from in one's imaginative project? After all, it is often the case that, when we envisage some state of affairs, our representation of it will contain elements which we do not attribute to the object envisaged. When I visually imagine a landscape, my visual image may be blurry or fragmentary, but I do not attribute blurriness or fragmentariness to the landscape envisaged. While we can thus quite intelligibly specify the absence of certain features of one's representation from the objects represented, this is, according to Nietzsche, not possible for

---

[18] I am thinking here especially of the kind of practical intentionality Heidegger calls 'circumspect handling' (*umsichtiges Besorgen*) of what is 'available' (*zuhanden*). See, for a good explication of this, Hubert Dreyfus, *Being-in-the-World* (Cambridge, Mass.: MIT Press, 1991), 60–87. Cf. also John Campbell's analysis of 'working concepts' and causally indexical thoughts in his *Past, Space and Self* (Cambridge, Mass.: MIT Press, 1994), 42–51. The practical modes of understanding described by Heidegger and Campbell clearly do not detract from Nietzsche's point, since they both involve a sort of 'envisaging' of what the corresponding linguistic expressions are about (e.g. when following the instruction 'Do it *like this*').

those features which he calls their perspectivalness. This is the clear implication of his rhetorical exclamation: 'As if a world would still remain over
after one deducted the perspective!' (WP 567). 'Perspective' here refers to
the specific manner in which any spatio-temporal object or its properties
are presented in an adequate mode of conceiving which goes beyond
'empty words' by modelling itself, however remotely or analogously, on
sense perception. Hence Nietzsche in one passage revealingly calls perspectivalness 'only a complex form of specificity' (WP 637)—the very form of
specificity, that is, which also characterizes perception. There is, then, an
asymmetry between this 'form of specificity' and the specific properties
exemplifications of which may well be components of a quasi-perceptual
conception of an object while not being attributed to the object conceived.
When we 'deduct' the perspectivalness from our representation—unlike
when we discount (say) its fragmentariness—the object does not
remain over: the 'representation' ceases to represent any possible particular.
Hence the incoherent nature of such an attempt to 'represent without
representation'.

Among the objections to be expected against this Nietzschean argument
two are likely to be prominent. Even if one grants for the moment
Nietzsche's move (to be considered below) from inconceivability, in his
sense, to impossibility, this only shows, it may be said, that those aspects of
objective reality which can be given a strong realist interpretation are not
of the kind which could even in principle be adequately conceived by means
of a kind of thinking which stands to sense perception in anything like the
relation that obtains between visualizing and seeing. In other words, what
is objectively real in the strong realist sense is not the sort of item that
could in principle be an object of sense perception for some creature
suitably positioned in time and space and with a suitable sensory
apparatus[19]—which means that it cannot be or actualize itself as a quality.
The classical candidates for such non-qualitative, putatively absolute properties are certain abstract structural ones, for example quantitative relations
of functional co-variation, which we have good reasons to believe are
exemplified in physical objects and processes. Granted for now that these
properties can themselves be conceived non-perspectivally, is the idea that
representation-independent objective reality might consist exclusively of
such quantitative relations—the numbers here not being regarded as
indices for qualities—an intelligible one? Well, not unless one is prepared
to countenance the idea that objective reality is itself neither spatio-
temporal nor capable of exercising causal power and hence obsolete for

---

[19] Cf. Colin McGinn, *The Subjective View* (Oxford: Oxford University Press, 1983), 80–2, 111 ff.

causally explaining our knowledge of it. It is difficult not to agree with Nietzsche when he dismisses this view briskly: 'The reduction of all qualities to quantities is nonsense' (WP 564).

The second main objection is likely to concern Nietzsche's move from our inability to 'understand', in his sense, the idea of non-perspectival objects, to their impossibility. This modal claim is certainly to be interpreted as asserting more than a merely physical impossibility dependent on the obtaining of contingent laws of nature. What is at issue is rather an impossibility as strong as that attaching to the denial of conceptual or logical truths. This is evident not only from his talk about 'contradiction' in the notebook passage from 1881, it emerges just as clearly from many later remarks in which he unambiguously states that concepts like *thing*, *object*, and *essence* are 'relational', and that the kind of relation involved is a representational one (e.g. WP 555–6, 560, 562, 568, 583; KGW VIII. 1. 5. 19). In several of these remarks, as well as in other passages, this point is explicitly linked by him to a rejection of what he calls things-in-themselves. It is difficult to resist the conclusion that what he means by 'things-in-themselves' here are (at least) objects of the sort postulated by strong realism:[20] actual object-like items

---

[20] A quite different interpretation of Nietzsche's critique of 'things-in-themselves' has been proposed by Maudemarie Clark in her *Nietzsche on Truth and Philosophy* (Cambridge: Cambridge University Press, 1990). According to her, Nietzsche, at least from 1887 onwards, holds a 'common sense realism', acknowledging that many things are actual and exemplify certain properties although they are not actually and may never be represented. This implies that we have an idea of the obtaining of a state of affairs which does not involve reference to concepts, beliefs, theories, or other representations (p. 45). What Nietzsche's dismissal of the thing-in-itself rejects is only the following two propositions: (1) there might be real items which cannot be known by any conceivable knowers, whatever their cognitive capacities; (2) a theory which ideally satisfies the best possible human standards of rational acceptability might fail to be true (pp. 44–50). Among these best standards are comprehensiveness, coherence, predictive success (pp. 48, 86). Now it would be easy to define an appropriate idealization of Clark's standard of comprehensiveness over sets of beliefs, according to which the best possible theory to be aspired to by us (our regulative ideal) is one which, besides satisfying various other standards, includes existentially quantified propositions representing all states of affairs conceivable by a being with idealized cognitive capacities (Clark's theory allows for such an idealization of cognitive capacities). Clearly, no actual singular state of affairs could in principle remain beyond the reach of a theory which satisfied this standard. It thus emerges that the denial of (2) in fact places no additional constraints at all on what can be the case, and Nietzsche's rejection of things in themselves as read by Clark consequently amounts to no more than the denial of (1). In several places she seems to acknowledge this (pp. 50, 102). But, as she herself remarks, it is 'not clear that anyone' has ever subscribed to (1) anyway (p. 47). Kant certainly did not, for Kant's thing-in-itself is knowable by a possible (conceivable) knower, namely by a being with intellectual intuition. Clark's reading thus has the peculiar consequence that Nietzsche's critique of the thing-in-itself would not affect Kant's own concept of it. But it is surely one of the few unambiguous contents of the passage she regards as the main evidence for her reading (TI IV) that Kant's concept of the thing-in-itself is rejected in it. As far as the textual warrant for Clark's interpretation is concerned, we shall see in Sect. 4 that the explicit wording of TI IV is incompatible with it.

without characteristics marking them as represented.[21] Even if one concedes Nietzsche's point about the inconceivability, by means of representations having sensory or quasi-sensory intuitive content, of particulars without perspectival properties, why should this imply their impossibility? Why should the limits of conceivability in this sense coincide with the limits of what is metaphysically possible rather than merely indicating a psychological inability on our part? When Nietzsche says that the notion of a thing-in-itself is a 'contradiction in terms' (BGE 16), his response to this objection is, in effect, that there is no relevant asymmetry here to the belief that a state of affairs represented by a proposition of the form 'fx and not-(fx)' is impossible. What reason have we for believing that a calculus which contains the law of non-contradiction should unrestrictedly apply to this and every possible world, such that a sequence of symbols of the above form, with its variables interpreted, respectively, to range over individuals-at-a-time and monadic properties, is 'necessarily' false? Is it not that we find it simply utterly perplexing to combine the component meanings, the better we come to understand them, in the manner we are asked to combine them? When we attempt to comprehend what is said in a proposition of this form, we simply cannot imagine any arrangement of the world it might describe. This 'cannot' indicates, however, not merely an ordinary imaginative *lack* or limitation (a 'privation')—as when I say that I cannot visualize a chiliagon. In that sort of case, it is easy to think of a being with much greater imaginative powers who can perform the feat in question. In the present instance, by contrast, the 'cannot' signifies a *positive* characteristic of my cognitive attempt which *increases* as my grasp of the meaning components improves and which terminates in utter perplexity and incomprehension, so that I cannot make sense of the suggestion that a being without my contingent cognitive limitations might actually be able to imagine the contradictory state of affairs.[22] There is no significant difference, Nietzsche suggests, between one's grasp of impossibility in such a case and the perplexity one encounters when attempting to comprehend the idea of an actual, non-perspectival, spatio-temporal object.

---

[21] Some of his remarks in the notebooks indicate that this is not all he means by 'thing-in-itself'. He occasionally concludes from the incoherence of the idea of non-relational (non-perspectival) objects to the incoherence of the notion of something's having a 'constitution in itself', i.e. purely intrinsic properties. It should, however, be stressed that this move can be found only in a few places in the notebooks (e.g. WP 558–9). I have discussed and criticized it in *Nietzsche and Metaphysics*, 109–11 and 281–4.

[22] See also Simon Blackburn, *Spreading the Word* (Oxford: Clarendon Press, 1984), 216–17. For a more elaborate statement, especially of the last point concerning the crucial difference between the 'unimaginability' relevant here and contingently varying ordinary imaginative limitations, see Edmund Husserl, *Logical Investigations*, trans. J. N. Findlay (London: Routledge, 1970), *Sixth Investigation*, §§30–5, ii. 749–59.

One way of seeking to resist this conclusion might be this. An anti-perspectivist may concede that we cannot adequately conceive of the intrinsic properties of a non-perspectival object as they are in themselves. This is so because our conception of its qualitative specificity is bound to be closely related to how the object appears or can appear to a perceptual awareness, and it seems to be a conceptual truth that any perceptual aware-ness is perspectival—in the sense of, from a point of view *on* the object—involving an (at least apparent) interaction, that is, a relation between the object and the knower. But could we not say that, since perception and any mode of conceiving ultimately based on it ('imagining') can thus only pres-ent us with *effects* of the object's intrinsic nature, that nature as it is in itself is in principle inaccessible to such modes of conceiving. If we also wish to retain at least a residue of meaning empiricism with its characteristic view of what it is to have an adequate conception of something, it would seem to follow that the intrinsic properties of a non-perspectival object are not adequately conceivable as they are in themselves, but only as they affect knowing subjects. Nevertheless, the argument might continue, *what* we are acquainted with in sense perception is (in part) intrinsic, non-perspectival properties, although we can only in principle be acquainted with them in a perspectival mode of presentation.

For the Nietzschean perspectivist, this solution would be a merely verbal one. Given that our concepts are constituted by their cognitive roles and the latter are essentially dependent on the modes in which the items falling under the concepts are or can be presented, it would still follow that we have no concepts of *non-perspectival objects as they are in themselves*, and that we therefore fail to grasp any coherent sense in the italicized phrase. It is unclear whether Nietzsche would accept the theoretical possibility of a sort of *via negativa*, i.e. of a demonstration by a priori argument both that among the ultimate furniture of the universe there must be items with causal powers and that not all of them can be perspectival. In any case, no such argument commanding reasonably widespread assent has yet been forthcoming.

3. AFFECTIVITY AS A CONDITION OF KNOWLEDGE OF THE REAL

Apart from drawing on visual perception, Nietzsche's examples of the alleged perspectivalness of all representations of a spatio-temporal world often emphasize their evaluative or interest-based character and the way in which they are constitutively related to the 'will'. Cognition is said to depend on 'will' and on 'affects' (GM III. 12), interests (WP 588), 'valuations' (WP

616, 675), and 'concerns' (WP 555; KGW VIII. 1. 5. 19), in short, on acts or states which belong to the affective and appetitive sphere. However, it is not a simple task to determine the scope of the claims that are being made or suggested by Nietzsche in this connection. The prima facie defensible possibilities of interpretation here range from ascribing to him relatively uncontroversial considerations concerning the interest-dependence of all classification and conceptualization to much stronger theses. I shall argue that there is sufficient, clear, textual evidence for attributing to him three thoughts of increasing strength and radicality: (1) all representations are interest-dependent; (2) the distinction between self and external, objective reality presupposes affectivity and the experience of volitional agency; (3) what can count as objectively real for us is essentially related to our dominant interests or concerns.

1. The claim that all representations are interest-dependent is explicitly stated in GM III. 12. Brian Leiter, in his careful reading of this passage, formulates it as follows: 'Necessarily, we know an object from a particular perspective: that is, from the standpoint of particular interests and needs.'[23] This a priori truth applies both at the level of our experiential encounter with the world and at more theoretical levels of representing it. Thus any perceptual representation of an object requires more than merely exposure to the environmental array and a passive receiving of data from it. What is needed for the representation of an object is a selective focusing on some of these data which only through such attentional 'interest' become available for potential future representations and thus for the constitution of an *object* of representation. If the context of perception is a dynamic one—e.g. a moving object—my representing it requires me to direct my attentional interest to a feature of my environment in a dynamic way—in other words, I need to *track* the object. As Nietzsche observes, those who maintain the possibility of a purely passive ('will-less') subject of knowledge ask of us 'to think of an eye that is inconceivable, an eye that is supposed to have no direction at all, where the active and interpreting powers through which alone seeing becomes a seeing of something are supposed to be suspended or lacking' (GM III. 12).

At the level of descriptive classifications of the world and of the theories (including our everyday conceptualizations) through which we articulate our understanding of it, there is an equally ineliminable involvement of interests. Which features we select in grouping worldly items depends clearly on our purposes, and the world does not prescribe any system of classification which subjects of knowledge are rationally compelled to adopt irrespective

---

[23] Leiter, 'Perspectivism in Nietzsche's *Genealogy of Morals*', 345.

of what their classification-guiding interests might be. For creatures like ourselves the prediction of events is a central interest and many of our classificatory concepts (especially in science) are governed by this interest. But we can think of creatures for whom this is not a dominant interest and who classify things according to quite different criteria. In many contexts our criteria of classification are provided by what strike us, owing to our attention-based noticing of some aspects rather than others, as phenomenal similarities. Often such similarities are by no means evident to the uninitiated observer and rather require a technical training (think of the stylistic classifications in the visual arts or in music theory). The world does not prescribe 'correct' classifications, no matter what the purposes of the classifiers may be, and these purposes themselves cannot be adjudicated between (as more or less 'rational', say) independently of what subjects are disposed to find most worth while and important to them. No classifications and no theories making use of them are thus intrinsically better, more adequate, or more appropriate independently of the purposes they serve, nor is any classification or theory thinkable which is not governed by any purposes at all.[24] None of these claims is likely to be found controversial, unless one believes in values or norms which impose obligations on subjects irrespective of whether they are disposed to recognize them as such. Nor do any of these claims imply that the *objects* represented or their properties are themselves constituted by or dependent on the interests of human or other subjects of knowledge.

2. In GM III. 12 Nietzsche diagnoses the idea of a 'will-less subject of knowledge' as a 'conceptual fiction' and adds that a putative awareness of the world in which 'active . . . powers' are supposed to be lacking or neutralized is an 'incoherence' (*Widersinn*). Now if a will-less subject cannot represent anything *as* anything at all, then it is unclear that it could still be regarded as a subject. In other words, Nietzsche is here also making a point about necessary conditions of subjectivity or selfhood. It is a thought familiar from the Kantian tradition that subjectivity—in a sense which requires the possibility of experiences being ascribed by a self to itself—demands

---

[24] One's epistemology will rationally vary in accordance with the purposes co-constituting different areas of inquiry. The method for knowing about how to predict phenomena will clearly be different from the method(s) for knowing about (say) the aesthetic properties objects appear as having, and these methods in turn will differ from the ways in which one best learns about *other* interest-involving perspectives. If different regions of inquiry require different methodologies, and if human cognitive capacities are finite, it follows that the very interests which disclose one aspect of reality to us will tend to occlude another. For example, if one's cognitive engagement with the world is guided by an interest in smoothly manipulating things, the dominance of the type of cognitive effort needed for this will tend to interfere proportionally with one's ability to understand other perspectives with other guiding interests. For an illuminating discussion of these issues and of Nietzsche's own guiding interests, see Richardson, *Nietzsche's System*, 264–80.

that representations be interpretable in specific ways. In particular, it has often been claimed that for self-consciousness to be possible a subject must be able to interpret its representations as glimpses of an objective world, the latter expression in turn being understood as referring to a world of 'weighty' objects which are independent of any particular state in which they are being represented and which are furthermore subject to various fairly stringent laws of connectedness.[25] In a number of passages Nietzsche wrestles with the very same question of the conditions of the possibility of a distinction between a subject and an 'objective' reality 'external' to it—such a reality being a necessary correlate of any potentially self-conscious subject, according to both Kant and Schopenhauer.[26] Nietzsche's contribution on this issue emphasizes a different aspect of the 'independence' that is definitive of the objectively real in so far as the latter is involved in the constitution of a self–world divide.

What is necessary for us to be able to conceive of ourselves as subjects encountering a world of real, external objects? Nietzsche's answer is that the concept of objective reality involves the idea of an actual or possible *efficacy* associated with some representational contents ('appearances', in his terminology; WP 588). This idea of the causal efficacy of objects is obtained from the *resistance* posed by appearances to the subject's experience of its spontaneous, self-moving *agency*. If this thought is conjoined with the more familiar Kantian and Schopenhauerian claim about the necessary dependence of empirical self-consciousness—and thus of subjectivity in one central sense of this expression—on representations as of 'external', 'independent' objects, it entails Nietzsche's conclusion in GM III. 12 that the concept of a will-less subject representing determinate objects is incoherent. But in fact we do not need to rely on Kant and Schopenhauer to supply one of the premises for this conclusion, for it follows from some of Nietzsche's own considerations. In his remarks on the concept of the subject, one theme that remains constant is the emphasis on its dependence on the idea of causal power:

The degree to which we feel life and power . . . gives us our measure of 'being', 'reality', not-appearance. The subject: this is the term for our belief in a unity underlying all the different impulses of the highest feeling of reality. (WP 485)

The concept 'reality', 'being' is taken from our feeling of the 'subject' . . . as the cause of all actions, as an agent. (WP 488)[27]

---

[25] See P. F. Strawson, *The Bounds of Sense* (London: Methuen, 1975), esp. 97–112, for a classical statement of this reading of Kant.

[26] Immanuel Kant, *Critique of Pure Reason*, B 274–8; Arthur Schopenhauer, *The World as Will and Representation*, trans. E. F. J. Payne, 2 vols. (New York: Dover, 1969), First Book, §7 (esp. i. 32–4).

[27] We need not occupy ourselves here with what is Nietzsche's main target of criticism in these remarks: the tendency to think of the subject as a substance from which causal powers *emanate*.

Elsewhere he insists that the experience of the subject's power essentially requires 'resistances' (e.g. WP 689, 693, 702). Combining these by no means marginal but frequently repeated observations yields the conclusion that subjectivity requires independent—in the sense of resistant—objects. Nietzsche's point, then, can be taken to be about the interdependence of the notion of a real object and of self-consciousness. Both of these emerge together, presupposing the phenomenon of resistance to what is experienced as spontaneous agency. Most of his remarks in this context concentrate on what is to him the crucial element in the object's independence: its resistance to the subject's 'will' or experienced agency. This is in sharp contrast to the Kantian emphasis on the rule-governed *order* in the contents of experience as what is constitutively required for the distinction between a sphere of independent objects and a subjective order of experientially encountering these objects. According to Nietzsche, what makes the object 'independent' is its experienced (or experiencable) efficacy, and this in turn requires an agency or active 'performance' on the part of the subject: 'Thus it is the highest degrees of performance that awaken belief in the ... reality of the object' (WP 533). 'So, being is grasped by us as that which acts on *us*, which *proves itself through its efficacy*' (KGW VIII. 1. 5. 19).

What is the kind of 'performance' which Nietzsche might be thinking of here? Is he referring to *bodily* agency and to experiences of resistance involving tactile pressure, as Dilthey's theory does in much more detail a few years later?[28] This is clearly not Nietzsche's point: 'A thing = its properties: and these are equivalent to what *concerns us* about this thing: a unity under which we gather the relations *relevant to us* ... an object is the sum of experienced *obstructions*' (KGW VIII. 1. 2. 77). Evidently Nietzsche is speaking here of our ordinary everyday conception of a real object which is, according to him, presupposed by higher-level theories about the physical world (see below). And it is quite clear that the 'obstructions' which might be relevant in this connection are not seen by him as dependent on *any one* sense modality. This is fortunate, for such a restriction would undermine the generality of his claim, which is a conceptual one. What is essential to

---

[28] Wilhelm Dilthey, 'Beiträge zur Lösung der Frage vom Ursprung unseres Glaubens an die Realität der Aussenwelt', in *Gesammelte Schriften*, vol. v (Leipzig: Teubner, 1923). Dilthey's thesis is that 'consciousness of willed movement and of the resistance which it meets . . . simultaneously engender consciousness of the self and of real objects' (p. 98). He is careful to distinguish the experience of resistance from sensations of tactile pressure, but nevertheless holds that occurrence of the latter is a necessary condition for the former to be possible. He is criticized on this score by Max Scheler, whose related theory is in this respect closer to Nietzsche's idea. Cf. Max Scheler, *Erkenntnis und Arbeit* (Frankfurt am Main: Klostermann, 1977), 239. For a recent continuation of this debate, see Thomas Baldwin, 'Objectivity, Causality and Agency', and James Russell, 'At Two with Nature: Agency and the Development of the Self-World Dualism', both in J. L. Bermúdez, A. Marcel, and N. Eilan (eds.), *The Body and the Self* (Cambridge, Mass.: MIT Press, 1995).

Nietzsche's position is thus a highly general point: that it be possible for the subject to distinguish between event sequences that are dependent on what the subject experiences as its agency and others that are not so, and such a distinction would seem to be in principle possible even for a being that lived in (say) a purely visual world. What is minimally and uncontroversially required for an awareness of agency is the experience of certain representational contents ('appearances') changing in accordance with what might be called the subject's 'unconditional' desires with present-tense contents, i.e. desires concerning the present which are not checked by countervailing ones or by other considerations. It is very unclear as well as controversial what, if anything, is necessary beyond this. Indeed, it is far from obvious whether the subject, in acting, necessarily has to be presented to itself as embodied in order to have an experience of agency.[29]

Nietzsche's present point, then, may be summarized as follows. The distinction between a self and real objects external to it is only possible for a point of view or perspective which involves desires and 'concerns' (and thus valuations), and which furthermore experiences itself both as a spontaneous agent and as obstructed or resisted in its agency by items in its experience. The concept of the objectively real is constitutively linked to this experience of the efficacy of some 'appearances' which manifests itself in their resistance to the sort of desires which, when they are effective, we call volitions (or intentions-in-action).[30] Grasping the significance of this thesis is complicated by the fact that Nietzsche has already argued (see (1) above) that the very *individuation* of objects presupposes interests and active interpretation. That this is a separate point can be seen very clearly by considering cases of vivid imagining where we certainly individuate objects without, however, regarding them as real. To be thematically (attentively) aware of a particular, even a particular with spatial properties, is to be distinguished from being aware of something as a real, 'external' object. It therefore seems that a distinction is needed, in order to explain this contrast, between the minimal

---

[29] When I am thinking through a philosophical problem, or trying to visualize some historical scene, I have an experience of agency or activity. I may perhaps as a matter of fact also have a simultaneous background awareness of my body, but there is no essential connection between these experiences. It seems perfectly possible for a subject to have an experience of the first kind without simultaneously having one of the second. Husserl claims that having representations as of enduring, three-dimensional objects necessitates the subject's self-presentation as self-moving 'lived body', involving, among other things, kinaesthetic sensations (*Ideen zu einer reinen Phänomenologie und phänomenologischen Philosophie* (The Hague: Martinus Nijhoff, 1952), Second Book, e.g. 55–8). But it would be very implausible to maintain that *any* representation as of a particular, extended item would be a priori impossible from a merely geometric point of view.

[30] Nietzsche's account requires that we can make sense of the idea of volitions in relation to objects or event sequences where willing is generally ineffective (e.g. 'willing that it should rain'). The intelligibility of such talk is defended and explicated by T. L. S. Sprigge, *Facts, Words and Beliefs* (London: Routledge, 1970), 288–97.

activity involved even in attentional selection, that is, in the individuation of objects, and further, affectively less neutral, relations to 'the will' required at some stage for what is thus individuated to be conceptualizable as a real object.[31] For this to be possible some attentionally selected objects must have engaged a more substantial affective or appetitive response of some kind, for instance a desire that the object appearance be maintained, or an experience of it as unpleasant or painful and a desire that it should cease. This does not mean that everything regarded as a real object must have engaged the will in some such way, since many such objects acquire this status by virtue of associative or other lawlike links with others which have.[32] There is another important asymmetry between the ways 'the will' is involved in object individuation and the self–world distinction respectively. It is possible to individuate experiential items by merely being directed onto them in selective attention and without being able to *think* of oneself as an agent (presumably animals and infants do this). But the mere *experience* of agency and resistance are not sufficient for distinguishing between the self and objective reality. This requires the ability to think of oneself as an agent (see below).

To elucidate Nietzsche's point further and also to simplify matters, we may ignore for a moment his observation that any individuation of object-like particulars already involves interest and activity and suppose, like classical empiricism, that the perception of such items could conceivably be a purely passive affair of registering pre-structured data. We may even suppose these data to display a high degree of rule-governedness, connectedness, and qualitative continuity, so as to be intrinsically hospitable to an interpretation of them as appearances of 'weighty', enduring objects. Even if we assume, then, that a subject might find itself in this way entirely passively enjoying experiences as of spatial particulars, this would not yet allow for a distinction between a self and real objects. With however much orderliness numerically distinct items might succeed one another 'according to a rule', thus encouraging in principle a reidentification of enduring objects, every datum would be just that—one more image, perceived, indeed, as from some point of view, but this point of view would be one without a possible interiority. It could not be the perspective of a *subject* on a *world*.[33]

---

[31] This important distinction is absent in James Russell's paper, whose argument otherwise is in close agreement with the points made here. (See 'At Two with Nature: Agency and the Development of the Self-World Dualism', 134–5.)

[32] Cf. Dilthey, 'Beiträge', 114–17.

[33] Therefore not every conceivable point of view is *ipso facto* a 'subjective' one. For a point of view on the world to belong to a subject (a self), affectivity and appetition need to be involved in the fairly substantial way described above. Nietzsche's use of 'perspective' always assumes the presence of these elements. Hence Volker Gerhardt is correct to observe that Nietzschean perspectives 'require *subjects* who relate to something other than themselves' ('Die Perspektive des Perspektivismus', *Nietzsche-Studien*, 18 (1989), 268).

I should like to finish the discussion of this aspect of Nietzsche's thinking with two cautionary remarks. First, nothing in what has been said so far implies that the concept of objective reality cannot detach itself at least to a considerable extent from the kind of resistances a subject originally or normally encounters. For example, in the inventory of items making up objective reality with which physical science operates, colour properties as they are experienced do not figure, although we very often find ourselves apparently affected by such sense-individuated properties in our ordinary *Lebenswelt*. We shall discuss Nietzsche's view on just how far the concept of objective reality can abstract from the life-world in (3) below. Secondly, Nietzsche is drawing attention only to what is, according to him, a necessary, not a sufficient, condition of a self–world distinction. As I have already indicated, it is clear that such a distinction requires conceptual abilities going well beyond the mere experience of agency and resistance. In order to distinguish my 'self' from external objects affecting me, I need to be able to *think of* myself as an agent rather than just be aware of my agency. What the further conditions of such a self-conception, or of any substantial self-consciousness, might be is a question on which much philosophical effort has been expended in recent decades. Among the claims that have been made in this regard are that self-consciousness non-contingently requires the belief that there are objects which continue to exist when unperceived, or that it requires the subject to think of itself as a physical object. It has also been widely held that self-consciousness requires intersubjectivity, either in the rather uncontroversial sense that the possession of the psychological concepts needed for self-consciousness involves the in-principle ability to apply them to others; or as the more substantial claim that for a subject to be self-conscious it is necessary that it has experiences and thoughts as of actual others; or indeed as the highly ambitious thesis that self-consciousness implies the actual existence of other subjects. Irrespective of the merits of the arguments mustered in this context as attempting to establish entirely general truths about the necessary conditions of self-consciousness *überhaupt*, nothing of what I have attributed to Nietzsche in this respect is incompatible with these further claims.[34] However, it is incompatible with a

---

[34] A note of caution may, however, not be inappropriate in relation to such claims. There is sometimes a tendency in discussions of these issues to think of self-consciousness involving a self–other distinction as an all-or-nothing affair and, in particular, to assume that such substantial self-consciousness requires the ability to determine one's existence in (objective) time, in Kant's famous phrase from the 'Refutation of Idealism'. A less schematic view of substantial self-consciousness has good reason to recognize that it is a matter of degree and to take cognizance of the empirical evidence suggesting that there are rudimentary forms of it that do not involve the capacity for autobiographical (narrative) reflection. See e.g. D. N. Stern, 'The Early Development of Schemas of Self, Other, and "Self with Other"', in J. D. Lichtenberg and S. Kaplan (eds),

strictly Kantian account of (phenomenal) objectivity. It might be objected here that Kant is making precisely Nietzsche's point when he maintains that any representation of an object—in the minimal sense of an instantiation of a general concept—involves the spontaneity of the understanding. Kant in fact says explicitly that every act of *attention* involves the spontaneity, i.e. activity, of the understanding.[35] This can indeed be read as corresponding to Nietzsche's observation reported in (1) above. But unlike Nietzsche, Kant does not give a special role to the will in relation to the constitution of empirically real outer objects. What is essentially involved in the constitution of such objects is for him not the resistance of some representational contents to what the subject experiences as its spontaneous agency, but rather the thoroughgoing rule-governedness among spatial representational contents. A spatial 'appearance' that cannot be integrated into such an order is, by virtue of this fact alone, not an appearing of a real object but an illusion. In fact, Kant insists (following Hume on this point) that we have no intuition of efficacy at all with respect to objects of outer sense.[36] Nietzsche would respond that if this were the case, neither a representation of external empirical reality nor self-consciousness would be possible.

3. Nietzsche's prima facie most radical thought in connection with his use of 'perspective' to indicate the dependence of representations on affectivity or appetition is the idea that what can count as objectively real for us is necessarily related to our dominant interests and concerns:

But we have only drawn the concept 'real, truly existing' from that which 'concerns us'; the more we are affected in our interest, the more we believe in the reality of a thing or an entity. 'It exists' means: I experience myself as existing in relation to it . . . So 'being' is grasped by us as that which acts on *us*, which *proves itself through its efficacy*. (KGW VIII. 1. 5. 19; cf. WP 533, 588)

. . . something that of is no concern to anyone *is* not at all. (WP 555)

The most natural interpretation of these and similar passages is that

(EID) our concept of objective reality constrains the range of possible candidates for this status to items that are relevantly related to our actual dominant concerns.

For convenience, we may call this Nietzsche's thesis of *essential interest-dependence* (EID). It is a fundamental theme of virtually all of Nietzsche's writings, even in the early period up to 1876, that the interests and 'values'

Reflections on Self-Psychology (Hillsdale, NJ: Analytical Press, 1983). Also A. Meltzoff, 'Foundations for Developing a Concept of Self', in D. Cicchetti and M. Beeghly, *The Self in Transition* (Chicago: University of Chicago Press, 1990).

[35] Immanuel Kant, *Critique of Pure Reason*, B 157.

[36] Ibid., A 49/B 66.

actually governing normal humans, consciously or otherwise, tend not to be cognitive or even purely contemplative ones, but rather practical ones, often—albeit by no means invariably or exclusively—involving desires for the subject's own survival and affective well-being (see e.g. HH 34; BGE 6; WP 480, 677).[37]

Now among the sorts of particular items which are of most forceful concern to normal humans as they actually are are arguably those that they are liable to encounter as *solid*—as exerting tactile pressure. If, for instance, the deliverances of a person's various sensory modalities, which normally tend to function in well-adapted synchronicity, suddenly began systematically to conflict with each other, so that the contours of apparent objects as presented to his sight suddenly no longer corresponded to their shapes as revealed by his sense of touch, it is to be expected that he would soon begin to rely on his tactile experiences as revealing 'what's really out there' and to regard his visual experiences as illusory. Assuming that there were no systematic correlations exploitable as signs between the deliverances of sight and touch respectively, he would begin to think of himself as having to find his way around the world rather like a blind person does. If this happened to humans collectively, we would regard ourselves as having visually lost contact with the actual world, even if it turned out that our visual experiences displayed highly coherent patterns both internally and in relation to other people's visual experiences. Presumably we would then consider ourselves to be suffering collectively from highly coherent visual hallucinations.[38] It is plausible to think that this tendency to associate what can be encountered as tactile resistance with what is real has its origin in the fact that many of our fundamental practical interests are so strongly linked to this sense modality. In no other respect do we normally experience ourselves as so exposed to, and potentially vulnerable by, the world.

Nietzsche is not committed, however, to a quasi-phenomenalist view according to which what is objectively real is what is an actual or possible datum of the sense of touch. On the present reading he is rather suggesting that what is objectively real cannot be *completely* detached from what we actually encounter in experience as most strongly affecting our interests

---

[37] In Nietzsche's later motivational psychology such desires are interpreted as ultimately either constituted by or derivative of a more fundamental generic desire for the experience of power or growth (*Machtgefühl*). (See e.g. BGE 230; WP 688–9; KGW VII. 3. 40. 61).

[38] One can easily make this story more complex and less clear-cut. What if the visual appearances were associated with auditory, especially linguistic, signals, and people could interpret themselves as interacting with other, visually presented, subjects? What if this apparent interaction took the form of an exchange about the nature of their common situation? It is not clear that such hypothetical subjects, as long as they retained normal human interests, could still regard themselves as living in a unified world at all.

(whatever that may be). If what has been said in the preceding paragraph about the hierarchy, in this respect, of sensory modalities is correct, we can conclude that what is objectively real for us, on a Nietzschean view, must be *relevantly related* to the contents of certain *sorts* of sense experiences of ours. One central kind of relevance here pertains to the kind of items which figure in our attempts to explain, by means of covering laws with predictive power, the occurrence of such experiential contents. It is because we have a vital interest in the prediction of such experiences that laws which have predictive power concerning them count as being 'explanatory' in a significant way. The best explanations of this kind may contain substantival terms most plausibly construed as referring to 'theoretical' entities which cannot themselves be encountered in the sort of sense experiences they help to explain (for example, electrons or electromagnetic fields). This does not, on Nietzsche's analysis, disqualify them from being regarded as objectively real. But given his empiricist conception of thought (see Section 2 above), such putative items can only intelligibly be interpreted along realist lines if they are in principle perceivable by subjects appropriately located and endowed with suitable faculties of perception and thought. Furthermore, the status as real accorded to them is parasitic on their role in the prediction of experiences whose contents are of significant concern to us. It is thus, according to Nietzsche, not merely the fact that items figure in causal (nomological) explanations which qualifies them for the label 'real'. Modifying our earlier story of a de-synchronized experience a little, it seems quite conceivable that the course of our experience was such as to warrant the postulation of distinct, mutually irreducible causal orders. Nietzsche's point is that in such a case only those explanatory items would count as real which had a causal role in relation to experiential contents that would *actually matter* to us. It is in this sense that objective reality is relative to human interests.

Now it is evident that what motivates this Nietzschean view is a more general construal of 'objective reality' as expressing an implicitly relational concept, in the sense of its being essentially indexed to subject-implying perspectives. Rather like a pure perspectival representation such as '*x* is on the right' is implicitly relational and should be more perspicuously indexed to a representing subject—i.e. '*x* is on the right of S (relative to S's axis of vision)'—so '*x* is objectively real' should be explicated as '*x* is objectively real for S-type subjects, given their interests'. What Nietzsche says about the concept of objective reality in relation to *human* subjects is thus a special case of his more general relational elucidation of this concept. It follows that the truth about objective reality would be different for subjects with different fundamental interests: 'There are many kinds of eyes. Even the sphinx has eyes—and consequently there are many kinds of "truths"' (WP 540).[39]

Perspectivism on the reading proposed here rules out global scepticism, at least if one grants that we cannot be radically mistaken about *all* our own central concerns. Assuming, for instance, that certain sense-based contents are the representational contents which in fact concern us most strongly, it is impossible according to EID that we should be comprehensively mistaken about the veridicality of our experiences presenting contents of this type. But it is certainly conceivable, as far as perspectivism is concerned, that those among our current explanatory theories which go significantly beyond the theoretical components involved in perception itself—in particular, our scientific and metaphysical theories—are comprehensively mistaken.

Nietzsche's rejection as incoherent of the idea of absolute objects (ERD) implies that all actual objects necessarily have features that mark them as represented. The considerations concerning interest-dependence which I am presently discussing have here been interpreted as presupposing the truth of ERD and can be seen as specifying further constraints on what can intelligibly count as such an object. Indeed, only if all possible particulars are perspectival in the sense specified by ERD does there appear to be any plausibility in the claim that all particulars that can count as real for us are necessarily relevantly related to our actual ruling interests. For if ERD is true, the only remaining rival candidates for the status of objective reality are object-like items figuring in other perspectives with quite different ruling interests (e.g. contemplative ones of a kind appearing strange to us). But if ERD is false and absolute objects are possible, it is unclear what good reason could be given for stipulating that their properties a priori could not be inaccessible to the methods of inquiry co-constituted by our quite contingent concerns. In Section 4 this issue will be pursued further and an alternative interpretation of Nietzsche's ideas on the interest-dependence of objective reality will be sketched which does not require concurrence with his denial of the possibility of absolute objects. Before that, however, the question needs to be addressed whether Nietzsche's position as outlined so far amounts to a version of ontological phenomenalism or idealism.

With regard to phenomenalism the answer is straightforward. None of the ideas attributed to Nietzsche above commit him to the view that there is nothing more to objects like trees or mountains than actual or possible experiential contents of subjects of a certain sort. Among the various problems associated with ontological phenomenalism, the most fundamental is

---

[39] The fragment continues: 'and consequently there is no truth'. Here as in other passages Nietzsche uses 'truth' in several distinct senses, thus creating the rhetorical effect of paradox. But his actual point is clear: there are many relative truths, but there cannot be any absolute truths.

probably that it can give us no explanation, in principle, of why the sub-junctive conditionals which by its lights give most of the content of beliefs about material objects are true. Nothing in Nietzsche's view as presented so far requires him to accept such a strongly counter-intuitive position, which is in this respect comparable to the (allegedly) Humean idea of causality as simply consisting in contiguity and regular concomitance or succession. For Nietzsche there may certainly be something categorical about the world which is the truth-maker of a subjunctive like 'If I were to look in *that* direction now, I would have an experience as of the sun setting'. But what-ever arrangement of categorical features of the world may make such sen-tences true if they are true, it cannot include absolute, non-perspectival objects.

With respect to idealism, it is doubtful whether this label is helpful when characterizing Nietzsche's view—unless indeed one uses it as a blanket term to cover any position that rejects what I have called strong realism. Historic-ally, 'idealism' has generally been used in a more discriminating way for metaphysical doctrines which accord ontological priority to the subject or to 'spirit', either in the sense of considering it as capable in principle of existing independently of objects, while objects are dependent on it, or in the sense of considering objects as in some sense 'produced' by, or 'emanating' from, the subject or from 'spirit' or 'thought'. The former description would apply to Berkeley, the latter, presumably, to figures like Fichte and Hegel.[40] Nietzsche suggests nothing of this sort. As I have interpreted him, neither subjects nor objects should be thought of as substances capable of absolute, independent existence. Subjects, furthermore, do not 'produce' objects but find themselves passive in relation to their recalcitrant presence in sense-based experience.[41] Nor does Nietzsche subscribe to the proto-idealist 'veil of ideas' doctrine according to which what is immediately perceived is 'in' the mind. While Kant had already argued (contra Berkeley) that our obser-vational access to outer, three-dimensional objects is just as non-inferential and direct as to our mental states revealed by inner sense,[42] Nietzsche often suggests the more radical view that bodily phenomena are more directly accessible to observation than 'inner' states (e.g. WP 489, 659).

[40] With respect to Kant's transcendental idealism the issue is complicated by Kant's multi-level account of the subject. But it is clear that he considers spatio-temporal objects to be dependent on 'us' while the noumenal self, 'the being which thinks in us' (A 401), or, in another phrase, 'the determining in me' (B 158), which I have no intuition and thus no knowledge of, is equally clearly not regarded by Kant as dependent on such objects, but is thought as substance (A 450/B 478) in the sense of having independent existence.

[41] For not dissimilar observations on the issues broached in this and the previous sentence, cf. John McDowell, *Mind and World* (Cambridge, Mass.: Harvard University Press, 1994), esp. 10 and 25.

[42] Immanuel Kant, *Critique of Pure Reason*, A 367–75.

4. THE LIFE-WORLD AND OTHER WORLDS:
PERSPECTIVISM AS A NEW AGENDA
FOR PHILOSOPHY

It was suggested above that Nietzsche's analysis of the notion of objective reality as explicated in Section 3 (EID) derives whatever plausibility it may have from tacitly taking for granted ERD, i.e. the conclusion of his argument (discussed in Section 2) attempting to establish the impossibility of non-perspectival objects. Once absolute objects are thus excluded from the picture, it may perhaps seem acceptable to argue that real objects relative to some type of subject S are, or are constructed from, certain actual or possible 'appearances' standing in appropriate relations to the interests of S-type subjects. But what if one does not accept ERD? In this concluding section I shall propose an alternative or, better, a supplementary interpretation of Nietzsche's argument which liberates it from the need to accept this premiss. While the conjunction of ERD and EID clearly amounts to a version of *metaphysical anti-realism*,[43] I shall refer to this reading, which has similarities with certain aspects of both pragmatism and phenomenology, as *metaphysical indifferentism*. This is a stance which is compatible with the truth of metaphysical anti-realism and hence may supplement it, but it is equally consistent with a strong realism about (some) spatio-temporal objects. The core of the anti-realist reading of perspectivism developed so far might be paraphrased, roughly, as 'absolute objects are impossible'; the metaphysically indifferent interpretation as 'if absolute objects are possible, they are not worth caring about'.

To appreciate the attraction of such indifferentism, consider, first, what EID without the support of ERD commits its adherents to. According to it, our concept of objective reality imposes the constraint that anything that can count as objectively real for us should be relevantly related to those representational contents which most strongly affect us, given our actual dominant interests. The meaning of 'relevantly' is in turn determined by those very interests. Given the kinds of concerns we actually find ourselves with, those aspects of causal relations relevant for prediction play a very prominent role here, but Nietzsche's remarks imply that this prominence is not one required by the very concept of the objectively real. EID entails that even if there were (in some sense) instances of absolute objects, these could not have the status of *reality* for some class of subjects unless subjects of this type experienced themselves as appropriately affected in their interests by

[43] Metaphysical anti-realism is the denial of what I have called strong realism. It is of course compatible with what is sometimes referred to as minimal realism, i.e. the view that a true episodic belief is true in virtue of something other than itself.

them. Unless they were thus affected, those objects could presumably for them constitute only something like the 'shadow kingdom ... beside true existence', a belief in which Nietzsche attributes to the ancient Greeks (WP 586).

To make Nietzsche's point here more vivid and to highlight its problems, imagine a subject whose notional world is entirely detached from *our* world which we shall assume, for the purposes of the argument, to be a world containing non-perspectival particulars. Let us call this imaginary monadic subject *Leibniz*. *Leibniz* may have a spatial position, but he is from our point of view disembodied, although not from his own. Indeed, one may assume his monadic notional world to contain everything regarded as necessary for self-conscious experience and thought by one's preferred transcendental arguments. There are in it items which he can interpret as appearances of persisting things comporting themselves in accordance with invariable laws, there are also items which he can interpret as other subjects linguistically interacting with him, and so forth. All that matters for the purposes of the present argument is that *Leibniz* is not affected by the absolute particulars with which we, *ex hypothesi*, interact. In fact, to make sense of Nietzsche's point even a weaker assumption would be sufficient, namely that *Leibniz* is not affected by the non-perspectival particulars in our world in any way that importantly *matters* to him. But let us continue with the more clear-cut, stronger version of the story. It might be objected that the hypothesis is incoherent since the existence of *Leibniz* would be unverifiable. This worry should not detain us for long. First, while it is true that it is part of the point of the hypothesis that there should be no interaction between *Leibniz* and absolute, e.g. physical, particulars populating our world, hence no physical possibility of a verification of his existence by techniques involving such items, there might in principle be other means of empirically confirming his existence or indeed of demonstrating it a priori. (The historical Gottfried Wilhelm Leibniz after all thought that the existence of other monads could be proved a priori.) But, more importantly, an *ad hominem* response may suffice here. Since Nietzsche's point is directed primarily against an absolute (strong realist) conception of objective reality and proponents of such a conception are committed to a non-epistemic construal of real objects, an objection to the hypothesis on verificationist grounds from this quarter is hardly to be expected and thus need not be countered in this context.

With *Leibniz* thus installed securely for present purposes, we may rephrase Nietzsche's point as follows. As far as our concept of objective reality is concerned, *Leibniz*, in being ignorant about the absolute particulars in our world, is not ignorant about any truths concerning objective *reality*, since these items are utterly irrelevant to him. Once the issue between Nietzschean perspectivism as expressed in EID and strong realism is sharpened in this way, we may not feel confident of just what 'our' concept of the objectively real would commit us to in such a case; i.e. how we would be disposed to use the phrase 'objective reality' in relation to this hypothetical situation. Most probably we would, contra Nietzsche, be inclined to say that *Leibniz* is indeed ignorant of some parts or aspects of reality. This indicates that we have or are capable of having what might be called *pure* cognitive interests which are not subservient to other (e.g. practical, manipulative-technological, aesthetic, communicative) concerns. On the other hand, most people would on reflection almost certainly also find it bizarre to label the phenomena showing up in *Leibniz*'s experiential world '*mere*' phenomena or '*merely* subjective' or even 'illusory'.[44] The bizarreness of this would be even more pronounced if it turned out that *Leibniz* had no pure cognitive interests and thus, in being ignorant of non-perspectival particulars, lacked nothing whatever that mattered to him. Nietzsche thus seems correct when he claims that our concept of objective reality, as normally used, applies paradigmatically to aspects of our 'phenomenal', experiential world which are experienced as affecting us, or regarded as capable of affecting us, in certain important ways. If we suppose ourselves for a moment to be in the position of *Leibniz*, can we really on reflection make sense of the idea that we would, in that case, be entirely cut off from *reality*, at least as we (now) standardly understand that expression? The conflicting intuitions elicited by the considerations just adduced suggest that we do not use a phrase like 'objective reality' univocally; in different contexts of use it expresses different concepts whose extensions may conceivably diverge as in our illustration.

Arguably, therefore, the most fruitful way of reading Nietzsche's remarks on this issue—and one he himself often explicitly invites—is ultimately not as making a point about how a certain term or phrase is standardly used. Such claims tend to be of very limited force against proposed conceptual revisions unless a good argument can be given for resisting such revisions. Rather, he is above all concerned to draw the reader's attention to the arcaneness, the other-worldliness, of a conception of objective reality and of an associated pure cognitive interest which permit a detachment of reality from the experiential contents which otherwise matter to us. Even if there could be non-perspectival objects—i.e. ignoring the argument of Section 2— the question which is most important from Nietzsche's point of view

---

[44] Kant would agree, provided these phenomena were sufficiently law-governed: 'If, now, I . . . say that all things, as outer appearances, are side by side in space, the rule is valid universally and without limitation. Our exposition therefore [!] establishes the *reality*, that is, the objective validity of space in respect of whatever can be presented to us outwardly as an object, but also at the same time the *ideality* of space in respect of things when they are considered in themselves through reason' (*Critique of Pure Reason*, A 28/B 44).

remains: why should we care about them? Why should it matter to us whether our familiar ('phenomenal') world, the world of possible appearances for us, is a potentially infinite set of appearings of absolute objects, or whether it consists instead of Berkeleian ideas, or of Leibnizian monadic perceptions, or is an 'objectification' of a Schopenhauerian Will?

It is true, there could be a metaphysical world; the absolute possibility of this can hardly be opposed . . . If the existence of such a world had been demonstrated as well as one likes, it would still be clear that knowledge of it would be the most useless of all knowledge: even more useless than a knowledge of the chemical analysis of water must be to a sailor in danger of shipwreck. (HH 9)

Even in the well-known passage from *Twilight of the Idols* sometimes used as evidence for Nietzsche's rejection of the notion of a thing in itself as self-contradictory, what he in fact explicitly says is *not* that it is incoherent, but that knowledge of what it purports to apply to would be *futile*: 'The "true world"—an idea which is no longer of any use, not even as an obligation—an idea which has become useless, obsolete, *hence* a refuted idea: let us get rid of it' (TI IV). What is it that makes (some) metaphysical knowledge 'useless', according to these passages? The expression 'metaphysical world' usually refers, in Nietzsche's relatively early writings from where the first quotation is taken, specifically to conceptions such as Schopenhauer's 'World-Will' whose character in itself is supposed to be not directly accessible to human cognition. What the Will is in itself cannot manifest itself as it is in itself in human experience. In this sense, the truth of the hypothesis that there is a cosmic Will can *make no difference* to possible human experience and knowledge of it is thus 'useless'.[45] The same would be true for absolute particulars. For these also could not manifest themselves as they are in themselves in human experience. Of course, if the assumption of absolute particulars was *constitutively* involved in our best common-sense and scientific theories, i.e. in explanations with predictive power, then such items would make a difference to possible human experience. But it is highly implausible to hold that successful scientific theories rationally require a strong realist interpretation.[46] According to Nietzsche's metaphysical indifferentism, whether we metaphysically 'explain' the predictive success of some of our empirical theories by postulating absolute objects, or by Berkeleian ideas sustained by an all-perceiving God, is irrelevant from the point of view of any human

[45] It may be said that it only makes no difference if one is not motivated by pure cognitive interests. But if one *is* motivated by such interests and believes Schopenhauer's metaphysics, one may, for example, be depressed by it. But in this case it is the *belief* which makes the experiential (here: affective) difference, not its truth.

[46] For a detailed discussion of this issue, see my *Nietzsche and Metaphysics*, 46–57 and 150–62.

interests *except* purely cognitive ones, and it is for this reason that knowledge of the 'true world' is useless.[47]

Much of Nietzsche's later writing, perhaps most famously sections 23–8 of the third essay of *On the Genealogy of Morals*, is devoted to showing not the incoherence, but the poverty and undesirability, of a view of the world in which metaphysical questions and approaches that permit the categorization of the objects of our mundane interests—interests other than pure cognitive ones—as 'mere' appearances, as somehow systematically lacking in or distorting reality, are regarded as of central or even overriding importance. The attitude that accords them such importance he calls the 'will to truth' and identifies as the 'core' of the 'ascetic ideal', or of 'religion' in a wide sense (GM III. 27): 'Religion used to correspond to the *popular conception* of nature. Today the popular conception is materialism. Consequently what exists of religion today needs to speak to the people in a materialist language' (KGW VII. 1. 4. 221). There are strong indications in Nietzsche's writings that what ultimately motivates his attacks on the idea of non-perspectival real objects is the opposition of what he unashamedly calls his 'taste' to the futility and life-undermining other-worldliness of an attitude which grants great significance to such metaphysical questions or approaches: 'It is of cardinal importance that one should abolish the *true world*. It is the great inspirer of doubt and devaluator in respect of the world *we are*' (WP 583). Recognizing that it is this motivation which gives the characteristic urgency to Nietzsche's criticisms may also enable us to explain an initially puzzling feature of his statements on this issue. Occasionally his denial of a non-perspectival reality is tempered by much more tentative, indeed agnostic, remarks: 'How far the perspectival character of being reaches or even whether it also has some other character . . . cannot be established' (GS 374). This strongly suggests that what matters for Nietzsche in this debate is ultimately not whether absolute objects are *possible*, but whether we should be interested in them, even if they are. His occasional prevarications on the question of their possibility also seem to indicate a hesitation to make his critique depend entirely on a metaphysical argument of the very kind which, if the history of philosophy is to be taken as evidence, may have little hope of commanding general assent (not because it is an anti-realist argument, but because it is a metaphysical one). The most promising explanation of the historical fact of ongoing contestation in

---

[47] At least if one considers God in Berkeley's metaphysics only in his idea-producing and idea-sustaining role, excluding the possibility of any more direct divine self-revelations ('miracles'), and ignoring any moral and soteriological aspects of the belief in God. The latter aspects clearly *do* relate to human concerns other than purely cognitive ones. It would therefore be quite illegitimate to conclude from Nietzsche's argument that metaphysics *per se* cannot have any practical relevance.

metaphysics may well be, as Nietzsche openly recognizes by his very hesitation, that our 'intuitions' in these remote regions of intermittent human
curiosity tend to be less than completely firm, let alone irresistible. In fact
Nietzsche himself in some moods is drawn to a metaphysical narrative
incompatible with perspectivism as explicated earlier. Sometimes he sur-
mises that '(objective) reality in itself' is not an unintelligible expression but
that it refers to an ontologically independent reality beyond all possible
specific conceptualizations—a realm of flux or radical 'becoming', of virtually instantaneous qualitative change without recognizable patterns or regu-
larities. Our categories of the understanding, which have developed under
evolutionary constraints, impose a certain relatively stable form on this
chaos and thereby make it conceptually knowable (e.g. WP 515–17, 520; TI
III. 5). I shall not enter into a discussion of the very considerable philosophical difficulties associated with this variant of a naturalized and radical-
ized Kantianism.[48] What is of interest here, and more importantly what is
likely to have interested Nietzsche about it, is that its implications, as far as
knowledge is concerned, do not differ significantly from those of Nietzsche's
dominant perspectivism as outlined in Sections 2 and 3. For it also makes it
impossible to know objects 'as they are in themselves' and confines all possible human knowledge, at least if it is to have any specificity at all, to the
world as it shows up for us. This 'world we are' (WP 583), for which
Nietzsche often simply uses the term 'life', is the world as we encounter it in
everyday experience and, in addition rather than to the exclusion of it, in
more specialized pursuits parasitic on it (such as natural science). It is a
world which includes appearances as of relatively persisting objects and of
other subjects besides us, a world of 'appearance, change, becoming, death,
want, desire' (GM III. 28).

But, it may be asked, what could be 'life-denying' about trying to *explain*
metaphysically why the contents of experience are the way they are, and why
certain subjunctive conditionals about our perceptual beliefs are true?[49]
Nietzsche would presumably concede that there is nothing intrinsically
objectionable about such an epistemic interest. But he would add a number

---

[48] Briefly: there is the epistemological question how Nietzsche knows of this intrinsically
unconceptualizable reality in itself (unconceptualizable except in the most general and relatively
empty terms as 'becoming', etc.). More importantly, the putative idea of an objective reality which
cannot be known *in principle* (WP 517, 520) would seem to fall victim to the many familiar
objections, some of them discussed in this paper, against the very intelligibility of such a notion.
Finally, this idea seems to be a version of the time-honoured distinction between 'prime matter' or
'stuff' and 'form', or between 'content' and 'scheme', a distinction about which there are good
reasons to be suspicious. For one well-known criticism, see Donald Davidson, 'On the Very Idea of a
Conceptual Scheme', in his *Inquiries into Truth and Interpretation* (Oxford: Clarendon Press, 1984).

[49] We have seen that for Nietzsche such beliefs are recognizable as such, although of course not
infallibly, by their intrinsic character, involving the experience of resistance (see Sect. 3).

of important caveats. First, the kind of 'explanation' in question should not be mistakenly assimilated to explanations in everyday and in scientific contexts. In the latter we have fairly clear and broadly agreed criteria for what makes explanation A 'better' than explanation B (in science, explanatory virtue is very closely linked to predictive success). In metaphysics we have no such criteria. Assuming for the moment that there are sophisticated versions of physicalist realism, idealism, panpsychism, or theist creationism which are internally coherent, there simply is no procedure agreed among competent inquirers for determining what would make any one of these metaphysical 'explanations' better than another. None of them essentially make any predictions at all, and all of them are in principle compatible with the results of scientific research.

Secondly, Nietzsche would resist a framework of research which made 'explanations' of this kind their *primary* concern, rather than a subsidiary aspect of investigating the 'life'-world. A philosophy which conceived of itself as first and foremost metaphysics would be subject to Nietzsche's criticism of the 'ascetic ideal', provided, that is, it regarded itself as an important pursuit.

Thirdly and crucially, Nietzsche's most persistent and uncompromising attacks are directed against metaphysical 'explanations' which, rather than saving the appearances they are supposedly explaining, wish to demote them to 'mere' appearances or to 'illusions'. He argues that reflection on our use of the term 'reality' reveals that we tend to use it—at least primarily or normally—for those (re)presentational contents which affect us most strongly and *as* they affect us. Various metaphysical doctrines, from Platonism to many versions of materialism, propose conceptual revisions entailing that those objects of concern are 'illusory' or '*merely* apparent'. Indeed, on some of these doctrines, concerns and interests themselves, as they normally manifest themselves to us (i.e. as affective aspects of experiential episodes), also involve false interpretations of the real. Nietzsche strongly urges resistance against such rationally far from mandatory conceptual revisions. On his psychological analysis of the will to truth and its connection with the ascetic ideal, their motivations are best explained as ultimately originating in, at best, an indifference to 'life' or, less harmlessly, in *ressentiment* against it.[50] We are least likely to lapse into such indifference or *ressentiment* if we concentrate in our cognitive pursuits on an elucidation of the structures of the life-world—scientific explanation being conceived not as conflicting with, but as one part of, this endeavour. It is this advice of Nietzsche's which became his most important and most influential legacy to subsequent continental European philosophy.

[50] For elaboration, see my *Nietzsche and Metaphysics*, 111–36.

4

THE ETERNAL RECURRENCE

ALEXANDER NEHAMAS

> It's the difference between making the most out of life and making the least, so that you'll get another better one in some other time and place. Will it be a sin to make the most out of that one too, I wonder; and shall we have to be bribed off in the future state as well as in the present?
>
> (Henry James, *"The Author of Beltraffio"*)

Whatever else we may be tempted to say of Nietzsche's ideas, it is unlikely that we shall describe many of them as sensible. Time after time, Nietzsche tears at the fabric of common sense, at the sense of ordinary language, at the language of reasonable thought. This is a fact on which he insists and of which he is proud. "How *could* I mistake myself," he asks in the Preface to *The Antichrist*, "for one of those for whom there are ears even now? Only the day after tomorrow belongs to me. Some are born posthumously," while to Carl von Gersdorff he writes, "There's no one alive today who could write anything like *Zarathustra*."[1]

By insisting so strenuously on his unique position in the history of thought, Nietzsche may have done himself a great disservice. For he seems to have licensed the attribution to him of views which are often impossible to accept; and which are then either defended as ideas whose time has not yet come or dismissed as the thoughts of someone who was more interested in shocking than in teaching. Of none of them is this more true than of that most peculiar of his many peculiar ideas, the eternal recurrence.

From Alexander Nehamas, "The Eternal Recurrence," *Philosophical Review*, 89 (1980), 331–56. Used by the permission of the publisher, Cornell University Press.

I thank Walter Kaufmann for discussing these problems with me on a number of occasions and for helpful comments. Richard Rorty and Gilbert Harman read an earlier version of this paper and both gave me kind and useful advice. The paper has been improved by the comments of the editors of *The Philosophical Review*. The financial support of the National Endowment for the Humanities is gratefully acknowledged.

[1] Peter Fuss and Henry Shapiro, *Nietzsche: A Self-Portrait from his Letters* (Cambridge, Mass.: Harvard University Press, 1971), 74.

I

The eternal recurrence is most commonly interpreted as a cosmological hypothesis. As such, it holds that everything that has already happened in the universe, and everything that is happening right now, and everything that will happen in the future, has already happened, and will happen again, preceded and followed by exactly the same events in exactly the same order, infinitely many times. Each of these cycles is absolutely identical with every other; in fact, it would be more correct to say that there is only one cycle, repeated over and over again in infinity. There can be no variations, and hence no interactions, between such repetitions. Everything that we are now doing, we have already done in the past (though it is impossible to remember, since that would constitute an interaction between two of the cycle's repetitions) and we shall do again, exactly as we are doing it now, infinitely many times.[2]

Though some writers simply cannot believe that Nietzsche actually accepted this theory,[3] such an interpretation can find support in Nietzsche's own writings. On the other hand, the evidence is not absolutely telling. First, this cosmological doctrine is not to be found in a number of passages where Nietzsche discusses the recurrence. Further, much of what Nietzsche wrote about the recurrence and about its psychological impact does not commit him to this cosmological hypothesis. The psychological use to which he puts the eternal recurrence only commits him to a weaker view which is, as we shall see, quite independent of any theory of the physical universe. This weaker view, I shall suggest, makes a much more serious claim to our attention than the cosmological theory with which Nietzsche's commentators, and sometimes Nietzsche himself, have identified it.

Nietzsche may at times have suspected that this cosmology was philosophically useless to him. This may explain why he never published a

---

[2] Such a treatment of the recurrence or of its cosmological (as opposed to its psychological) aspects can be found in these recent writers: Arthur Danto, *Nietzsche as Philosopher* (New York: Macmillan, 1965), ch. 7; Walter Kaufmann, *Nietzsche: Philosopher, Psychologist, Antichrist*, 3rd edn. (New York: Vintage, 1968), ch. 11; Joe Krueger, "Nietzschean Recurrence as a Cosmological Hypothesis," *Journal of the History of Philosophy*, 16 (1978), 435–44 (with complete references); Bernd Magnus, "Nietzsche's Eternalistic Countermyth," *Review of Metaphysics*, 26 (1973), 604–16, and *Nietzsche's Existential Imperative* (Bloomington: Indiana University Press, 1978); Ivan Soll, "Reflections on Recurrence," in Robert Solomon (ed.), *Nietzsche: A Collection of Critical Essays* (Garden City: Doubleday, 1973), 322–42; Arnold Zuboff, "Nietzsche and Eternal Recurrence," in Solomon, (ed.), *Nietzsche*, 343–57. As we shall see, Soll and Magnus are concerned with the possibility rather than the actuality of the truth of this hypothesis.

[3] Tracy B. Strong, *Friedrich Nietzsche and the Politics of Transfiguration* (Berkeley: University of California Press, 1975), 261. Though my understanding of the recurrence differs from Strong's, I am greatly indebted to his discussion, and to discussion with him.

"proof" of the recurrence despite the fact that, as a cosmology, the recurrence is inseparable from its proof. Since it is essentially a theory for which no empirical evidence can be given,[4] its credibility depends just on such a proof. This is not a minor matter, for Nietzsche describes the recurrence as "the fundamental conception" of *Thus Spoke Zarathustra*,[5] a book whose hero he characterizes as "the teacher of eternal recurrence."[6] But to teach a theory of the universe is at least to try to show that it is true, and it is not clear that Nietzsche seriously made such an effort in his published work. It is true that the section "On the Vision and the Riddle" (Z III. 2, quoted below, p. 123) can be taken to include an attempt to show that such a theory is true without violating the work's lyrical style. But Nietzsche called himself as well "the teacher of eternal recurrence" in *The Twilight of the Idols*, a book in which a rigorous proof of this doctrine would have been quite in place, but from which it is totally absent.[7]

Nietzsche sketches out a proof of such a cosmology in his notes, which his editors published after his death.[8] But it is not easy to determine what his actual purpose was from these fragmentary entries. And this is even more true of the similar passages in sections 1053–1069 of *The Will to Power*, which his sister, who put the volume together after his death, did not even arrange in chronological order.[9]

The unpublished proof is incomplete and ultimately unsatisfactory. In order to derive the conclusion that the world infinitely repeats itself, at least the following two premisses are necessary:

(1) The sum-total of energy in the universe is finite.
(2) The number of states of energy is finite.

XII, 90 suggests that Nietzsche thinks that (2) follows from (1) but, as Danto has shown, this is not correct.[10] Premiss (2) must be included as an

---

[4] Cf. Danto, *Nietzsche as Philosopher*, 204, and Kaufmann's discussion of the view's "supra-historical" character, *Nietzsche*, 319–21.

[5] EH III, Z 1.

[6] Z III. 13.

[7] TI X. 5.

[8] Most of these are collected in vol. xii of the *Grossoktavausgabe* (Leipzig: Naumann, 1901). Translations from the *Nachlass* are mine (hereafter, XII).

[9] Cf. WP 1053–67, and pp. xv–xvi of *The Will to Power*, ed. W. Kaufmann (New York: Vintage, 1968).

[10] Danto, *Nietzsche as Philosopher*, 206. This criticism, accepted by Magnus, "Nietzsche's Eternalistic Countermyth," 605–6, is also made by Krueger. Marvin Sterling ("Recent Discussions of Eternal Recurrence: Some Critical Comments," *Nietzsche-Studien*, 6 (1977), 261–91, esp. 265–8) has tried to show that this entailment holds if we attribute to Nietzsche a particular ontology. He identifies the sum-total of energy with the number of "force-centers," which he considers as Nietzsche's basic ontological units. He assumes that these interact either totally or not at all. And he argues that if we interpret "states of energy" as sets of interacting force-centers it will follow

independent assumption: and its justification is far from obvious. And behind all such considerations is Simmel's classic refutation which, though it grants only a finite number of states of energy, shows that there is no guarantee that a particular combination of these states will ever occur again.[11]

In some passages, Nietzsche seems to give the eternal recurrence a different interpretation. For example, in section 55 of *The Will to Power* he describes it as the "most scientific of all hypotheses." On the assumption that by "scientific" Nietzsche means "objective," this has been taken as evidence that the hypothesis in question is physical or cosmological. But the assumption is unjustified. First, we must recall Nietzsche's fundamental suspiciousness of science: "It is perhaps dawning on five or six minds that physics, too, is only an interpretation and exegesis of the world (to suit us, if I may say so!) and not a world-explanation";[12] "most of what today displays itself . . . as 'objectivity,' 'being scientific,' . . . 'pure knowledge, free of will,' is merely dressed up skepticism and paralysis of the will" (BGE 208). Secondly, the relevant part of this section begins as follows: "Let us think this thought in its most terrible form: existence as it is, without meaning or aim, yet recurring inevitably without any finale of nothingness: 'the eternal recurrence.'" This suggests that what is at issue is the thought that the universe as a whole continues as it is indefinitely—not that the same events in it are repeated. Finally, Nietzsche, who describes this view as "nihilistic," glosses "scientific" as follows: "We deny end goals; if existence had one it would have to have been reached." This shows that "scientific" is much closer in sense to "not-teleological" than to "objective" or "in correspondence with the facts" (a view which, in any case, Nietzsche repudiates as incoherent).[13] The interpretation of the recurrence which we shall discuss below clearly satisfies this last sense of "scientific."

All the other references to the eternal recurrence in section 55 of *The Will to Power* also seem to concern the endless, purposeless unfolding of the world, and not its actual repetition. Section 56 of *Beyond Good and Evil* discusses the desire that the recurrence be true, and is thus neutral on what the recurrence itself is. As we shall see, section 341 of *The Gay Science*[14] does not presuppose the truth of the cosmological hypothesis, and neither does

that, since there are no degrees of interaction, their number is finite. But even if this doubtful ontology is attributed to Nietzsche, the argument still falls prey to Simmel's refutation (see below).

[11] Georg Simmel, *Schopenhauer und Nietzsche* (Leipzig: Duncker & Humblot, 1907), 250–1. Cf. Kaufmann, *Nietzsche*, 327. Soll ("Reflections on Recurrence," 327 ff.) suggests that a random recombination of states might avoid Simmel's criticism, but rightly concludes that Nietzsche's determinism precludes such a construal of recurrence.

[12] BGE 14.

[13] Cf. Danto, *Nietzsche as Philosopher*, 68–99.

[14] GS 341.

Ecce Homo II. 10. On the other hand, *Ecce Homo*, "The Birth of Tragedy," section 3, clearly speaks of the "doctrine of the 'eternal recurrence,' that is, of the unconditional and infinitely repeated circular course of all things" (EH III, BT 3).

When we turn to *Zarathustra* itself, the book of which the recurrence is "the fundamental conception," we find two passages which present us with what appears to be a cosmology, "On the Vision and the Riddle" (III. 2) and "The Convalescent" (III. 19).[15] The rest of the references to the view are not committed as to its exact signification. We must now look at these two sections.

In "The Convalescent," Zarathustra finally manages to face what is there called his "abysmal thought." This thought, which is somehow connected with the recurrence, is so terrible that he remains insensible and impassive for seven days. At the end of this period, his animals hail him as "the teacher of eternal recurrence"; and it is *they*, not Zarathustra, that declare that they "know what you teach: that all things recur eternally, and we ourselves too; and we have already existed an eternal number of times, and all things with us" (Z III. 13). We should notice, however, that Zarathustra himself, who affectionately and condescendingly calls his animals "buffoons and barrel organs" and who accuses them of turning his thought into a "hurdy-gurdy song",[16] remains silent and does not once acknowledge the view which they attribute to him.

The text itself may suggest that the "abysmal thought" is not the cosmological hypothesis: "The great disgust with man—*this* choked me and had crawled in my throat . . . my sighing and questioning croaked and gagged and gnawed and wailed by day and night: 'Alas, man recurs eternally! The small man recurs eternally!'" (Z III. 13). That the "abysmal thought" is the recurrence of the "small man" is also suggested by section 6 of the essay on *Zarathustra* in *Ecce Homo*: "Zarathustra is . . . he that has had the hardest, most terrible insight into reality, that has thought the 'most abysmal idea,' [and] nevertheless does not consider it an objection to existence, not even to *its eternal recurrence*—but rather one reason more for being himself the eternal Yes to all things" (my italics). This statement would be difficult to interpret if we took the "abysmal idea" to be the thought that the universe recurs eternally, since that idea is described as a possible *objection* to existence and to its eternal recurrence. If, on the other hand, we identify that thought with the recurrence of the type of person represented by the "small

---

[15] Cf. Danto, *Nietzsche as Philosopher*, 202; Krueger, "Nietzschean Recurrence as a Cosmological Hypothesis," 440; Soll, "Reflections on Recurrence," 335 n. 5. Even Strong finds in the former section "the main exposition of eternal return" (*Friedrich Nietzsche*, 262).

[16] Cf. Strong, *Friedrich Nietzsche*, 265–6.

man" (cf. the "last man" in the "Prologue" to *Zarathustra*), a type which aroused Zarathustra's contempt and disgust, the passage can be read smoothly. Moreover, we can see that despite Nietzsche's categorical wording in *Zarathustra*, all that these two statements presuppose (in order to explain Zarathustra's reaction) is not the assertion of the cosmological doctrine but only his supposition that if he were to exist again then everything about the world (good as well as bad, including the small man) would have to exist again. This supposition, I shall argue, is all that the eternal recurrence need be taken to assert.

In "On the Vision and the Riddle" Zarathustra confronts his "spirit of gravity," a lame dwarf whom he is carrying on his shoulders (cf. Z IV. 13. 10). To destroy that dwarf, who claims that "all truth is crooked; time itself is a circle",[17] Zarathustra, standing by a gateway, says:

Behold ... this moment! From this gateway, Moment, a long, eternal lane leads *backward*: behind us lies an eternity. Must not whatever *can* walk have walked on this lane before? Must not whatever *can* happen have happened, have been done, have passed by before? And if everything has been there before—what do you think, dwarf, of this moment? Must not this gateway too have been there before? And are not all things knotted together so firmly that this moment draws after it *all* that is to come? Therefore, itself too? For whatever *can* walk—in this long lane out *there* too, it *must* walk once more.

And this slow spider, which crawls in the moonlight, and this moonlight itself, and I and you in the gateway, whispering together, whispering of eternal things—must not all of us have been there before? And return and walk in that other lane, out there, before us, in this dreadful lane—must we not eternally return?

This passage clearly states the cosmological doctrine. But it is important to notice that, as we shall see in detail, the psychological consequences which Nietzsche draws from the recurrence do not presuppose this doctrine, but only a weaker supposition which is consistent with this text.

This weaker view is that in this, and in every moment, is implicit everything that has occurred in the past and everything that will occur in the future. We shall see presently that Nietzsche believes that every event in the world is inextricably connected with every other; he believes that if anything had occurred differently, everything would have occurred differently, that if anything happened again, everything would happen again. He thinks that the history of the world or (in more modest terms) the history of each person is implicit in every moment: "Don't you know that? In every action you perform the history of every event is repeated and abridged" (XII. 726). In this sense, nothing that has happened to us is contingent. This is a point of which Zarathustra is becoming increasingly aware, as is shown by a

---

[17] Cf. Strong, *Friedrich Nietzsche*, 264.

passage to which we shall have to refer again: "The time is gone when mere accidents could still happen to me; and what could still come to me now that was not mine already? What returns, what finally comes home to me, is my own self and what of myself has long been in strange lands and scattered among all things and accidents" (Z III. 1). This essential connection between the world's temporal stages implies that if any one of them recurred at any time, all of them would also have to recur. And, therefore, that every cheap and detestable part of the world (including the "small man"), which is as necessary to what the world is as are the best of its parts, would recur if anything at all recurred. This is, as we have seen, the "abysmal thought" which Zarathustra has to face and to accept in "The Convalescent." At this stage of the narrative, however, the thought prompts him to have a "vision": he sees a shepherd, choking because a snake has crawled into his mouth and there bitten itself fast. He yells to the shepherd to bite the snake's head off, and asks, in a "riddle," who that shepherd is. The answer is that the shepherd (who heeds Zarathustra's advice and is transformed, "no longer shepherd, no longer human—one changed, radiant, laughing!" (Z III. 2)) is Zarathustra himself, once he has succeeded in accepting this thought: it is given, in terms of the very same imagery, in "The Convalescent," where Zarathustra finally becomes able to want to undergo again all that is cheap and detestable about the world for the sake of what is not.

Perhaps Nietzsche realized that this view is independent of the cosmology that he sometimes entertained (and this might be why he never published his proofs of that hypothesis), or perhaps he did not. On balance, the evidence suggests that he did not. Logically, however, the use he makes of the eternal recurrence does not require the truth (or even the coherence) of this highly doubtful cosmology, whose defects have obscured the serious and valuable elements in Nietzsche's view.[18]

II

Such a version of the eternal recurrence as we have begun to sketch is already anticipated in section 341 of *The Gay Science*:

---

[18] That Nietzsche did think of the recurrence as a cosmology is suggested by the fact that writers with whom he was familiar had argued for such a view, e.g., Heine (cf. Kaufmann, *Nietzsche*, 317–19) and Schopenhauer (cf. *The World as Will and Representation*, trans. E. F. J. Payne (Indian Hills, Colo.: Falcon's Wing Press, 1958), i. 273–4, 279; ii. 489; this reference was pointed out to me by the editors of the *Philosophical Review*). Nietzsche himself was willing to find the doctrine in the Pythagoreans, Heraclitus, and the Stoics (cf. Kaufmann, *Nietzsche*, and Magnus, *Nietzsche's Existential Imperative*, ch. II). But we must then account for his notorious insistence on the radical novelty of the idea of the recurrence. Perhaps what he took to be novel in the recurrence is the metaphysical view which we shall discuss below, and not the cosmology itself.

The greatest weight.—What, if some day or night a demon were to steal after you into your loneliest loneliness and say to you: "This life as you now live it and have lived it, you will have to live once more and innumerable times more; and there will be nothing new in it, but every pain and every joy and every thought and sigh and everything unutterably small or great in your life will have to return to you, all in the same succession and sequence—even this spider and this moonlight between the trees, and even this moment and I myself. The eternal hourglass of existence is turned upside down again and again, and you with it, speck of dust!"

Would you not throw yourself down and gnash your teeth and curse the demon who spoke thus? Or have you once experienced a tremendous moment when you would have answered him: "You are a god and never have I heard anything more divine." If this thought gained possession of you, it would change you as you are or perhaps crush you. The question in each and every thing, "Do you desire this once more and innumerable times more?" would lie upon your actions as the greatest weight. Or how well disposed would you have to become to yourself and to life *to crave nothing more fervently* than this ultimate eternal confirmation and seal?

This passage, as Ivan Soll has convincingly argued,[19] does not presuppose the truth of the claim that the world, or one's life, eternally repeats itself—or even that this is a credible notion. Nietzsche is simply not interested in that question. He is, however, interested in the attitude that one must have toward oneself in order to react with joy and not with despair to the demon's question, to the thought that one's life will occur, the same in every detail, again and again.[20]

It is absolutely crucial for our purposes that Nietzsche considers only two reactions to the demon's question: total exhilaration or total despair. He does not, in particular, consider the possibility that one might remain indifferent to this thought. This indifference could be of two sorts.

The first sort of indifference, indifference to the *actual* fact of recurrence, is well described by Danto:[21]

It does not matter that we pass away and return and pass away again. What counts is what we eternally do, the joy of overcoming, whatever our task may be, and the meaning we give to our lives. And all of this for the sake of the thing itself, not for any consequences: for it leads to what it has led to and always will.

This same reaction is envisaged by Nikos Kazantzakis:

I subdue the last, the greatest temptation: hope. We fight—because so it pleases us; we sing—though there are no ears to hear us.

Where are we going? Shall we ever win? What is this whole battle about? Don't ask! Fight![22]

---

[19] "Reflections on Recurrence," 323.

[20] Cf. Magnus, "Nietzsche's Eternalistic Countermyth," 607.

[21] *Nietzsche as Philosopher*, 212.

[22] Nikos Kazantzakis, *ΑΣΚΗΤΙΚΗ—Salvatores Dei* (Athens: Sympan, n.d.), 49, 58; the translation is mine.

Such a reaction does contain an affirmation, but this is not, I think, what Nietzsche has in mind. For this affirmation depends on a fundamental indifference to the fact that what we are doing we have already done and shall, inevitably, do again.[23] But Nietzsche in no way wants indifference; on the contrary, Zarathustra, with his emphasis on the notion of self-overcoming, exacts from his followers even the acceptance of the past, as we shall see in detail below: "A new will I teach men: to *will* this way which man has walked blindly, and *to affirm it*" (Z I. 3; my italics).

The second sort of indifference is discussed by Soll, who is concerned with the psychological consequences of the *possibility* of the recurrence of one's life. He argues that since, by definition, one cannot now anticipate one's experiences in future recurrences nor then remember one's present, and since psychological continuity is at least necessary for concern with our self, the possibility that my life may occur again "should actually be a matter of complete indifference."[24] To this extent, Soll seems to be right: my *future* experiences, if there will be any, are of no concern to me *now*. Nietzsche, however, fails to consider this possibility altogether.

Should we conclude from this that Nietzsche, who is convinced of the crucial consequences of the recurrence and of its capacity to generate the "highest" affirmation of *this* life, misunderstood the implications of one of his most crucial ideas?

It seems to me that Nietzsche's failure to consider indifference as a possible reaction to the recurrence reveals that he did not always think of his view as a cosmological theory, to which indifference would have been an appropriate reaction. In what follows, therefore, I will offer an interpretation of the recurrence which makes no appeal whatever to the structure of the

---

[23] I am tempted to think that this is the only possible nonfatalistic reaction to the cosmological version of the recurrence. Gilbert Harman has objected that the recurrence, so construed, only entails determinism, which does not in turn entail fatalism. But I think that the fact that an event has already occurred in the past makes its occurrence in the present necessary in a way in which the idea that human actions, like all other events, are caused does not. Nietzsche, who accepts determinism (cf. Soll, "Reflections on Recurrence," 329; Zuboff, "Nietzsche and Eternal Recurrence," 349–50) also believes that our beliefs and thoughts can function as causes of our actions (XII. 117).

[24] Soll, "Reflections on Recurrence," 339. Soll's argument seems to depend on a view of identity and continuity similar to that recently argued for by Derek Parfit, "Personal Identity," repr. in John Perry (ed.), *Personal Identity* (Berkeley: University of California Press, 1975), 199–223. But Soll does not mark clearly the distinction between identity and continuity, and this misleads Sterling ("Recent Discussions of Eternal Recurrence," 273–4) into an unwarranted criticism of Soll's argument. Zuboff ("Nietzsche and Eternal Recurrence," 350–2, 357) argues that the recurrence is a matter of indifference because not only one's current life, but also a large number of possible alternatives to it, will recur eternally. This seems unlikely; cf. Krueger, "Nietzschean Recurrence as a Cosmological Hypothesis," 442–3, Soll, "Reflections on Recurrence," 327–32. Soll's view that Nietzsche is concerned with the possibility that the world may recur is shared by Magnus: e.g., *Nietzsche's Existential Imperative*, 116 ff.

physical world. To simplify matters, let us consider the single repetition of a particular life; the case can then be generalized to the whole world.

The most common view of the recurrence considers it to be the *unconditional assertion* of a cosmology:

(A) My life *will* recur in exactly identical fashion.

The likely psychological consequences of holding this view are either utter resignation or indifferent joy in doomed effort. Its difficulties caused Soll to interpret the recurrence as the *conditional assertion* of a cosmology:

(B) My life *may* recur in exactly identical fashion.

But the psychological consequence of this view, too, seemed to be utter and unqualified indifference, a reaction which Nietzsche does not consider. Suppose then that we construe the recurrence as the *assertion of a conditional*:

(C) If my life were to recur, it would recur in exactly identical fashion.

This construal has nothing to do with physics. It does not presuppose the truth of the cosmology we have discussed, or even its coherence (since it does not assert that my life ever could recur). On the other hand, it has much to do (though one hesitates to use the word in connection with Nietzsche) with metaphysics. It concerns the relation of a subject to its experiences, or more generally of an object to its properties, and it has direct and serious psychological implications.

We must first ask, however, what justifies this conditional. Why can't we be offered the possibility of living again, but also the option of doing some things differently? One always wants, for example, to have had at an earlier age knowledge which one acquired only later on—and so to have followed a different path to the present, or even a path to a different present. One may with good reason want to change parts of one's past, or of one's present, or of what one foresees to be one's future.

Why then does Nietzsche's demon offer only the return of the very same life, and not of a similar one instead? The reason, I suggest, is not to be found in Nietzsche's physics or in his theory of time (though he may have thought so himself at times), but rather in his rejection of the notion of the substantial subject, conceived as something over and above its experiences and actions. This, in turn, is a special case of his rejection of the notion of the thing-in-itself. And, therefore, Nietzsche's ultimate reason for believing that if one's life were to recur it would have to be identical to the present one is his very central doctrine of the will to power, of which the rejection of the thing-in-itself is, in turn, one aspect:

The "thing-in-itself" is non-sensical. If I remove all the relationships, all the "proper-ties," all the "activities" of a thing, the thing does not remain over. (WP 558)

This view is found often in Nietzsche's published writings:

There is no "being" behind doing, effecting, becoming; "the doer" is merely a fiction added to the deed—the deed is everything . . . our entire science still lies under the misleading influence of language and has not disposed of that little changeling, the "subject" (the atom, for example, is such a changeling, as is the Kantian "thing-in-itself").[25]

Nietzsche's favorite illustration of this idea is the lightning:

The popular mind separates the lightning from its flash and takes the latter for an *action*, for the operation of a subject called lightning . . . (ibid.)

Through the presence of the image of the lightning, therefore, the following passage provides a connection between the will to power and the eternal recurrence and, thus, also support for the interpretation which I am proposing:

If only a moment of the world recurred—said the lightning—all would have to recur. (XII. 724)

Nietzsche thinks that there is no subject, no thing, left over beyond the sum-total of its characteristics and effects, its experiences and actions. If any of these were different, their subject, being their sum-total, would also have to be different. He seems to think that, strictly speaking, all properties are equally essential to their bearer (and thus that there is ultimately no distinc-tion between essential and accidental properties); if any property is different, the subject itself is a different subject. And he also seems committed to the stronger view that if any object were different, every object would be differ-ent. For if some of a thing's effects were different, then some other things would have to be affected differently by it; thus they would be "in them-selves" different and affect still other things differently—the chain, perhaps, rounding back to its hypothetical first member and beginning anew. This view is expressed most explicitly in *The Will to Power*, section 557:

The properties of a thing are effects on other "things": if one removes other "things," then a thing has no properties, i.e., there is no thing without other things, i.e., there is no "thing-in-itself."

And it provides the metaphysical foundation of Zarathustra's famous statement:

---

[25] GM I. 13; cf. BGE 12, 17; TI III. 5. This view of Nietzsche has had a decisive influence on French existentialism, especially on Sartre: cf. *The Transcendence of the Ego* (New York: Farrar, Straus & Giroux, 1957), 73–4. For discussion, see John T. Wilcox, *Truth and Value in Nietzsche* (Ann Arbor: University of Michigan Press, 1974), 114–26. Strong (*Friedrich Nietzsche*, 261) claims that there is no connection between the will to power and the recurrence.

Have you ever said Yes to a single joy? O my friends, then you have said Yes too to all woe. All things are entangled, ensnared, enamored; if ever you wanted one thing twice, if ever you said, "You please me, happiness! Abide, moment!" then you wanted all back. All anew, all eternally, all entangled, ensnared, enamored . . . (Z IV. 19)

To question this metaphysics, which would require an examination of the will to power, is more than we can attempt here. Other serious questions, as we shall see, confront us in any case.

The explanation of why the demon offers us only the very same life, which we can only accept or reject in its entirety, is therefore to be found in this metaphysics: a different life would constitute a different person. To want to be in any way different is, on this view, to want to be in every way different. And since, as Nietzsche claims, everything is essentially connected with everything else in the world, to want our self to be different is also to want everything in the world to be different. And this in turn explains why Nietzsche envisages only two reactions to the demon's question: total exhilaration or total despair. If we accept any part of our self, then we accept our entire self, and all the world as well; and if we reject any part of it, then we reject our entire self, and all the world with it.

We can state this interpretation of the eternal recurrence by generalizing thesis (C) above to include not only an individual life, but everything in the world:

(C′) If anything in the world recurred (including an individual life, or even a moment of it), then everything in the world would recur in exactly identical fashion.

I suspect that in *The Gay Science* Nietzsche had not thought of his view as it is expressed in (C′), and had probably not yet connected it with the will to power.[26] At the time of that book his question was only this: How would one react to the possibility of living one's life over again? What he then saw in August of 1881, "6000 feet beyond man and time" (EH III, Z 1), what probably does constitute the fundamental conception of *Zarathustra*, an idea whose implications are present and striking throughout the book, is the hypothesis that if we were to have another life it would have to be, if it were to be *our* life at all, the very same life that we have already had. And for it to be the same life, it would have to be part of the very same world in which we have already lived, which would therefore have to recur exactly as it has

---

[26] Cf. Kaufmann, *Nietzsche*, 188–9.

already occurred, down to its most minute, and to its most detestable, aspects.[27]

This life and this world then turn out to be (even if they were to be repeated) the only life and the only world there are: "This life—your eternal life!" (XII. 126). This is what Zarathustra "the godless," who asks his listeners to "remain faithful to the earth, and . . . not [to] believe those who speak to you of other-worldly hopes" (Z, "Prologue"), has quite paradoxically discovered in the eternal recurrence. Yet whatever one's metaphysics implies, it seems a peculiar view to suppose that every one of my actions is equally important to me and to what I am. Insignificantly different actions (for example, wearing slightly different clothes on an immaterial occasion) make up only insignificant differences in my person. Should not one's model allow for such variations in significance?

Strictly speaking, Nietzsche is committed to the view that every one of a person's actions is equally a part of that person's identity. But if we concentrate on the psychological aspects of the recurrence, we may be able to find a different answer, for though the occurrence of an action is given, its significance may still be variable.

The first thing to notice is that it is slightly perverse of me to want to repeat my life exactly as it has already occurred except for something (like having on one occasion worn slightly different clothes) which I begin by considering as insignificant. Why should I, after all, want that event to be different if it does not matter to me that it has occurred? Nietzsche seems to be concerned with those aspects of our lives which actually are important to us—aspects which determine in our own eyes what sorts of persons we are. And though how to dress may be significant for some people, no one would be consumed with nausea and despair at the prospect of living through a trifle, whatever that would be, again. To want only insignificant character-

---

[27] It may be argued that the rejection of the substantial subject, though it may lead to the idea that all of a person's actions are equally essential, does not lead to a thesis like (C) or (C′). That is, it might be true that if all my actions were equally essential to me, then I would have the same career in every possible world. But this would not imply that if my career had two (or more) successive phases in this world, each of which might in a sense constitute a distinct life, these phases would have to be exactly alike. But how are we to understand the notion of a phase in this context? To consider the future occurrence a *phase* of *my* (total) life, we would have to have access to an enduring subject as the ground of that identification. But, for Nietzsche, the subject (the totality of my actions) disappears with my death. We could only identify *me* as living again if I were to be born just as I was born this time, and to grow up in the same way, and so on. But from this it seems to follow that if I were to live again, I and the whole world (given that everything is just the totality of its effects, and that any change in me would effect changes everywhere) would have to be exactly similar to what we are now. Thus we can ascribe this view to Nietzsche on the basis of his denial of the substantial subject without appealing to his stronger position that every part of a person's life necessitates every subsequent one and that therefore a single part could only recur if it were preceded and followed by exactly the same parts.

istics of our lives to be different is to want to be significantly like what we are.

What then is, and what is not, significant in how we view ourselves? To this question there is, for two reasons, no answer. First, because there is no answer which applies uniformly to different individuals:

> He . . . has discovered himself who says, "This is *my* good and evil"; with that he has reduced to silence the mole and dwarf who say, "Good for all, evil for all." . . . "This is *my* way; where is yours?"—thus I answered those who asked me "the way." For *the* way—that does not exist. (Z III. 11; cf. XII. 116)

Secondly, because there is not even a fixed answer as to what is significant for each individual. The relative significance of our experiences and actions is not determined once and for all; it is, rather, a characteristic over which we have serious control. Though Nietzsche believes that all our actions are equally important to our nature, he also believes that how they are related to our nature—what nature, in fact, they constitute—is an open question. How we perceive the relationships between our actions, which patterns we consider as seriously shaping our conduct, which actions belong to those and have lasting implications and which do not and are therefore exceptions and accidents—all these he sees as questions which are constantly receiving different answers. Nietzsche considers the awareness of this fluidity of the personality as one of the basic characteristics of the *Übermensch*; and it is this fluidity which underlies the emphasis on constant self-overcoming in the discussion of the *Übermensch* in the opening sections of book I of *Zarathustra*. Moreover, it is precisely here that we shall find the relationship between the eternal recurrence and the "highest affirmation" for which we have been searching.

As the section "On Redemption" (Z II. 20) suggests, the only way to justify one's life is to become able to accept it in its entirety; and the mark of this ability is the desire to repeat this very life (and hence everything else in the world as well) again in all eternity. Suppose, then, that one comes to accept Zarathustra's thought, that one begins to try to make oneself such as one would want to be again, and thus act as the *Übermensch* acts (cf. Z I. 1, 16).

Such a project would be faced with two grave difficulties. First, our power to control our future is not as absolute as Zarathustra sometimes suggests, since at any time our possibilities are limited by our past and our present; accordingly, Nietzsche's image of the "self-propelled wheel" seems too optimistic. Secondly, our past is now given to us; it consists of events which have already occurred, and over which we have no longer any control. There are certain to be among them experiences and actions, character traits, even whole phases of our personality and parts of our life, which we would with good reason not want to repeat ever again. These are fixed. How can we accept now these unacceptable parts of our past?

Such questions exercise Nietzsche in *Zarathustra*:

> To redeem those who lived in the past and to recreate all "it was" into "thus I willed it"—that alone I should call redemption ... willing liberates; but what is it that puts even the liberator himself in fetters? "It was"—that is the name of the will's gnashing of teeth and most secret melancholy. Powerless against what has been done, he is an angry spectator of all that is past. The will cannot will backwards; and that he cannot break time and time's covetousness, that is the will's loneliest melancholy.[28]

From this it seems that affirmation is impossible, unless by a stroke of unbelievable luck we have done nothing we regret, or unless by means of self-deception we can convince ourselves that we have not: the past forces us to repudiate whatever future it leads into. Since on Nietzsche's view every aspect of the personality is equally essential, it seems to follow that if there is any part of our life (or of the whole world, for that matter) that we are unable to accept, then we should be unable to accept all of it. Partial acceptance of the self presupposes that we can abstract our self from some of its characteristics, and that therefore these characteristics are only accidental to it.

Yet Nietzsche does suggest that there is a sense in which the past can be changed: "The will is a creator. All 'it was' is a fragment, a riddle, a dreadful accident—until the creative will says to it, 'But thus I willed it.' Until the creative will says to it, 'But thus I will it; thus shall I will it'" (Z II. 20). This does not, of course, involve literally undoing the past. Nietzsche is thinking of his view that every one of my past actions is a necessary condition for my being what I am. If, therefore, I am even for a moment such as I would want to be again, my past actions can be seen in retrospect to have been essential to, and therefore constitutive of, the self which I would want to repeat. What is thus changed is not the past, but its significance. This is accomplished by creating, on the basis of the past, a future which is at some point acceptable, and which therefore justifies what made it possible: "I taught them ... to create and carry together into one what in man is fragment and riddle and dreadful accident; as creator, guesser of riddles, and redeemer of accidents, I taught them to work on the future and to redeem with their creation all that has been."[29] To accept the present thus implies accepting all that has led to it.

---

[28] Z II. 20. The similarity in the vocabulary among the different sections of Nietzsche's work dealing with the recurrence should be noted. An attempt to spell out the view I am supporting is made by Pierre Klossowski, "Nietzsche's Experience of the Eternal Return," in David B. Allison (ed.), *The New Nietzsche* (New York: Dell, 1977), 107–20, esp. p. 115.

[29] Z III. 12. Nietzsche often speaks of the reinterpretation of the past as its "destruction" or "annihilation"; cf. Z I. 16, GM II. 24.

It is in this sense that one can now say of the past "Thus I willed it." The significance of the past lies in its relationship to the future; and insofar as the future is yet to come, the past's significance remains an open question.

Nietzsche believes that the past cannot be changed, as his view, that if one were to live again one would have to have the very same life, implies. He thinks that one should take the occurrence of the events of one's past as given, and on their basis achieve something which makes one willing to accept oneself. At that point, one accepts all that one has done, since past events are individually necessary and jointly sufficient for one to be what one is. In this sense one can turn even the accidents in one's past into actions, that is, into events for which one is willing to accept responsibility ("Thus I willed it"). In the ideal case, everything in the past is redeemed in this manner; one is "reconciled with time": "The time is gone when mere accidents could still happen to me; and what could still come to me now that was not mine already? What returns, what finally comes home to me, is my own self" (Z III. 6). This attitude presupposes the realization that the significance of the past depends on its importance to the future. Not to realize this is to brood over the past, to take its significance as given once and for all—like the "pale criminal," who "was equal to his deed when he did it; but he could not bear its image after it was done. Now he always saw himself as the doer of one deed . . . the exception now became the essence of him" (Z I. 6). This is the basis of the attitude which Nietzsche, in *The Genealogy of Morals* (I. 10ff.), calls *ressentiment*, and which characterizes the slave morality. In *Zarathustra* he writes that one should prove to an enemy that the enemy has done one some good, instead of wanting revenge (Z I. 18). Rather than staying with the "harm," one takes the enemy's action as material for further development (cf. Z II. 7). In the *Genealogy* the picture is more complicated: "To be incapable of taking one's enemies, one's accidents, even one's misdeeds seriously for very long—that is the sign of strong, full natures in whom there is an excess of the power to form, to mold, to recuperate, and to forget" (GM I. 10). One can thus either incorporate a past event into a complex, harmonious and unified pattern, or one can simply not take it seriously; in the latter case one sees it precisely as an exception, as an event of no significance, of no lasting consequence. In either case, the event cannot be resented. If the event *is* insignificant, resentment is out of place. If it is not, and if the attempt to assimilate it into one's personality succeeds, if one manages to see the things of the past fall together and change themselves, undergo that relegation that transforms melancholy and misery, passion, pain, and effort into experience and knowledge, resentment is again out of place. For no place remains for thinking that the consequences of a past action on the self (and therefore the self as well) remain unchanged. We would be making the same point by saying that one need not think that any action is in itself harmful (or, for that matter, beneficial); whether it is or not depends on its long-term implications for the whole of one's changing self.

III

The view we have attributed to Nietzsche is that the justification of one's life lies in those moments when one, in accepting the present, also accepts all of the past; for though perhaps one did not in the past will something, one would not now have it otherwise. In this ideal case everything about one would be, and would be seen to be, part of oneself; it would, accordingly, be manifested in one's every action: "Oh, my friends, that your self be in your deed as the mother is in her child—let that be *your* word concerning virtue" (Z II. 5).

This is, I think, a limiting case: a person who would be different in every way if his life were different in any, a life so organized and coherent that if anything in it were changed, everything in it would fall apart. Such a person would indeed see in the eternal recurrence the "highest affirmation." For in this limiting case one would want what would happen in any case if it happened at all: the eternal recurrence of every single part of one's life, which one would see as following inevitably from any other. And, to generalize, one would also in that case want what, in turn, would also happen: the eternal recurrence of everything else in the world—past or future, accidental or intentional, "good" or "evil."[30]

Such a person can only be considered as an ideal case of the perfect relationship that one could acknowledge to bear to one's experiences and actions; and insofar as it is ideal, this case can only be approximated. But we must notice how serious a role might be played by self-deception in one's thinking that one is close to achieving that sort of relationship. I might be willing, for example, to repeat my life only because I do not let myself see it for what it is; because I do not allow myself to see in the proper light, or to see at all, large and objectionable parts of it.

This, I think, is a serious difficulty, for Nietzsche's view gives us great freedom in determining what in fact constitutes part of our life and what does not. I might accordingly be exhilarated at the prospect of my life's repetition just because I am attending to only a small part of it. Nietzsche, it

---

[30] Here I disagree with Strong. He believes (*Friedrich Nietzsche*, 270–2) that what recurs is only a subset of the characteristics which make up a person, and which are selected in order to be perpetuated.

seems to me, was aware of this problem. This is supported by his description of the occasion for the demon's question as one's "loneliest loneliness," when presumably one would be most likely to be honest with oneself; it is also supported by his repeated emphasis on the difficulty with which Zarathustra comes finally to accept the recurrence. In both cases Nietzsche is trying to suggest how intense, and how very painful, a self-examination is necessary before the question can be answered affirmatively. But the point remains that to want nothing to be different (EH II. 10) presupposes having faced everything. And there is no independent way of establishing that this has actually been done. In addition, Nietzsche does not even try to provide one; the process of examination may have to go on forever.

That such self-examination may be unending, however, could well be a very acceptable consequence to Nietzsche, especially if the conjecture I am about to make is reasonable. For what I would now like to suggest is that the best intuitive model for Nietzsche's ideal case, the case in which if anything is different everything is different, may be a perfect story—a story in which no detail is inconsequential, nothing out of place or capricious, in which every "Why?" has an answer better than "Why not?"

This model carries with it a number of advantages. For one thing, it connects the eternal recurrence, in which the interpretation of the past is, as we have seen, so crucial, with Nietzsche's overarching metaphor of the world in general as a text to be interpreted.[31] In addition, since interpretation is a never-ending process, and the notion of a complete or total interpretation is an impossible purpose to aim at,[32] the model accounts for the fact that the examination of one's life with the purpose of putting all of it in the proper perspective may have to go on forever. A second advantage of thinking of the ideal life on the model of a story is that in likening that life to a work of art it does some justice to Nietzsche's early view that "it is only as an aesthetic phenomenon that existence and the world are eternally justified" (BT 5).[33] In this way it allows us to see that despite the many differences which separate *The Birth of Tragedy* from Nietzsche's later works, some of his concerns remain relatively stable over the years.

More importantly, however, this model brings into clear focus two central characteristics and, with them, two major difficulties of Nietzsche's view. Nietzsche believes, as we have seen, that as a matter of logical fact a person's

[31] BT 5; cf. Kaufmann, *Nietzsche*, 323. Cf. also Jean Granier, "Perspectivism and Interpretation," in Allison (ed.), *The New Nietzsche*, 190–200.

[32] Cf., for example, Peter Jones, *Philosophy and the Novel* (Oxford: Clarendon Press, 1975), 193. I should point out, however, that I do not think that any perspectivist conclusions follow from this fact.

[33] Cf. Kaufmann, *Nietzsche*, 323.

life cannot be in any way different and still be that person's life. His view that every property belongs to its subject essentially, that a subject is nothing more than its properties, and that properties are a thing's effects on other similar subjects (in short, his doctrine of the will to power) implies that no counterfactuals of the form, "If I had done such-and-such instead of such-and-such, then I would have . . . ," can ever be true. Accordingly, the ideal life is to realize that this is so and to make oneself into such a person that one would not *want* any such statement to be true. Our model provides an intuitive illustration of this peculiar view by focusing attention on the case of literary characters, whose world does seem to be exhausted by the descriptions of what actually happens in the stories in which they are found. A character, it may be argued, is nothing over and above what is said of it in the story. Accordingly, at least in a good story, every detail about a character is equally crucial; at least in the perfect case, everything noticeable about a character has a function in the story and is essential to the character being what it is. In a good story, to change one action of one character would be to cause the story to fall apart. To keep the story coherent (if that would be at all possible) many other changes would have to be made throughout—and, in that case, a different story would emerge. Furthermore, if one action of such a character were different, many others of that character's actions would cease to make sense in the context; and it might become a real question whether the character would still be the same. Could Anna Karenina not have fallen in love with Vronsky? Could she not have left her husband? Could she have loved her son less? Could she have been ultimately less conventional than she was? Could she not have been the sister of Prince Oblonsky? Such questions are at least difficult to answer in relation to literary characters, and this difficulty provides some motivation for Nietzsche's thinking of the ideal person in similar ways.

But though our model motivates this feature of Nietzsche's view, it also reveals one of its possible weaknesses. For even if it is true that literature cannot support counterfactuals of the sort we have been discussing (and I am not sure that it is), Nietzsche may still be accused of generalizing illegitimately from that case. He himself was notoriously unwilling to accept the distinction between fact and fiction.[34] But it can still be maintained that the fundamental difference between them is just the fact that the former is, while the latter is not, expected to support counterfactuals of the sort that he considers universally false. In short, the first essential characteristic of Nietzsche's view (and also, perhaps, its first central difficulty) is that it

---

[34] Danto, *Nietzsche as Philosopher*, 38–42, 72–6.

assimilates the ideal person to an ideal literary character and the ideal life to an ideal story.

The second characteristic (and its attendant difficulty) which this model brings out concerns what one feels compelled to consider as a moral aspect of Nietzsche's view. A literary character may be a perfect character and (represent) an awful person. If we assume that Nietzsche is looking at people on the model of such characters and at life on the model of a story, we may be able to explain why he is willing to leave the content of his ideal life unspecified. He is much more concerned (as one usually is in relation to literary characters) with how one's actions fit together into a coherent, self-sustaining, motivated whole than he is with the quality of the actions themselves. Our model also explains his view that actions do not have qualities in themselves but only in relation to one's whole life: the justification of a character's action, its full significance, can only be determined in terms of how it fits into the whole picture presented by the character and by the story in which it occurs. His view that one should not take one's misdeeds seriously, and his idea that virtue depends not so much on what is done but on whether what is done is an expression of one's whole self, of one's "own will" (Z I. 1) are also accounted for by this model; for these are exactly the questions we tend to ask of literary characters. The virtue of characters, as characters, depends precisely on this sort of coherence on which Nietzsche insists for people. Authors are not blamed for creating morally repugnant characters, at least so long as these characters are in some sense believable. To stay with an author whom Nietzsche clearly admired, the narrator of Dostoevsky's *Notes from the Underground*, perfect as a character, unspeakable as a man, is a case in point. It is true that sometimes we tend to react in a more direct moral way to literary figures; but I should think that in most cases where a character's immorality is held against the author, the character is either not well drawn, or its viciousness is gratuitous in that it does not function essentially in the story.

Again, then, though our model motivates Nietzsche's view, it also highlights its difficulty. To be the perfectly integrated person whom he so admires is quite compatible with being morally repulsive. This criticism, too, we should point out, depends on a moral outlook which Nietzsche made one of his major points of attack throughout his life. But one remains with the uncomfortable feeling that someone could achieve Nietzsche's ideal life and nevertheless be a repugnant human being. This does not matter so much for literary characters, who are not people, and with whom our concerns are different; but it does, one feels, matter for people.

One might perhaps try to think of this ideal life as a frame in which different particular lives might fit, and require independent arguments for excluding some of these. I do not know how one might do this, and Nietzsche does not seem interested in this approach. Still, in thinking of his ideal life on the model of a story, we should do well to think of it in terms of Proust's *Remembrance of Things Past*. In this fictional autobiography the narrator relates in enormous detail all the silly, insignificant, pointless, accidental, sometimes awful things he did in his rambling efforts to become a writer. He relates the time that he wasted, the acquaintances he made, the values he accepted at different times, his changes of mind, the way he treated his family, his lovers and his servants, the disjointed and often unflattering motives out of which he acted most of the time. Yet all these somehow finally enable him to become a writer. They enable him to see them all as parts of a unified pattern, the result of which is his determination to begin writing his first book. This book, he tells us, will relate all the silly, insignificant, pointless, accidental, sometimes awful things he did in his rambling efforts to become a writer and to begin writing his first book—which he has not yet begun, but which his readers have just finished reading. I am not suggesting that Marcel's actual life would have been Nietzsche's own ideal. But it does seem to me that the frame supplied by this perfect novel, which relates what becomes and is seen to be a perfect life, and which keeps turning back upon itself endlessly, is the best possible model for the eternal recurrence. To achieve such a life involves the reinterpretation of what is in a sense already there, since the whole self is implicit in its every action. Nietzsche seems to think that to lead an ideal life is to understand what that self is which is already there and to live according to that understanding. If this is so, we might finally be in a position to understand one of Zarathustra's most puzzling self-descriptions: "For *that* is what I am through and through: reeling, reeling in, raising up, raising, a raiser, cultivator and disciplinarian, who once counseled himself, not for nothing: Become who you are" (Z IV. 1). And in this way we may able to see the eternal recurrence, located now at the very center of Nietzsche's thought, as a provocative and serious theory of human personality.

5

NIETZSCHE'S DOCTRINES OF THE WILL TO POWER

MAUDEMARIE CLARK

There is an apparent contradiction between Nietzsche's view of knowledge and what I shall call his ontological doctrine of the will to power, the doctrine that the world is will to power. The proposal I will defend for dissolving this apparent contradiction is that we interpret the ontological doctrine as a self-conscious myth which is not intended to supply knowledge about the world, and that we distinguish from it a second, psychological doctrine of the will to power which Nietzsche believes does give us such knowledge.

The advantage of interpreting Nietzsche's ontological doctrine as a myth follows from the difficulties of reconciling it with his views about knowledge, if we think it is intended to supply knowledge. From the time of *Human, All Too Human*, Nietzsche rejected all claims to metaphysical or non-empirical knowledge of reality. He has also been interpreted as rejecting all claims to knowledge and truth, but I believe that John Wilcox has argued convincingly that Nietzsche's later position not only allows, but demands, the possibility of empirical truth,[1] and I shall treat his conclusion as given. It then follows that if the doctrine of the will to power is intended to supply knowledge of reality, it is consistent with Nietzsche's views on knowledge if and only if it is intended as an empirical doctrine. I do not believe it is plausible to so interpret it.

The most detailed account of the will to power as an empirical doctrine has been given by Walter Kaufmann, who writes that Nietzsche's will to power, unlike Schopenhauer's will, is not metaphysical, but is "essentially an empirical concept arrived at by induction."[2] The will to power first appears, in the aphoristic works prior to Zarathustra, as "a psychological drive in terms of which many diverse phenomena could be explained; e.g., gratitude, pity, self-abasement." Success in explaining such different types of behavior

From Maudemarie Clark, "Nietzsche's Doctrines of the Will to Power," *Nietzsche-Studien*, 12 (1983), 458–68.

[1] John Wilcox, *Truth and Value in Nietzsche* (Ann Arbor, Mich., 1974), esp. ch. 4–6.
[2] Walter Kaufmann, *Nietzsche: Philosopher, Psychologist, Antichrist* (New York, 1968), 204.

was the basis, Kaufmann believes, upon which Nietzsche then formulated the hypothesis that all human behavior could be explained in terms of the will, i.e., motivating desire, for power. Kaufmann takes this psychological doctrine to be the core which is then widened to include the behavior of all living beings, and generalized into "the still more extreme hypothesis that will to power is the basic force of the universe."[3] This latter doctrine may, of course, be called "metaphysical" for the same reason I have called it "ontological"—that it is taken to be true of all reality—but according to Kaufmann's interpretation, it is not "metaphysical" as I am using that term, in contrast to "empirical," for it is offered only as a hypothesis to account for the data of experience.

On Kaufmann's interpretation, then, Nietzsche's doctrine of the will to power is reconcilable with his claims about knowledge. For the doctrine does not tell us what the world is in itself (from no perspective at all), thereby violating his perspectivism, but only that from the human perspective it is will to power. That all knowledge is interpretation (rather than a mirroring of the "in itself") does not preclude the possibility that will to power is, as Kaufmann puts it, "the one and only interpretation of human behavior [and reality in general] of which we are capable when we consider the evidence and think about it as clearly as we can."[4] In other words, will to power might be the one and only interpretation that accounts for all the data, or is true in the sense of corresponding to the way things are from a general human perspective. In fact, Kaufmann thinks it obvious that the ontological doctrine is not true in this sense (nor in any other), and claims that it "need not be taken seriously, not even in an effort to understand Nietzsche."[5] Kaufmann seems to believe that the ontological doctrine plays little role in Nietzsche's philosophy, that it is merely an over-enthusiastic and ill-advised extension of the psychological doctrine which does have a central role to play. Thus, from the viewpoint of one interested in maintaining Nietzsche's stature as an important philosopher, the main advantages of the empirical interpretation of the will to power are that it explains how Nietzsche could arrive at the doctrine without violating minimal standards of consistency, and that it insulates the psychological doctrine from the ontological one, so that we can legitimately regard the former as worthy of the serious consideration Kaufmann thinks we should deny the latter. Kaufmann's interpretation would be undermined if it can be shown that the psychological doctrine of the will to power, as he understands it, does not deserve serious consideration as an empirical hypothesis. I shall now argue that it does not.

[3] Ibid. 207.
[4] Ibid. 206.
[5] Kaufmann, in Paul Edwards (ed.), *Encyclopedia of Philosophy* (New York, 1967), v. 510.

One of the major aims of Kaufmann's empirical interpretation of the will to power is to answer the objection that Nietzsche's doctrine does not explain anything, that by finding the will to power at work everywhere, it empties it of all meaning and reduces it to a "mere phrase," devoid of explanatory power or cognitive significance.[6] Kaufmann's answer is that "on the contrary, it is surprising how much of human behavior Nietzsche illuminates by calling attention to will to power and its hidden workings."[7] One can agree with Kaufmann, however, and yet claim that the enlightening character of explanations of behavior in terms of power is dependent on an implicit contrast with other motives, and is therefore lost as soon as all other motives are interpreted as will to power. For example, the enlightening character of contemporary accounts of rape in terms of power is dependent on an implicit contrast between desire for power and the sex drive: what the rapist supposedly wants is not sexual gratification but a sense of power. Doesn't this explanation lose its enlightening character if we accept the claim that all behavior is to be explained in terms of will to power, and therefore have to say either that there is no sex drive, or that its aim is also power?

The empirical interpretation of Nietzsche's doctrine can be maintained in the face of this kind of objection only if the will to power is defined so that at least some *possible* motives are not instances of it, and the contrast between power and other possible, though not actual, motives is preserved. Such a definition of will to power seems available in the understanding of power as the ability to do or get what one wants, the ability to enforce one's will. A sense of this ability to enforce his will is what the rapist is thought to want insofar as his behavior is explained in terms of power. This definition not only *allows* the possibility of a will that is not a will to power, but actually *demands* it, since the will a person wants to be able to enforce must be distinguished from the will to be able to enforce it, that is, from the will to power. It therefore seems useful to think of the will to power as a second-order desire for the ability to satisfy one's other, or first-order, desires.[8] But it

---

[6] Kaufmann, *Nietzsche*, 204.

[7] Kaufmann, in Edwards (ed.), *Encyclopedia of Philosophy*, 511.

[8] As drawn by Harry G. Frankfurt ("Freedom of the Will and the Concept of a Person," *Journal of Philosophy*, 68 (14 Jan. 1971)), the distinction between a first-order and a second-order desire is that the object of the latter is another desire whereas the object of a first-order desire is something other than a desire (of the same person). The distinction must be drawn somewhat differently if the will to power is to qualify as a second-order desire (or drive) because its object is not another desire (i.e., its aim is not to have, keep, or satisfy other desires) but the *ability* to satisfy other desires, whether or not one has these desires. I would therefore draw the distinction in terms of whether we can explain what the object of the desire is in an illuminating way without referring to other actual or possible desires, as we can when the object is food, drink, sex, or knowledge, but not when it is power or freedom.

would be possible to want the ability to satisfy any first-order desire one might come to have even though one has never had a first-order desire. The existence of a second-order desire for power therefore does not entail the existence of any first-order desires, and is compatible with the empirical hypothesis that human beings have no first-order desires, that "whatever is wanted is wanted for the sake of power,"[9] i.e., for the ability it gives to get what one wants. If there is nothing contradictory in this hypothesis, however, it surely is not deserving of serious consideration. Human life would have to be viewed as the attempt to gain the ability to satisfy first-order desires when we have none to satisfy. That such a picture fits parts of human life I have no doubt, but it is incomprehensible that beings who never had any other desire would have a desire to be able to satisfy their desires. It seems obvious that the desire for power, as I have defined it, must develop on a foundation of other desires, even though it may come to have more importance than any of them, and may certainly operate in contexts in which no first-order desire is operating.

I conclude that Nietzsche's psychological doctrine can be construed as an empirical hypothesis, but only at the cost of depriving it of all plausibility and suggesting that Nietzsche was less astute about psychological matters than one would have thought. The only alternative consistent with Nietzsche's view of knowledge is that the doctrine is not intended to provide knowledge. I therefore suggest that we interpret the psychological doctrine under consideration as a specialization of the doctrine of the world as will to power, and interpret the latter as myth, or, in the words of *The Birth of Tragedy*, as "a concentrated image of the cosmos" which helps us to interpret our lives and struggles.[10] In Nietzsche's earliest work, myth is closely associated with the truth which cannot be approached by science, but once Nietzsche abandons the belief in metaphysical truth, myth always stands in opposition to knowledge and truth. In the notebooks of the 1870's, he asks whether philosophy is an art or a science, and answers that "both in its purpose and its results it is an art," an "invention beyond the limits of experience . . . the continuation of the mythical drive. Thus it is essentially pictorial." In constructing its picture of reality, "philosophy uses the same means as science—conceptual representation."[11] But "considered scientific-ally, a philosophical system is an illusion, an untruth," the value of which

---

[9] Kaufmann, in Edwards (ed.), *Encyclopedia of Philosophy*, 511.

[10] BT 23. Translations are from Walter Kaufmann's editions of Nietzsche's works, unless otherwise indicated.

[11] Translated by Daniel Breazeale, *Philosophy and Truth: Selections from Nietzsche's Notebooks of the Early 1870's* (Atlantic Heights, NJ, 1979), 19.

"does not lie in the sphere of knowledge, but in that of life."[12] When I suggest that Nietzsche's doctrine is a self-conscious myth, I am following his own usage, and mean that the will to power gives us a picture or image of reality which is not intended to provide knowledge, but *is* supposed to play a role in the interpretation of experience and the furtherance of life.

Consider, for example, the following description of nutrition from the collection of notes called *The Will to Power*: "the protoplasm extends its pseudopodia in search of something that resists it—not from hunger but from will to power. Thereupon it attempts to overcome, appropriate, assimilate what it encounters: what one calls 'nourishment' is merely a derivative phenomenon, an application of an original will to become stronger."[13] Although this passage seems unlikely to change anyone's beliefs about protoplasm or nourishment, it might well give one a new image of the protoplasm—perhaps as a little Napoleon setting out with its pseudopodia to conquer the world. It therefore seems accurate to say that its effect is "essentially pictorial."[14] The effect is apparently achieved by focusing on aspects of the nutritional process related to strength—overcoming of obstacles and growth in strength—and by ignoring the protoplasm's need for food in order to survive. If this is correct, then Nietzsche's procedure fits the account of artistic idealization he gives in *Twilight of the Idols*: "idealizing

---

[12] Ibid. 17.

[13] WP 702.

[14] This is not to deny that the passage appears to offer an explanation of nutrition in terms of will to power, and therefore seems designed to serve cognitive interests, precisely the interests not served by myth, according to the passage cited in nn. 11 and 12. It is difficult to take seriously the explanation in terms of will to power, however, since no reason is given in its favor, or against the alternative explanation in terms of hunger. As a proposed explanation of an organism's behavior in the seeking and ingesting of food, "hunger" presumably refers to an internal mechanism which induces the behavior under conditions related to nutritional requirements, the organism's need for food. Given Nietzsche's claim that even "our knowledge of man today goes just as far as we understand him mechanistically" (A 14), he should find the existence of such mechanisms likely, and reject as superfluous teleology (BGE 13) the introduction of a will in order to explain what can probably be explained mechanistically. Of course, if Nietzsche is using "will to power" so that "'will' now serves only to denote a resultant" (A 14), then no teleological explanation is being offered. But then no other explanation of the behavior in question is being offered either, and the point of the passage is only that power (growth in strength and the overcoming of what is encountered) is the result of nutrition. But surely survival or preservation (the alternative to will to power in BGE 13) is also a result of nutrition, and probably a more important one for the purpose of explaining the existence of the behavior to be explained, since the power that results from the behavior will presumably contribute to the explanation only insofar as it also contributes to the probability that organisms that engage in the behavior will survive long enough to pass on the genes for the mechanism that induces the behavior. It therefore appears that the passage fails to give any plausibility to the claim that for cognitive purposes (i.e., for the purpose of understanding nutrition), power or will to power is more important than hunger or survival. Despite this failure, however, the passage rarely fails to make readers smile, and not in condescension. My explanation for this is that its main effect is to suggest not a new way of explaining the protoplasm's nutritional activity, but a new way of picturing or imagining it, in terms of our experience of power rather than our experience of hunger or deprivation.

does not consist . . . in subtracting or discounting the petty or inconsequential. What is decisive is rather a tremendous drive to bring out the main features so that the others disappear in the process." Thus need or hunger disappears in the picture Nietzsche paints of nutrition. But what determines the "main features"? The answer provided by the continuation of the passage makes even more obvious the connection to Nietzsche's doctrine of will to power: "In this state one enriches everything out of one's own fullness: whatever one sees, whatever one wills, is seen swelled, taut, strong, overloaded with strength. A man in this state transforms things until they mirror his power—until they are reflections of his perfection. This having to transform into perfection is—art."[15] Thus the "main features" of the object are not given, but are determined by the state or qualities of the artist. But if this is how Nietzsche determined that the world is will to power, then his ontological doctrine offers not knowledge of the world from a general human perspective, but an idealized picture of that world—a myth.

I want to argue now that the early sections of *Beyond Good and Evil*, which contain the first statements of Nietzsche's ontological doctrine in his own voice (as opposed to Zarathustra's), give us reason to believe that the doctrine is intended as a myth or idealization. Consider his characterization of Stoicism. He claims that while pretending to read the canon of his law in nature, the Stoic has actually imposed his morality, his ideal on nature. "You demand that she should be nature 'according to the Stoa' and you would like all existence to exist only after your own image—as an immense eternal glorification of Stoicism." He then adds that "what formerly happened with the Stoics happens today, too, as soon as any philosophy begins to believe in itself. It always creates the world in its own image."[16] But if Nietzsche's philosophy believes in itself, then it must also create the world in its own image, that is, in the image of its author's ideal. The plausibility of viewing Nietzsche's philosophy of the will to power as such a creation becomes clear, I believe, if we compare his doctrine with Schopenhauer's. Both philosophers portray the world as will, and in doing so, rule out a goal or end state of the world process that could be its justification or source of value. I believe the major difference between their portraits of such a world process is that Schopenhauer sees it in terms of need or lack—his world is a hungry will devouring itself[17]—whereas Nietzsche's is painted in tones of strength and abundance—his world is a superabundant will whose energy overflows.[18] I believe that each is a very selective picture—an idealization—of a world

---

[15] TI IX. 8–9.
[16] BGE 9.
[17] See, especially, ch. 28 of *The World as Will and Representation*, vol. ii.
[18] See, especially, WP 1067.

devoid of ultimate purpose or justification, and that it is plausible to trace the difference between them to a difference in ideals. Schopenhauer idealizes the ascetic, one who turns against life and willing, and his world is plausibly construed as the world of his ideal, i.e., the world as it appears to one who finds no value in the process of living. Nietzsche's ideal is opposite, the life-affirming person who does find value in the process, who possesses what Zarathustra calls the "gift-giving virtue," and should therefore qualify as "able to enrich everything out of one's own fullness."[19] Such a person would see the world under the aspect of abundance rather than lack, as the over-flowing of energy without ultimate goal, as play—in short, as will to power. If this is correct, Nietzsche's ontological doctrine reads his own ideal into the world—or shows us the world as it is from the perspective of his ideal.

But that would not make Nietzsche subject to his own criticism of philo-sophers. His objection is not that they read their ideals into the world, but only that they do not admit to doing so, pretending to arrive at their doctrines through a "pure, divinely unconcerned dialectic."[20]

They are all advocates who resent that name, and for the most part even wily spokes-men for their prejudices which they baptize "truths"—and very far from having the courage of conscience that admits this, precisely this, to itself; very far from having the good taste of the courage which lets this be known, whether to warn an enemy or a friend, or, from exuberance to mock itself.

If it is plausible to regard the will to power as Nietzsche's own ideal read into the world, we should be able to find evidence of his attempt to make known its character as myth and the projection of value.

I believe we find such evidence in two important passages of *Beyond Good and Evil*. The first contains the principal argument for Nietzsche's onto-logical doctrine found in the works he published. The central section of this passage reads as follows:

The question is in the end whether we really recognize the will as *efficient*, whether we believe in the causality of the will: if we do—and at bottom our faith in this is nothing less than our faith in causality itself—then we have to make the experiment of positing the causality of the will hypothetically as the only one. "Will" of course can affect only "will" . . . In short one has to risk the hypothesis whether will does not affect will whenever "effects" are recognized.[21]

It should be noted that Nietzsche does not assert the major premise of this argument, the causality of the will. It is put in hypothetical form—if we do believe in the causality of the will. Accordingly, the argument's conclusion is put in the subjunctive: "The world viewed from inside, the world defined and determined according to its 'intelligible character'—it would be 'will to

---

[19] See n. 14.　　　[20] BGE 5.　　　[21] BGE 36.

power' and nothing else." That is, the ontological doctrine of the will to power should be our conclusion *if* we accept the premises, that the will is causal, that only the will is causal, that will affects only will. But does Nietzsche accept these premises? He does not say here that he does, and he explicitly rejects them elsewhere. In *The Gay Science*, he calls "the faith in the will as the cause of effects" a "faith in magically effective forces," adding that "when Schopenhauer assumed that all that has being is only a willing he enthroned a primeval mythology."[22] And a similar position is presented in *Twilight of the Idols*.[23] In fact, Nietzsche's critique of the causality of the will is well-known. Why has it not been concluded, then, that he does not accept the argument he gives for the doctrine of the will to power?[24] The only good reason against drawing this conclusion is that Nietzsche does identify the ontological doctrine as "my proposition" in the passage, and the only natural interpretation seems to be that he is providing an argument for a conclusion he accepts.[25] But there *is* an alternative reading, one that makes the passage consistent with Nietzsche's unequivocal rejection of the causality of the will: that he is providing the same kind of argument for his doctrine that other philosophers have provided for theirs, but is letting us in on his belief that his doctrine receives no legitimate support from such arguments. His motives would be honesty, and exuberance—perhaps to mock not only himself, but also his readers. His motivation may also have something to do with the distinction he mentions in a nearby passage "between the exoteric and the esoteric, formerly known to philosophers . . . whenever one believed in an order of rank and *not* in equality and equal rights."[26]

I want now to consider the passage containing Nietzsche's apparent admission that his doctrine of the will to power is "only interpretation." It begins with the claim that "nature's conformity to law" exists only owing to "interpretation and 'bad philology'." "It is no matter of fact, no 'text,' but rather only a naively humanitarian emendation and perversion of meaning, with which you make abundant concessions to the democratic instincts of

---

[22] GS 127.

[23] TI VI. 3.

[24] In *Nietzsche as Philosopher* (New York: Macmillan, 1965), 231, Arthur Danto suggests a way of resolving the apparent contradiction between Nietzsche's argument for the world as will to power and his rejection of the causality of the will: that we take the latter to reject only the claim that will can affect matter, on the grounds that will can only affect will. But this does not solve the problem since the proposition that will can only affect will is clearly part of the mythology Nietzsche claims Schopenhauer enthroned in GS 127.

[25] This is the argument Müller-Lauter gives against Schlechta's claim that hypothetical and subjunctive forms Nietzsche uses in the passage indicate that he is not asserting the doctrine of the will to power here. See Wolfgang Müller-Lauter, "Nietzsches Lehre vom Willen zur Macht," in *Nietzsche-Studien*, 3 (1974), 8–9.

[26] BGE 30.

the modern soul: 'Everywhere equality before the law; nature is no different in that respect, no better off than we are'."[27] Nietzsche is not rejecting the contents of what we call the "laws of physics." Instead, the science of physics seems to provide the "text" in question. His point is that we conceive the relations between phenomena calculated by physics as "laws" only because we read into them democratic prejudices. With "opposite intentions and modes of interpretation," he goes on to say, we could instead conceive these relations as "the tyrannically inconsiderate and relentless enforcement of claims of power." In other words, by reading into nature values opposite to democratic ones, we could interpret nature as will to power. This is the context for Nietzsche's remark: "Supposing this too is interpretation—and you will be eager enough to make this objection?—Well, so much the better." One might take Nietzsche to be claiming here only that his doctrine of the will to power is, like science, a simplification of the data available from the human perspective rather than a mirroring either of this data or of things in themselves. His admission that his doctrine is "only interpretation" would then be consistent with the claim that, in accord with traditional criteria such as simplicity and accounting for the data, it is the best interpretation of nature from the human perspective, that it is true. In the context, however, it seems clear that Nietzsche is placing his doctrine on a par not with physics, but with the belief in "nature's conformity to Law," which results from "bad philology" and democratic prejudice. His "so much the better" is a response to an imagined critic who points out that he has not demonstrated a difference between the democratic interpretation of nature and his own—except, of course, that they represent different values. If this is correct, then Nietzsche is admitting that in accord with traditional criteria, his doctrine of the will to power is not a good interpretation of nature, that it reads his values into nature. Of course, if we used different criteria for grading interpretations—e.g., "ideas by which one could live better, that is to say, more vigorously and cheerfully than by 'modern ideas'"[28]—one might grade the will to power more highly, and Nietzsche clearly would. But it would have been dishonest to call this doctrine "true," thereby suggesting that it meets traditional criteria for good interpretations—at least without giving all the clues I am suggesting Nietzsche gave that it is "true" only according to new criteria, and that it meets our old criteria for art and myth.

But if Nietzsche's ontological doctrine is the *result* of reading his values into the world, his claim that the world is will to power can have no legitimate role in arguments for his values or against other values. Nor can the doctrine that all human behavior aims at power, if that is merely a

---

[27] BGE 22.   [28] BGE 10.

specification of the ontological doctrine. Yet it is clear that Nietzsche uses the will to power in such arguments and gives no sign of regarding them as illegitimate. I believe we can account for such arguments in terms of a second doctrine of the will to power, which Nietzsche mentions when, immediately following his admissions that the ontological doctrine is "only interpretation," he claims to be alone in understanding psychology as the "doctrine of the development of the will to power."[29] Nietzsche's psychology is also "interpretation," of course, but he would claim that it meets traditional criteria for good interpretations, or is true.[30] In accord with Nietzsche's view of truth, this means that his second doctrine of the will to power is an empirical one, and, in accord with my previous argument, *that* means that will to power must be regarded as one desire among others, and not as the essence of all desire. But that is how Nietzsche often treats the will to power in psychological contexts, as in the *Genealogy*, when he calls it "the strongest, most life-affirming drive."[31] I believe that this phrase also indicates the basis for the role of power in Nietzsche's revaluation. Will to power is the most life-affirming drive in the sense that the satisfaction of this drive, a sense of power, of the ability to enforce one's will, is necessary for the affirmation of life, whereas a sense of powerlessness induces depression and a tendency to passive nihilism. This is, I believe, the main thesis of Nietzsche's psychological doctrine of the will to power,[32] and it bears a remarkable similarity to a hypothesis psychologists are now studying under the title of the "learned helplessness model of depression."[33] If this thesis is

[29] BGE 23.

[30] This is a major reason why I do not believe that the fact that the ontological doctrine of the will to power might be true according to a new criterion for truth (e.g., increase in the feeling of power) should lead us to suppose that Nietzsche is adopting this criterion and is therefore calling his doctrines "true" only in a new sense. Nietzsche's psychological claims presuppose the old sense of truth, as does the claim that the doctrine of the will to power increases the sense of power. If, as Müller-Lauter claims, the doctrine of the will to power (and any other doctrine) is true "if it only serves power" (Wolfgang Müller-Lauter, *Nietzsche. Seine Philosophie der Gegensätze und die Gegensätze seiner Philosophie* (Berlin: Walter de Gruyter, 1971) 111), we would have to know if it is true in the old sense that the doctrine serves power in order to determine the truth of the doctrine in the new sense.

[31] GM III. 18. Another example is Nietzsche's comment on the Greeks (TI X. 3): "I saw their strongest instinct, the will to power." The obvious implication is that they had other instincts. And when he claims that "philosophy is this tyrannical drive itself, the most spiritual will to power" (BGE 9), Nietzsche is contrasting philosophers with scholars, among whom "you may really find something like a drive for knowledge, some small, independent clockwork that, once well wound, works on vigorously without any *essential* participation from all the other drives of the scholar" (BGE 6). In this context, the drive for knowledge is contrasted with, not taken to exemplify, the will to power.

[32] I believe that GM is an extended argument for this claim, and that it also figures prominently in Zarathustra's analysis of the ascetic ideal in "On Redemption," Z II. 20.

[33] See, for instance, *Journal of Abnormal Psychology*, 87 (Feb. 1978), which is devoted entirely to the learned helplessness model of depression.

true, then one whose ideal is the affirmation of life is committed to placing a positive value on power and the will to power (assuming that the latter is necessary for the possession of a sense of power). It is then more obvious how the ontological doctrine of the will to power, which I have called a myth, reflects Nietzsche's ideal, for this myth glorifies the psychological will to power by picturing the universe as this desire "writ large." It therefore glorifies precisely what is necessary for the affirmation of life.

I hope these brief remarks on Nietzsche's psychological doctrine have suggested an approach to understanding how the will to power functions in his arguments concerning values. I believe that these arguments can be properly understood and evaluated only when Nietzsche's empirical doctrine of the will to power is freed from the encumbrance of an apparently metaphysical doctrine whose true value lies in its role as art and encouragement to the affirmation of life, but which only leads to confusion when taken as an attempt to satisfy the cognitive aims of inquiry.[34]

[34] I would like to acknowledge support for the writing of this paper provided by a summer grant from the Columbia University Council for the Humanities, and to thank Arthur Danto, Lorraine Daston, Richard Kuhns, Bernd Magnus, Sidney Morgenbesser and James Walsh for helpful comments on earlier drafts.

6

NIETZSCHE'S POWER ONTOLOGY

JOHN RICHARDSON

1 THE METAPHYSICS OF WILL TO POWER

In his early manuscript on the first philosophers, Nietzsche speaks of "a metaphysical doctrine, which has its origin in a mystical intuition and which we meet in all philosophies, together with ever-renewed attempts to express it better—this proposition that 'all is one'" (PTAG 3). And we meet it, apparently, in Nietzsche himself. He says many times, in many ways and many contexts, that things are will to power (*Wille zur Macht*).[1] Let's begin with this familiar core to his philosophy, with what I've called his 'ontology' or 'metaphysics': this is his account of what the world most basically 'is'. Here, as later with the hackneyed contrast between master and slave, we must work to reach beneath the level of grasp with which long familiarity has left us content, just as Nietzsche himself must struggle to free his terms from the complex layers of meaning deposited by earlier philosophers. What is this 'power' that things essentially will? Does it encompass all and only what that word (or the German *Macht*) refers to in everyday use? How do

From John Richardson, *Nietzsche's System* (New York: Oxford University Press, 1996), 18–52. The paper includes references to other chapters and sections of *Nietzsche's System*.

[1] Kaufmann, in his helpful history of Nietzsche's approach to his mature use of the concept (W. Kaufmann, *Nietzsche: Philosopher, Psychologist, Antichrist*, 4th edn. (Princeton: Princeton University Press, 1974), 200), cites Z I. 15 as its first published appearance; Z II. 12, a fuller account, says (through Zarathustra saying what life itself says): "Only where there is life is there also will: not will to life but—thus I teach you—will to power!" Here and often elsewhere the point is restricted to 'life' (e.g., BGE 13, GS 349, WP 254); Nietzsche's main interest is of course in *human* will to power. But he extends this 'power biology' or 'power psychology' into a 'power ontology' in many other places; see especially BGE 22, 36, WP 634, 692, 1067. (Note also here WP 582: "'Being'—we have no other representation of it than as '*living*'—How can something dead 'be'?") There are many less-explicit statements of such a 'global' view, such as references to "the absolute homogeneity of all happening" (WP 272) and "a *power-willing* occurring in all happening" (GM II. 12). My project below will be to show how often this power-ontological vision of the world is implicit in what Nietzsche says. It's worth noting that he makes his point (whether about life or being) using each of the traditional terms usually translated 'essence': *Wesen* (in BGE 259, GM II. 12, WP 693) and *Essenz* (BGE 186). See again the Introduction on the complaints that Nietzsche's notebooks give (a) the only evidence for a power ontology, and (b) evidence that can be discounted.

things 'will' this power? Is it in just the way we usually think we ourselves will? Or, as could rather be expected, does Nietzsche intend more precise and idiosyncratic senses for such basic terms in his thought? We must hope indeed for senses precise enough to support the use we shall see he will make of these terms, in laying out his own values, as well as in many others of his most distinctive views. And if we do discover an articulable and complexly structured point here, we'll have found an important general way he resembles his metaphysical predecessors.

When we first hear Nietzsche's claim, and as long as we allow our understanding of it to be guided by his terms' surface suggestions, we suppose he is speaking of a human willing that aims at power over other persons as its ultimate end. That is, we take him to be saying that all people 'first' or 'basically' want power—which we interpret as political, economic, or personal rule over others—and that with a view to this they then adopt their distinctive behaviors, as different routes toward a single end. His point seems to be that as a matter of psychological fact a condition of authority over other persons is our 'highest end', all our other goals being chosen and pursued only as means to this. His position seems analogous to psychological hedonism, only substituting this power for pleasure.

This reading finds support not merely in the sound of his phrase. Some of Nietzsche's own remarks encourage it, including his attacks on psychological hedonism and the way he proposes his own view as a substitute for it.[2] And many of Nietzsche's more casual readers have taken his will to power thesis in this way. In turn, this reading has important implications for the way one interprets his values, as grounded in that thesis. Because he seems to fix level of power as the true standard for value, this reading suggests that the Nietzschean ideal will be (only) such individuals as Napoleon. It encourages the comparison of Nietzsche with Plato's Callicles and Thrasymachus, and perhaps even the suspicion that he wasn't very much misappropriated by the Fascists.[3] In short, this intuitive grasp of his notion of power underlies several important grounds for aversion to Nietzsche.

This simple reading seems less common today than it once was.[4] But

---

[2] See GM III. 7, TI I. 12, WP 688, 702. Nietzsche accepts psychological hedonism in *Human, All Too Human* (I. 18, 103–4).

[3] So says Stern; see n. 27 in this chapter.

[4] Kaufmann (*Nietzsche: Philosopher, Psychologist, Antichrist*, 180) shows that Nietzsche did indeed use 'power' to mean 'worldly power' in early writings, such as UM, but that this use was abandoned. M. Haar, "Nietzsche and Metaphysical Language," trans. C. Welch and L. Welch, in D. B. Allison (ed.), *The New Nietzsche: Contemporary Styles of Interpretation* (first pub. New York: Dell, 1977; Cambridge, Mass.: MIT Press, 1985): "We must accordingly discard from the very start, as a great misconception, any interpretation of the Will to Power that is *solely* psychological or anthropological."

although many now see its inadequacy, I think it hasn't yet been replaced with a full enough positive conception of the will to power. We must work to grasp this notion, and other Nietzschean ideas, on the basis of his most grounding, philosophical remarks. We must build strictly from these our understanding of comments couched in more ordinary terms and not immediately read the latter in an ordinary way. Or at least we should once fully attempt to develop his meaning this way. As we follow this route, we discover (I hope) a more subtle and even plausible view.

More particularly, we discover that the natural analogy to psychological hedonism (taking this with a familiar notion of pleasure, as explained in § 1.1 below) is misleading in several respects. To begin with, 'will to power' is most basically applied not to people but to 'drives' or 'forces', simpler units which Nietzsche sometimes even calls 'points' and 'power quanta'.[5] These are the simplest 'units' of will to power, or the simplest beings that are such will; we grasp Nietzsche better if we begin with these and only later make the complex extension to persons. This breadth of his use of the phrase already suggests that we mustn't hear 'will' with the narrowly human referent it most connotes.[6] Indeed, we'll see he believes that our usual notion of the will is not just too narrow—it's not even true of us; he'll claim that precisely because we are constituted out of drives or forces, we don't 'will' anything in the way we ordinarily suppose. But these points are best postponed until we attempt the extension to persons.

Turning for now to the other term, 'power', we see that this, too, must be read with a special sense. That broad application of 'will to power' again shows that power can't be so distinctively human an end as the political and economic domination that first come to mind. Indeed, power will be a quite different type of end from such domination, or from pleasure. It can't be a highest end in the familiar way pleasure is for psychological hedonism, because neither drives nor their ends of power are as completely homogeneous as this would require them to be. We must come to see several connected points here. Drives pursue distinctive activities not chosen as

---

[5] Already in BT 1 the Apollonian and Dionysian are 'drives'; TL makes metaphor formation 'the fundamental human drive'. BGE 36 suggests that the only 'reality' we have access to is that of our drives and that "thinking is merely a relating of these drives to one another". The terms 'drive' and 'force' are very common in the notes collected into *The Will to Power*; see especially those gathered under the heading "The Will to Power in Nature". At other times, Nietzsche uses more abstract terms for his basic beings: 'mastering centers' (WP 715), 'dynamic quanta' (WP 635). Other suggestive terms used in this role are 'instinct' (TI IX. 39) and 'affect'. See especially G. Parkes, *Composing the Soul: Reaches of Nietzsche's Psychology* (Chicago: University of Chicago Press, 1994) on Nietzsche's early and persistent attention to 'drives'.

[6] Of course, one must also say that Nietzsche chooses 'will' because he thinks our human will a potentially most-revealing case. Thus WP 490: "the only *force* there is, is of the same (*gleicher*) kind as the will". But we need to learn to understand this human will better.

means to the end of power. And 'power' doesn't name some determinate state describable without reference to those activities—in the way that 'pleasure' is usually presumed to name a specific experience, the same for all. This means that power is 'individuated', necessarily different in content in different wills; this grounds the familiar individualism in Nietzsche's values. Together, these points make the structure of his theory quite different from psychological hedonism, so that indeed its effect is less to supply a new end than to introduce a new telic structure, in place of that most natural to us.

1.1. Power as Growth in Activity

I take it to be evident from the expression itself that 'will to power' is a potency for something, a directedness toward some end. So I take it that Nietzsche, despite his repeated attacks on (what he calls) 'teleology', really has such a theory himself: the beings or units in his world are crucially end-directed, and to understand them properly is to grasp how they're directed or aimed.[7] Above all, it's to grasp how they're aimed at power, an end somehow essential to them.

This telic reading is reinforced by Nietzsche's very common treatment of the drive (*Trieb*) or force (*Kraft*) as the typical unit of this will.[8] He adopts these terms from biology and physics and means to build on the sense they have there: "The victorious [physicists'] concept 'force' . . . still needs to be completed: an inner world must be ascribed to it, which I designate as 'will to power'" (WP 619). Of course, his choice of these as his units also shows that this essential directedness is not (inherently) conscious; he proposes to describe a nonconscious intentionality. Whether this in itself is plausible must eventually be faced.

---

[7] Nietzsche attacks 'teleology' often and emphatically. This rejection is expressed as early as PTAG 19; see also, for example, WP 552 and 666. But such criticisms seem directed against several specific forms of such a view: against what we might call a 'conscious teleology' (the claim that 'mind' directs the course of things) or a 'steady-state teleology' (the claim that the end aimed at is some stable condition) or a 'holistic teleology' (the claim that the world in general is a unit with its own end). The telic schema I attribute to Nietzsche differs from all of these. So WP 675: "that one takes doing *something*, the '*goal*' (*Ziel*), the 'aim' (*Absicht*), the 'end' (*Zweck*), back into the doing, after having artificially removed this from it and thus emptied the doing". R. Schacht (*Nietzsche* (London: Routledge & Kegan Paul, 1983), 242) argues that "'will to power' is not a teleological principle, identifying some state of affairs describable in terms of 'power' as a goal to which all forms of behavior of living creatures are instrumentally related." In denying that power is a concrete condition (such as pleasure might be), I take myself to be in agreement with this.

[8] KSA 10. 1 [3] (1882): "Everything is force." (For *Nachlass* notes not included in *The Will to Power*, I give the location in the *Kritische Studienausgabe* (KSA): volume number, followed by notebook number, followed by the note number in brackets. I also include the date of the note in parentheses, which allows it to be located in the *Kritische Gesamtausgabe* (KGW) as well.)

More immediately useful is something else this choice of cases reveals: just as scientists speak of a variety of drives or forces, so Nietzsche takes the units of will to power to be deeply diverse in their types, differentiated by their distinctive efforts or tendencies.[9] The sex drive, for example, is one pattern of activity aiming at its own network of ends—perhaps these are centered on seduction or coupling or orgasm—whereas the drive to eat aims at a very different network. But now how are these *internal* ends, which distinguish the drives from one another, related to that essential end of power, which they all have in common? Nietzsche thinks of this relation in a very different way than we expect.

Power is not, first and most clearly, merely one among the ends that individuate drives. By contrast, political power is such an internal end, the object of one type of drive in particular, one pattern of effortful pursuit. Nietzschean power must somehow motivate all these pursuits, so it has to be an end of a different sort. What could it be such that a striving for it could 'enter (essentially) into' all of these other drives, instead of being an alternative to them?[10]

I think we have a natural response: we expect that power is a 'highest end', for whose sake all those internal ends are adopted as means. Achieving the latter is either a partial achieving of power itself or a step toward it. Thus the drive's overall strategy is to maximally accomplish its internal end, because it's in that very act—in each state or event of its satisfaction—that it achieves power. This natural way of thinking of the relation between lower and higher ends is displayed in the most familiar version of psychological hedonism: all our other goals are valuable to us, because in achieving or having them, we experience pleasure. So our particular projects are really just routes converging toward a single condition—different doors chosen by each but through which each hopes to arrive at the same place.

Nietzsche says some things that suggest this view. It seems clearest in his occasional attempts to explain the content of the diverse drives as having evolved, in the distant past, out of an undifferentiated will to power; that bare and primitive form of this will originally selected the main types of internal ends as means to its satisfaction. For example, WP 651 speaks of hunger as a specialized form of will to power, which once arose from it through a division of labor; presumably, the drive coalesced toward the end

---

[9] In D 119's extended account of our drives, some examples are "our drives of tenderness or humorousness or adventurousness" and "of annoyance or combativeness (*Kampflust*) or reflection or benevolence".

[10] So I take it that Nietzsche expresses himself less aptly when he speaks of will to power as a *particular* drive; in GM III. 18 it is "the strongest, most life-affirming drive"; in TI X. 3 it is the Greeks' "strongest instinct".

of eating, because that act is a specific way of taking power over something else, of 'incorporating' it. Nietzsche also thinks that drives continue even now to draw strength from such ways their ends involve 'taking power'. So the sex drive impels us, as an effort to appropriate or possess another person.[11]

Despite such supports, I think that natural conception of power, as an end achieved by means of these lesser ends, misses the major novelties in Nietzsche's notion in two ways: (1) by overstating how far drives' distinctive ends are chosen as means to power, it misses how the goal of power crucially presupposes such internal ends as given; (2) by locating achievement of power in the maximal achievement of those internal ends, it misses how power involves growth of the drive itself, and hence improvement in those ends.

1. Those cosmogonic stories about the origins of the main drive types stand at odds with Nietzsche's much more common deployment of his notion of will to power: to explain not why (e.g.) the sex drive wants sex but how. He has in view drives or forces already having distinctive characters of their own, *about* which they will power. So it's not that the sex drive (at some metaphysical core) possesses a sense of power in the abstract, for whose sake it chooses sexuality as a means to an end; rather, it's already polarized into valuing only specifically sexual power. Nor is the person such an undifferentiated will, choosing by turns those internal ends; instead, we're composites of many preformed drives, rising by turns to expression and prominence.

Power can't play that role of highest end, because it's essentially enhancement in an activity already given. A drive finds itself already pursuing given ends through a given project; that it wills power explains not why it has this project but how it now tries to improve what it has: it tries to raise to a higher level the activity it finds distinctive of it. To be a will to power, it must already want something other than power. Thus each drive is a specific way of pursuing power in a project whose overall lines were drawn beforehand. So Nietzsche thinks of drives as belonging to largely stable types, not able to redirect themselves onto radically different routes toward power; the sex drive doesn't transform itself into an urge to eat. Instead, he strikingly thinks, drives change through 'sublimation' or 'spiritualization' of their distinctive pursuits—by their amendment not their replacement. Thus the sex drive becomes 'the love of all mankind' but remains inherently sexual.[12]

---

[11] This 'cosmogony' looks similar to Anaximander's, which places the origin of things in the *apeiron*. BGE 36 and WP 658 suggest such a view. KSA 10. 7 [77] (1883): "*And one and the same amount of force-feeling can discharge itself in a thousand ways:* this is 'freedom of the will'—the feeling, that in relation to the necessary explosion a hundred actions serve equally well." See GS 14 on the sex drive. And note how GS 360 also points this way.

[12] BGE 189 and TI V. 1, 3. In *Nietzsche's System* §III.4.1, I describe this movement of spiritualization, showing just how it's always a development of a preestablished project.

This means that power has a different logic from ends like pleasure or political power. It can't be a highest end in the same way they are, because it's not a concrete or 'first-order' end like them. It's not definitionally separable from some (or other) 'drive', some preexisting pattern of effort, with its own internal ends; power isn't an independent state, that could be described without supposing some such effort as given. Pleasure, by contrast, is usually considered a concrete state, one that many activities can produce—as sex or eating does—but itself an experience distinct from these causes or means.[13] Nietzschean power can't have this independence, because it is (roughly) improvement in whatever a drive's activity already is; it's growth or development *in* that pattern of effort and therefore amounts to a different 'concrete condition' for each different drive.[14] Thus power, as something willed by every drive, 'lacks content', requiring a contingent filling out from some given case. So by this new telic logic, the routes to power don't converge on a common target. Willing their own development leads drives in diverging directions. This point is the main metaphysical root for Nietzsche's individualism in values: "The deepest laws of preservation and growth command . . . that everyone invent for himself *his* virtue, *his* categorical imperative" (A 11).[15]

To put the point another way, the will to power doesn't and can't steer the drive 'from the ground up'. In commending it to us, Nietzsche doesn't propose it should be an ultimate directing aim, remaking us entirely by its own standards; he takes himself to diverge here from philosophers' usual way of promoting their 'ideals of reason'. However, we still need to specify how this will to power bears on those given projects, that is, what its second-order guidance of them is.

2. Again our usual telic conception suggests an answer: these drives 'will power' inasmuch as they will the 'full achievement' of their internal ends, at the expense, if need be, of all competing drives' efforts. So the will to power is just the will to maximally satisfy the given internal end; it's the drive's aim to achieve that end as quickly and lastingly as it can. This might seem to

---

[13] Some, however, have viewed pleasure more in the way I go on to treat power, making pleasure a 'function on' some activity—always the pleasuring *of* that particular activity. There are suggestions of such a view in Aristotle (*Nicomachean Ethics*, 10. 5), for example.

[14] This is perhaps a point intended by Heidegger (*Nietzsche*, trans. D. Krell, J. Stambaugh, and F. Capuzzi (first pub. Pfullingen: Günther Neske, 1961; San Francisco: Harper & Row, 1979–87), i. 42) and Deleuze (*Nietzsche and Philosophy*, trans. H. Tomlinson (New York: Columbia University Press, 1983), 85). M. Clark's account (*Nietzsche on Truth and Philosophy* (Cambridge: Cambridge University Press, 1990)) is partly similar: "It amounts to thinking of the will to power as a second-order desire for the ability to satisfy one's other, or first-order, desires (cf. Frankfurt)" (211; see then 227 ff.). (This is a later version of Ch.4 in this volume.) I diverge from this in point 2 following. See also Schacht, *Nietzsche*, 222–3.

[15] I develop this point in §III.1.3.

render the point trivial. Yet, it's precisely this usual conception that Nietzsche means his notion of power to deny. Here his target is another part of our telic logic: we expect that a drive (or directedness) aims at ends by (above all or exclusively) aiming to *accomplish* them—a state or event in which it achieves satisfaction and rests content, its effort either ceasing or shifting into merely maintaining that state. We presume a type of end we might call a 'steady state', its ideal achievement the unbroken continuance of a condition or repeating of an event. But Nietzsche's promotion of power as a second-order end is a denial that drives do or should pursue their internal ends in this manner.

To begin with, power is a movement of growth or enhancement rather than a persisting state (or repeated event). As will to power, a drive's essential end is movement beyond what it now is or does. And this doesn't just mean that it wants to be more than it is; a drive's essential aim isn't even to arrive at some better state. If we think of the ends distinguishing drives as states of achievement, then will to power's object will be the passage toward and into these states and not their occupation. This shifts importance from those ends to their pursuit, to the effortful and not-yet-satisfied approach toward them. So BGE 175: "In the end one loves one's desire and not what is desired."[16]

On the one hand, we can think of the passage toward those internal ends as itself such a movement of growth, and so a case of power itself. At least among the most familiar drives, this passage takes an episodic and cyclical form: the end is achieved at intervals, with the drive waning in vitality just after that, its interest in the end only gradually reviving and then growing in intensity (and power to absorb us) as it reapproaches that end. Within each periodic cycle, the drive retraces the same ascending arc, asserting itself ever

[16] WP 125: "For so sounds the teaching preached by life itself to all that lives: the morality of development. To have and to will to have more—growth, in a word—that is life itself." In fact there are two general strategies, or two choices of terminology, available to us for accommodating this point about power within a telic schema. We can present it as a point either about the ('internal') character of the ends that drives pursue, or about the ('external') way they pursue those ends. Thus on the one hand, we might reinterpret the distinguishing ends of our drives, redescribing them such that their 'maximal achievement' would be this perpetual heightening in a characteristic activity. This would treat 'power' as a component in drives' ends; the will to power thesis would then demand that we change our common conception of the ends they pursue (though not of the way they pursue them). So the goal of the sexual drive would be not intercourse or orgasm but the continual heightening of its sexual activity (broadly understood). Or on the other hand, we might say that drives 'will power' by ultimately aiming not at maximal achievement of their goals but at the enhancement of their activity of pursuing them. Here that aim would be a 'higher end' not in the sense that all others are adopted for its sake, but in the sense that it regulates the manner of their pursuit. This is the terminology I adopt for stating Nietzsche's point. It involves a drastic revision in the type of telic structure most natural to us, but this aptly reflects the drastic nature of Nietzsche's claim.

more vehemently and effectively; so it finds a first form of power, in each episodic rush toward its end.

But Nietzsche considers such 'intra-episodic' growth to be much less important than another sort: growth from cycle to cycle, in the pattern or structure of the project itself. A drive that merely repeats itself—the habit— misses a fuller or truer power: instead of trying just to eat or seduce again and again, it should try to raise its whole pattern of effort 'to a higher level'. Nietzsche calls this truer, 'inter-episodic' growth 'sublimation' (*Sublimierung*).[17] We humans are preeminent as wills to power, because of our capacity for it—for the pace at which our drives are able to break habitual patterns and evolve new forms.

This makes the connection between power and a drive's internal end even less direct than we expected: not only does power not lie in this end's achievement, it doesn't even mainly lie in progress toward it but in improving this progress. Moreover, the criteria for this 'improvement' aren't set by the end—it's not just an improvement in the route's efficiency for achieving the end. Rather, as we'll gradually see, it lies in an enrichment or elaboration of the drive's activity pattern. For this reason, it will often involve deferring or postponing achievement of the end—hence a loss in efficiency. Indeed, it can involve a revision of the internal end itself: its 'location' may shift, as in the shift in focus from swallowing to tasting. Although will to power indeed supposes a defining allegiance to its given end, it also tries to work changes in it. (We'll see that this is its form of allegiance to it—to help it 'become what it is'.)

So a drive wills power by trying to develop its activity pattern. And its effort is properly here, because (for Nietzsche) this activity is just what the drive is. We mustn't imagine it as an agent or source of that activity, as what causes or engages in it. Nietzsche insists that the 'doer behind the doing' is a fiction; really there are no such abiding things, only processes.[18] (I examine this claim in the account of the 'theory of becoming' in chapter 2.) So the world consists of behavior patterns, each striving to enhance itself, to extend

---

[17] Kaufmann (*Nietzsche*, 218 ff.) helpfully surveys Nietzsche's uses of 'sublimation' but misses the important point at hand. He takes sublimation to occur when the undifferentiated will to power, displaced from its (for example) sexual expression, directs itself toward quite different, nonsexual ends; all that remains constant is will to power itself. But would it then be apt to call this 'sublimation of the sex drive'? In the examples Nietzsche gives, we find a greater continuity: ends are modified, not replaced. So WP 312: "[One] has refined cruelty to tragic pity, so that it may be *disavowed* as [cruelty]. In the same way sexual love [has been refined] to *amour-passion*; the slavish disposition as Christian obedience". I take 'spiritualization' to be an especially effective form or means of sublimation, for Nietzsche.

[18] GM I. 13: "there is no 'being' behind doing, effecting, becoming; 'the doer' is merely a fiction added to the doing—the doing is everything." WP 631, like many other passages, associates this fiction with the structure of our language. See also WP 550, 551, and 625.

its own scope of activity. Thus the sex drive is strictly the activity of trying to seduce (etc.), which, as will to power, is also trying to improve itself in a certain way. Processes themselves are willful, in this twofold directedness. They aim at ends, but not so as to dissolve or release their own tensed effort by a full and lasting accomplishment of these ends; nor do they aim just to continue themselves. Rather, each such activity pattern wills its own 'self-overcoming' (*Selbstüberwindung*): it wills to rise toward a new and higher level of effort—perhaps indeed a level at which its internal ends are also overcome and replaced by descendants—one that will then have to be overcome in turn.[19]

In a way, this makes drives 'selfish': each essentially aims at its own development or growth. But it also begins to open up a sense in which this is not so. Nietzsche calls this crucial growth a 'self-overcoming' to make a further point, to be increasingly important as we proceed. With that favorite expression, he means that a drive presses or tends beyond the borders to its 'identity'; its will is to pass beyond itself, by evolving into some stronger 'descendent' drive or pursuit. And if the activity doesn't itself persist in this future it wills, its intent is less clearly selfish.[20] We'll see that the ambiguous boundaries around a drive, and the ambiguous nature of its interest in what lies beyond them, have a crucial bearing on Nietzsche's own values.

An important qualm must be addressed, however: doesn't it seem that some drives just do want to satisfy their (internal) ends, just do aim at those episodic end states themselves, again and again in the same way? This may suggest that we've gone too far in attempting to specify a content for the end of power; perhaps we've already strayed over the boundary between the power ontology and the perspectivism it generates. Perhaps there's just no one way that drives will power; perhaps here it already 'depends on the individual' (drive), on its own interpretation of power. So perhaps I've forced on Nietzsche a greater specificity in the notion of power than he would accept.

This danger—of assigning too determinate a content to the 'power' he says all things will—must make us cautious as we proceed. I address the issue more fully in §1.2. There, as here, the problem will be complicated by a further factor.

---

[19] So Z II. 12 (entitled "On Self-Overcoming"): "And life itself told this secret to me: 'See,' it said, 'I am that, *which must always overcome itself* ' ". See also GM III. 27.

[20] WP 488: "No 'substance', rather something that in itself strives after strengthening, and that wants to 'preserve' itself only indirectly (it wants to *surpass* itself—)." KSA 10. 1 [73] (1882): "The *highest love of self* (*Ich*), when it expresses itself as heroism, is close to pleasure in self-destruction (*Untergange*), so to cruelty, self-assault."

Nietzsche is well aware that some wills—some persons—do aim at steady-state ends and want only to rest in them; this is indeed a common charge in his critical diagnoses. But he can still see them as 'essentially' wills to power, because he understands this essence in a way we might not expect: a thing can 'fall away from' its essence or achieve it in only a 'deficient' way. His ontology treats a sort of being that comes in degrees.[21] Thus drives that will ends of that stable sort are failing to will appropriately to their own essence; to understand them is to see them as misdirected this way. This and other ways that wills aim askew—with a distorted sense of power—Nietzsche stigmatizes as 'reactive'; only the active achieve essence, by willing power itself.

We'll have to face some obvious questions this odd use of 'essence' raises—for example about the testability of claims concerning it. The power ontology may seem too slippery if it shifts between the claim that everything does will power and the claim that everything should.

In any case, Nietzsche says many times that will to power aims at growth and not mere stability; for example: "the only reality is the *willing to become stronger of every center of force*—not self-maintenance, but appropriation, willing to become master, to become more, to become stronger" (WP 689).[22] We'll see that several others of his key ideas are rooted in this point. So it seems safe to take at least this much to belong to power itself, secure above the level of perspectival differences: power is growth, in level of activity or in 'strength'.[23]

---

[21] GM II. 12 equates the role of will to power as the essence of life with "the principal priority . . . that the spontaneous, attacking, encroaching, newly-interpreting, newly-directing, and form-giving forces have", whereas adaptation "follows only after this", as "an activity of the second rank, a mere reactivity". See A 6 (quoted in §3) and WP 485. But note, too, the skepticism in WP 583: "That a correlation stands between *degrees of value* and *degrees of reality* . . . is a metaphysical postulate proceeding from the assumption that we *know* the rank-order of values".

[22] BGE 73 reads: "Whoever reaches his ideal even thereby comes out above it." See also WP 688 and 696–7 . More generally, WP 708: "becoming has *no goal-state*, does not flow into 'being'." In D 108: "Development does not will happiness, but development and nothing further." And WP 649: "the *feeling-more*, the feeling of *becoming stronger*, wholly apart from any uses in the [Darwinian] struggle, seems to me the genuine *progress*". This is most of the force of his attack on Darwin, whose theory is in other ways importantly similar. Nietzsche takes Darwin to say that living things pursue their own preservation; this seems to him too static (and even cowardly) a goal. See BGE 13, for example.

[23] So understood, strength and power are distinct: whereas the former occurs as a state—as a level or amount (of strength)—the latter occurs as a passage between two such states. Thus Nietzsche just spoke of 'willing to become stronger' (*Starker-werden-wollen*), and in WP 488 he speaks of striving toward 'strengthening' (*Verstärkung*). To keep his point clear, we might try not to follow him in his frequent looser uses of 'power' for a level of strength. WP 663: "All that happens out of aims is reducible to the *aim of increasing power*." See also WP 633.

1.2. Power as Over Others

We must try to develop this account of will to power a step further, by giving this 'growth' or 'enhancement' a more definite sense. In willing power, a drive strives to become stronger, to grow in its distinctive activity. But this is still quite vague. What is the criterion or measure for growth? What makes it the case that a drive's strength is expanding or increasing rather than diminishing? Again, we must try to press beyond our everyday use of these terms, which measures growth in such an unsorted variety of ways. Unless we can do so, 'power' won't have a sense definite enough to support an ontology with much content. Moreover, it won't support the valuative claims Nietzsche roots in it, because (as we'll see) these amount to a 'power consequentialism' and so depend on 'power' being given a definite enough measure to serve as a useful deliberative and evaluative criterion.

It's clear from the bulk of Nietzsche's remarks that growth has to do with a drive's relation to other drives: one drive typically enhances its strength relative to, or even at the expense of, others. Usually, at least, power is power 'over others'. This may indeed be taken as a second main aspect of power, alongside its aspect as growth—a more disturbing aspect, for obvious reasons. Here we must try to avoid the temptation that presses on sympathetic interpreters to diminish this aspect and thus 'tame' Nietzsche's power notion. And with this aspect, too, we have to press for more specificity. Not only are there many everyday ways to hear this 'power-over-others' but Nietzsche's own remarks seem to describe it diversely. Because some of these sorts of power over others are themselves more socially acceptable or attractive than others—so that Nietzsche is more palatable if these are what he thinks essential to us—this choice is a focal point for disagreement among his interpreters. We may catalog the possibilities in this way:

1. A drive's strength level is measured by the perspectives on it of other drives (and its perspective on them), in particular perhaps by whether they 'look up to it' or not, by whether they think it better or worse than themselves. So drives grow by improving the views others take of them (and maybe by deflating their own views of others). As concrete cases of this motivational structure, the strivings for fame and for love come to mind. WP 677 seems to speak so: "What is *common* [to the artistic, scientific, religious, and moral views of the world]: the mastering drives will to be viewed also as *the highest courts of value in general*, indeed as *productive* and *ruling authorities (Gewalten)*." This first option brings the perspectivism close to the heart of the power ontology; it leaves

little independent content for that ontology. By contrast, the next several readings make power something more 'objective'.

2. A drive's strength level is measured not in relation to other drives but by some independent or absolute standard; yet it is (usually) only possible to improve this level at the expense of others—as it were, by expanding into territory that was theirs. So the diminishing of others is a means—even a practically necessary means—to self-improvement but does not constitute it. Begging some questions, we might take pursuit of wealth as a project typically adopted from this sort of motivation: one wants wealth (taking this to include the fine things money buys) for its own sake and asks oneself whether the best means to it requires depriving others. Does pursuing power require struggling against others only as such a best or usual means? Nietzsche might think of power this way in WP 728: "It belongs to the concept of the living that it must grow—that it must extend its power and consequently (*folglich*) take into itself foreign forces."[24]

3. A drive's strength level is measured relative to others, by their comparative performances in independent pursuits: Does it do these things better or worse than they? These shared pursuits are thus crucially *contests*; their point is to set up tasks, with scales for success, against which the competing wills test themselves and are compared. So, unlike in (2), power is relational: a drive's essential aim is to improve with respect to others. Simplifying again, we might take an athlete's will to be first to belong to this type; his winning requires that others lose, as something more than a mere means. Nietzsche's great stress on 'rank order' (*Rangordnung*) might express this sense, as also his admiration for the Greek *agon*.[25]

4. A drive's strength level is measured by whether it is able to rule or master others in some way (which then needs to be specified). So its current level consists roughly in its ruling *abc* and its being ruled by *xyz*, whereas growth or decline lies in ruling more or fewer (or ruling these more or less fully). Like (1) and (3), this would make power essentially 'over others'—indeed, in a blunter way than by merely impressing or surpassing them. It suggests a cruder sort of *agon*, in which the competing wills work more directly on one another, instead

---

[24] A. C. Danto (*Nietzsche as Philosopher* (New York: Macmillan, 1965), 220) suggests this account: "Each force occupies a territory (an area of space) and is pretty much what it is as the result of counter-forces meeting and opposing its territorial expansion."

[25] See the draft "Homer's Contest" (1872) in *The Viking Portable Nietzsche*, ed. W. Kaufmann (New York: Viking, 1968). Kaufmann seems to have this reading in mind—see n. 28 in this chapter.

of at independent tasks: the goal is to subdue, and not just outperform, the other—as in wrestling, for example, by contrast with racing. BGE 259 speaks for this sense: "life itself is *essentially* appropriation, injury, subjugation of what is foreign and weaker".[26]

Of these possible readings, each supportable by things Nietzsche says, the last has the harshest effect. It places aggression nearest the core of the beings he claims we are. Struggle against others is here not just a means to an end (2); a means would have alternatives (at least logically possible ones), but (4) makes struggle essential to us, and indeed to all beings. Moreover, it suggests a more desperate sort of struggle than those for fame (1) or victory (3): it requires forces to grow, it seems, not just by impressing or outperforming others but by oppressing and subjugating them. If power is also Nietzsche's ultimate value, (4) would mean he commends an ideal that is much harder to accept.[27] This surely is some of the attraction the other three readings have had for many interpreters.[28]

Of course, the goals named by these different senses are, in a way, not mutually exclusive; they can 'nest within' each other, one being pursued as a means to another. Thus fame could be wanted as a means to wealth or vice versa—and so perhaps with each other pair. This might explain why Nietzsche sometimes singles out each. Or, we might suspect that he hasn't really pried them apart. But even if he hasn't explicitly separated these alternatives, deliberately chosen from among them, and persistently held that choice in mind, one sort of power over others might still be most operative in his thinking and best connected with his other main thoughts. So does any of the four have such priority, so that the others are best grasped as means or approximations to it (and not vice versa)?

Here again, we may feel a reluctance noted earlier in our hunt for will to power. Perhaps we should respond to this question by rejecting its demand for a choice. Perhaps Nietzsche thinks that which way power over others is pursued just depends on which drive is doing the pursuing. He'd then be

---

[26] Schacht (*Nietzsche*, 220) presents will to power as "the basic tendency of *all* forces ... to extend their influence and dominate others". See, too, J. P. Stern, *A Study of Nietzsche* (Cambridge: Cambridge University Press), 117 ff.

[27] Stern, *A Study of Nietzsche*, 120: "If there is anything in the recent 'Nietzschean' era that comes close to an embodiment of 'the will to power', it is Hitler's life and political career".

[28] Kaufmann (*Nietzsche*, 201), in the course of his influential effort to render Nietzsche more palatable, emphasizes how will to power is a *self*-overcoming and suggests that it's only in this that competition with others occurs: "In Nietzsche's vision the world becomes a Greek gymnasium where all nations vie with each other, each trying to overcome itself and thus to excel all others." O. Schutte (*Beyond Nihilism: Nietzsche without Masks* (Chicago: University of Chicago Press, 1984), 76 ff.) helpfully surveys some of the interpretations of will to power and argues that to be viable the notion must be purged of the suggestion of domination, which she takes Nietzsche to have included in it.

allowing that diversity of types quite deliberately. The measure for growth would vary with the drive, so that it wouldn't be possible to specify any further content for the 'power' aimed at by all drives alike. We might all the more expect this given that we've already seen drives vary in the activities they will to enhance: maybe these different activities pursue quite different types of 'power over others', so that ingestion and seduction (e.g.) have nothing concrete in common. Have we come as far as Nietzsche is willing to go, in specifying an essential content for drives as will to power?[29]

This reason not to choose from those options might also be counted as a choice of (1)—or rather of a near cousin to it. It lets the content to power over others be determined perspectivally: not (principally) by the direct comparisons drives make of one another, as in (1), but by their differing conceptions of what 'power over others' involves. It makes all the ways perspectives interpret this (ranging, e.g., from killing to persuading the other) count equally well as cases of it: all further specific content to power would arise only *for* a viewpoint and would vary by viewpoint. (One version might so allow perspectives to determine power 'conceptually' but then make it a factual matter whether the concept thus specified is satisfied (e.g., whether the other *is* killed); a more thorough perspectivism would put even this satisfaction 'in the eye of' the perspectives.)

I return to this perspectival problem in §2, but won't come to final grips with it until chapter 4. Here my answer can be little more than to reaffirm my guiding approach. But we can at least notice certain raw evidence that Nietzsche rejects a 'subjectivist' notion of power. First, it seems he can't think a will's power is 'in the eye of' the will itself, because he holds that wills can be wrong as to whether they grow. Growing doesn't just lie in my thinking I do; that can often be 'wishful thinking', a mistake about my real status.[30] Second, it seems he can't think a will's power depends on other wills' views of it, because he so clearly denies that power is a matter of reputation or recognition. Instead, will to power aims at a real condition, specified independently of any perspectives *about* power.[31] This point is reinforced by what we've seen of Nietzsche's odd use of 'essence': most drives might

---

[29] GS 13: "it is a matter of taste whether one prefers the slow or the sudden, the assured or the dangerous and audacious increase of power—one seeks this or that spice depending on one's temperament." See also BGE 194.

[30] WP 917 speaks of "*artificial* strengthening: whether it is by stimulating chemicals or by stimulating errors", and gives several examples of the latter. WP 48 says that "the experience of *intoxication*" has sometimes misled, because it "*increases* the feeling of power in the highest degree . . . therefore, naively judged, *power*". HH I. 545 says that vanity seeks to seem to itself to rule.

[31] A more 'realist' account of power is implied by passages saying that the interaction between two drives proceeds according to their preexisting degrees of strength. WP 633: "It is a matter of a struggle between two elements of unequal power: a new arrangement of forces is reached according to the measure of power of each of them." See also WP 634 and 855.

misconceive their essential end. This insistence on the prevalence of error about power makes Nietzsche far more a realist than an idealist about it: a drive's enhancing its activity or strength is a real change in its activity or in its real relation to other drives.

Moreover, I think the great weight of evidence suggests that, among the ways power might thus be 'real', Nietzsche thinks mainly of (4). He most often and most emphatically identifies growth as increased 'mastery' (*Herrschaft*) of others; the second is not just a means to the first. So he says, "every single one of [the basic drives of human beings] would like only too well to represent just *itself* as . . . the legitimate *master* (*Herr*) of all the rest of the drives. For every drive seeks to be master (*ist herrschsuchtig*)" (BGE 6).[32] We might have found the other lines more attractive, as giving Nietzsche's valuation of power an easier chance to be acceptable to us. But most of what he says really requires this more aggressive vision, which calls up immediate sentiments against itself, and must say so much more in its own defense to seem plausible or attractive.

Once again, Nietzsche's willingness to give this further specificity to the will to power as the essence of all things is still compatible with his recognizing that some drives don't, in fact, will such mastery but rather the ends specified in (1), (2), or (3) above. He thinks these drives have 'fallen away from' their own essence as will to power, an essence that in some sense is still theirs. They have, as it were, misidentified the end they essentially will and have misguidedly shunted their efforts onto a diverging track.

Incorporating this result into our previous findings, we say that drives are 'will to power' in that they essentially pursue the continual enhancement of their distinctive activities, enhancement that consists in increasing their mastery of others. So the level of a drive's activity, its strength, is measured by 'how much' it rules over others.

Yet this can't satisfy us either. We must press to see whether this notion of mastery can itself be given a more concrete content. And we must make it concrete, if we can, in a way that reveals some principle of unity in this dual

---

[32] Z II. 12 presents will to power as "the will to be master". BGE 259: " 'Exploitation' . . . belongs to the *essence* of the living, as an organic basic function". GM I. 13 says that strength expresses itself as "a willing to subjugate, a willing to throw down, a willing to become master, a thirst for enemies and resistances and triumphs". GM II. 11: "life functions *essentially*, that is in its basic functions, by injuring, assaulting, exploiting, destroying, and simply cannot be thought of without this character." WP 490: "the only *force* that there is, is of the same (*gleicher*) kind as that of the will: a commanding (*Commandiren*) of other subjects, which thereupon alter." WP 369: "There is no egoism that remains by itself and does not encroach . . . 'One furthers one's I always at the expense of others'; 'life lives always at the expense of other life'.—Whoever does not grasp this, has still not taken the first step toward honesty with himself." UM II. 1 already speaks of a force that "masters and directs". D 113: "The striving for distinction is the striving for subjugation of the nearest". See also BGE 19, 230, and WP 481.

account of will to power. Why might increased domination also be an enhancement of that distinctive activity?

My suggestion is this: drive A rules B insofar as it has turned B toward A's own end, so that B now participates in A's distinctive activity. Mastery is bringing another will into a subordinate role within one's own effort, thereby 'incorporating' the other as a sort of organ or tool. As his important term 'incorporation' (*Einverleibung*) suggests, Nietzsche very often thinks of this process by analogy with physical ingestion.[33] But he thinks it not physically and spatially, but 'psychically'—or, better: in applying it to wills, he thinks it telically. Drive B's activity comes to be telically contained within A's, and this is the crux to the mastery involved in Nietzschean power.[34]

This makes B's serving A a matter of the former's willful intentions, but not in such a way that ruling is 'in the eye of the ruled'. It lies not in B's viewing itself as serving A but in its setting its sights by reference to A's own project, which it may or may not notice that it does. Thus there's a fact to the matter how far A rules B, a fact that both A and B can (and usually do) mistake, a fact not 'transparent' to either, even though it lies in the intentions (the willing) of B. Indeed, Nietzsche mainly describes the many subtler ways of being ruled and subsumed than by intending to serve: all the other ways of fixing one's course out of fascination with another will, even (or especially) in rejecting reaction *against* it. In all such cases, one has been induced to adjust one's own aim into some reference to the other; the other thus 'shows up' in one's activity, whether in positive or negative image.

This account finds important support in its ability to explain why growth should necessarily involve or include rule over other drives. We can understand better the dimension in which the will 'grows stronger' by developing this mastery as incorporation. As we've seen, each will is a pattern of behaviour—a habit, as it were—but one that aims not merely to continue itself but to grow. Each such activity is bounded or disrupted by the different efforts of other wills, by other such self-asserting patterns. Such resistance shows the behavior limits of its scope—how much is 'not-it'—but also how to overcome these limits: by compelling or inducing the collaboration of those independent forces, by bringing their practices into service of its own.

---

[33] BGE 230 speaks of a will's "appropriating force, its 'digestive force', to speak in a picture— and really 'the spirit' is most similar (*gleicht*) to a stomach." GM II. I entertains the similar 'inpsychation' (*Einverseelung*). GS 14: "Our pleasure in ourselves so wills to preserve itself, that it again and again changes something new *into ourselves*; that is what possession means." See also HH I. 224, WP 656 and 769.

[34] WP 552: "domination (*Übermacht*) over a lesser power is achieved, and the latter works as function of the greater".

On the one hand, so aligning different wills to its own effort gives the behavior a new facility or smoothness: served by those wills, it can more easily and more often secure its internal ends. But as we saw in §1.1, Nietzschean power lies chiefly not in those intra-episodic satisfactions but in developing the first-order project itself: it lies in enriching the effort at those ends, and so also those ends themselves. For this, incorporation must work a different way than by marshaling 'efficient servants'—transparent functionaries to its ends. To help to the more important sort of power or growth, the forces subjected must keep their own characters and not be utterly made over into mere facilitating tools; they must add their own telic patterns and viewpoints to its fabric. It's only by coming to rule persistingly different forces that a will expands not just quantitatively, reproducing its own pattern in others, but qualitatively: to include those still-foreign behaviors as phases or elements in its own thus fuller effort. I think this is a key point in Nietzsche's distinctive notion of power: it knits together power's main aspects as growth and domination, by specifying the best ('truest') way of growing by ruling. We'll notice many important recurrences of this point as we proceed.

This completes our first sketch of Nietzsche's 'will to power'. The metaphysical notion now has content enough for us to go on to see how it's situated in his thought as a whole, and especially how it supports his perspectivism. Of course, many puzzles about this notion remain; let's finish this section by marking one major issue we must return to.

We still need to settle whether (and how) mastery can be reciprocal. If A grows stronger by ruling B in the way described, does it follow that B cannot at the same time be growing by ruling A? Is B necessarily diverted from its own ends, and thus diminished, when A employs it in this way? Or can drives simultaneously rule and encompass one another? And does A rule B any the less if B also rules A? These issues are important for Nietzsche's values: if the will's egoism, which these values seem to aid and abet, necessarily pursues the destruction or diminishing of others, those values will be the more troubling to us. In the following, and especially in chapter 3, I develop and weigh the main Nietzschean resources for reaching a less brutal lesson than this: (what I call) the *agon* and spirit points.

2 WILLS TO POWER AS PERSPECTIVES

We've anticipated that Nietzsche takes his power ontology to generate a 'perspectivism' and indeed that the relation between these will be the key topic of this book. We're now able to take a first look at the way this perspectivism arises. This Nietzschean 'doctrine' has been often discussed.[35] But it's important to keep clear, as is not often done, how the 'perspectives' this teaching speaks of are those of drives or wills to power. His power ontology, with its distinctive conceptions of wills and of power, stands prior to this perspectivism as (something like) its objective precondition, and thereby gives to that teaching some unexpected features. Or at least, this is the relation between ontology and perspectivism that Nietzsche usually suggests and whose tenability we're exploring now (by that two-level strategy announced in the Introduction).

We've seen that, as will to power, a drive aims at ongoing growth in its distinctive activity. Nietzsche's perspectivism begins in the thought that this *telic* directedness goes together with an *intentional* one, with being a perspective, 'at' or 'on' some intentional content. Just by virtue of striving in the way it does, every drive involves, is partly, a particular 'view': a view of its purpose or end and of the surroundings as helps or hindrances to that end. In thinking this an aspect of all will to power, Nietzsche attributes views to far more than just human beings; he calls perspective "the basic condition of all life" (BGE, Preface). And (still more generally) he speaks of "this necessary perspectivism according to which every center of force—and not only the human being—construes the whole rest of the world from itself, i.e., measures, touches, forms, according to its own force" (WP 636).[36]

We must try to see how a drive's telic thrust can, in itself, already involve a distinctive perspective on the world. In willing its own power or growth, the drive acts and reacts toward other things in accordance with this aim, by whether they help or hinder its pursuit. It senses, and differentially responds to, different things in its environment. And (Nietzsche thinks) these patterns of effort and avoidance in themselves constitute an 'interpretation', of things in their relevance to its aim. They constitute this viewpoint whether or not they occur consciously. Each drive's end-directed activity already 'polarizes' the world toward it, giving everything a significance relative to it. So, for example, the sex drive views the world as inspiring or requiring a sexual response; the world appears with erotic potential as its meaning or sense.

I think there are three important points here that distinguish Nietzsche's

---

[35] The account by Danto (*Nietzsche*, 68 ff.) has been especially influential. See also Schacht, *Nietzsche*, 61 ff., A. Nehamas, *Nietzsche: Life as Literature* (Cambridge, Mass.: Harvard University Press, 1985), 49 ff., and B. Leiter, "Perspectivism in Nietzsche's *Genealogy of Morals*," in R. Schacht (ed.), *Nietzsche, Genealogy, Morality: Essays on Nietzsche's "On the Genealogy of Morals"* (Berkeley: University of California Press, 1994) for other statements of this teaching.

[36] WP 643: "The will to power *interprets*: . . . it demarcates, determines degrees, differences of power. Mere differences of power could not perceive themselves as such: there must be something there that wills to grow and interprets the value of every other thing that wills to grow." WP 567: "every center of force adopts a *perspective* toward the whole *remainder*, i.e. its wholly determinate *valuation*, mode of action, and mode of resistance." See also WP 481.

perspectivism from those more 'cognitivist' cousins we usually find in idealism. First, he denies that these perspectives are necessarily conscious, though he applies to them many of the intentional or cognitive terms we might normally restrict to consciousness. "Our most sacred convictions, the unchangeable in regard to our supreme values, are *judgments of our muscles*" (WP 314). Second, this perspective is not something prior to the activity or even something separate that accompanies it, as we take plans or pictures (even unconscious ones) to be. Nietzsche stresses its unity with the doing itself, with the way it tends in a certain direction, adjusts to other behaviors, and in general differentially acts on, and is affected by, the world. This perspective is an aspect or ingredient in this. Third, this essential or original perspective—this way things appear to the striving will—is deeply valuative. Values are not a secondary estimation of beings previously met and picked out in some neutral or objective way. To this primary viewpoint, things already appear as potentials or opportunities: they appear *as* they bear on the will's own end.

In order to follow Nietzsche into this vision of the perspectives essential to beings, we have to struggle on each of these points, because the opposite positions are so natural and tempting to us: we find it hard not to think of viewpoints as (1) conscious, (2) separate from 'doing', and (3) chiefly theoretical (in aiming at 'facts'). To reinforce Nietzsche's revisions, let's go back through these points in different order.

Beginning with (3), we mustn't think that these perspectives aim basically at truth, at mirroring the world. It's not that the drive takes a theorizing view aimed to see how the world truly is, as a step before applying that neutral information back to its practical ends. It views the world from its interests: "It is our needs *that interpret the world*; our drives and their For and Against" (WP 481). And so Nietzsche stresses that even perception isn't neutral: "There is no doubt that all sense perceptions are wholly permeated with *value-judgments* (useful, harmful—consequently, agreeable or disagreeable)" (WP 505). How far it's possible to overcome this willful interest and to aim at truth itself is a major issue in chapter 4. But if a neutral view of things can somehow be achieved, it would have to remain dependent on this more basic perspectivity.

This way that perspectives are rooted in interest shows the deep place Nietzsche finds (in his power ontology) for 'value' (*Wert*). This lies in what each will 'sees' as conducing to its own development: the conditions that help or allow it to grow. "But willing = willing a goal. Goal includes an evaluation" (WP 260).[37] Value lies in the way the world is 'polarized' for each

---

[37] WP 715: "'Value' is essentially the viewpoint for the increase or decrease of these mastering centers".

will and not in any theories or beliefs about value. It lies in how things 'matter' to the will and so depends on that deep receptiveness of will that Nietzsche calls 'affect' (*Affekt*) or 'feeling' (*Gefühl*). A perspective on the world always involves an 'experiencing' of it, as it bears on the drive's pursuit of power.[38] This conjunction of willing, viewing, valuing, and feeling is already evident in HH I. 32: "A drive towards something or away from something, without a feeling that one is willing the beneficial or avoiding the harmful, a drive without some kind of knowing appraisal of the value of its goal, does not exist in human beings." The main polarity in feeling is that between pleasure and pain which Nietzsche (metaphysically) defines as the will's experience either of growth or of frustration and decline.[39]

But this talk of feeling and experience, of pleasure and pain, mustn't tempt us back to another mistake (1)—not only are perspectives not detached, they're also not (originally) conscious. We'll eventually see (§III.5.1 and §IV.3.1) how Nietzsche explains the rise of consciousness out of drives, as an unusual and secondary event. Drives or forces proceed mainly 'beneath the level of consciousness' even in persons—not to mention in the animals, plants, and nonliving things in which or as which Nietzsche also finds them. So when he says that a drive 'aims' at certain ends, 'views' the world in a consequent way, and 'experiences' certain values within it, none of this is supposed to entail that the drive is conscious. "For we could think, feel, will, and remember, and we could also 'act' in every sense of that word, and yet none of all this would have to 'enter our consciousness'" (GS 354).

If it's hard for us to think so, it's even harder to see all of these as (2) not self-sufficient events, separate in particular from the physical behavior they accompany. So even as we try to render them 'nonconscious', we tend just to displace these views and feelings into a 'sub- or unconscious' stream of cognition, still proceeding apart from bodily actions, still observing and guiding them from outside. But for Nietzsche these intentional events are just aspects of the will, as the directed activity of some body. The power ontology, as a monism, means to fuse the physical and the intentional, as aspects of a single being; neither is a thing in its own right, but each is a structural feature of will to power. Nietzsche's attacks on materialism and idealism are guided by this aim to find a middle ground between them.

---

[38] BGE 19 analyzes 'willing' to involve "a plurality of feelings, namely the feeling of the state *away* from which, the feeling of the state *towards* which"; it goes on to say that the will "is above all an *affect*, and specifically the affect of the command (*Commando*)". WP 688 says that "will to power is the primitive form of affect".

[39] WP 688: "pleasure is only a symptom of the feeling of power achieved, a consciousness of a difference". See also WP 693 and 699.

Thus his notion of perspectives is both richer and poorer than we first expect. They each involve a valuing and feeling we mightn't expect in them, but they're also stripped of the consciousness, and the independence from bodily acts, that we do expect viewpoints to have. Nietzsche takes away the latter, in part to allow perspectives to be posited as universally as the power ontology implies. But of course it still seems highly dubious to extend viewing/valuing/feeling beyond people to animals, plants, and even inorganic forces.[40]

This analysis of Nietzsche's notion of perspectives is not itself enough to specify that 'perspectivism' that we're so particularly interested in. The latter doctrine involves some inference from that notion, against 'realism' or 'objectivity'—as, for example, in the familiar note: "no, facts is precisely what there is not, only interpretations" (WP 481).[41] Not until chapter 4 will we fully face this problem of specifying—and disarming—Nietzsche's perspectivism. But our two-level strategy requires a provisional account of it, of how it could not conflict with (and undermine) the power ontology.

So the (tentative) point must be that Nietzsche's vision of a world of perspectives presumes that each of these has the essential structure of will to power, is a certain pattern of activity, aiming at its own growth; this much, this form, is 'objectively' true of them. But what the distinctive content of that activity might be is determined in the viewpoint of each will and can only be grasped 'subjectively', by itself (or by somehow taking its view). What it 'does' is not a merely physical process, open to the public scrutiny of other perspectives; it depends on what it, in its unique way, is *trying* to do. And this requires, perhaps, that we adjust or retune the way we've implicitly been thinking of the drive's activity. We mustn't think this to have a real character or content independent of the drive's intentions; it gets its sense in the directedness of the drive. Each will is self-defining. Thus the sex drive's pattern of activity is 'sexual' only for its own willful perspective; from outside this perspective, there's no particular way that it is, no particular thing that it does. Without taking a drive's distinctive perspective, all that can be said about it is that it's a will to power, albeit with all that (rather elaborate) formal structure we've described. Only this stands 'above' determination by particular viewpoints. So we explain, for the moment, the power ontology's insulation from the perspectivism.

---

[40] I can't answer this difficulty directly but will try to reduce the implausibility gradually, by developing the peculiar way Nietzsche's ontology means 'being' or 'reality'.

[41] WP 556: "There is no 'fact-in-itself' (*Thatbestand an sich*), *but a sense must always first be laid in, so that there can be a fact*". See also WP 567.

3 WILL TO POWER'S BASIC FORMS: ACTIVE VERSUS REACTIVE

Another key aspect of this power ontology needs to be clarified. I've remarked several times that not all drives pursue mastery in the way this metaphysics describes. Nietzsche supposes that some drives 'fall away from' their essence as will to power, failing to achieve one or another element in the full structure we've just surveyed. But this is puzzling: How is such failure compatible with the claim that all beings are will to power?

We must go on to see how will to power can occur in either of two basic forms, which I call 'active' (*aktiv*) and 'reactive' (*reaktiv*).[42] The contrast is indeed so basic to Nietzsche that he marks it with many other pairs of terms: the most important are 'health' (*Gesundheit*) and 'sickness' (*Krankheit*), 'ascent' (*Aufgang*) and 'decline' (*Niedergang*), 'overfullness' (*Überfülle*) and 'poverty' (*Verarmung*). And he claims special insight into this difference: "I have a subtler sense of smell for the signs of ascent and decline than any human being before me; I am the teacher *par excellence* for this" (EH I. 1). The distinction rests on the notion of will to power: the active drive wills power itself, whereas the reactive has somehow turned aside from its essential end. So the contrast marks the dimension of Nietzsche's metaphysical values, those embedded in the power ontology itself.

Two important issues arise here. First, we must weigh how this contrast helps with the problem just noted: If the reactive drive does not will power, why call it a will to power? Nietzsche seems to shift between saying that will to power is what everything is, and saying it's what everything should be; surely we must be suspicious here. Second, our leading problem also comes up: How could Nietzsche offer any such values, consistently with his perspectivism? If, as we saw in §2, values mark the bias or bent of particular willful perspectives, won't this hold, too, for these judgments about 'sickness' and 'decline'? How can they aspire to that metaphysical status? To weigh these problems, we must first make more vivid to ourselves the dimension of this active/reactive contrast.

---

[42] I've been influenced by Deleuze here; indeed, these terms 'active'/'reactive' are more his than Nietzsche's, who shifts freely among many different contrast pairs ('healthy'/'sick' etc.). But I think Deleuze is right that 'active'/'reactive' best states the gist of the others as well. (I'm less sure how similar to his my analysis of this contrast has grown to be.) The terms are most prominently used in GM II. 11, which distinguishes at length between the active and reactive affects; see also GM II. 12. GM I. 10 says of resentment: "its action is fundamentally reaction". Sometimes the contrast term for 'active' is 'passive'. WP 657: "What is 'passive'?—To be *hindered* in the forward-grasping movement: thus an act of resistance and reaction. What is 'active'?—grasping out for power." KSA 12. 7 [48] (1886–7): "What do *active* and *passive* mean? is it not becoming-*master* and becoming *subjugated*".

This contrast is closely connected with that between master and slave, but we shouldn't conflate them. Whereas the latter are types of persons, 'active' and 'reactive' apply to wills more generally, including to each of the multiple drives in persons. Nietzsche has stories to tell about how persons are formed out of these drives and then how those types are developed by psychological and social-historical processes; I discuss these accounts in §4 below and §I.5. It will emerge that the master *is* active and the slave reactive but that they're so in richly specific ways; before developing these, we need the more abstract distinction.

So what might Nietzsche mean by active and reactive? Perhaps we think first of the traditional contrast between having the causes of one's behavior within or without. Does a drive originate its own activities—is it 'free', as the 'cause of itself'—or is its behavior determined by external forces? This certainly approximates to Nietzsche's intent but can't be quite right, because it ignores his emphatic attacks on both causation and freedom as incompatible with the world's essence as will to power. Or, as he also puts it, that essence shows how our notions of causation and freedom need to be (not given up but) revised.[43] So we must stop thinking of causation as a merely external relation between purposeless things and reinterpret it as the struggle among purposive wills. And we must replace that notion of the *causa sui* with the type of freedom wills *can* have; this will be Nietzsche's rewriting of the Kantian autonomy.

On the one side, 'reacting' doesn't mean being caused to act by an external force, where this force is conceived as delivering an impetus that compels such action. Not only must we avoid thinking of this causation mechanically (e.g., with the familiar billiard balls), we mustn't frame it on the model of one will obeying a stronger other, under duress. Reacting is indeed a matter of 'obeying' but in a stronger sense, in which one will obeys another only by adopting, 'internalizing', the latter's views and values, and indeed by adopting them in preference to its own. It obeys not especially in what it does but in what it views as worth being done. A reactive will is one with a tendency— a habit or an instinct—to obey in this special sense.

So a drive obeys (in this sense) not when some constraining force temporarily displaces it from pursuing its own goals, while it keeps these goals for itself and regrets being so diverted from them. It obeys by being persuaded into willing and valuing foreign goals as superior to its (original) own, by being colonized by the other will and induced to adopt the latter's perspective in preference to its own. So reacting is more a consequence of temptation than constraint. Thus a weak drive need not be reactive; the power

---

[43] WP 658, 633. I treat this topic in §III.5.2.

ontology deploys these terms differently.[44] A weak drive may be forced to obey in the ordinary sense, but without doing so in our stronger one: unable to enact its distinctive behavior, it may still keep its allegiance to it, waiting for its opportunity. Yet we can also see how being forced to obey in the former sense can promote obedience in the latter: a drive that finds itself always compelled by some force stronger than itself is easily tempted toward and into that other's view-point, as able to constrain, perhaps by virtue of some strength intrinsic to the viewpoint itself.[45]

There's a second way we need to reinterpret obeying if we're to use it to explain reactivity. A drive 'obeys' foreign forces even in reacting against them; it obeys by taking over their values, whether positively *or negatively*. When a drive takes its task as the struggle against what some other is, it still sets its sights by reference to that other and is still diverted from its own development. It gives that other drive further presence in the world by installing it within itself as a guiding mark, if only as what it negates. It therefore obeys (in our sense) even when it obsessively denies. Thus, if one is sick, "[o]ne does not know how to get loose of anything, to become finished with anything, to repel anything—everything injures. Human being and thing obtrude too closely; experiences strike one too deeply; memory is a festering wound" (EH I. 6).

Now in fact, Nietzsche most often uses 'reactive' (and its relatives) for wills of just this sort: for those obsessively, resentfully struggling against others; his analysis of 'resentment' is a highly characteristic teaching. He distinguishes (we might say) two main species of reactivity: the herd animal and the person of resentment, the former obeying by following, the latter obeying by reacting against. Although Nietzsche pays much attention to the herd instinct, he takes far more interest in resentment: it's both harder to notice than simple conformity (being more devious), and also more important to understand (being indeed more distinctively human and the source of most of our values).[46] I pursue these subtypes further, when I look at Nietzsche's analysis of the 'slave' type of person, in §I.5.2.

[44] So, perhaps, Deleuze, *Nietzsche and Philosophy*, 53: "Forces are said to be dominant or dominated depending on their difference in quantity. Forces are said to be active or reactive depending on their quality."

[45] GS 347: "the less one knows how to command, the more urgently one desires someone who commands, who commands strictly—a god, prince, class, physician, father confessor, dogma, or party conscience." Nietzsche goes on to speak of this as a "*disease of the will*". BGE 199 suggests that a "herd instinct of obedience" is inherited. See WP 721 and 738.

[46] Perhaps Nietzsche's emphasis shifts, early to late, from the herd type to resentment. Will that straightforwardly obeys or copies is a major theme of *Daybreak*, for example at D 104. His later accounts of the herd instinct stress how this hates exceptions, so that he now finds resentment even in conformity; see the other notes on the herd type grouped as WP 274–87. Resentment is already noted in HH I. 60: "but to think revenge without possessing the force and courage to carry it out, means to carry about a chronic suffering, a poisoning of body and soul".

Turning now to the positive notion, the active is Nietzsche's rewriting of freedom: it's a will that is not so tempted away from its own distinguishing activities and values. This is why, contra Kant, "'autonomous' and 'ethical' (*sittlich*) exclude one another" (GM II. 2). 'Ethics' (*Sittlichkeit*) is both a custom (*Sitte*) one conforms to and a custom that expresses resentment; it fuses both species of reactivity, both types of diversion from self.[47] By contrast, the active will keeps allegiance to itself and to the values favoring its own activity. It has an eye, indeed, for what's distinctive to itself, and a confidence in the worth of what it finds there.[48] As such, it 'commands', though once again not in the usual sense. A drive may command (compel) in that usual way, even out of a resentful animosity toward the other; the strength to rule others so no more implies activeness than (we saw) weakness ensures a reactive obeying. Instead, the active will commands others 'internally', by interpreting them and their values from the viewpoint of its own, thus granting them only a subordinate role in a world still revolving about itself. Once again, Nietzsche's further refinements on this valuative notion will concern us as we proceed. We'll see how his own ideal (often named 'overman') is an elaborate specification of a form of activeness.

Now let's recall the first problem: If reactive drives don't will power itself, how can they still be wills to power? How can Nietzsche justify attributing this essence to them? Or does he just mean that this is what those drives 'should' will, and if so, how could he justify this? But he so often makes both the factual and valuative claims, as if they were a single point, that we really must try to see how to combine them. Notice how they're fused, for example, in A 6: "Life itself counts for me as the instinct for growth, for duration, for an accumulation of forces, for *power*: where the will to power is lacking there is decline."

As already suggested, I think Nietzsche so combines these points because he operates with a sense of 'essence' that is clear in the tradition, yet still surprising and odd to us. With his power ontology, he means an essence that is 'differentially realized', achieved to different degrees, in different cases.[49]

---

[47] Or perhaps Nietzsche chiefly finds the herd conformity in *Sittlichkeit* (with its link to *Sitten*), whereas the element of resentment bulks larger in *Moral*. (This is another reason not to translate them both as 'morality'.)

[48] UM II. 10: "The Greeks gradually learned *to organize the chaos* by following the Delphic teaching and reflecting upon themselves, that is, back upon their real (*achten*) needs, and letting their seeming-needs die out. Thus they again took possession of themselves". WP 918: "For what does one have to atone worst? For one's modesty; for having given no hearing to one's ownmost needs; for mistaking oneself; . . . for losing a fine ear for one's instincts".

[49] By better 'realizing' its will to power essence, a will achieves a higher degree of being or reality. In §II.1.2, I compare this with Plato's teaching. See also R. Nozick, *The Examined Life: Philosophical Meditations* (New York: Simon & Schuster, 1989), 128 ff., whose criteria for 'being more real' are partly like those I attribute to Nietzsche.

But we need to be cautious here: the active will doesn't 'realize' its will to power essence in the sense that it 'becomes conscious' of it. It's not that all drives 'deep down' will power, and only the active ones do so deliberately, in self-awareness. In fact, Nietzsche thinks that conscious wills tend to be *re*active, whereas simpler, nonhuman wills are more easily and usually active. So we need some other way to parse the distinction than with consciousness.

Nietzsche's claim of essence is in part the claim of a certain logical priority of the active, a teleological priority: the reactive will's way of aiming presupposes the active.[50] It does so not in the sense that there can only be reactive wills because others are active, but because the reactive is intrinsically a *failing* to be active. It belongs to its motivational structure that it gets meaning from others because it can supply none itself; it belongs to the way it wills that it adopts its course as second best. By contrast, the active will 'realizes' its essence not consciously, and not cognitively, but telically, in aiming at what it, as a will to power, wants first and foremost. (This shows how Nietzsche's claim of a will to power essence can depend on his psychology, on his diagnosis of the reactive type.)

On the other hand, the claim about essence is also, ineliminably, a claim of the valuative priority of the active; we can't suppose the logical point can fully generate and justify the preference that Nietzsche's power ontology expresses.[51] Indeed, since this preference gives priority to the 'highest forms', the essential is for him less what (logically) must come first but more what's achieved at the end of long effort and development. We find the essence of things when we find the highest and best they can become.

What of our second problem: How are these values embedded in the power ontology, compatible with the perspectival analysis of values, given just now in §2? Values were explained there as expressing the distinctive interests of behaviors bent on their own development. So how can Nietzsche's values of power and activeness not be idiosyncratically *his*—accounts of what *his* growth or progress would be?

For now, I'll merely reiterate how the two-level account (generally and tentatively) answers this: the perspectival thesis applies only to values lying at a level 'below' that of power itself. It applies to that idiosyncratic activity content, that power is (in each case) growth *in*; any such content has value only for those particular viewpoints that presuppose it. But the value of power lies in a 'form' of allegiance or commitment to that content which is essential to every will and doesn't vary by perspective. Thus power's

[50] Recall GM II. 12 on "the principal priority . . . that the spontaneous, attacking . . . forces have; 'adaptation' follows only after their working".

[51] Compare GM I. 5's account of the Greek masters' word for themselves: "*esthlos* means, in its root, the one who *is*, who has reality (*Realität*), who is real (*wirklich*), who is true".

essential value is not inconsistent with, but indeed a presupposition for, the perspectival values of particular wills.

4 PERSONS AND SOCIETIES AS SYNTHETIC WILLS

I've now sketched the deep structure of the power ontology to some detail and length. But there's still another way this choice of starting point might seem distorting: most of Nietzsche's thoughts are at a much less abstract level and seem to have little to do with any such metaphysical claims. So I must go on to show how this ontology infuses and structures his other main thoughts—and that we understand them crucially better by grasping them so.[52] In the rest of this chapter, then, I survey, much more quickly, the rest of the Nietzschean system, seeing how it builds on the abstract positions just sketched.

In order to pass from these abstract wills to power to Nietzsche's more usual topics, we must take a certain structural step: we must see how simple wills to power combine into more complex, *synthetic* wills; we must look, as it were, at Nietzsche's 'chemistry'. Although we've artificially focused so far on single drives or forces, his interest is mainly in persons and societies, complexes synthesized out of countless such simple parts. Indeed, it's in application to these complexes that Nietzsche's thoughts about will to power find their main plausibility and interest. This study of combination is all the more important because with it a new valuative standard emerges: internal complexity or 'richness' is a Nietzschean value at least partly independent of activeness, and even in some tension with it.

This combining of wills occurs at a hierarchy of levels, beginning with that of atomic forces.[53] But let's focus on the most important and least implausible stages, of synthesis into persons and societies. A crucial point in both analyses is that the (person's or society's) parts both do and do not combine to constitute a real being, a higher-order will in its own right. Nietzsche finds a great ambiguity here and is often inclined to deny that any

---

[52] As I noted in the introduction, and will examine in §IV.5, the ontology 'supports' these other views not by serving as an a priori foundation for deduced conclusions, but by conceptually structuring those views—a structuring whose worth we're to judge empirically.

[53] Nietzsche's freedom in applying his concept of will to power to 'wills' of so many different types might arouse a certain suspicion. He might seem to be proceeding more from an unreflective enthusiasm for the notion—leading him to apply it indiscriminately wherever his attention falls—than from any worked-out schema for the levels at which it occurs. Or he might seem to suppose it is a sort of cosmic force that 'enters into' or 'possesses' beings already otherwise constituted in their different levels or types. Interpreters seem often to hear him this way. And yet I think attention and effort can discover an intriguing account of the way these 'higher-order' wills are formed from simpler ones.

such synthetic being, any person or society, really exists. But while holding this reservation in view, we must ask how are persons made up out of drives, and societies out of persons? What new form does will to power take in these, as beings of this new complexity?

A person, then, isn't a simple will for Nietzsche but an organized complex of numerous drives of various strengths.[54] Of course, we must understand these drives in our Nietzschean way: not as 'doers behind the doing' but as activity patterns or behaviors themselves. Each habit or practice enacted in a person's life tries to extend and enrich itself, by crowding out competing practices or making them serve it. So these drives struggle to dominate one another, but this struggle is not just a chaos of forces successively overpowering one another. They reach (shifting) balances of power by arriving at relatively stable relations of command and obedience toward one another. A person is just such a balance among simpler wills, an interweaving of those behaviors, allowing each to express itself proportionately to its strength. For the most part, Nietzsche thinks of this compromise as a being in its own right, as a 'synthesis' of those parts. He treats it as a new will with some independence from those that compose. It shows this in sometimes restraining them—even the strongest drive is now somewhat moderated in its expression. This synthetic will thus restrains these parts, because it now wills power itself—tries to develop itself, as this synthesis. Thus a person's identity lies in the system of his drives, but this system isn't simply their sum but the power relations, the 'order of rank', among them. And so Nietzsche analyzes the expression 'who he is' with "in what rank order the innermost drives of his nature are set toward one another" (BGE 6).[55]

Indeed, this is the structure of every living thing: "A multiplicity of forces, connected by a common mode of nutrition, we call 'life'" (WP 641). Thus Nietzsche's analysis makes persons the same in type as animals, more

---

[54] Compare the accounts of this drive constitution in G. Parkes, *Composing the Soul: Reaches of Nietzsche's Psychology* (Chicago: University of Chicago Press, 1994) and L. P. Thiele, *Friedrich Nietzsche and the Politics of the Soul: A Study of Heroic Individualism* (Princeton: Princeton University Press, 1990), 51 ff.

[55] See BGE 36 again. BGE 12 commends the phrase "soul as social structure of the drives and affects", and BGE 19 says "our body is only a social structure of many souls". GM II. 1 says "our organism is arranged oligarchically"; KSA 10. 7 [94] (1883): "The most general picture of our essence is *an association of drives*, with constant rivalry and particular alliances with one another." WP 492 states that the 'subjects' we suppose ourselves to be are really "regents at the head of a communality"; it speaks further of "rank order and division of labor as the conditions that make possible the individual (*Einzelnen*) and the whole." And WP 524 describes "a kind of leading committee where the different *chief desires* make their voices and power count." See also WP 490 and 647. Nietzsche already thinks with this model at UM IV. 9; he speaks (with sympathetic reference to Wagner's drama) of calculating "the grand course of a total passion out of a multiplicity of passions running off in different directions". And D 119 speaks of "the totality of *drives* which constitute [a person's] essence", D 422 of "one's fifty particular (*eignen*) drives".

continuous with them than if some quite new component, such as mind or reason, were introduced. Human beings are distinguished simply by bearing more such drives, and drives that are more opposed to one another.[56] Not only is there no detached theoretical subject standing above this struggle among our drives, there is also no preexisting 'overwill', no simple second-order will whose function it is to control them. So at BGE 117: "The will to overcome an affect is ultimately only the will of another, or of several other, affects." Thus when Nietzsche attacks 'the will'—for example, when he says, "There is no 'will': it is only a simplifying conception of the understanding" (WP 671)—he is usually not expressing doubts that bear against his own proposed will to power; he's rejecting his predecessors' faith in such a simple self or faculty.[57]

We still need to examine more closely the logic of this combining of wills, what I've just called their 'synthesis'. Consider first the relation between a pair of drives, the one dominating and using the other for its ends, the latter pursuing goals imposed on it by the first. Then the complex composed of this pair can't be understood by attempting to 'sum together' the two forces, as if these were vectors pressing off in different directions. The weaker drive joins in the project commanded by the stronger and thereby enhances it; but as always struggling to assert itself within this relation, it also modifies that project with something of its own. Unlike vectoral forces, these projects adjust to one another, proportionately to their relative power; each thereby finds some expression within the other. As before, we should stress how all of this occurs in the concrete behaviors of these drives—now, in the ways their respective activities are intertwined in the daily life of the person. For the most part, the weaker practice is taken as a stage within the stronger and must shift direction to better serve this role. Yet the dominant project, even by thus absorbing the other as an epicycle within it, takes on new character itself.

In such a case, in which one drive quite rules the other, we identify the resulting complex with the dominant drive: this is still its activity, now enriched by that other, which it has absorbed or made (mostly) like itself. But

---

[56] Nietzsche stresses this continuity as early as "Homer's Contest" (1872), which begins: "When one speaks of *humanity* (*Humanität*), the idea is basic that this is something that *separates* and distinguishes human beings from nature. In reality, however, there is no such separation". A 14: "We no longer derive the human being from the 'spirit' or the 'deity'; we have placed him back among the animals." WP 966: "As opposed to the animals, the human being has bred large an abundance of *opposing* drives and impulses (*Impulse*) within himself: thanks to this synthesis, he is master of the earth." See also BGE 291, GM III. 13, WP 259.

[57] D 109: "While 'we' believe we are complaining about the vehemence of a drive, at bottom it is one drive *that is complaining about another*". A 14: "today we have taken from [the human being] even the will, in the sense that no faculty (*Vermögen*) may any longer be understood by it." Also TI III. 5, VI. 3, WP 692.

if we think of a case in which the drives are more evenly balanced, with one perhaps dominant in some respects or contexts but the other dominant in other respects, we won't still attribute the activity of the resulting whole to either of its members. They now form a unit with a distinctive activity of its own, not to be identified with either of the others, nor even with their (vectoral) sum. Think, for example, of eating with other persons: our interests in food and in social interaction here intertwine, and not merely in the sense of being pursued simultaneously. Two practices now express themselves within one another and so join to form a new and more complex practice. Nietzsche thinks this practice has, as it were, a life of its own: 'social eating' will tend to repeat and develop itself. Thus there arises a second-order power unit, one that can itself be entangled with other such pursuits and so enter into still higher syntheses.[58]

We should imagine the person, then, as such a unit, though one vastly more complex, because it is a synthesis of many parts, which are themselves syntheses of simpler parts; the different organs of the body, or rather their functionings, are such lower-order complexes. Thus a person is formed of a vast network of power balances, struck at a hierarchy of levels. What differences between persons become important—turn out to reflect our deep structure—given this analysis? I catalog some of the main dimensions along which such systems of drives might vary:

1. How many different drives does a person bear? Nietzsche does not suppose there's a standard set intrinsic to all human beings; some will be far more complex in this way than others. His overstress on 'breeding'—his notion of these drives as mainly inherited ('in the blood')—is misleading here: we must bear in mind his Lamarckism. My drives are the product of the lives my parents led; rather than some common human endowment, they're those particular practices I've been (we will say) trained up into. So they include not just eating, for example, but even quite specific meal rituals and tastes.[59]

2. How compatible with one another are a person's drives? Of course all drives are by their nature as will to power at odds with one another; it's

---

[58] WP 642: "To what extent a striving-against lies even in obeying; its own power is by no means given up. In the same way, there is in commanding an admission that the absolute power of the opponent has not been vanquished, incorporated, disintegrated." WP 488 says that a subject "can transform a weaker subject into its functionary without destroying it, and to a certain degree form a new unity with it." WP 636 speaks of each body as striving to extend its force but meeting other bodies whose similar efforts oppose it; it therefore "ends by coming to an arrangement ('union') with those of them that are sufficiently akin to it: thus *they then conspire together for power*. And the process goes on—".

[59] See BGE 200, 224 on the great internal diversity of moderns. BGE 264: "One cannot wipe from the soul of a human being, what his ancestors have done most gladly and continually."

their essence to try to rule one another. But (pairs of) drives will vary in how opposed and irreconcilable their distinguishing activities are. Because each drive seeks dominance by impressing others *to* its activity, how far it will thereby try to turn those others *from* their own natures will vary. So a person is made up of drives that are more or less 'tolerant' of one another, more or less capable of 'harmonious' relation.[60]

3. What are the relative strengths of a person's drives? Are one or two much stronger than the others, or are all on roughly equal footing? If the latter, it may be harder for stable power relations to form, especially if the many equal rivals are incompatible with one another in the way just described. Such a person might more nearly approach the condition of that chaos of succeeding impulses mentioned before.[61]

4. How thoroughly have a person's drives been synthesized with one another? Nietzsche thinks the unity of a person is never complete—this is why he sometimes denies any persons exist—but a matter of varying degree.[62] This most important difference among persons depends on some of the other differences in ways we've seen; it deserves special attention.

Let's think a bit further about the privative case. Here the constitutive drives haven't found any balance with one another, or only a very unstable one. There isn't, that is, any overall pattern of behavior, any comprehensive practice in which they all find their expression, but instead just a sequence of their separate, private doings. Instead of being channeled to contribute to some such overall effort, each drive squirms to break loose in a spasm of pure self-assertion, followed by its total suppression by some equally unrestrained drive. Such a person will lack 'self-control', which is now shown by Nietzsche to be a different condition than we usually think. What's missing isn't strength of 'the will', as a part or tool of 'the self', but the capacity of this set of drives to combine in the way described.[63] And they

---

[60] See again BGE 200.

[61] WP 778: "the against-one-another of the passions; two, three, a multiplicity of 'souls in one breast': very unhealthy, inner ruin, disintegrating, betraying and increasing an inner conflict and anarchism". See also TI IX. 41.

[62] WP 488: "*No* subject 'atoms'. The sphere of a subject continually *growing* or *decreasing*, the midpoint of the system continually *shifting*". See also WP 635.

[63] WP 46: "Weakness of the will: that is a simile that can mislead. For there is no will, and consequently neither a strong nor a weak will. The multiplicity and disgregation of the impulses, the lack of system among them results in a 'weak will'; their coordination under the dominance (*Vorherrschaft*) of a single one results in a 'strong will'". See Nehamas, *Nietzsche*, 170 ff. (a later version of Ch. 10 in this volume), on the task of unifying the self.

may lack this capacity merely because of such 'chemical' incompatibilities as we've noted.

We'll see that the extent of unification achieved by a person's drives is a major valuative standard by which Nietzsche ranks him. This value can be understood as a new form of the activeness we've already seen his ontology values. When we rise to the level of complex wills, the active/reactive distinction can be drawn not just by whether the will commands others 'outside' itself but by whether it commands the simpler wills that it comprises.[64] Indeed, Nietzsche supposes that such self-mastery is a crucial precondition (or at least aid) for mastering others. Is the synthesis able to hold its constitutive forces to their contributing roles and prevent them from asserting themselves disruptively against it? A person can either 'command' or 'obey' his parts, whereas the simple drive can do neither—neither restrain nor give way to itself. Thus the poorly synthesized person exhibits a new form of reactivity; he obeys away from himself, by obeying too small a part of himself. Nietzsche thinks this brand of reactivity is typical of persons: just because we're distinguished from other living things by our greater complexity of parts, it is harder for us to achieve synthesis. This is why man is 'the sick animal', 'all too human'.[65]

Thus the standard of unity, by which Nietzsche often rates persons, might be counted a special application of the value of activeness (already placed in his system). But Nietzsche will also rate persons by another standard, somewhat in tension with this one: by their degree of complexity, by their multiplicity of parts. How does this other value emerge? Activeness was valued, recall, as a well-directed pursuit of one's own power. But power amounted to growth by incorporation: having one's activity come to encompass the behaviors of others. So growth involves an advance in internal complexity; a will that is now complex, is so because of successful power willing in the past, by itself or others. However, such achieved complexity makes it ever more difficult to continue to will power healthily. The greater the richness of parts at hand, the harder it is to marshal them together. We can see, then, how the values most deeply rooted in the power ontology—those of power and activeness—support an oxymoronic standard for rating persons: the extent to which they show a 'complex unity'.

We mustn't stop, however, at the level of the person in exploring the synthetic forms of will. Nietzsche's discussions of societies and their

[64] So is the whole active only at the expense of the parts, by forcing them into a reactive obedience? We'll see that Nietzsche thinks personal unity ('self-control') can be secured by a 'taming' or 'suppression' of the drives, but need not be.

[65] GM III. 13, A 14, KSA 9. 12 [163] (1881) identifies 'the human individual' as "the highest and *most imperfect* being (*Wesen*)".

practices show that these should be treated in parallel to persons: they, too, are made up from simpler parts—from drives or persons or simpler complexes of these. They, too, become synthetic units of will to power in their own right, able to pursue their own development and to command their members to serve that end.

Nietzsche often speaks of peoples or races as having or being wills to power. Yet it's tempting not to take such applications of the concept quite strictly. We might suspect that they're merely shorthand ways of referring to the behavior of the persons who make up those groups, to the sum of the ways they themselves will power. This seems confirmed when we notice that he even applies that concept to such amorphous beings as religions: sometimes, he says, "they themselves will to be ultimate goals and not means among other means" (BGE 62). It's hard to see how he could mean this literally; is it a case of that loose or metaphorical expression we so expect from him?

There's indeed less evidence that Nietzsche has fully thought out a definite sense for such talk, that he pays as much attention to the task of analyzing societies in his power terms as he does with persons. We'll later find other important differences between his treatments of these two, which suggest he indeed has more qualms against treating societies as real beings than we've seen he has against persons. Still, there are many indications of another tendency, which gives them just the analysis we expect, given the power ontology.[66]

We can extract this line from the striking discussion of punishment in the second essay of *On the Genealogy of Morals*. Nietzsche argues that we mustn't conflate the origin and the purpose of this social custom or practice; they're different because, in general, everything that comes into being "is again and again interpreted to new views, confiscated, remodeled, and redirected to a new use by some power superior to it" (GM II. 12). He illustrates this with the case of an organ in a living body: as the organism as a whole grows, it assigns ('commands') that part to ever new roles. The institution of punishment, he thinks, has a similar place within an encompassing being; this practice, as "a certain strict sequence of

---

[66] From early on, Nietzsche tends to view societies as living beings. UM II. 1 gives as examples of living things "*a human being or a people or a culture*"; UM II. 4 says, "a people to whom one attributes a culture has to be in all reality a living unity (*Eines*)", and offers the analogy of many threads wound into a knot; UM II. 10 says, "Hellenic culture was no mere aggregate . . . The Greeks gradually learned *to organize the chaos*". HH I. 99 says that morality arises "when a greater individual or a collective-individual, for example the society, the state, subjugates all other single ones . . . and orders them into a unit (*Verband*)." See also GM II. 11 (a legal order is "a means of creating *greater* units of power"), GM II. 20 ("the conclusive rank order of all the people's elements, in every great racial synthesis"). See also BGE 259 and WP 728.

procedures" (GM II. 13), is directed to a series of uses by the society as a whole, or by other forces within it. Punishing thus takes on a series of 'meanings', which Nietzsche catalogs at some length.

So his picture seems to be this. Such a custom is a particular system of interactions among persons, but one that has taken on a life of its own, as a synthetic will to power. It thus tends to continue and extend itself and in doing so shows independent power over its parts: it draws persons into performing it. This system of behavior persists in a fairly constant form from one generation to the next. But it's also always changing, because it is always being jostled by other such practices competing with it. Together, these compose a still larger power unit: the society as a whole, the system of these systems of behavior, their organization into a network of power relations. This higher-order unit acts back on its parts in just the same way, commanding them into the roles in which they most contribute to its overall effort—or at least, the healthy, active society will command in this way.

This parallel analysis shows that societies will crucially vary in the same ways we saw persons do; we shall ask the same questions of them:

1. How many different types of persons and customs enter into this society? Nietzsche uses the standard of complexity at this level as well: he'll rank societies by the richness or diversity of their parts.
2. How compatible with one another are the society's parts? Along with their diversity, the contentiousness of these parts helps to determine how far they can be synthesized into a stable whole.[67]
3. Are a few of these persons or practices dominant over the rest, or are there many, roughly equal in strength? The distinction between aristocratic and democratic societies of course falls here. We'll explore Nietzsche's preference here and how it's related to his ranking of the parallel types of persons.
4. How thoroughly synthesized are these parts? Once again, the most important question about any society is how fully formed it is as a will in its own right. The more tightly knit its parts are into a whole, the more power it has over them and the less free they are to upset the balance in a solitary self-assertion.[68]

This raises a certain problem: activeness of the society looks incompatible with activeness of the person. The former involves a subordination of society's members to its comprehensive project: it limits them to roles it requires. So in the fully formed and active society, it seems persons would be least

[67] D 272 speaks of "crossed races, in which, together with a disharmony of bodily forms . . . there must always go a disharmony of habits and value-concepts."
[68] See again D 272.

allowed to develop themselves in idiosyncratic directions, which we've seen their power requires.[69] Thus we can expect that Nietzsche's judgments on the value of 'freedom' will be most important, because they'll reflect his judgment on the relative values of a person and a society. To anticipate: it's a striking feature of his thought that although he values persons as greater quanta of power formed as syntheses of lesser drives, he doesn't follow the parallel by valuing societies as still greater quanta formed from those persons themselves; this is a clue to the differences in the ways these two synthetic power units are formed. I reconfront these issues in chapters 2 and 3, as I dig more deeply into Nietzsche's social views.

[69] WP 719: "A *division of labor* among the *affects* within society: so that individuals (*Einzelnen*) and classes cultivate an *incomplete*, but for that reason *more useful* kind of soul." D 9 develops the incompatibility between the 'ethics of custom' and individuality.

7

MAKING LIFE WORTH LIVING: NIETZSCHE ON ART IN *THE BIRTH OF TRAGEDY*

RICHARD SCHACHT

No higher significance could be assigned to art than that which Nietzsche assigns to it in the opening section of *The Birth of Tragedy*. "The arts generally" are said to "make life possible and worth living" (BT 1). Art was never far from Nietzsche's mind, even when dealing with matters seemingly far removed from it. He includes a number of artists among the "higher" types of human being whom he takes to stand out from the greater part of humankind hitherto, and likens to artists both the "philosophers of the future" he envisages and the "overman" he declares to be "the meaning of the earth." Indeed, he even aspired to art himself, investing much effort and a good deal of himself in poetic and musical composition.

Nietzsche's interest in art was by no means either exclusively academic or merely personal. In his original preface to BT, he speaks disparagingly of readers who may "find it offensive that an aesthetic problem should be taken so seriously," and who are unable to consider art more than a "pleasant sideline, a readily dispensable tinkling of bells that accompanies the 'seriousness of life.'" Against them, he advances the startling contention that "art represents the highest task and the truly metaphysical activity of this life" (BT, Preface). And he goes on to maintain that "the arts generally" serve to "make life possible and worth living" (BT 1). It remains to be seen what he has in mind in saying this, as well as in terming art "the truly metaphysical activity of this life." But these passages provide an ample indication of the centrality of art both in the cluster of issues he deals with in BT and also in his thinking about them.

From Richard Schacht, "Making Life Worth Living: Nietzsche on Art in *The Birth of Tragedy*", in his *Making Sense of Nietzsche: Reflections Timely and Untimely* (Urbana: University of Illinois Press, 1995), 129–52; first pub. in R. J. Sclafani and G. Dickie (eds.), *Art and Aesthetics: Theories and Critiques* (New York: St Martin's Press, 1977).

I

Nietzsche makes no attempt to conceal the influence of Schopenhauer on both his conception of reality and his thinking about the arts. Schopenhauer may fairly be said to have been his primary philosophical inspiration, in a twofold way. On the one hand, Nietzsche was initially convinced of the soundness of much of what Schopenhauer had to say about the world, life and the arts. But on the other, he was deeply unsettled by Schopenhauer's dark conclusions with respect to "the value of existence" and the worth of living. Most of his contemporaries tended to dismiss Schopenhauer as a morbidly pessimistic crank even while being appreciative of his stylistic brilliance. But Nietzsche saw that he had raised profoundly serious questions about life, which could no longer be answered as theologians and philosophers traditionally had answered them, and to which new answers had to be found if those given by Schopenhauer himself were not to prevail. Schopenhauer had concluded that existence is utterly unjustifiable and valueless, except in the negative sense that the inevitable preponderance of suffering endows it with an actual disvalue; and that, for anyone who considers the matter soberly and clearsightedly, oblivion must be acknowledged to be preferable to life.

Schopenhauer's reason for taking this darkly pessimistic position was that in his view existence in general and life in particular are characterized by ceaseless struggle and striving, inevitably resulting in destruction and (among sentient forms of life) involving incessant suffering of one sort or another. The whole affair, as he saw it, is quite pointless, since nothing of any value is thereby attained (the perpetuation of life merely continuing the striving and suffering). No transcendent purposes are thereby served; no pleasure, enjoyments, or satisfactions attainable can suffice to overbalance the sufferings life involves, thus excluding a hedonic justification of living; and so life stands condemned at the bar of evaluative judgment. It is, in a word, absurd. Ceaseless striving, inescapable suffering, inevitable destruction—all pointless, with no meaning and no justification, no redemption or after-worldly restitution, and with the only deliverance being that of death and oblivion: this is Schopenhauer's world as *Wille und Vorstellung*— the pre-Christian apprehension of life attributed by Nietzsche in BT to the Greeks, recurring again in the modern world as Christianity enters its death throes.

Nietzsche does not question the soundness of this picture in BT; and, even though he later rejected the Schopenhauerian metaphysics, he continued to concur with this general account of the circumstances attending life in the world. To live is to struggle, suffer, and die; and, while there may be more to living than that, no amount of "progress" in any field of human enterprise can succeed in altering these basic parameters of individual human existence. Even more significantly, for Nietzsche as well as for Schopenhauer and Nietzsche's Greeks, it is not possible to discern any teleological *justification* of what the individual is thus fated to undergo, either historically or supernaturally. We can look neither to a future utopia nor to a life hereafter that might serve to render our existence endurable and meaningful.

How can one manage to endure life in a world of the sort described by Schopenhauer, once one recognizes it for what it is—endure it, and beyond that *affirm* it as desirable and worth living despite the "terrors and horrors" that are inseparable from it? "Suppose a human being has thus put his ear, as it were, to the heart chamber of the world will," Nietzsche writes, "how could he fail to *break*?" (BT 21). He terms this general recognition of the world's nature and of the fate of the individual within it "Dionysian wisdom"; and he compares the situation of the Greek who attained it to that of Hamlet—and implicitly to that of modern man (with a Schopenhauerian-existentialist world view) as well: "In this sense the Dionysian man resembles Hamlet: both have once looked truly into the essence of things, they have *gained knowledge*, and nausea inhibits action; for their action could not change anything in the external nature of things. . . . Now no comfort avails any more. . . . Conscious of the truth he has once seen, man now sees everywhere only the horror or absurdity of existence. . . . He is nauseated" (BT 7).

Nietzsche desperately wanted to find some sort of solution to this predicament—though he cloaked his longing in the guise of a more detached interest in the question of how it has been possible for "life" to manage to "detain its creatures in existence" even when the erroneous beliefs that commonly shield them are no longer in operation. For this reason his attention was drawn to a people who were already very much on his mind owing to his professional concerns and who constituted a perfect subject for a case study along these lines: the early Greeks. They were no brute savages, mindlessly and insensitively propelled through life by blind instinct; rather, they were highly intelligent, sensitive, and well aware of the ways of the world. Moreover, they were sustained neither by anything like Judeo-Christian religious belief nor by any myth of historical progress and human perfectibility. Yet they did not succumb to Schopenhauerian pessimism; on the contrary, they were perhaps the most vigorous, creative, life-affirming people the world has known. Thus Nietzsche was drawn irresistibly to them, asking of them: how did they do it? What was the secret of their liberation from the action- and affirmation-inhibiting nausea that seemingly ought to have been the result of their own Dionysian wisdom? The answer, he believed, lay in that which was the most striking and glorious achievement of their culture: their art. Thus the passage cited continues: "Here, where the danger to [the] will is greatest, *art* approaches as a saving sorceress, expert at healing. She alone knows how to turn these nauseous thoughts about the horror or absurdity of existence into notions with which one can live" (ibid.).

This is the guiding idea of Nietzsche's whole treatment of art and its significance for human life in BT. The main themes of this work are summarized in the following lines from its concluding section, which expand upon this idea by making reference to the key concepts of the "Dionysian" and "Apollinian" and bring to the fore the most central and crucial notions in Nietzsche's entire philosophy of art—the notions of *overcoming* and *transfiguration*:

Thus the Dionysian is seen to be, compared to the Apollinian, the eternal and original artistic power that first calls the whole world of phenomena into existence—and it is only in the midst of this world that a new transfiguring illusion becomes necessary in order to keep the animated world of individuation alive. . . . Of this foundation of all existence—the Dionysian basic ground of the world—not one whit more may enter the consciousness of the human individual than can be overcome again by this Apollinian power of transfiguration. (BT 25)

II

Before turning to a closer consideration of these themes, a fundamental ambivalence in Nietzsche's thinking about the relation between art and life—in BT and also subsequently—must be noted. From first to last, Nietzsche was deeply convinced that art requires to be understood not as a self-contained and self-enclosed sphere of activity and experience detached from the rest of life, but rather as intimately bound up with life and as having the greatest significance in and for it. This is reflected in his later observation (in his "Self Criticism") that art in BT is viewed "in the perspective of life"— a circumstance he regards as one of the signal merits of the work, its many inadequacies not withstanding. And it is one of the most decisive and distinctive features of his general philosophical position that its development is characterized by a kind of dialectic between his understanding of life and the world and his understanding of art—each affecting the other and bringing about changes in the other as the other worked changes upon it.

The underlying unity of the notions of art and life in Nietzsche's thinking is to be seen in BT in his treatment of the basic impulses operative in art— the Dionysian and the Apollinian—as identical with basic tendencies discernable in ourselves and nature alike. And the consequences of his conviction of the existence of this unity are apparent in the subsequent development of two notions that came to figure importantly in his later writings: those of the "overman" and the "will to power." For I would suggest that the latter is to be understood as an outgrowth of the dual notions of the Dionysian and Apollinian "art impulses of nature," in which they are *aufgehoben* in the threefold Hegelian sense of this term: they are at once negated, preserved, and superseded. And I would also suggest that the "overman" is to be construed as a symbol of human life raised to the level of art, in which crude self-assertive struggle is sublimated into creativity that is no longer subject to the demands and limitations associated with the "human, all-too-human."

The overcoming of the initial meaningless and repugnant character of existence, through the creative transformation of the existing, cardinally characterizes both art and life as Nietzsche ultimately came to understand them. And this means for him both that life is essentially artistic and that art is an expression of the fundamental nature of life. "Will to power" is properly understood only if it is conceived as a disposition to effect such creatively transformative overcoming—in nature, human life generally, and art alike. And the overman is the apotheosis of this fundamental disposition, the ultimate incarnation of the basic character of reality generally to which all existence, life, and art are owing.

In BT, of course, neither "will to power" nor "overman" makes an appearance, and the relation between art and life is discussed in other terms. One of the most notable features of the discussion, however, is Nietzsche's readiness to employ the term "art" not only to refer in a conventional manner to sculpture, music, and the other standard "art forms" (kinds of work of art, their production, and their experience), but also in a broader, extended sense. For example, Nietzsche suggests that "every man is truly an artist" to the extent that it is part of the experience of everyone to engage in the "creation" of "the beautiful illusion" of "dream worlds" (BT 1), even though no "works of art" in the usual sense are thereby produced. Furthermore, turning his attention from such (Apollinian) "dreaming" to the experience of what he calls "Dionysian ecstasies," Nietzsche speaks of the Dionysian throng as *being* "works of art" themselves: here "man . . . is no longer an artist, he has become a work of art. . . . The noblest clay, the costliest marble, man, is here kneaded and cut" (ibid.).

Most striking of all, however, Nietzsche refers constantly to "nature herself" as "artistic," and terms both the Apollinian and the Dionysian tendencies "art-impulses" of *nature*. Thus he initially presents them "as artistic energies which burst forth from nature herself, without the mediation of the human artist," and goes on to say, "with reference to these immediate art-states of nature every artist is an 'imitator'" (BT 2). And he is not merely suggesting that nature is thus "artistic" as well as humanity, albeit in different ways; for he contends that these two "art-states of nature" are "the only two art impulses" (BT 12), and he even goes so far as to attribute the true authorship of *all* art to "nature" rather than to human agency considered in its own right. "One thing above all must be clear to us. The entire comedy of art is neither performed for our betterment or education, nor are we the true authors of this art world." The human artist is said to be merely "the medium through which the one truly existent subject celebrates his release in appearance." Artists and the rest of us alike are "merely images and artistic projections for the true author," which is the fundamental principle of reality—the world will—itself; and we "have our highest dignity in our significance as works of art," as creations of this ultimate "artist," rather than as producers and appreciators of art objects (BT 5).

Yet Nietzsche also speaks of art very differently, and in a way that suggests a much less direct and even contrasting relation between it and the world. Thus, for example, he writes that "the highest, and indeed the truly serious task of art" is "to save the eye from gazing into the horrors of night and to deliver the subject by the healing balm of illusion from the spasms of the agitations of the will" (BT 19). He repeatedly asserts that art in all of its forms deals in "illusion" and even "lies." Art spreads a "veil of beauty" over a harsh reality—and, when he speaks of it as a "transfiguring mirror" (BT 3), the emphasis is on "transfiguring," which precludes any accurate reflection. Thus he writes that "art is not merely imitation of the reality of nature but rather a metaphysical supplement of the reality of nature, placed beside it for its overcoming" (BT 24).

Here the concluding passage of the entire work, cited earlier, should be recalled, in which Nietzsche returns to this theme of the necessity of overcoming whatever consciousness of the world's nature is attained by means of an art of "transfiguration" capable of covering over what has been glimpsed with a "splendid illusion" (BT 25). It was the "terror and horror of existence" from which the Greeks needed to be saved; and "it was in order to be able to live" that they developed their art: "all this was again and again overcome by the Greeks with the aid of the Olympian *middle world* of art; or at any rate it was veiled and withdrawn from sight" (BT 3). Nor does this apply only to nontragic art forms; for Nietzsche asserts that "the tragic myth too, insofar as it belongs to art at all, participates fully in this metaphysical intention of art to transfigure" (BT 24).

Even while thinking along these lines, however, Nietzsche envisages a fundamental link between "art" and "life," in that the latter is held to have been the source of the Greek's salvation from the desperate situation in which it also placed him: "Art saves him, and through art—life" (BT 7). Life thus is cast in a dual role, with the consequence that the relation of art to it is also a dual one. But can the world of art at once be thought of as a world "supplementing the reality of nature, placed beside it for its overcoming," and therefore distinct from it and contrasting to it—and at the same time be understood as the creation of this very nature itself, expressing its own basic "artistic impulses," and therefore fundamentally as homogeneous and even identical with it? In BT, Nietzsche tries to have it both ways, but it is far from clear that it is possible to do so.

III

In any event, it should be clear by now that Nietzsche in BT thinks of what art *is* in terms of *what art does* and *how art does it*; and that for him the answers to these two questions are to be given in terms of the notions of *overcoming* (*Überwindung*) and *transfiguration* (*Verklärung*). These two notions recur repeatedly throughout BT and figure centrally in most of his major pronouncements about art—regardless of what art forms he may be considering, and notwithstanding any basic differences between them.

It should further be evident that this "overcoming" is to be understood in relation to certain human needs that Nietzsche regards as fundamental and profoundly compelling, thereby endowing art with an extraordinary importance transcending that of mere enjoyment or satisfaction derived from entertainment or self-expression. And his interpretation of art in terms of "transfiguration" also clearly involves him in a fundamental break with Schopenhauer and all other cognitivist philosophers of art; for if art is essentially a matter of transfiguration its ministrations to our needs will necessarily proceed otherwise than by heightening our powers of insight and understanding.

Nietzsche's frequent references to "illusions" in a number of contexts make this obvious, but the point applies even where this latter notion does not (notably, in the case of music). Even where some sort of "truth" about reality is purported to come through in art, he takes it to be essential to the artistic character of the expression that a transfiguration of the "true" content has occurred in its artistic treatment—and its artistic character and quality attaches entirely to the element of transfiguration, rather than to this content and its transmission.

It is important to bear in mind the general applicability of the notions of overcoming and transfiguration when turning to Nietzsche's discussion of the art impulses and art forms he is intent upon distinguishing, both to interpret properly what he says about them individually and to avoid the error of supposing that he takes them to be entirely different phenomena united by nothing more than a shared name. He does begin by speaking of "the science of aesthetics" and of "the continuous development of art," thereby implying some degree of unity of both the discipline and its subject. Yet he immediately introduces the notion of the "duality" of "the Apollinian and Dionysian," asserts that "art" is but a "common term" until the two are "coupled with each other" (BT 1), and goes on to analyze them along very different lines—even to the point of maintaining that these notions represent "*two* worlds of art differing in their intrinsic essence and in their highest aims" (BT 16). These "art impulses" and "worlds of art," however, while very different indeed for Nietzsche, are nonetheless both "*art* impulses" and "worlds of *art*." That they have more than merely this same "art" denomination in common is testified to by the fact that their "coupling" had a fruitful artistic issue: tragedy.

Neither in Apollinian nor in Dionysian art, Nietzsche contends, do we encounter unvarnished representations of the world, as it is in itself, as it presents itself to us in experience, or as it might be conceived by a thinker concerned with the natures of the types to which all existing things belong. The impulses to the creation of art for Nietzsche are not cognitive impulses of any sort. If they stand in any relation at all to knowledge, he holds that this relation may best be conceived instead as an *antidotal* one. And it is undoubtedly in part to stress the extent of his departure from any cognitively oriented interpretation of art that Nietzsche introduces his discussion of the Apollinian and the Dionysian by dwelling upon their connection with the phenomena of dreaming and intoxication. Each of these phenomena, he maintains, manifests a deeply rooted and profoundly important aspect of our nature, and each answers to a powerful need. And the strength of the hold art exerts upon us can be understood only if it is recognized that the different art forms have their origins in these basic impulses, and emerge in answer to these strong needs.

Nietzsche's discussion of Apollinian and Dionysian duality in BT is intended to bring out both the radical difference between what he thus takes to be the two basic life-serving and art-generating impulses these names designate, and also the possibility of their interpenetration—and, further, the great importance (for "life" and art alike) of the results when this occurs. At the outset of his discussion of the Apollinian and Dionysian duality he singles out two art forms as paradigms of each—"the Apollinian art of sculpture and the non-imagistic, Dionysian art of music" (BT 1)—but then moves immediately to a consideration of the more fundamental experiential "states" (also termed Apollinian and Dionysian) to which he takes all such art forms to be related: dreaming and intoxication.

Nietzsche contends that human beings are so constituted that they are impelled to each by basic dispositions, and respond to each with powerful but differing positive feelings. Thus he suggests that there is something in "our innermost being" that "experiences dreams with profound delight and joyous necessity" (ibid.), while it is likewise the case that "paroxysms of intoxication" are accompanied by a "blissful ecstasy that wells up from the innermost depths of man, indeed of nature" (ibid.). It is these feelings of "profound delight" on the one hand and of "blissful ecstasy" on the other that are held respectively to characterize the experience of the Apollinian and Dionysian art forms. These forms touch the same deep chords in our nature and so produce the same sort of response. And this is taken to be the key to understanding how it is that they are able to perform their life-sustaining functions (to the extent that they manage to do so).

As Nietzsche views them, dreaming and intoxication are not merely analogs to art, or pre-forms of art, or even experiential sources of artistic activity. There is an important sense in which they themselves *are* artistic phenomena—only the "artist" in these cases is no human being, but rather "nature," working in the medium of human life. In this context, the Dionysian and Apollinian require to be conceived "as artistic energies which burst forth from nature herself, without the mediation of the human artist— energies in which nature's art impulses are satisfied in the most immediate and direct way" (BT 2). Nietzsche does not mean this to be construed merely metaphorically; for it is his contention that human artistic activities are to be regarded as of a piece with these more basic life processes—developments of them, to be sure, but outgrowths sufficiently similar to them to warrant regarding "every artist as an 'imitator'" in relation to "these immediate art-states of nature." Thus he also contends that "only insofar as the genius in the act of artistic creation coalesces with this primordial artist of the world, does he learn anything of the eternal essence of art" (BT 5).

It may be noted in this connection that for Nietzsche it is in this respect— and only in this respect—that art may properly be conceived as involving "the imitation of nature." That is, art imitates nature in that the same sort of thing goes on in the former instance as goes on (among other things) in the latter. But precisely because creative transformation is involved in the former no less than in the latter (as part of the very "imitation" in question), true art no more involves the attempt exactly to represent nature as it confronts us than dreaming and intoxication faithfully record it—nor yet again does true art merely give expression to the contents of experiences had while in these states.

Having said this, it must immediately be granted that Nietzsche does employ the language of "representation" in speaking of the relation between both Apollinian and Dionysian art forms and the content of what might be termed the "visions" characteristic of the associated experiential states more broadly and fundamentally conceived. It has already been noted that he is willing to speak with Schopenhauer of (Dionysian) music as a "copy" of the "primal unity" underlying all appearances. It has also been observed that he conceives of Dionysian art as effecting a kind of identification of the individual with this underlying reality through a captivating revelation of its nature as conveyed by "the Dionysian artist" who has glimpsed it and "identified himself with" it. To this it must be added that he also speaks of the employment of "the beat of rhythm," and tonal architectonics in Apollinian music "for the representation of Apollinian states" (BT 2). And, while it is "mere appearances" rather than the reality underlying them with which all such states are held to be concerned, the "beautiful illusions" of Apollinian plastic art are suggested to be, if not such appearances themselves, at any rate "appearances of" *those* appearances (BT 4).

In short, Nietzsche holds that there is at least a kind of "mirroring" relation between what is discerned in Dionysian states and what one finds in Dionysian art, and also between what is envisioned in Apollinian states and what one finds in Apollinian art. Indeed, it can even be said that for him the efforts of artists of both sorts serve at once to share and to heighten experiences centering upon the contents of the respective sorts of vision. Were this not so, the "joy in existence" deriving from the "blissful ecstasy" generated by the one and the "profound delight" arising from the other (through the generation and intensification of which these types of art are held to perform their life-sustaining function) could not be stimulated by art.

The solution to this difficulty is to be found in the fact that for Nietzsche art transforms even as it thus "represents." It is no simple faithful mirror of the contents of these states, but rather "a transfiguring mirror" (BT 3). And it is one of the central points of his discussion of these two types of art that they not only transfigure even as they mirror, but moreover transfigure the already dissimilar contents of the visions associated with the two kinds of state in quite different ways. In view of this double difference, it is perhaps understandable that Nietzsche could have been moved to speak of "two worlds of art differing in their intrinsic essence" (BT 16).

The basic contrast he is concerned with establishing here may be expressed in terms of the distinction between *images* and *symbols*, and the double difference just mentioned bears importantly upon it. In the case of what Nietzsche calls Apollinian art, the chaotic play of crude and ephemeral appearances associated with such basic Apollinian experiential states as dreaming and imagination undergoes a transformative process, issuing in the creation of enduring, idealized images—"beautiful illusions," as he terms them, illusory because nothing either in the flux of appearance or beyond it corresponds to them, and of greater beauty than the haphazardly constituted contents of this flux. They are transfigurations of appearances—images akin to the stuff of dreams but also contrasting markedly with them.

In the case of Dionysian art, on the other hand, the transformation from which it issues is of the experience of the inexhaustible, dynamic "primal unity" that is "beyond all phenomena and despite all annihilation" associated with such basic Dionysian states as intoxication and orgiastic revelry. What *this* transformation gives rise to is "a new world of symbols," in which "the essence of nature is now . . . expressed symbolically" (BT 2); and it is the resulting *symbolic forms* in which Dionysian art consists. These symbolic forms are transfigurations of ecstatic states—expressions akin to immediate Dionysian ecstasy, but differing markedly from it, no less than from the underlying reality glimpsed in it. Thus Nietzsche holds that "Dionysian art . . . gives expression to the will in its omnipotence, as it were, behind the *principium individuationis*" (ibid.). Yet he insists that even so paradigmatic a case of such art as music is not to be thought of as identical with this will: "music, according to its essence, cannot possibly be will. To be will it would have to be wholly banished from the realm of art" (BT 6). For were it the same as will, it would lack the transfigured character of all art.

Thus it is Nietzsche's contention that there is one sort of art in which the works produced have a symbolically expressive character, and another sort in which the works produced do not, having instead the character of idealized images or "beautiful illusions." And it is one of the seemingly curious but important points of his analysis that the kinds of art generally regarded as most clearly "representational" fall largely into the latter category, while those generally thought of as primarily "nonrepresentational" belong in the former. The idealized images of Apollinian art are not to be thought of as having the function either of faithfully representing or even of symbolically expressing anything at all. They are rather to be thought of as beautiful illusions, to be contemplated simply for what they are in themselves, and to be enjoyed solely on account of their intrinsic beauty. They are, as Nietzsche says, a "supplement of the reality of nature, placed beside it for its overcoming" (BT 24). And, if there is any significant relation between them and this "reality," it does not consist in their genetic link to the experiential phenomena of which they are transfigurations, but rather in their ability to lead us to think better of the world of ordinary experience by regarding it in the "transfiguring mirror" they constitute, "surrounded with a higher glory" (BT 3). Through Apollinian art, the world of ordinary experience is not actually transformed and its harshness eliminated. But to the extent that the idealized images created through the transformative activity of the

Apollinian artist admit of association with that which we encounter in this world, our attitude toward the latter benefits from this association, as our delight in these images carries over into our general disposition toward anything resembling them.

Once again, however, it is not knowledge that we thereby attain, but rather only an altered state of mind, brought about by "recourse to the most forceful and pleasurable illusions" and "seducing one to a continuation of life" (BT 3). One may have reservations about the psychological validity of these latter contentions, or about the effectiveness of the process indicated (as indeed Nietzsche himself came to have subsequently). These reservations do not affect Nietzsche's main point here, however, concerning the status of those works of art he terms Apollinian. They are beautiful illusions—idealized images that neither represent nor symbolize, but rather delight precisely by virtue of the beauty they possess as a result of the creative transfiguration accomplished in their production.

In the case of Dionysian art, matters stand quite differently. The Dionysian artist too is creative, and not merely someone with insight and the ability to communicate it—notwithstanding Nietzsche's assertion that, in the paradigm case of such art, "he produces [a] copy of [the] primal unity as music" (BT 5). It may be that there is a kind of "re-echoing" of the nature of this fundamental reality in instances of Dionysian art, as Nietzsche goes on alternately to put the point. In terms of this metaphor, however, such art is no less a "transfiguring echo-chamber" than Apollinian art is a "transfiguring mirror," for the artistic "re-echoing" does not stand in the same near-immediate relation of identity to this "primal unity" as does the more basic Dionysian phenomenon of intoxication, but rather comes back in an altered form, the creative production of which involves "the greatest exaltation of all [human] symbolic faculties."

Thus, Nietzsche goes on to say, "the essence of nature is now to be expressed symbolically; we need a new world of symbols" (BT 2)—and it is this "new world of symbols" that constitutes both the language and the substance of Dionysian art. The issue is somewhat confused by Nietzsche's use of the term Dionysian to refer to the "primal unity" itself ("the Dionysian basic ground of the world," etc.) and also to insight into its nature and the plight of the individual in such a world ("Dionysian wisdom"), as well as to such art, which draws upon our "symbolic powers" and thereby transfigures even while giving expression to the former. But, once again, it must be borne in mind that for Nietzsche, like other art forms, "it belongs to art at all" only insofar as it "participates fully in this metaphysical intention of art to transfigure" (BT 24). For he believes that we could not endure the full glare of an unmediated encounter with the world's essential nature, and that it is only *as transfigured* through its expression in the entrancing symbolic forms of the Dionysian arts that a nondestructive identification with it is possible.

In short, in these arts the world's nature is expressed in a form that attracts rather than repels us—a symbolic form, the attractiveness of which is bound up with the transfiguration involved in this symbolization and made possible by the character of the "new world of symbols" under consideration. Dionysian art does not have the character of a "veil of illusion" radically different from the reality of nature and "placed alongside it for its overcoming," as does Apollinian art for Nietzsche. Yet it does have a somewhat analogous character and function in that it expresses the reality of nature in a manner enabling us to overcome our abhorrence of it and derive "joy in existence" from identification with it, by means of a quasi-"illusory" medium of transfiguring symbolic forms.

The most fundamental and crucial ideas Nietzsche seeks to advance in this connection are that art is essentially not representational (or imitative) with respect to the world either as we perceive it or as it is apprehended in cognition, but rather that it is transfigurative; that, on the other hand, the transfigurations it involves are more than mere pleasing expressions of emotions or fancies in sensuous form; and that they are not all of the same kind. One does not have to subscribe to the version of the appearance/reality distinction that he accepts here (but later rejects), or to his contention that art is the "highest task and truly metaphysical activity of this life," or to his conviction that it has the purpose of performing the kind of "overcoming" function he describes in relation to the "terror and horror of existence" to follow him this far—and farther still.

IV

Nietzsche takes the notions of transfiguration and illusion to apply not only to works of Apollinian and Dionysian art conceived as objects of aesthetic experience, but also to the subjects of such experience insofar as they become absorbed in them. The entire significance of art is missed, for him, if one does not recognize that the consciousness of those experiencing these art forms undergoes a transformation analogous to that occurring in their creation—and that, with this transformation, the experiencing subject's very psychological identity is in a sense transfigured, even if only temporarily, and in a way that does not alter the basic reality of one's human nature and existence in the world. The latter circumstance is what renders it appropriate to speak of illusion here—though Nietzsche is no less concerned to indicate the value of such illusion "for life" than he is to point out its illusory character.

The subjective transformation associated with the objective one involved in the creation of the work of art, however, has a very different character in the two general sorts of cases under consideration. Thus Nietzsche contends that they constitute two fundamentally distinct stratagems by means of which "the insatiable will" at the heart of nature conspires to "detain its creatures in life and compel them to live on" (BT 18). He discusses them in terms of what occurs in the case of the "Dionysian man" and in the case of the "Apollinian man," and for the sake of convenience I shall follow him in this—with the understanding, however, that these expressions refer to contrasting types of psychological states rather than to distinct groups of human beings.

The Dionysian does not exchange his physiological and sociocultural identity and situation in the world for another, or escape them altogether, in the course of the "destruction of the *principium individuationis*" of which Nietzsche speaks. As an experiential phenomenon, however, this destruction is very real: the Dionysian is psychologically transformed into one for whom the only reality of which he is aware—and therefore that with which he himself identifies—is that which is expressed in the movements, tonalities, or other symbolic forms in which he is immersed. Thus Nietzsche contends that, through the experience of Dionysian art, "we are really for a brief moment primordial being itself, feeling its raging desire for existence and joy in existence; the struggle, the pain, the destruction of phenomena, now appear necessary for us" (BT 17). As one in a state of intoxication may be said (quite appropriately, even if only psychologically) not to "be oneself," one immersed in the surge and flow of an instance of this type of aesthetic experience "loses oneself" in it. One's consciousness is caught up in it and one's self-consciousness is altered accordingly, whether this transformation manifests itself behaviorally in an enraptured cessation of ordinary activity, in outward inaction masking inward tumult, or in entrance into overt participation in the event as well. Such experience is of being blissful, but also in the original and literal sense of the term *ekstasis*, which denotes a standing out from beside or beyond oneself.

To the extent that one's own existence may be conceived as being actually a moment of the reality expressed in Dionysian art and with which one thus comes to feel at one through its mediation, this transformation may be said to have the significance of a dispelling of the illusion involved in one's ordinary consciousness of oneself as something distinct from it and to be characterized in other terms. But, to the extent that such experience leads one to identify oneself so completely with this reality that one feels oneself to enjoy even those of its features that actually characterize it only as a whole, with which one is not truly identical, this transformation may also be said to have the significance of the fostering of another, different illusion. Thus Nietzsche suggests that, here no less than in the case of Apollinian art, we are dealing with a way in which, "by means of an illusion," life conspires "to detain its creatures in existence" despite the harshness of the conditions it imposes upon them—in this instance, through "the metaphysical comfort that beneath the whirl of phenomena eternal life flows on indestructibly" (BT 18).

The illusion in question is not that "life flows on indestructibly" despite the ephemerality of phenomena—for it does. We may be "comforted" (and more) through the transformation of our psychological identity enabling us to achieve a sense of unity with this indestructible and inexhaustible underlying reality, of which we are truly manifestations. But, while such comfort may be termed metaphysical, this transfiguration is not, for it leaves our actual status in the world unchanged and the basic conditions of our human existence unaltered—as we discover that when the moment passes the Dionysian aesthetic experience comes to an end, and we "return to ourselves," our psychological identities transformed back again into their original non-Dionysian state. The only enduring comfort is the recollection of the rapture of the Dionysian experience and the knowledge that it remains available to us. But a profound danger attends this kind of "overcoming," of which Nietzsche is acutely aware: the letdown may be great, the disparity between Dionysian states and ordinary life distressing, the illusion discerned, and its recognition found disconcerting—and thus the long-term effect of such experience may be detrimental rather than conducive to life (BT 7). It is for this reason, more than any other, that Nietzsche has reservations about Dionysian art and experience generally, despite the evident fascination they have for him.

Nietzsche's Apollinian type constitutes a very different case, being the product of quite another kind of psychological transformation. As in the previous case, this transcendence is held to be not only merely temporary but also fundamentally illusory, and the resulting transformation only psychological rather than genuinely ontological. Here, too, Nietzsche sees the cunning hand of nature at work, in this instance "detaining its creatures in life" through rendering the Apollinian "ensnared by art's seductive veil of beauty fluttering before his eyes" (BT 18).

The realm of Apollinian art is a kind of "dream world, an Olympian *middle world* of art" (BT 3) that is neither the everyday world nor the underlying world of will, but rather a created world by means of which the latter is "veiled and withdrawn from sight" and the former is supplanted as the focus of concern. And entrance into this world is possible, Nietzsche holds, only for a kind of dreamer, or Olympian spectator, detached from the kinds of involvements and concerns that both characterize the everyday world and endow us with our ordinary psychological identities. Indeed, it requires that one *become* such a "pure spectator"—or rather, that the images presented are such that they induce a kind of contemplative consciousness through which one's psychological identity is transformed into that of such a subject. They stand outside of time and change, need and strife; and to become absorbed in them is for Nietzsche to have one's consciousness comparably transformed. If, in the experience of Dionysian art, one is enraptured, one may be said here to be entranced. And, in a state of such entrancement, it is as if one had become a part of this world of images—not as one of them, but as a placeless, disembodied center of awareness, a subject fit for such objects and answering to their nature.

While Apollinian art involves "the arousing of delight in beautiful forms," this is not to be construed merely in the sense of providing us with pleasure, but rather in terms of an overcoming of the distress associated with our human condition through what is felt to be a kind of redemption from it. "Here Apollo overcomes the suffering of the individual by the radiant glorification of the *eternity of the phenomenon*; here beauty triumphs over the suffering inherent in life" (BT 16). For the Apollinian "is absorbed in the pure contemplation of images" (BT 5), the beauty of which strongly attracts us and brings us under their spell, causing us to banish all else from our minds and seemingly to become nothing but the delighted awareness of them. Our delight is genuine, and our psychological transformation real— even though on a more fundamental level both the objects of such consciousness and this self-consciousness are merely two aspects of the Apollinian illusion, which is but "one of those illusions which nature so frequently employs to achieve her own ends" (BT 3).

This illusion, however, is by no means as insubstantial as the term might seem to suggest. One indication of this, on Nietzsche's account, is the very fact that it is powerful enough to enable "nature" to achieve its end of "seducing one to a continuation of life" by means of it (BT 3). And if it is the case, as Nietzsche claims in this same sentence, that Apollinian art is thus "called into being, as the complement and consummation of existence," it follows that it is no *mere* illusion that leaves the reality of human life unaffected. It does not fundamentally alter the human condition. But, if it is in some significant sense the "consummation of existence," it may be truly said to effect a significant transformation of "existence"—or at least that portion of it that is the reality of human life. Art is indeed our creation; but we also are (or at least can be) recreated or transfigured by art.

The kind of experience and spirituality that become attainable in relation to the idealized images of Apollinian art may not constitute an elevation of those who attain to them entirely beyond the reach of the entanglements of ordinary life and the deeper harsh realities of existence in this world. Yet they do render the existence of those attaining to them qualitatively different from that of those who remain entirely immersed in the quotidian, or who further succeed only in finding occasional respite through Dionysian experience. It is Nietzsche's appreciation of the magnitude of this qualitative difference that accounts for his celebration of the achievement of the archaic Greeks in their creation of Apollinian art, both plastic and epic.

V

Nietzsche conceives tragic art to be no less Apollinian than Dionysian in origin and nature. At the very outset of the book he advances this contention with respect to the archetype of it, asserting that "by a metaphysical miracle of the Hellenic 'will,'" the "tendencies" associated with each "appear coupled with each other, and through this coupling ultimately generate an equally Dionysian and Apollinian form of art—Attic tragedy" (BT 1). The burden of his entire discussion of tragedy is that its emergence presupposed not only the prior development of the art of Dionysian transfiguration, but also the *retransfiguration* of the latter under the influence of the likewise previously developed art of Apollinian transfiguration.

The birth of tragedy for Nietzsche was an event of the greatest actual and possible future significance. For it did not merely involve the appearance of a qualitatively new art form, thus opening another chapter in the development of art. It also made possible a further qualitative transformation of human life, which he conceives to have been and to be of far greater moment than is generally recognized. The possibility of tragic art did not end with the expiration of Attic (Greek) tragedy, and is not wedded to the dramatic form of the works produced by the classical tragedians. Nor is Nietzsche here thinking in addition merely of Elizabethan tragic drama, together with the tragic opera of his own time, but rather of what he characterizes more generally as *tragic myth*.

Moreover, and even more importantly, he does not conceive of tragic art as a phenomenon the significance of which is confined to but a single sphere of human experience and cultural life. Rather, he views it as the potential foundation and guiding force of an entire form of culture and human existence, which alone is capable of filling the void left by the collapse of "optimistic" life-sustaining myths (both religious and philosophical-scientific).

And he looks to it to assume anew the function of "making life possible and worth living," which neither Apollinian nor Dionysian art as such is capable any longer of performing. The former may continue to entrance and delight us, and the latter to enrapture and excite us, and both may continue to transport and transform us in their respective fashions—but the power of the illusions they involve to sustain us has been lost.

In this connection it is both crucial and illuminating to bear in mind the passage cited earlier from the last section of the book, in which Nietzsche contends (clearly with tragic art specifically in mind) that, with respect to the basic character of the world and of existence in it, "not one whit more may enter the consciousness of the human individual than can be overcome again by [the] Apollinian power of transfiguration" (BT 25). To be able to endure the awareness of these stark realities of which we are capable and which cannot in the long run be prevented from emerging, and to be able further to embrace and affirm life despite the attainment of such an awareness, a transformation of this consciousness is necessary. In its starkest, simplest and most vivid form, according to Nietzsche, it would be overwhelmingly horrible, "nauseating," paralyzing and unendurable, save in temporary transports of Dionysian ecstatic self-transcendence that cannot be sustained and so constitute no adequate long-term recourse.

For Nietzsche, tragic art alone is truly equal to this task. As has been seen, he holds that it enables us to experience the terrible not as merely terrible, but rather as sublime; and that it achieves something akin to a Dionysian effect upon us, which however is not identical with it—for it does not take the kind of life-endangering toll that Dionysian intoxication does, inducing an experiential state that differs as significantly from such intoxication as it does from Apollinian dreaming. In the long run it has the character of a tonic rather than a depressant; its aftermath is held to be *exhilaration*, rather than either the overall exhaustion that follows upon Dionysian excitement or the exasperation that Apollinian exaltation leaves in its train. And, considered more immediately, it might be said to *enthrall*, rather than to entrance or enrapture. So to describe what tragic art does is not to give an analysis of it; but Nietzsche's conception of its nature requires to be comprehended in light of this understanding of its effects.

Tragic art too, for Nietzsche, may be said to constitute a kind of "transfiguring mirror." It is a mirror, however, in which we see reflected neither "appearances" idealizingly transfigured nor the character of the reality underlying them symbolically expressed. We are confronted instead with "images of life"—reflections of the human condition (which is also our own) highlighting both the individuation it involves and the fate bound up with the latter in a world in which all individual existence is ephemeral, harsh, and ridden with strife and suffering. What we encounter, however, is not a stark and brutally "realistic" portrayal of this condition as such. We see it in transfigured form—even though this transfiguration of it does not consist in its radical transmutation into a merely imaginary idealized condition *contrasting* to the actual human condition on these counts. And it likewise does not involve the effective obliteration of the salient features of human life through the diversion of attention from the entire domain of individuation to the collective, the impersonal, the merely vital, and the enduring aspects of life underlying it. Rather, the kind of transfiguration occurring here is one that pertains to our perception of individual human existence—*as* existence that is individual rather than merely a part of an inexhaustible and indestructible flow of life, and that is human rather than above and beyond the conditions to which human beings are subject.

This transfiguration pertains first to the character of the dramatic figures with which we are confronted—or, rather, it comes about first in the context of our confrontation with them, but it does not remain confined to this encounter, serving rather to alter our apprehension of the human condition more generally. It is in this sense above all that tragic art may be said to serve as a transfiguring mirror: it works a transformation upon our consciousness of the human reality that is also our own, at the same time as it reflects that reality for us to behold.

Tragic art presents us neither with an ideal to be admired and emulated nor with an avenue by means of which to escape all thought of the hard realities of life. The latter are very much in evidence, and the tragic figure caught up in them is one with whom, as an individual, we empathize—but with whom, as a character, we do not identify. Yet the manner of presentation of such figures, which renders them tragic and not merely pathetic, does much more than merely purge us of our self-directed feelings of fear and pity through an empathic discharge. It can have a powerful positive impact upon the way in which we perceive our human condition and experience the reality of our own lives, by revealing them to us in a very different light from that in which we would otherwise tend to view them. The point might be put by saying that the tragic artist, not through the persona of the tragic figure per se but in the larger structure of the tragic drama, interposes a medium between us and the reality of human existence that does more than simply give expression to the latter; for the medium further shapes and colors our consciousness of reality and is able to help us attain an affirmative attitude toward it precisely by virtue of doing so.

In short, tragic art provides us with a way of apprehending this reality that enables us to come to terms with it—and not only to endure but also to affirm what we thereby see, as we thereby learn to see it. In this way it resembles Dionysian art. And for Nietzsche this similarity of tragic art to the Dionysian arts is by no means merely fortuitous. In tragic myth, as in music and dance, something transcending mere appearances is symbolically expressed—and in being so expressed it is transformed for our consciousness. Here, however, the symbolic forms employed are not primarily those characteristic of these Dionysian art forms, but rather are drawn from the initially nonsymbolic domain of Apollinian art.

Life regarded as tragic is no longer life seen as merely wretched and pathetic; and the "displeasure" associated with "the weight and burden of existence" is overshadowed and forgotten when the latter takes on the aspect of tragic fate rather than mere senseless suffering and annihilation. The fate of tragic figures, when nobly met rather than basely suffered, enhances rather than detracts from their stature, and these figures serve as a symbolic medium through which individual existence more generally is enhanced for us. It is in these terms that the exquisite stimulant distinctively characteristic of tragic art is to be conceived, even though it is strongly supplemented by the presence of that which is characteristic of Dionysian art as well.

The unique achievement of tragic art is thus held to be that it fundamentally alters our apprehension of human existence and the circumstances associated with it, which result in the suffering and destruction of even such extraordinary figures as the central characters of tragic drama and myth. Through it, these circumstances cease to stand as *objections* to human life and its worth and emerge instead as features of it that—as part of the larger whole human lives are and can be—actually contribute to its overall significance and attractiveness. And thus, Nietzsche suggests, it serves to bring it about that existence can "seem justified" *aesthetically*—"only as an aesthetic phenomenon" (BT 24). Nietzsche's use of the term "only" here is highly important, for his general point is that it is *only* in this way, in the last analysis, that it is possible for us to find human life and our own existence endurable and worthwhile without recourse to illusions that radically misrepresent the actual nature of our human reality and the world more generally.

VI

As has been observed in connection with Apollinian and Dionysian art, there is for Nietzsche a significant sense in which all images, like appearances more generally, are to be considered illusory. And so, for that matter, are all symbols, for neither may be supposed to correspond even approximately, let alone exactly, to the actual nature of reality. No relation of resemblance obtains between these sorts of experiential phenomena and the constitution of this underlying reality itself; the difference is qualitative, and profound. But it is by no means only in this very basic (and relatively uninteresting) respect that Nietzsche takes tragic art too to involve the generation of illusion.

It has already been observed that this illusion centers on the "image of life" with which we are confronted in the tragic figure. While such figures are not simply "realistically" drawn, or fictitious but true-to-life individuals, or representatives of the elemental characteristics of "Dionysian universality" (as is the chorus), they are not mere Apollinian beautiful illusions either. Like Apollinian idealized images, however, they constitute something on the order of a "supplement of the reality of nature," and of that of ordinary human existence along with it, "placed beside it for its overcoming." The "core of life they contain" is the same as our own, but this core is artistically transformed into images of life expressing possibilities that are more human than mere glorious appearances, and yet that differ markedly from the commonplace, in ways moreover answering to no predetermined human essence or foreordained human ideal. They thus can in no sense be said to confront us with the "truth" of human existence. And, since what they confront us with is something other than truth, they may be said to present us with a kind of illusion. It is in this sense that Nietzsche's remarks to this effect are to be understood.

Yet this illusion is no *mere* illusion, and the transformed consciousness of ourselves that emerges when we view our own lives in the light of the manner of those of these tragic figures is not *merely* illusory, for the creations in which they consist are not distorted or erroneous representations of something that has a fixed and immutable character and cannot be otherwise. And they also are not simply imaginary substitutes temporarily usurping a position in our consciousness that is normally and more properly occupied by our ordinary conception of our own mundane reality. Rather, they are symbols of *human possibility*. And as such they serve to carry us beyond the mere acknowledgment of intractable aspects of the human condition, enabling us to discern ways in which the latter may be confronted and transformed into occasions for the endowment of life with grandeur and dignity.

By means of these symbols, human life thus may come to take on an aesthetic significance sufficing to overcome the distressing character of its harsh basic features. It stands revealed as a potentially aesthetic phenomenon, "justifiable" accordingly in our estimation even in the face of its hardest circumstances. And of paramount importance for Nietzsche is the fact that tragic art works this feat in a non-Apollinian way; it does not confine this perception of the tragic figures themselves, while precluding its application to our lives. These figures stand as symbols serving to facilitate our apprehension of the possibilities they express, together with "the core of life they contain," *as our own*—and so to alter the aspect of our own lives.

To say that this is all illusion, as Nietzsche does, is neither to deny the reality of this alteration nor to downplay its significance. Rather, it is to make the point that our lives thus acquire an experiential character that is no part of their fundamental objective nature, and that this occurs through the transforming mediation of created images enabling us to discern aesthetic significance in human existence—notwithstanding that its basic circumstances warrant the attribution to it of no significance whatsoever.

What is at issue here, once again, is the "aesthetic justification" not simply of the world generally, but also (and more importantly) of human existence, as we do and must live it. And this is something that presupposes the super-session of Dionysian as well as Apollinian (and also ordinary) conscious-ness. Tragic art is held to be capable of accomplishing this result only by virtue of the "fraternal union of Apollo and Dionysus" occurring in it, not by a victory of the latter over the former. The quasi-Apollinian tragic figure may be "annihilated," but the entire Apollinian element is not. And while "the Dionysian predominates" in "the total effect of the tragedy" (BT 21), it does not emerge in sole possession of the field. If human existence is to be "justified" *despite* its inescapable harsh conditions and fate, it cannot be exhibited in such a way that only the suffering and destruction it involves are made to stand as its final truth, with all aesthetically justifying character-istics being reserved to the "primordial unity" that flows on beneath the surface of individuation and appearance.

The consciousness of human existence and of ourselves that Nietzsche terms "tragic" is neither purely Apollinian nor merely Dionysian, for the tragic myth in accordance with which it is shaped places this existence we share in a new and different light. A new way of seeing it becomes possible, in that our relation to the reality that is at once the ground and the abyss in our existence comes to be regarded as amenable to Apollinian transform-ation. Here our own existence as individuals is not something to which it is necessary to be oblivious to experience aesthetic enjoyment, as in the cases of Apollinian delight and Dionysian rapture in their separate and more basic aesthetic forms. Rather, human life itself becomes the focus of a kind of aesthetic satisfaction identical with neither but related to both, through its treatment in a way that brings our capacity for responses of both sorts into play in relation to it. To be sure, the underlying character of the world itself and of the human condition is not thereby altered, but the aspect of human existence is, even while it is apprehended against the background of this Dionysian reality.

In a sense, tragic art may thus be said to accomplish the Apollinianization of the Dionysian, in our consciousness of the latter if not also in its actual nature. But it may perhaps more appropriately be said to accomplish a complex and radical transformation of something else, in a less one-sided manner: the aspect of our human existence, at once along partly Apollinian and partly Dionysian lines. What is thus transformed is not tragedy, for the accomplishment of tragic art is not the transformation of tragedy into something else. Tragedy, rather, is the *issue* of this artistic transformation, through which existence comes to be experienced as tragic. This is indeed an artistic accomplishment, since tragedy no less than beauty may be said to exist only in the eye of the beholder, whose sensibility has been formed and cultivated by art. It is no brute fact of human existence, but rather an acquired aspect it may come to bear through the transfiguring agency of the tragic artist.

It is in this way that the tragic myth comes to be endowed with what Nietzsche terms its "intense and convincing metaphysical significance" (BT 21)—and also its most profoundly illusory character, for it leads us to feel something to be the deepest and highest "truth" of human existence—the tragic character it is capable of coming to bear, with all the sublimity and majesty devolving upon it therefrom—which is no part of either its fundamental nature or any intrinsic essence legitimately attributable to it. We are led to view life as though it were a means to the end of actualizing the aesthetic values associated with human existence as it is revealed in the transfiguring mirror of tragic myth.

VII

In BT, Nietzsche placed his hope for a revitalization of Western civilization—in the face of the collapse of both otherworldly religiousness and rationalistic-scientific optimism—in a reemergence of a tragic sense of life. But, as he readily acknowledged, such a view of life cannot be sustained in the absence of tragic myth and an acceptance of the understanding of human existence associated with some instance of it. It is for this reason that he devoted so much discussion in this work to the importance of myth and to the need for a new and compelling form of tragic myth in the modern Western world.

Nietzsche obviously thought, when he wrote BT, that Wagner was well on the way to accomplishing the task he thus envisioned. The details of his discussion of this and related matters, however, are of relatively little intrinsic interest—especially since he soon after lost his enthusiasm for

Wagner and abandoned his commitment to the ultimacy and indispens-ability of that form of art he associates here with tragic myth. He further seems to have become convinced that art generally has a significance in relation to life and that it also has a variety of features to which his analysis of it in BT does not do justice. In any event, he subsequently approached the arts somewhat differently, placing less emphasis upon differences between the various art forms and the kinds of experience associated with them and concerning himself more with the phenomenon of artistic creativity generally.

Although Nietzsche devoted at least some (and often considerable) atten-tion to art in nearly all of his later writings, however, he never again sub-jected it to a comparably comprehensive, intensive, and sustained analysis or treated it with a similar breadth of vision. He subsequently deepened and modified his understanding of art in certain important ways and recast his views with respect to it. Yet he retained most of the fundamental notions in terms of which he interprets it in BT, in one form or another, and continued to give them central roles in his subsequent discussions—not only of art, but also of human life, and of what he came to call its "enhancement"—and the "overcoming of nihilism" along with it. And he not only heralded his *Thus Spoke Zarathustra* at the conclusion of the original edition of *The Gay Science* with the words "*Incipit tragödie*" (GS 342), but also continued to conjoin the motifs of art, tragedy, and the affirmation and enhancement of life to the end. However much his thinking changed, he never abandoned his early conviction of their profound interconnection.

8

NIETZSCHE: THE REVALUATION OF VALUES

PHILIPPA FOOT

> This problem of the *value* of pity and of the morality of pity . . . seems
> at first sight to be merely something detached, an isolated question
> mark; but whoever sticks with it and *learns* how to ask questions here
> will experience what I experienced—a tremendous new prospect opens
> up for him, a new possibility comes over him like a vertigo, every kind
> of mistrust, suspicion, fear leaps up, his belief in morality, in all moral-
> ity, falters—finally a new demand becomes audible . . . we need a *cri-
> tique* of moral values, *the value of these values themselves must first be
> called in question* . . .
>
> (GM, Preface, 6)[1]

What Nietzsche expresses here, his sense of the fearful strangeness of his
thoughts, is something intensely felt and not unfitting given the facts of the
case. For in his lonely, highly daring mental voyage he had come to a view of
life which was quite unlike that of any of his contemporaries, and which
brought him to challenge ways of thought and behaviour centuries old. He
was ready, he said, to call in question Christian morality and even all morality, and when he had questioned he condemned. Yet Nietzsche saw as clearly
as anyone that morality could fascinate and inspire. "Thou shalt" he said is
the name of a great dragon "sparkling like gold" (Z I, "On the Three Metamorphoses", 10). He knew that what he was doing was almost unthinkable;
he was branding as evil what seemed most certainly good.

Now one would expect that such a challenge from an undoubted genius
must either be defeated or else shake the world. But neither of these things
have happened. It is true that Nietzsche's theories (or a travesty of them)
played a brief and inglorious part on the world's stage when he was pro-
claimed as a prophet by the Nazis, but by and large he has neither been
accepted nor refuted, and this seems a remarkable fact. How is it, one may
ask, that philosophers today do not even try to refute Nietzsche, and seem to

From Philippa Foot, "Nietzsche: The Revaluation of Values", in R. C. Solomon (ed.), *Nietzsche:
A Collection of Critical Essays* (Garden City, NY: Anchor Books, 1973), 156–68.

[1] Translations, unless otherwise stated, by Walter Kaufmann.

feel morality as firm as ever under their feet? Why do we not argue with him as we argue with other philosophers of the past? Part of the answer seems to be that a confrontation with Nietzsche is a difficult thing to arrange. We find it hard to know where we could meet him because of the intrinsically puzzling nature of a project such as his. Nietzsche had demanded a critique of moral values and announced that he was calling in question "the value of these values themselves". But how can one value values? The idea of such a thing is enough to make one's head spin. It is, therefore, with a rueful sense of the difficulties that I shall try, in this essay, to confront Nietzsche, or at least to help to prepare the ground for a confrontation.

A problem arises at the outset. In the passage I quoted he spoke of the morality of pity but also of "all morality". Which shall we take his target to be? I shall consider first Nietzsche's special objection to Christian morality, with its teaching of the virtues of humility and compassion, and its rejection of "the world".

Nietzsche wanted to show Christian morality as a "slave morality" rooted not in anything fine or admirable but rather in weakness, fear, and malice: these were its origins and to these origins its present nature conformed. In this morality the good man is the humble and compassionate man, the one who is not to be feared. But originally, he insists, it was quite otherwise. In the beginning it was the strong, noble, privileged aristocrat who called himself good, and called those who lacked his own qualities bad. These old concepts were turned on their heads when the perspective of the weak prevailed. For then the contrast of what was good and bad (*schlecht*) gave way to the contrast between what was good and evil (*böse*); the weak branded those they feared evil, and praised the "propitiatory" qualities natural to men like themselves who were incapable of aggression. Where the old valuation had been positive the new was negative; the "members of the herd" must first brand the enemies they feared as evil before they could see themselves as good. Moreover Nietzsche detects a large amount of malice under the professions of Christian humility and goodwill. When the weak call the strong evil the move is not merely defensive; it is also an expression of that peculiar malice which Nietzsche referred to as *ressentiment*. Those who cultivate humility and the other propitiatory virtues to cloak their weakness nourish an envious resentment against those stronger than themselves. They want revenge for their inferiority and have a deep desire to humiliate and harm. The wish to punish seems to Nietzsche one of the most evident signs of this hidden malice, and he sees the idea of free will, and accountability, as invented by those who desired to inflict punishment. Nor is punishment always directed outward; the man of self-sacrificing virtue is resentful and venomous also towards himself. "But thus I counsel you, my friends:

Mistrust all in whom the impulse to punish is powerful" (Z II, "On the Tarantulas").

The man professing Christian virtues is, Nietzsche insists, a sick individual, deeply malicious to himself and others. He has been taught to reject life as it is, to despise his own sensuality, and to torment himself and others in the name of his ideals. Even these ideals are inimical to health, since what is preached is compassion, and this Nietzsche sees as a kind of sickness in itself. Pity, he says, is a *temptation* to be resisted at all costs; he thinks of it as a kind of poison to the compassionate man, who becomes infected by the sufferings of others. "The suffering of others infects us, pity is an infection" (WP 368).[2] Nor does he believe that pity relieves suffering. Now and then it may do so, but more often the object of our compassion suffers from our intervention in his affairs. He suffers first from the fact that we are helping him. "Having seen the sufferer suffer, I was ashamed for the sake of his shame; and when I helped him I transgressed grievously against his pride" (Z II, "On the Pitying"). "It seems to me that a human being with the very best of intentions can do immeasurable harm, if he is immodest enough to wish to profit those whose spirit and will are concealed from him . . ." wrote Nietzsche in a letter to his sister in 1885.[3] Nor did Nietzsche think that good motives lay behind most charitable acts. Charitable and helpful people "dispose of the needy as of possessions. . . . One finds them jealous if one crosses or anticipates them when they want to help" (BGE 194). Concern for others often betrayed a man's dissatisfaction with himself; men who were dull tried to cheer themselves up with the sight of their neighbour's misfortunes, while those who had a low opinion of themselves would try to buy back a better opinion from those on whom they had conferred a benefit. Nietzsche saw the preoccupation with others as an evasion, and a sign of spiritual ill-health; what is important is to love oneself "so that one can bear to be with oneself and need not roam" (Z III, "On the Spirit of Gravity", 2). The man who loves himself will be the one who most truly benefits others; in his own rejoicing he will forget how to contrive pain for them.

What shall we say of Nietzsche's attack on Christian morality as it has so far been described? With what weapons is he attacking, or on what ground? Several different lines of attack can be discerned. In the first place he is suggesting that what is praised as Christian virtue is largely a sham, and that true goodwill would be produced not by teaching the morality of compassion but rather by encouraging "a healthy egoism". Secondly he is saying that judged by its own aims this morality is bad. Men suffer pity as a

---

[2] Translation by Walter Kaufmann and R. J. Hollingdale.
[3] Quoted in *The Portable Nietzsche*, ed. Walter Kaufmann (New York: Viking, 1956), 441.

sickness, and by their pity they do more harm than good. Each of these charges would be damaging if it could be shown to be supported by the facts. But what of Nietzsche's account of the origins of Christian morality, and his insistence that it represents the ascendancy of the weak over the strong? If proved would this be damaging or not? Could one reply that virtues such as compassion and justice are indeed of special interest to those liable to misfortune and vulnerable to oppression, and that they are none the worse for that? Such a reply would miss the point of Nietzsche's attack. He is trying to show the "good and virtuous" as representatives of a mean and base section of mankind, as fawning, timid, incapable people who express in hidden form the malice they are afraid to express openly. He wants to suggest that they are both despicable and dislikable, and if he could really do this he would have struck a most telling blow. For how could a society which came to see things in Nietzsche's fashion have a morality of this kind? It is not, after all, enough for a moral system that particular actions should be rewarded or punished as in a system of laws. If a certain man is to be seen as a good man, and certain actions as good actions, then he and they must be generally esteemed. And no one is esteemed if he is the object of scorn and dislike. If Nietzsche could show that we have no reason either to admire the man of Christian virtue or to be grateful to him, he would have knocked away a psychological base without which this morality cannot stand.

In representing Christian morality as the weapon used by the weak to defend and exalt themselves Nietzsche was trying to show it and them in a disagreeable light. But it was much more important to him to show that in favouring the weak at the expense of the strong Christianity was the most powerful of the forces making for the degeneration of the human race. "Nothing has preoccupied me more profoundly than the problem of decadence" he wrote (CW, Preface). And he saw as decadent the type of man encouraged by Christian teaching, describing him as an accommodating, industrious, gregarious individual who was mediocre, and dull. Against this portrait he set that of a stronger "higher" type of individual, bold, independent, and ready to say "yes" to life. Such a man would not be much concerned about suffering, whether his own or that of others. Among his equals he would behave with restraint; to the weak he might be dangerous, but if he harmed them it would be rather from disregard than from malice. The weak man, however, is afraid of suffering for himself and preoccupied with the misfortunes of others. He tries to build himself a safe life which shall not require too much exertion. "One has one's little pleasure for the day and one's little pleasure for the night: but one has a regard for health" (Z I, "Zarathustra's Prologue", 5). He preaches the morality of compassion, though filled with secret ill will towards others.

Much controversy has surrounded Nietzsche's writings on the "higher" and "lower" types of man. Is he to be taken as glorifying the cruel tyrant, the "beast of prey", or did he have some less repulsive ideal? The answer seems to be neither an unqualified yes nor an unqualified no. There is no doubt that in the comparison of men he preferred as the more healthy type "even Caesare Borgia" to the mediocre submissive modern man. And there are some embarrassingly awful passages in which he speaks of the superior man's ruthlessness towards his inferiors as if it could be seen as something merely pranksome. But the cruel man is certainly not his ideal, and there are some to whom he refuses to preach egoism at all.

There are the terrible ones who carry around within themselves the beast of prey and have no choice but lust or self-laceration. And even their lust is still self-laceration. They have not even become human beings yet, these terrible ones: let them preach renunciation of life and pass away themselves! (Z I, "On the Preachers of Death")

In Nietzsche's eyes the important distinction was that of the "ascending" and "descending" types of men. One great question was to be asked about the history of any race: did it represent decline or ascent? And each individual should be scrutinized "to see whether he represents the ascending or the descending line of life" (TI IX. 33). Nietzsche saw himself as the one, the only one, who saw clearly the contrast between ascending and declining mankind. "I have a subtler sense of smell for the signs of ascent and decline than any other human being before me; I am the teacher *par excellence* for this . . ." (EH I. 1). It was in this context that he preached egoism to the strong:

Every individual consists of the whole course of evolution. . . . If he represents the ascending course of mankind, then his value is in fact extraordinary; and extreme care may be taken over the preservation and promotion of his development. (It is concern for the future promised him that gives the well-constituted individual such an extraordinary right to egoism.) If he represents the descending course, decay, chronic sickening, then he has little value: and the first demand of fairness is for him to take as little space, force, and sunshine as possible away from the well-constituted. (WP 373)

And it was in this context that Nietzsche spoke least ambiguously about the fate he envisaged for the weak. "The weak and the failures shall perish: first principle of *our* love of man" (A 2).

It was no wonder then that Nietzsche had a special hatred of Christianity. He saw it as the religion of the weak designed for their protection and glorification, and he saw it as the most powerful influence for decadence and decline. Above all he thought Christian morality harmful to the stronger and healthier type of man. By preserving the incapable and "misbegotten", and by insisting that they be the object of compassionate attention, it would cause even the strong to be infected with gloom and nihilism. And even more importantly it would lead the "higher" type of man to mistrust his own nature, and would create conditions in which it was impossible for him to find his health. To require a peaceable benevolence from such a man, to preach humility and pity to him, is necessarily to injure him.

To demand of strength that it should *not* express itself as strength, that it should *not* be a desire to overcome, a desire to throw down, a desire to become master, a thirst for enemies and resistances and triumphs, is just as absurd as to demand of weakness that it should express itself as strength. (GM I. 13)

The strong man condemned by society for doing what his nature demands will suffer from guilt and self-hatred, and may well be turned into a criminal.

The criminal type is the type of the strong human being under unfavourable circumstances: a strong human being made sick. . . . His *virtues* are ostracized by society; the most vivid drives with which he is endowed soon grow together with the depressing affects—with suspicion, fear and dishonour. (TI IX. 45)

Nietzsche does not shrink from the conclusion that for some men ruthlessness may be the condition of health. It is the counterpart of his belief that "everything evil, terrible, tyrannical in man, everything in him that is kin to beasts of prey and serpents, serves the enhancement of the species 'man' as much as its opposite does" (BGE 44). If God is dead nothing guarantees that evil may not be the condition of good.

If . . . a person should regard even the affects of hatred, envy, covetousness, and the lust to rule as conditions of life, as factors which, fundamentally and essentially, must be present in the general economy of life (and must, therefore, be further enhanced if life is to be further enhanced)—he will suffer from such a view of things as from seasickness. And yet even this hypothesis is far from being the strangest and most painful in this immense and almost new domain of dangerous insights . . . (BGE 23)

It is, then, for the sake of the "higher" man that the values of Christian morality must be abandoned, and it is from this perspective that the revaluation of values takes place. Is it Nietzsche's intention to present us with a clash of interests—the good of the strong against that of the weak? Obviously he has this intention, but just as obviously this is not all that he wants to suggest. A more puzzling aspect of his doctrines comes before us when we remind ourselves of what he says about the *value* of the "higher" type of man. "The problem I pose is . . . what type of men shall be *bred*, shall be *willed*, for being higher in value, worthier of life, more certain of a future" (A 3). And again Nietzsche says: "We have a different faith; to us the democratic movement is . . . a form of the decay, namely the diminution, of man, making him mediocre and *lowering his value*" (BGE 203, italics added). What does he mean when he speaks of the *value* of one type of man as greater than that of another? Nietzsche himself has remarked elsewhere that one can never too carefully consider the question "value for what?" And in these terms one might try to explain what he says about the value of certain men. Perhaps he means that the contribution they make to life in general— by their optimism and fearlessness for instance—makes them *valuable* to us all. Or perhaps he is judging their value by the contribution they make to the future. Are they not a bridge to the superior man who may come in the future—to the *Übermensch*? Neither suggestion tells the whole story, and the second simply shifts the problem. If the "Overman" or "Superman" is the one who gives some men value, this must be because he has value himself. In fact Nietzsche seems to want to say that anyone who is strong, independent, and so on—anyone who fits his description of the higher type of man— is one who *has value* in himself, and we are left with this puzzling idea. Is Nietzsche merely talking nonsense, or can we make sense of the word "value" as it is used here? The answer seems to be that we can. For it does make sense to say that *we value* strong and exceptional individuals, whether or not Nietzsche's picture of these individuals rings true. We do find patterns of reaction to exceptional men that would allow us to see here a valuing rather similar to valuing on aesthetic grounds, even if it is one for which we have no special name. I am thinking of the interest and admiration which is the common attitude to remarkable men of exceptional independence of mind and strength of will. Such men hold our attention, and are often willingly served. When Nietzsche says that what is at stake is whether "the *highest power and splendor* actually possible to the type man" is ever to be attained (GM, Preface, 6) it suggests that he is appealing to our tendency to *admire* certain individuals whom we see as powerful and splendid. He himself even says, in one passage, that "This is at bottom a question of taste and of aesthetics: would it be desirable that the 'most respectable', i.e., most tedious, species of man should survive?" (WP 353). But I think that the passage is untypical, and in any case does not quite describe the facts as they are; if there is an element of respect in the common reaction to strong and remarkable men then the analogy with an aesthetic valuation should not be pressed too far. Perhaps what we should do is simply to suggest a similarity between the way we attribute *value* (aesthetic value) to art objects and the *value* that Nietzsche attributes to a certain kind of man, both resting on a set of common reactions, and on reactions that have much in common.

If this were a correct account of the matter what would we conclude? Would Christian morality, or any other, be vulnerable to Nietzsche's attack? From the comparison with aesthetic values one would say that it might be vulnerable, not because something had been proved against it but because men might come to care more about producing and preserving interesting and "splendid" individuals than about the ends of morality. For consider what the implications would be were it to be discovered that the human race would become physically uglier if morality flourished, or that justice and kindness destroyed beauty of some other kind. This could be considered irrelevant by those for whom moral values were more important than aesthetic values, and one might count as similarly irrelevant the discovery that "the highest power and splendor" was inconsistent with moral ends. Nevertheless morality might decline.

So far we have been considering Nietzsche's objections to one specific moral system—that of Christianity. But he had spoken of an attack on "all morality" and was ready to call himself an immoralist. Does he really have arguments reaching so far? Some of his arguments against Christian morality will be brought also against other moral systems. But with others this will not be possible. Nietzsche could not, for instance, accuse Aristotle of preaching a morality of pity, nor of extolling humility. On the contrary Aristotle's description of the *megalopsychos* who possesses the virtue of greatness of soul and "deserves and claims great things" (*Nicomachean Ethics*, 1123ª15) has much in common with Nietzsche's picture of the "higher" type of man. Let us ask which part of Nietzsche's doctrines could justify us in thinking that morality—all morality—was indeed his target.

Is it relevant, for instance, that Nietzsche had no place in his ideology for the concept of *guilt*? About this he was quite explicit. He saw efforts to make men feel guilty as expressions of malice, and rejected guilt as a reaction to anything he himself would do. "Not to perpetrate cowardice against one's own acts. Not to leave them in the lurch afterwards! The bite of conscience is indecent" (TI I. 10). This seems to prove nothing about whether Nietzsche was, as he said, rejecting all morality; it does not seem impossible that a man should have a morality without accepting guilt as a response to moral failure. It would have been different had he been rejecting the aim of self-discipline, but this Nietzsche never did. Like Callicles in Plato's *Gorgias* Nietzsche objects to the "taming" of the strong man by society, but where Callicles urges that the strong should throw away all restraint and allow their passions full rein Nietzsche was scornful of such a suggestion. He does indeed oppose those who would weaken or even destroy a man's passions, but insists that a strong will belongs only to one who has imposed discipline and unity on his desires. So instead of objecting to morality on the ground that it involves discipline of the passions he says that this is its one merit. "What is essential and estimable in every morality is that it constitutes a long compulsion . . ." (BGE 188). Obviously drawing on his own experience he insists that what is most *natural* is a kind of self-discipline. "Every artist knows how far from any feeling of letting himself go his 'most natural' state is—the free ordering, placing, disposing, giving form in the moment of 'inspiration'—and how strictly and subtly he obeys thousandfold laws precisely then . . ." (BGE 188).

To this extent, then, Nietzsche is at one with the moralist: he is preaching self-discipline and control of the passions. Nevertheless it may be argued that he is rightly to be called an immoralist. It is relevant here to recall that the word "morality" is derived from *mos* with its plural *mores*, and that in its present usage it has not lost this connexion with the *mores*—the rules of behaviour—of a society. For Nietzsche keeps some of his sharpest vituperation for those who try to impose social rules and a code of behaviour which shall be uniform throughout the community. He repeatedly rages against those who preach "Good and evil, good and evil, the same for all".

> Let us finally consider how naive it is altogether to say: "Man *ought* to be such and such!" Reality shows us an enchanting wealth of types, the abundance of a lavish play and change of forms—and some wretched loafer of a moralist comments: "No! Man ought to be different." He even knows what man should be like, this wretched bigot and prig: he paints himself on the wall and comments, "*Ecce homo!*" (TI V. 6)

What will create health in one will enfeeble another, and each man must discover the rule of his own health. To desire that men should be virtuous

> means that they should cease to be distinct
> means that they should begin to resemble one another in their needs and demands—more clearly that they should perish—
> The will to a single morality is thereby proved to be a tyranny over other types by that type whom this single morality fits: it is a destruction or a levelling for the sake of the ruling type (whether to render the others no longer fearsome or to render them useful). (WP 315)

It may be suggested that Nietzsche, even if he will not accept rules of behaviour to be taught to all men, does at least set up ideals of character valid for all. Is it not the case that he refuses to praise anyone who is not, e.g., courageous and independent? This is of course true, and it does give some overlap, both in form and content, between a moral system and a set of teachings such as Nietzsche's. Nevertheless an injunction such as "seek your own health" is so neutral as to actual behaviour as to fail to reestablish the link with social norms. And even injunctions such as this one were not preached to everyone, since Nietzsche thought that many men were simply incapable of health and strength. There were, as we have already seen, cruel monsters to whom Nietzsche would not preach egoism. And as for the members of "the herd" he said that he had no wish to change them; the spirit of the herd should rule within the herd. He is not, he insists, trying to preach his kind of virtue generally: it belongs only to the rare and exceptional man.

These considerations should, I think, incline us to the view that Nietzsche is an immoralist rather than a special kind of moralist. And one is led in the same direction by the fact that he was prepared to throw out rules of justice in the interests of producing a stronger and more splendid type of man. I suggested that this implied a quasi-aesthetic rather than a moral set of values. Morality is necessarily connected with such things as justice and the common good, and it is a conceptual matter that this is so.

Why then should we still have a feeling, as I think we do, that Nietzsche has a great deal in common with the moralist and that he is not simply arguing from an incompatible and irreconcilable point of view? I think that this is due to the fact that in much of his work he can be seen as arguing about the way in which men must live in order to *live well*. It is the common ground between his system and that of traditional and particularly Greek morality that makes us inclined to think that he must be a moralist after all. For while Nietzsche loathed utilitarianism, with its concern for the greatest happiness of the greatest number, and its tendency to take pleasure and the absence of pain as the motive of all human action, he himself was interested, one might say, in the conditions in which men—at least some men—would flourish. The issue is hard to get clear because Nietzsche, as well as introducing quasi-aesthetic criteria which are irrelevant in this context, also appeals to an idea of human good that is opposed to that of his opponents, and there is no concept that has proved more intractable than that of human happiness or human good. We are inclined to say at first sight that happiness is equivalent to contentment, and only to see that this cannot be the case when we notice, for example, that we count someone as unfortunate, not fortunate, if he suffers brain damage and thereafter lives the life of a happy child. But this correction shows that however little we are able to give an account of the idea of human good we have reason to agree with Nietzsche that a man is harmed if he is taught to be content with small pleasures and made unfit for enterprises requiring daring and independence. So, insofar as Nietzsche is suggesting that morality in general, and Christian morality in particular, has this effect he is at least arguing on moral ground. And of course there were more obvious ways in which the "good and virtuous" had been "harmed". For Nietzsche saw them as resentful, hating themselves and others, and without strong purpose or desire. No man can live happily if he lives like this.

The conclusion of this discussion must be that Nietzsche's "revaluation of values" is a most complex matter, and there is no single answer to the question as to what he was attacking or as to what the basis might be for the attack. It is not, therefore, surprising that we should shy away from the attempt to say whether he was right. I shall, however, try to say one or two things about this. First of all I would like to point out that everything depends on his theories and observations of human nature. If his attack on

Christian morality and on other moralities is going to be worth anything he has got to be *right* about the effect of teaching pity and justice—that it merely hides the *ressentiment* of the weak while it does injury to the strong. And he would have to be right in seeing compassion as necessarily harmful to the compassionate man and of little use to the unfortunate. Moreover he would have to be right about the possibilities of a "healthy egoism" in the strong, even when this egoism could involve ruthlessness to those who are less fortunately placed. Now on some points in his psychological observation Nietzsche undoubtedly was right; he was right for instance to teach us to be wary of one who finds other men most satisfactory when they are in need of his help, and to be wary also of the one who hates himself. At certain points his observation, and his anticipation of depth psychology, shows him as a brilliant psychologist. But one could not see Nietzsche as one who had a great knowledge of life and of the human heart. He describes convincingly what he knew thoroughly, as he knew the life of the lonely genius, the creative artist or thinker. It is, however, noticeable that his picture of the strong noble man fails to carry conviction when it deviates from this model; what he says about the conditions for this man's health seems to stem largely from his belief that the overriding and underlying principle of human behaviour was the will to power. Now it is notorious that general theories about the springs of action are traps for philosophers, and Nietzsche, who tried to work on a world historical scale, is an obvious victim of the delusion of having seen things whole. This would have to be shown, but *prima facie* one has no reason to trust Nietzsche's views of human nature beyond a very limited perspective, and one quite inadequate for his case. There is no reason to suppose that we really are in the dilemma that he insists on—that we either sacrifice the weak or else deform the strong. And in a way events have caught up with Nietzsche. How could one see the present dangers that the world is in as showing that there is too much pity and too little egoism around? One wonders what Nietzsche himself, in some ways a most humane man, would have said if he were living now, and could see inhumanity on its present scale, and in its present blatant forms.

9

NIETZSCHE AND THE MORALITY CRITICS

BRIAN LEITER

I. INTRODUCTION

Nietzsche has long been one of the dominant figures in twentieth-century intellectual life. Yet it is only recently that he has come into his own in Anglo-American philosophy, thanks to a renewed interest in his critical work in ethics.[1] This new appreciation of Nietzsche is reflected in the work of many philosophers. For Alasdair MacIntyre, for example, Nietzsche is the first to diagnose the failure of the project of post-Enlightenment moral theory—even though, according to MacIntyre, Nietzsche wrongly thinks that such theory is the last hope for moral objectivity.[2] For Annette Baier, he is one of those "great moral philosophers" who show us an alternative to the dominant traditions in modern moral theory, an alternative in which we "reflect on the actual phenomenon of morality, see what

From Brian Leiter, "Nietzsche and the Morality Critics," *Ethics*, 107 (1997), 250–85. (Some footnotes shortened or cut.)

For helpful comments on earlier versions of some or all of this material, I am grateful to Elizabeth Anderson, Frithjof Bergmann, Maudemarie Clark, Stephen Darwall, Ken Gemes, David Hills, Thomas Pogge, and, especially, Peter Railton. I have also benefited from the comments and questions of philosophical audiences at Rutgers University (New Brunswick), and the Universities of Arizona (Tucson), California (San Diego), and Texas (Austin). Finally, I thank the editors and anonymous referees for *Ethics* for their useful comments on the penultimate draft.

[1] Interestingly, the last explosion of Anglo-American philosophical interest in Nietzsche— roughly, from 1900 until the end of World War I—was also driven by an interest in his ethics (and esp. its connection to evolutionary theory and positivism). See, e.g., Maurice Adams, "The Ethics of Tolstoy and Nietzsche," *Ethics*, 11 (1900), 82–105; Alfred W. Benn, "The Morals of an Immoralist—Friedrich Nietzsche," *Ethics*, 19 (1908–9), 1–23, 192–211; A.K. Rogers, "Nietzsche and Democracy," *Philosophical Review*, 21 (1912), 32–50; William M. Salter, "Nietzsche's Moral Aim," *Ethics*, 25 (1915), 226–51, 372–403; Bertram Laing, "The Metaphysics of Nietzsche's Immoralism," *Philosophical Review*, 24 (1915), 386–418. One may hope that no philosopher today would write, as one dissenter from the Nietzsche revival did then, that "nothing . . . quite so worthless as 'Thus Spoke Zarathustra' or 'Beyond Good and Evil' has ever attracted so much attention from serious students of the philosophy of morals" (Herbert Stewart, "Some Criticisms on the Nietzsche Revival," *Ethics*, 19 (1909), 427–8).

[2] Alasdair MacIntyre, *After Virtue* (Notre Dame, Ind.: University of Notre Dame Press, 1981), esp. 107–11.

it is, how it is transmitted, what difference it makes."[3] For Susan Wolf, he represents an "approach to moral philosophy" in which the sphere of the "moral" comes to encompass those personal excellencies that Utilitarian and Kantian moral theories seem to preclude.[4] For other recent writers, he figures as the exemplar of a philosophical approach to morality that these writers either endorse (e.g., Philippa Foot) or reject (e.g., Thomas Nagel, Michael Slote).[5] Indeed, in looking at the claim common to critics of morality like Slote, Foot, Wolf, and Bernard Williams—that "moral considerations are not always the most important considerations"—Robert Louden has recently asked, "Have Nietzsche's 'new philosophers' finally arrived on the scene: 'spirits strong and original enough to provide the stimuli for opposite valuations and to revalue and invert "eternal values" '?" (BGE 203)[6]

In this paper, I propose to investigate and delineate more precisely the real similarities and differences between Nietzsche "the immoralist" and the recent critical writers in moral philosophy. Doing so will require first saying something about the distinct strands in the recent critical literature, since not all of these have made equal—or equally interesting—claims on Nietzsche. After surveying briefly the landscape of recent critical work, I will examine in detail just one aspect of this work—that associated with those philosophers I will call the "Morality Critics." I hope to show that, notwithstanding some superficial similarities, Nietzsche is in fact engaged in a critique of morality in terms quite foreign to recent discussion in the Anglo-American world. For what distinguishes Nietzsche, I will argue, is that he is a genuine critic of *morality* as a real cultural phenomenon, while recent Anglo-American writers are only critics of particular *philosophical theories of morality*. Nietzsche, unlike these writers, situates his critique of morality within a broader "cultural critique," in which morality is attacked as only the most important of a variety of social and cultural forces posing obstacles to human flourishing. This approach to critique places Nietzsche,

---

[3] Annette Baier, "Theory and Reflective Practices," in her *Postures of the Mind* (London: Methuen, 1985), 207–27, 224.

[4] Susan Wolf, "Moral Saints," *Journal of Philosophy*, 79 (1982), 419–39, 433.

[5] See, e.g., Michael Slote, *Goods and Virtues* (Oxford: Clarendon Press, 1983), 79; Thomas Nagel, *The View from Nowhere* (New York: Oxford University Press, 1986), 196; Philippa Foot, "Nietzsche: The Revaluation of Values," Ch. 8 in this volume, esp. p. 216; see also her "Morality as a System of Hypothetical Imperatives?" repr. in her *Virtues and Vices* (Berkeley: University of California Press, 1978).

[6] Robert Louden, "Can We Be Too Moral?", *Ethics*, 98 (1988), 361–80, 361. Louden begins his essay by quoting Nietzsche's call for "a *critique* of moral values, *the value of these values themselves must first be called in question*" (GM, Preface). Translations, with occasional minor emendations, are by Walter Kaufmann and/or R. J. Hollingdale; for purposes of making emendations, I rely upon KSA.

not in the company of Anglo-American morality critics, but rather in that European tradition of modernist discontent with bourgeois Christian culture that runs, we might say, from Baudelaire to Freud, with faint echoes audible in the critical theories of Adorno and Marcuse.[7] Like these critics, Nietzsche is concerned with the condition of a culture, not the shortcomings of a theory, and in particular with the character and consequences of its moral culture. Because of this fundamental difference between Nietzsche and recent Anglo-American philosophy, Nietzsche's critique also represents a far more *speculative* challenge to morality. In the concluding section of this paper, I will pose some critical questions about the plausibility of Nietzsche's attack.

II. THEORY CRITICS AND MORALITY CRITICS

We must begin, however, with some distinctions: first, between morality and moral theory; and, second, between types of criticism of moral theory. When I say that recent Anglo-American work has been critical only of particular *theories* of morality, but not of morality itself, the distinction I have in mind is simple enough: it is the difference between, on the one hand, morality as an everyday cultural phenomenon, the stuff of common sense and common opinion, guiding the conduct of ordinary people; and, on the other hand, morality as more or less systematized, improved, and codified in some theoretical framework produced by a philosopher. Of course, most moral theorists presumably think that their theory captures what is essential to morality as an everyday cultural phenomenon. They may or may not be right in this claim. But even if the theory does capture what is *conceptually* central to morality as an everyday cultural phenomenon, a critic may still worry about the effects of the unsystematic, uncodified, unimproved moral beliefs that comprise the daily life of the culture. Such a critique might invite the philosophical rejoinder that the deficiencies of "ordinary" morality simply need to be cured by good philosophy. I shall, in fact, return to this type of objection after we have set out Nietzsche's own critique in greater detail.

Recent Anglo-American criticism, in contrast to Nietzsche, has taken as its target moral theory, but it has done so in two quite distinct senses. Let us call the "Theory Critics"—philosophers like Annette Baier, Charles Larmore, Charles Taylor, and sometimes Bernard Williams—those who

---

[7] See the useful overview in Robert Pippin, *Modernism as a Philosophical Problem* (Oxford: Basil Blackwell, 1991), 4–7, 30.

think that our "particular moral assessments and commonsense moral principles" are not the sort of things about which one should or can have a
theory (in some precise and technical sense of the word "theory").[8] The
qualification here is important, for the position of the Theory Critics is not a
rank anti-intellectualism or some sort of ethical particularism.[9] What, then,
are the marks of "theory" in this objectionable sense (hereafter Theory)? A
survey of the recent literature suggests that a Theory is *often* characterized
by two aims in particular:

> (1) Reduction: Theory tries to reduce all value to a single, unitary
> source;[10]

and

> (2) Mechanical Decision: Theory tries to articulate an explicit, mechan-
> ical decision procedure for generating answers to ethical questions (or
> explicit criteria for ethical decision and a decision procedure for their
> application).[11]

These pernicious aspects of Theory are closely related, for it is precisely
Theory's reduction of value to a single source that makes possible Theory's
goal of a Mechanical Decision procedure, namely, one that uses the privileged basic value to "churn out" (we might say) moral directives.[12] Against

---

[8] See Stephen Darwall, Allan Gibbard, and Peter Railton, "Toward *Fin de siecle* Ethics: Some
Trends," *Philosophical Review*, 101 (1992), 115–89, 181. This forms the subject matter of *normative*
theory, which these authors, following Baier, identify as the primary target of those I am calling
the Theory Critics.

[9] See Jonathan Dancy, "Ethical Particularism and Morally Relevant Properties," *Mind*, 92
(1983), 530–47.

[10] Bernard Williams, *Ethics and the Limits of Philosophy* (Cambridge, Mass.: Harvard University Press, 1985), 16–17, cited hereafter in the text as ELP; Thomas Nagel, "The Fragmentation
of Value," repr. in *Mortal Questions* (Cambridge: Cambridge University Press, 1979), 131–2;
Charles Larmore, *Patterns of Moral Complexity* (Cambridge: Cambridge University Press, 1987),
138; Charles Taylor, "The Diversity of Goods," repr. in his *Philosophy and the Human Sciences:
Philosophical Papers 2* (Cambridge: Cambridge University Press, 1985). Elsewhere in ELP
Williams worries about a different kind of reductionism, i.e., the attempt to reduce all practical
reasoning and all obligation to *moral* reasoning and *moral* obligation. See esp. ch. 10.

[11] Bernard Williams, Preface, in his *Moral Luck* (Cambridge: Cambridge University Press,
1981), p. x; Larmore, *Patterns of Moral Complexity*, p. ix, ch. 1; Taylor. Something similar seems
to be Annette Baier's target in "Theory and Reflective Practices," and "Doing without Moral
Theory?" (repr. in *Postures of the Mind*, 228–45), esp. in her talk of the theorist's hierarchical
ordering of moral principles "in which the less general are derived from the more general" ("Doing
without Moral Theory?", 232) on the model of a legal system ("Theory and Reflective Practices,"
214) (where the latter is thought of, in a pre-Legal Realist sense, as involving the deduction of
particular decisions from general rules).

[12] Taylor aptly calls this the ambition for a "single-consideration procedure," a label which
suggests the unity of Reduction and Mechanical Decision, and objects that such a procedure
cannot do justice to "the real diversity of goods that we recognize" ("The Diversity of Goods,"
245, 247).

these aims, the Theory Critics argue that value is not unitary (there is, in Taylor's phrase, a "diversity" of goods) and that (partly as a result) Mechanical Decision procedures are simply impossible in the ethical life: ethical decision and action, these critics say, requires practical wisdom, virtues, or sensitivity to the particular context, all things which (allegedly) cannot be captured within the confines of Theory.

Anyone familiar with the recent literature knows that it appears to contain more complaints—and certainly more epithets—than just these: Moral Theory is said to be too abstract, too general, too systematic, too foundationalist, too simplistic, and too contemptuous of non-Theoretical forms of reflection.[13] I would suggest, though, that all these complaints are most helpfully thought of as variations on the critique of Reduction and Mechanical Decision. For example, it is *because* Theory reduces value to a single source that it is too simplistic. Similarly, it is *because* Theory wants a Mechanical Decision procedure that can generate answers in any particular case that Theory ends up being too general and too abstract.

Focusing the critique of Theory in this way is useful because of a certain tension in the writings of the Theory Critics, for a common refrain among them is that the rejection of Theory (in the technical sense) does not entail the rejection of ethical reflection.[14] But if reflection is not simply to lead us back into Theory, then we must have some *clear* idea of what Theory is— something more than that it is an account of morality that is too simple or too abstract. Indeed, it would seem that if something is to count as reflecting at all—as opposed, say, simply to emoting—then it *must* aim for some degree of abstraction, simplification, generality, and coherence. To reflect at all must involve abstracting from the particular case and identifying (some of) the general features which permit comparison and harmonizing with other cases. Theory in the objectionable sense must require something else, otherwise all reflection would involve Theory. I have suggested that this something else is captured by the joint aims of Reduction and Mechanical Decision: it is these that mark the line between bad Theory and good ethical reflection.

Yet these considerations suggest something further. For some degree of

[13] See Baier, "Theory and Reflective Practices" and "Doing without Moral Theory?"; and Williams, *Ethics and the Limits of Philosophy*, esp. 115–17, 127, 202.

[14] For example, Baier argues for ethical reflection without "normative theory in the Kantian sense" while noting that "reflectiveness about our practices requires at the very least noting whether they are counterproductive to their expressed aims" ("Theory and Reflective Practices," 226). Williams wonders throughout *Ethics and the Limits of Philosophy* "why reflection should be taken to require theory" (p. 112) and claims that "philosophy in the modern world cannot make any special claim to reflectiveness" (p. 3). Taylor goes further and concedes that even if there are a plurality of goods, "people . . . are faced with the job of somehow making them compatible in their lives" ("The Diversity of Goods," 236) and that, as a result, "the demand for a unified theory" is a "demand we cannot totally repudiate" (p. 245).

abstraction, generality, and coherence—the minimal requirements of all reflection—are also surely among the minimal desiderata of all *theory* construction. In that case, we ought to say that theory in this minimalist sense really is part of ethical reflection. Thus, by ordinary usage, it would be misleading to describe the complaint of the Theory Critics as directed at theory per se, since they only target those theoretical ambitions (i.e., Reduction and Mechanical Decision) that go beyond the minimal requirements. The difference between the Theory Critics and the mainstream of the modern tradition is, ultimately, one of degree, not kind.[15]

Those I will call the "Morality Critics," by contrast, are those—like Michael Slote, Michael Stocker, Susan Wolf, and, again, Bernard Williams—who criticize moral theory, not because of its theoretical ambitions, but because of its *moral* commitments (more precisely, either the substantive *content* of the morality endorsed or the *weight* assigned in practical reasoning to moral demands). Admittedly, the Morality Critics often present themselves as critics of morality itself—in that sense they echo Nietzsche—but, on examination, it is clear that their targets are specific theories of morality, consequentialist and deontological. The Williams of *Ethics and the Limits of Philosophy* is illustrative in this regard, for he might seem, at first sight, a counterexample to this characterization.[16] After all, Williams calls "morality" "the peculiar institution" and says this morality "is not an invention of philosophers … [but rather] the outlook, or, incoherently, part of the outlook, of almost all of us" (ELP 174). He goes on to worry about the "several natural ways in which" this morality's special notion of obligation "can come to dominate a life altogether" (ELP 181–2). In passages like these, Williams seems to be objecting *not* that the best moral *theory* requires obligation to dominate life, but rather that once moral obligation is allowed to "structure ethical thought" (ELP 182), it has a "natural" tendency to rule out all other considerations.

Yet appearances here are deceiving. While Williams plainly wants to align himself with Nietzsche as a critic of morality as a genuine cultural phenomenon—hence the rhetoric about "the peculiar institution" and morality not being "an invention of philosophers"—it is far from clear that the notion of moral obligation he discusses is anything other than a

---

[15] This is clearest in the case of writers like Nagel and Larmore, who explicitly affirm both the tenability of moral theory and the indispensable role of something like Aristotle's practical wisdom or judgment in our moral life. See Nagel, "The Fragmentation of Value," 135–7; and Larmore, *Patterns of Moral Complexity*, ch. 1, p. 151 ("My intention … has not been to deny the possibilities or importance of moral theory. I do not believe that the complexity of morality is so great, so boundless, that it baffles any attempt at systematization.").

[16] I take the preceding sentence to be a more obviously apt characterization of some of Williams's earlier work in ethics.

philosopher's "invention" or, at best, such a severe systematic reworking of the ordinary notion as to be only a distant relative of the unsystematic, uncodified notion of obligation actually at work in our culture.

Morality's purportedly threatening notion of "obligation," for example, is constructed by Williams entirely from the works of Kant and Ross, with no gesture at showing what relation their philosophically refined notions of "obligation" bear to those in play in ordinary life. Yet where is the evidence, one might ask, that real people treat "moral obligation[s] [as] inescapable" (ELP 177) and that they accept the idea that "only an obligation can beat an obligation" (ELP 180)? Surely the evidence is not in the way people actually live, in the way they actually honor—or, more often, breach—their moral obligations, a point Nietzsche well understood.[17] What is the evidence that, in our relativistic culture, individuals think that "moral obligation applies to people even if they do not want it to" (ELP 178)? Even Williams, in leading up to the specter of morality dominating life, says that "the thought can gain a footing (*I am not saying that it has to*) that I could be better employed than in doing something I am under no [moral] obligation to do, and, if I could be, then I ought to be" (ELP 181, emphasis added). But surely this "thought" might only gain a footing for Kant or Ross, or some other philosopher who followed out to its logical conclusion a deontological *theory*. It is a pure philosopher's fantasy to think that real people in the moral culture at large find themselves overwhelmed by this burdensome sense of moral obligation. Like the other Morality Critics, Williams writes as though he is attacking "morality," when what he is really attacking is "morality" as conceived, systematized, and refined by philosophers. Such a critique may be a worthy endeavor, but it is far different from worrying about the "dangers" of ordinary morality as understood—unsystematically and inchoately—by ordinary people.

What, then, distinguishes a Morality Critic from a Theory Critic if both are ultimately talking about moral *theory*? Roughly, the idea is this: for the former, there is always room, *in principle*, for a better theory to thwart the criticism, while for the latter, Theory (in the technical sense) is the heart of the problem, not part of the solution. These points are well illustrated in Stocker's well-known paper "The Schizophrenia of Modern Ethical Theories."[18] Stocker argues that "if we . . . embody in our motives, those various things which recent ethical theories hold to be ultimately good or right, we will, of necessity, be unable to have those motives" (p. 461) and thus be

---

[17] See the further discussion in "Nietzsche's Critique: A Critical Assessment" below.

[18] Michael Stocker, "The Schizophrenia of Modern Ethical Theories," *Journal of Philosophy*, 73 (1976), 453–66, cited in this section by page number.

unable to realize the associated goods (e.g., friendship, love, pleasure). Stocker claims, however, that a suitable ethical theory must be one in which reasons and motives can be brought into harmony, such that one can be moved to act by what the theory identifies as "good" or "right." Stocker's point isn't, then, that theorizing in ethics is a misguided enterprise; it's just that we need better theories, ones in which theoretical reasons can also serve as motives for action. Like a Morality Critic, Stocker holds that adherence to morality as it is (read: moral theory as it is) is incompatible with having the motives requisite for certain personal goods ("love, friendship, affection, fellow feeling, and community," p. 461); unlike a Theory Critic, he allows, or at least implies, that a better (i.e., nonschizophrenic) theory could solve the problem.[19]

We need, however, a more precise characterization of the Morality Critics, since the preceding account would also capture types of criticism that appear to have no affinity whatsoever with Nietzsche's. What I have in mind, of course, is the tradition of deontological criticism of consequentialism and of consequentialist criticism of deontological theories.[20] Such criticisms are not about theory per se but about the moral commitments of the theories. Yet worries about the rationality of constraints on good maximization, or about consequentialist violations of the autonomy and dignity of individuals, would not seem to be the sorts of worries that call to mind the writings of Nietzsche. We need, then, a sharper characterization of the "Morality Critics," one which excludes intramoral debates between Kantians and consequentialists.

Yet this very way of stating the problem also suggests its solution. What characterizes the Morality Critics is precisely that they criticize morality *extra*morally, from the standpoint of nonmoral goods and considerations. Such a tentative characterization, of course, generates its own problems— first, because we need a clearer grasp of the distinction between the moral and the extramoral; and second, because of the potentially question-begging designation of certain sorts of goods and considerations as extramoral (defenders of morality, as we shall see, often argue that these goods and reasons are included within the moral point of view, suitably construed).[21]

[19] See esp. the concluding pages of Stocker's piece. Susan Wolf presents a slightly different case than other Morality Critics in this regard; see "Moral Saints," 435–7.

[20] For example, of the former type, John Rawls, *A Theory of Justice* (Cambridge, Mass.: Harvard University Press, 1971), esp. 26–7; of the latter type, Samuel Scheffler, "Agent-Centered Restrictions, Rationality, and the Virtues," *Mind*, 94 (1985), 409–19, esp. 409.

[21] A third difficulty is that some writers construe demands of, e.g., partiality and integrity to be essentially moral demands, apart from their role in deontological and consequentialist theories. See David Brink, "Utilitarian Morality and the Personal Point of View," *Journal of Philosophy*, 83 (1986), 417–38, 418–19; Larmore, *Patterns of Moral Complexity*, 132–3. This construal is not, I think, suggested by the writings of most Morality Critics themselves and, in any event, can be dealt with in the way suggested in the text.

Yet if we agree to treat the "moral" as exhausted by deontology and consequentialism, then we can say that the Morality Critics are those philosophers who criticize the moral commitments of theory from the standpoint of (*apparently*) nonmoral goods and considerations.

But let us now try to state this view even more precisely. A Morality Critic takes as her target—to borrow Susan Wolf's phrase—"a perfect master of a moral theory" ("Moral Saints," 435), deontological or consequentialist. The Morality Critic then argues that such a perfect master is precluded from realizing certain nonmoral goods and excellences—let us call them "personal goods."[22] This follows from the truth of two theses:

Incompatibility Thesis (IT): Acting in accordance with morality is (at least sometimes) incompatible with realizing or enjoying these personal goods;[23]

and

---

[22] Nagel speaks of morality posing "a serious threat to the kind of personal life that many of us take to be desirable" (*View from Nowhere*, 190). Wolf claims that the "moral saint" cannot realize "a great variety of forms of personal excellence" ("Moral Saints," 426). Bernard Williams argues that both Kantian and utilitarian theories will sometimes require us to abandon our "ground projects," those projects "which propel [a person] in the future, and give him (in a sense) a reason for living" ("Persons, Character, and Morality," in A. Rorty (ed.), *The Identities of Persons* (Berkeley: University of California Press, 1976), 209–10). See Bernard Williams, "A Critique of Utilitarianism," in J. J. C. Smart and Bernard Williams, *Utilitarianism: For and Against* (Cambridge: Cambridge University Press, 1973), 77–150, esp. 115–17, and *Ethics and the Limits of Philosophy*, esp. 181–2 (worrying that a Kantian notion of obligation can "come to dominate life altogether"). Slote argues that a commitment to morality would require us to "deplore and disavow" (*Goods and Virtue*, 85) certain otherwise admirable traits like "single-minded devotion to aesthetic goals or ideals" (p. 80)—because of their essential tendency also to produce immoral behavior. Michael Stocker is probably an exception to the characterization offered in the text. While most Morality Critics view the nonmoral goods and considerations as largely *prudential* in character, Stocker is concerned with phenomena like "love" and "friendship" whose value is probably not prudential. See "The Schizophrenia of Modern Ethical Theories."

[23] For example, Wolf: "The admiration of and striving toward achieving any of a great variety of forms of personal excellence are character traits it is valuable and desirable for people to have . . . In thinking that it is good for a person to strive for [this] ideal . . . , we implicitly acknowledge the goodness of ideals incompatible with that of the moral saint" ("Moral Saints," 426). The truth of IT is defended in slightly different ways by the Critics, depending on whether they are taking consequentialism or Kantianism as the target. (For consequentialism, and specifically Utilitarianism, see Wolf, "Moral Saints," 427–30; Williams, "A Critique of Utilitarianism," 93–118, "Persons, Character, and Morality," 199–200, 210; for Kantianism, see Wolf, "Moral Saints," 430–3; Williams, "Persons, Character, and Morality," and *Ethics and the Limits of Philosophy*, ch. 10.). However, as a number of writers have noted, there is a common element in both deontological and consequentialist theories that is supposed to generate IT, i.e., their commitment to an *impersonal* point of view and *impartial* value. Because of this commitment, these theories cannot (according to the Critics) do real justice to the importance of our various *personal* and *partial* attachments and projects: such projects and attachments can always be sacrificed when impersonal and impartial considerations demand it. Our most important personal project is, after all, just one among many from the moral point of view, which is precisely why (according to the Critics) morality cannot do justice to its significance and value. See Nagel, *View from Nowhere*, 189–91.

Overridingness Thesis (OT): Moral considerations are always the practically determinative considerations, and thus override all competing considerations.

It is the conjunction of IT and OT that generates the problem: for (by IT) moral considerations will conflict with "personal" considerations, and (by OT) personal considerations must lose. Since it would be intolerable actually to abandon these personal considerations, however, Morality Critics take this conflict to show that we must reject OT: moral considerations are not always the practically determinative considerations.[24] Defenders of morality, by contrast, typically reject IT: they argue that personal goods and moral goods are not incompatible because, for example, morality includes personal goods within its (suitably objective) purview or because morality includes supererogatory duties or virtues, such that morality can recognize morally praiseworthy conduct without always demanding its performance in a way that would inevitably override personal considerations.[25]

We will find it convenient, I think, to borrow Nagel's language (*View from Nowhere*, 193 ff.) and speak of the general issue here in terms of a conflict between the "Good Life" (one in which personal considerations are dominant) and the "Moral Life" (one in which moral considerations govern)—or between "living well" and "doing right." According to IT, the Good Life and the Moral Life are incompatible; according to OT, the Moral Life must prevail, at the expense of the Good Life (given IT). Note, too, where Nagel locates Nietzsche in the debate thus framed: "The good life overrides the moral life. This is Nietzsche's position ... The view is that if, taking everything into consideration, a moral life will not be a good life for the individual it would be a mistake to lead it" (*View from Nowhere*, 196). This passage aptly describes the core of the supposed relation between Nietzsche and the Morality Critics: like them, Nietzsche is supposed to side with the

---

[24] Wolf challenges "the assumption that it is always better to be morally better" and concludes that "our values cannot be fully comprehended on the model of a hierarchical system with morality at the top" ("Moral Saints," 438). Slote claims that the possibility of admirable immorality should "[loosen] ... our attachment to the 'overridingness' thesis" (*Goods and Virtue*, 107). Williams concludes, "Life has to have substance if anything is to have sense, including adherence to the impartial [moral] system; but if it has substance, then it cannot grant supreme importance to the impartial system" ("Persons, Character, and Morality," 215). Owen Flanagan identifies "this assumption of the sovereignty of the moral good" as the target of critics like Wolf, Williams, and Slote (Owen Flanagan, "Admirable Immorality and Admirable Imperfection," *Journal of Philosophy*, 83 (1986), 41–60, 41). Note that for at least Williams, morality already does its damage—in the form of "alienation"—once it asks us to view our personal projects as up for grabs in moral deliberation (whether or not morality ultimately requires us to abandon them).

[25] On the "objective purview" response see, e.g., Peter Railton, "Alienation, Consequentialism and the Demands of Morality," repr. in S. Scheffler (ed.), *Consequentialism and its Critics* (Oxford: Oxford University Press, 1988), 93–133, esp. 113–17. On the "supererogation" response see, e.g., Stephen Darwall, "Abolishing Morality," *Synthèse*, 72 (1987), 71–89, esp. 78–83.

importance of the Good Life against the encroaching demands of the Moral Life. Even granting that Nietzsche is perhaps more extreme in his rejection of the demands of the Moral Life, he still counts as the first in a line of Morality Critics that includes Williams, Wolf, Slote, and others who (*a*) recognize the truth of IT and (*b*) part company with the tradition in their rejection of morality's OT. We shall have occasion to consider shortly how well this picture really captures Nietzsche's critical project. It remains to say, first, a few brief words about Nietzsche and the Theory Critics.

Nietzsche's notorious hostility to systematic theorizing—evidenced in his quip that "the will to a system is a lack of integrity" (TI I. 26)—would seem to make him a natural ally of the Theory Critics. It is true, moreover, that Nietzsche does not offer a normative ethical theory in the way that Kant or Sidgwick or any other representative of the tradition does.[26] Yet Nietzsche's reason for this has nothing to do with the sort of reasons that animate recent Theory Criticism. Nietzsche's hostility to normative theorizing grows, instead, out of his naturalism and fatalism,[27] which lead him to be deeply skeptical about the utility of propounding normative theories about what we ought to do. Thus, for example, he declares that "the single human being is a piece of *fatum* from the front and from the rear, one law more, one necessity more for all that is yet to come and to be" (TI V. 6). Given that this is Nietzsche's view, it is unsurprising that he should also say: "A man as he *ought* to be: that sounds to us as insipid as 'a tree as it ought to be'" (WP 332). Of course, Nietzsche does think that values can play a *causal* role in a

---

[26] A different question is whether he offers an ethical theory more akin to ancient ones—say, a type of virtue ethics, as some recent writers have suggested. See, e.g., John Casey, *Pagan Virtue: An Essay in Ethics* (Oxford: Clarendon Press, 1990), esp. 79–83; Lester Hunt, *Nietzsche and the Origin of Virtue* (London: Routledge, 1991). The difficulties with Hunt's account will serve to highlight the problems confronting this interpretation of Nietzsche. According to Hunt, Nietzsche's theory of virtue is "procedural": "it specifies which traits are virtues by indicating a certain process and declaring that any trait that arises from this process is virtuous" (p. 145). The relevant process is given by Nietzsche's "experimentalism," which requires us to experiment with different goals until we find those which bring about "a complete integration of the psyche" (p. 141), such that "one part of the self imposes order on other, potentially chaotic parts by successfully orienting the subordinate parts towards its own purposes" (p. 128). The traits that are conducive to the integrating goals are, says Hunt, virtues for Nietzsche. There is certainly something broadly right about this picture, though its vagueness is only one of its several problems. First, the theory seems not so much procedural as substantive, since it employs a substantive criterion (integration of the self) for identifying which goal-oriented activities involve virtues. Second, it seems to stretch Nietzsche's ambitions considerably to attribute to him something called a "procedural theory of virtue." Third, Hunt gives almost none of the detail about particular virtues that interest most contemporary writers (including, e.g., Casey), even relegating Nietzsche's own specific virtue lists to an endnote (p. 187 n. 4). While Hunt has a multitude of interesting things to say about Nietzsche, it is not clear that his account makes Nietzsche a virtue theorist of much practical or philosophical help.

[27] For a more substantial discussion of these oft-neglected themes in Nietzsche's work, see Brian Leiter, "The Paradox of Fatalism and Self-Creation in Nietzsche," Ch. 11 in this volume.

person's actions (cf. GS 335), or he would not be concerned to undertake a revaluation of values. He thinks, simply, that the causal efficacy of values is always circumscribed by the natural facts that make a person who he or she is.[28] It is the failure of traditional ethical theories to grasp this point that leads him to think they are useless. The philosophical motivation, then, for Nietzsche's opposition to normative theory simply bears no relation to that found in the Theory Critics.

I want to turn, then, to what seems a more immediate, and deep, affinity between Nietzsche and those philosophers I called the Morality Critics.

III. NIETZSCHE'S CRITIQUE OF MORALITY

Why does Nietzsche attack morality? I want to begin by setting out in summary form an account that I have developed in greater detail elsewhere.[29] Since Nietzsche uses the word "morality" (*Moral*) in both positive and negative senses,[30] I will introduce a "technical" term to mark "morality" as the object of his critique: what I will call henceforth "morality in the pejorative sense" (MPS).

All moralities are, for Nietzsche, characterized by a *descriptive* and a *normative* component; that is, they (*a*) presuppose a particular descriptive account of human agency in the sense that, for the normative claims to have intelligible application to human agents, particular metaphysical and empirical claims about agency must be true and (*b*) embody a normative agenda which creates or sustains the special conditions under which only certain types of human agents enjoy success. Any particular morality will, in turn, be an MPS for Nietzsche if it

(1) presupposes certain *particular* descriptive claims about the nature of human agents: for example, that agents act freely and thus are responsible for what they do ("the Descriptive Component");

and/or

(2) embodies a normative agenda which benefits the "lowest" human beings while harming the "highest" ("the Normative Component").

---

[28] For further discussion, see ibid.

[29] See esp. Brian Leiter, "Morality in the Pejorative Sense: On the Logic of Nietzsche's Critique of Morality," *British Journal for the History of Philosophy*, 3 (1995), 113–45, and also Leiter, "Beyond Good and Evil," *History of Philosophy Quarterly*, 10 (1993), 261–70. The former sets out the affinities and differences my account has with those common in the secondary literature.

[30] For some nonpejorative uses of the word "morality", see, e.g., TI V. 4 (where he speaks of the possibility of a "healthy morality" (*gesunde Moral*)), and BGE 202 ("higher moralities" (*Morale*)). On the nature and content of such a morality, see my "Beyond Good and Evil."

Note, first, that these two components are not of equal importance for Nietzsche, for what ultimately defines an MPS as against morality in a non-pejorative sense is the distinctive normative agenda. Thus, while Nietzsche criticizes at length the view of agency that he takes to be implicit in at least certain paradigmatic examples of MPS, he also holds that "it is *not* error as error that" he objects to fundamentally in an MPS (EH IV. 7). That is, it is *not* the falsity of the descriptive account of agency presupposed by MPS, per se, that is the heart of the problem. Thus, strictly speaking, it is true that a morality could be an MPS even if it did not involve a commitment to an untenable descriptive account of agency.[31] Because Nietzsche's most common specific target is, however, Christian morality, the critique of the Descriptive Component of MPS figures prominently in Nietzsche's writing. For purposes here, however, I will concentrate on the Normative Component, which constitutes the philosophical heart of Nietzsche's critique.

According to Nietzsche, the normative agenda of an MPS favors the interests of the lowest human beings at the expense of the highest. Before illustrating what such an agenda might look like, we need, first, to establish that this is, in fact, central to Nietzsche's conception of MPS and, second, to explore what Nietzsche means by higher and lower persons.

In the secondary literature, Nietzsche has been saddled with a variety of different accounts and critiques of MPS.[32] A popular thought, for example, is that Nietzsche objects to morality because of its claim of universal applicability.[33] Yet Nietzsche never objects to the universality of moral demands, per se, as an intrinsically bad feature of MPS; rather, he finds universality objectionable because he holds that "the demand of one morality for all is detrimental to the higher men" (BGE 228). Similarly, he holds that "when a decadent type of man ascended to the rank of the highest type [via MPS], this could only happen at *the expense of its countertype*, the type of man that is strong and sure of life" (EH III. 5, emphasis added). Finally, consider the illuminating preface to the *Genealogy*, in which Nietzsche sums up his basic concern particularly well:

---

[31] Smart's Utilitarianism is a good example of an MPS that embodies a normative agenda that is objectionable on Nietzschean grounds, while involving no commitment to an untenable metaphysics of agency. See esp. J. J. C. Smart, " 'Ought,' 'Can,' Free Will and Responsibility," in his *Ethics, Persuasion and Truth* (London: Routledge, 1984). Bernard Williams has gone so far as to suggest that because blaming can be justified on utilitarian grounds alone (and regardless of whether agents have free will), Utilitarianism is, at best, a "marginal member of the morality system"—where Williams takes Kantian morality to be the paradigmatic member (*Ethics and the Limits of Philosophy*, 178).

[32] See the overview in Leiter, "Morality in the Pejorative Sense," 113–17.

[33] See, e.g. Alexander Nehamas, *Nietzsche: Life as Literature* (Cambridge, Mass.: Harvard University Press, 1985), 209, 214, 223.

What if a symptom of regression were inherent in the "good," likewise a danger, a seduction, a poison, a narcotic, through which the present was possibly living *at the expense of the future?* Perhaps more comfortably, less dangerously, but at the same time in a meaner style, more basely?—So that precisely morality [MPS] would be to blame if the *highest power and splendor* (*höchste Mächtigkeit und Pracht*) possible to the type man was never in fact attained? So that precisely morality was the danger of dangers? (GM, Preface, 6; cf. BT, "Attempt at a Self-Criticism," 5)

In these and many other passages,[34] Nietzsche makes plain his real objection to MPS: simply put, MPS thwarts the development of human excellence, that is, "the highest power and splendor . . . possible to the type man." This is the very heart of Nietzsche's challenge to morality.

But who are Nietzsche's "higher types," these individuals who possess "the highest power and splendor"? Nietzsche alternately calls them "strong," "healthy," and "noble"; conversely, the lowest men are "weak," "sick," and "base." Higher types are also described by Nietzsche as nonreactive, creative, self-disciplined, and resilient; and they evince a Dionysian attitude toward life. Since a detailed exposition of these very general characteristics would take me far afield of my central topics in this paper, I propose to pursue a simpler two-step course.

A. First, Nietzsche provides in his writings two unequivocal and concrete examples of "higher" human beings: Goethe and Nietzsche himself.[35] Nietzsche, of course, often expresses admiration for other people— Napoleon, sometimes Caesar, the "free spirits" discussed throughout *The Gay Science*—but Goethe and Nietzsche himself stand out for the esteem they enjoy in Nietzsche's work. Taking these two, and in particular Nietzsche himself, as paradigm cases of human excellence will make it possible to say

[34] See D 163; BGE 62, 212; GM III. 14; A 5, 24; EH IV. 4; WP 274, 345, 400, 870, 879, 957. For example, in a work of 1880 he writes, "Our weak, unmanly, social concepts of good and evil and their tremendous ascendancy over body and soul have finally weakened all bodies and souls and snapped the self-reliant, independent, unprejudiced men, the pillars of a *strong* civilization" (D 163). While in a posthumously published note of 1885 he remarks that "men of great creativity, the really great men according to my understanding, will be sought in vain today" because "nothing stands more malignantly in the way of their rise and evolution . . . than what in Europe today is called simply 'morality'" (WP 957). Similarly, in a late note of 1888, he observes (in a passage plainly echoing the preface of GM), "Whoever reflects upon the way in which the type man can be raised to his greatest splendor and power will grasp first of all that he must place himself outside morality; for morality has been essentially directed to the opposite end: to obstruct, or destroy that splendid evolution wherever it has been going on" (WP 897).

[35] I should not be construed here as endorsing the idiosyncratic view defended in the last chapter of Nehamas. According to Nehamas, Nietzsche does not *describe* his ideal person—his "higher man"—but rather "exemplifies" such a person in the form of the "character" that is constituted by and exemplified in his literary corpus. Nietzsche, however, *describes* at great length and in many places (see D 201; GS 55; BGE 287; WP 943) the types of persons he admires, and he also describes himself as such a person (see EH I. 2). For further criticism of Nehamas on this and other points, see my "Nietzsche and Aestheticism," *Journal of the History of Philosophy*, 30 (1992), 275–90.

something reasonably concrete about the alleged harmful effects of MPS shortly. It will also help emphasize that, whatever Nietzsche's illiberal sentiments, he ultimately admired creative individuals the most: in art, literature, music, and philosophy, "the men of great creativity, the really great men according to my understanding" (WP 957). His critique of morality is, in an important sense, driven by the realization that the *moral* life is essentially inhospitable to the truly creative life, a point to which I shall return below.[36]

B. Second, I want to offer some greater—albeit brief—detail concerning at least one of the above-mentioned characteristics of higher men, namely, their "Dionysian" attitude toward life. An agent, for Nietzsche, has a *Dionysian attitude* toward life insofar as that agent affirms his life unconditionally, in particular, insofar as he affirms it notwithstanding the "suffering" or other hardships it has involved.[37] An agent *affirms* his life in Nietzsche's sense only insofar as that agent would gladly will its eternal return, that is, will the repetition of his life through eternity.[38] Thus, higher human beings are marked by a distinctive Dionysian attitude toward their lives: they would gladly will the repetition of their lives eternally. Note, too, that Nietzsche claims that this attitude characterized both himself and Goethe (on Nietzsche, see EH III, CW 4; on Goethe, TI IX. 49). We shall see shortly how this trademark attitude of higher types—their Dionysian attitude toward life—is implicated in Nietzsche's critique of the normative agenda of MPS.[39]

---

[36] This type of simplifying move, however, does not obviously help us get a fix on who "lower men" are supposed to be. Yet not saying more about "lower men" is not necessarily problematic for my project here of characterizing Nietzsche's conception of MPS. For the heart of Nietzsche's complaint is simply that MPS has a *deleterious effect on higher types* (i.e., those who manifest human excellence). It is true that Nietzsche also seems to think that MPS is in the interests of other persons—"lower men"—but this by itself is *not* objectionable; recall that Nietzsche says, "The ideas of the herd should rule in the herd—but not reach out beyond it" (WP 287). It is this "reaching out beyond," then, that is at issue because it is this that *harms* "higher men." If there were a social order in which MPS existed—and in which it served the interests of "lower" types—without having any effects on potentially "higher" men, then one would imagine that Nietzsche should have no objections. In that case, one could leave the issue of who "lower men" are pleasantly vague without any cost to the analytical task of getting clear about Nietzsche's critique of morality.

[37] So an agent who says, colloquially speaking, "I would gladly lead my life again, except for the time in my thirties when I was ill and depressed," would not affirm life in the requisite sense.

[38] For example, EH III, Z 1: "The idea of the eternal recurrence, this highest formulation of affirmation that is at all attainable" (cf. BGE 56).

[39] Some writers (e.g., Richard Schacht, *Nietzsche* (London: Routledge, 1983)) have argued that Nietzsche objects to MPS centrally because it is harmful to "life." The main difficulty with this approach, even as it is typically developed, is its vagueness: as Mark Platts remarks, "*Morality versus life* is not the best defined of battle lines" (*Moral Realities* (London: Routledge, 1991), 220). I argue elsewhere that when Nietzsche speaks of morality being harmful to "life," he really means harmful to "higher men"; see my "Morality in the Pejorative Sense," 132–4. Other writers (including Schacht again) have suggested that Nietzsche criticizes morality by reference to his preferred standard of "value" as "will to power." I ignore this possibility here, because it seems to make the notion of "will to power" more central to Nietzsche's mature thought than recent

What norms, then, comprise an MPS? Nietzsche identifies a variety of normative positions[40]—what we may characterize simply as "pro" and "con" attitudes—as constituting the distinctive normative component of MPS. So, for example, a morality will be an MPS if it embraces any one or more of the following sorts of normative views:

(1) Pro: Happiness
    Con: Suffering
       (GS 338; Z III. 1; BGE 202, 225)
(2) Pro: Altruism or selflessness
    Con: Self-love or self-interest[41]
       (GS 328, 345; Z III. 10; GM, Preface, 5; TI IX. 35;
       EH III, D 2 and IV. 7)
(3) Pro: Equality
    Con: Inequality
       (GS 377; Z IV. 13; BGE 257; TI IX. 48; A 43;
       WP 752)
(4) Pro: Pity
    Con: Indifference to the suffering
       (GS 338; Z III. 9; GM, Preface, 5; A 7)

Three observations about how to understand this picture of Nietzsche's critique are in order:

1. The various possible normative components of an MPS should be construed as *ideal-typical:* they single out for emphasis and criticism certain important features of larger and more complex normative views. Nietzsche himself remarks that while there is "a vast realm of subtle feelings of value and difference of value which are alive, grow, beget, and perish," we still need "attempts to present vividly some of the more frequent and recurring forms of such living crystallizations—all to prepare a *typology* of morals" (BGE 186). In criticizing MPS, we should see Nietzsche as criticizing some of the "frequent and recurring forms" that mark various ideal types of MPS.

scholarship would suggest is warranted. See Mazzino Montinari, "Nietzsches *Nachlass* von 1885 bis 1888 oder Textkritik und Wille zur Macht," in his *Nietzsche Lesen* (Berlin: de Gruyter, 1982); Maudemarie Clark, *Nietzsche on Truth and Philosophy* (Cambridge: Cambridge University Press, 1990), 212–27 (this is a later version of Ch. 5 in this volume). Textual worries aside, I doubt whether a good argument can even be made out that "will to power" provides Nietzsche with his standard of value. I make this case in "Nietzsche's Metaethics," *European Journal of Philos.* 8 (2000), 277–97.

[40] For a more complete discussion, see again my "Morality in the Pejorative Sense," 134–42.

[41] Nietzsche only advocates "severe" self-love, i.e., highly critical concern with the self, as the only self-love conducive to the full flourishing of the strong and healthy individual. See EH IV. 7, and the further discussion below.

2. In characterizing MPS in terms of its "pro" and "con" attitudes, I do not mean to suggest that MPS consists only of such "attitudes": to the contrary, associated with each of these attitudes could be various prescriptive and proscriptive commands, suitable to the plethora of particular circumstances to which such attitudes might be relevant. Yet Nietzsche is typically concerned with the underlying (ideal-typical) attitude—or "spirit"—of MPS, rather than the particular rules of conduct.

3. Let us say that that which MPS has a "pro" attitude toward is the "Pro-Object," while that which MPS has a "con" attitude toward is the "Con-Object." Keeping in mind that what seems to have *intrinsic* value for Nietzsche is "human excellence"—the sort of excellence qua creative genius exemplified by Goethe and Nietzsche, for example—we can say that Nietzsche's criticisms consist of two parts:

(*a*) With respect to the Pro-Object, Nietzsche argues either (i) that the Pro-Object has no *intrinsic* value (in the cases where MPS claims it does) or (ii) that it does not have any or not nearly as much *extrinsic* value as MPS treats it as having; and

(*b*) With respect to the Con-Object, Nietzsche argues *only* that the Con-Objects are *extrinsically* valuable for the cultivation of human excellence and that this is obscured by the "con" attitude endorsed by MPS.

In other words, what unifies Nietzsche's seemingly disparate critical remarks—about altruism, happiness, pity, equality, Kantian respect for persons, utilitarianism, and so on—is that he thinks a culture in which such norms prevail as morality will be a culture which eliminates the conditions for the realization of human excellence, the latter requiring, on Nietzsche's view, concern with the self, suffering, a certain stoic indifference, a sense of hierarchy and difference, and the like. Indeed, when we turn to the *details* of Nietzsche's criticisms of these various norms we find that, in fact, he focuses precisely on how they are inhospitable to human excellence. I want to illustrate this point here with just one example.

According to Nietzsche, the "spirit" of MPS is that happiness is good and suffering bad.[42] What, one wonders, could be harmful about this sort of seemingly innocuous valuation? An early remark of Nietzsche's suggests an

---

[42] One problem with this view is that its endpoint—the abolition of suffering and the reign of happiness—is an impossibility because Nietzsche holds that "happiness and unhappiness are sisters" (GS 338), that we must have both in order to have either. Although the unity of apparent opposites is a recurring theme in Nietzsche, it is not central to his objection to this aspect of MPS. A useful discussion of this theme can be found in Nehamas, *Nietzsche: Life as Literature*, 209–11.

answer: "Are we not, with this tremendous objective of obliterating all the sharp edges of life, well on the way to turning mankind into *sand*? Sand! Small, soft, round, unending sand! Is that your ideal, you heralds of the sympathetic affections?" (D 174). In a later work, Nietzsche says, referring to hedonists and utilitarians, "Well-being as you understand it—that is no goal, that seems to us an *end*, a state that soon makes man ridiculous and contemptible" (BGE 225). By the hedonistic doctrine of well-being, Nietzsche takes the utilitarians to have in mind "*English* happiness," namely, "comfort and fashion" (BGE 228),[43] a construal which, if unfair to *some* utilitarians, may do justice to our ordinary aspirations to happiness. In a similar vein, Nietzsche has Zarathustra dismiss "wretched contentment" as an ideal (Z, Prologue, 3), while also revealing that it was precisely "the last men"—the "most despicable men"—who "invented happiness" in the first place (Prologue, 5).

Thus, the first part of Nietzsche's objection is this: happiness is not an intrinsically valuable end; men who aim for it—directly or through cultivating the dispositions that lead to it—would be "ridiculous and contemptible." Note, of course, that Nietzsche allows that he himself and the "free spirits" will be "cheerful"—they are, after all, the proponents of the "gay science" (cf. GS). But the point is that such "happiness" is not *criterial* of being a *higher* person, and thus it is not something that the higher person— in contrast to the adherent of MPS—aims for.

But why is it that aiming for happiness would make a person so unworthy of admiration? Nietzsche's answer appears to be this: because *suffering* is positively necessary for the cultivation of human excellence, which is the only thing, on Nietzsche's view, that warrants admiration. Nietzsche writes, for example, that

> The discipline of suffering (*Die Zucht des Leidens*), of *great* suffering—do you not know that only *this* discipline has created all enhancements of man so far? That tension of the soul in unhappiness which cultivates its strength ... [W]hatever has been granted to [the human soul] of profundity, secret, mask, spirit, cunning, greatness—was it not granted to it through suffering, through the discipline of great suffering? (BGE 225; cf. BGE 270)

Now Nietzsche is not arguing here that—in contrast to the view of MPS— suffering is really *intrinsically* valuable; the value of suffering is only

---

[43] Nietzsche no doubt construes the doctrine thus uncharitably because he thinks that the "British utilitarians . . . walk clumsily and honorably in Bentham's footsteps" and that they have "not a new idea, no trace of a subtler version or twist of an old idea" (BGE 228). Mill, of course, was at pains to develop a subtler hedonistic doctrine than Bentham's, though it is an open question whether in the process he does not pour all the content out of the notion of "pleasure." In any event, Nietzsche drew no distinction between Bentham and Mill—referring to the latter (in an especially intemperate spirit) as "the flathead John Stuart Mill" (WP 30).

extrinsic: suffering—"great" suffering—is a prerequisite of any great human achievement.[44] Nietzsche's attack, then, conforms to the model sketched above: (1) he rejects the view that happiness is *intrinsically* valuable; and (2) he thinks that the negative attitude of MPS toward suffering obscures its important extrinsic value.

In regard to (2), it is worth recalling a biographical fact about Nietzsche, namely, that perhaps no philosopher in history knew suffering more intimately than he did.[45] For many years, he endured excruciating headaches and nausea, lasting for days at a time, during which he was bedridden and often alone. Yet notwithstanding his appallingly bad health throughout the 1880s, he produced in less than a decade the bulk of his remarkable philosophical corpus. In fact, he believed that his suffering contributed essentially to his work; here is a typical—admittedly hyperbolic—remark from *Ecce Homo*:[46] "In the midst of the torments that go with an uninterrupted three-day migraine, accompanied by laborious vomiting of phlegm, I possessed a dialectician's clarity *par excellence* and thought through with very cold blood matters for which under healthier circumstances I am not mountain-climber, not subtle, not *cold* enough" (EH I. 1). Thus, on Nietzsche's picture of his own life, it was absolutely essential and invaluable that he suffered as he did, hence his willingness to will his life's eternal return, *including all its suffering*. We might add, too, that if Nietzsche had taken seriously the MPS evaluation of happiness and suffering, then he should not have been able to maintain his Dionysian attitude toward life; to the contrary, rather than will its repetition, he should have judged his life a failure because it involved so much hardship.[47]

Now it may perhaps be quite true, even uncontroversial, that great achievements (certainly great artistic achievements) seem to grow out of intense suffering: there is no shortage in the history of art and literature of such cases. But granting that, we come up against a serious objection to Nietzsche's position, namely, why should anyone think an MPS is an obstacle to this phenomenon? This is what I shall call the "Harm Puzzle," and the puzzle is this: why should one think that the general moral prescription to alleviate suffering must stop the suffering of great artists, hence stopping them from producing great art? One might think, in fact, that an MPS could

---

[44] Compare GS, Preface, 3: "Only great pain is the ultimate liberator of the spirit. . . . I doubt that such pain makes us 'better'; but I know that it makes us more profound."

[45] For a general account, see Ronald Hayman, *Nietzsche: A Critical Life* (New York: Penguin, 1980).

[46] Compare this letter of Jan. 1880, quoted ibid. 219: "My existence is a fearful burden. I would have thrown it off long ago if I had not been making the most instructive tests and experiments on mental and moral questions in precisely this condition of suffering and almost complete renunciation."

[47] Nietzsche, in fact, reverses the MPS valuation, commenting, "Never have I felt happier with myself than in the sickest and most painful periods of my life" (EH III, HH 4).

perfectly well allow an exception for those individuals whose own suffering is essential to the realization of central life projects. How, then, does MPS "harm" potentially "higher types"?

IV. NIETZSCHE AND THE MORALITY CRITICS

This question serves as a natural point at which to revisit the apparent affinity between Nietzsche and the Morality Critics. As we saw earlier, these Critics argued that morality, because of its commitment to an impersonal point of view and a corresponding impartial standard of value, will prove incompatible with important personal projects and attachments that we all have: such projects, after all, are just one among many from the moral point of view, and thus may have to be sacrificed when morality demands it. These philosophers then argue that since it would be unacceptable actually to forgo these projects and attachments, we must reject the idea that moral considerations are necessarily the practically determinative considerations, overriding all others: sometimes the Good Life must override the Moral Life.

There are, of course, certain obvious differences between the views of these "Morality Critics" and the Nietzsche we have just explored. As Richard Miller has recently observed,[48]

Nietzsche often seems to recommend that the constraints of morality be ignored, but it would be a misreading of his intentions to infer that morality ought to be ignored by someone of middling abilities, or a primary interest in family life, or by someone whose characteristic striving is a successful leveraged buy-out. In contrast, the troubling recommendations at the center of current disputes are very broadly addressed. In particular, Bernard Williams' influential warnings about morality are addressed, primarily, to people with normal attachments and their own projects, projects which may be of ordinary sorts.

This difference in audience is clearly reflected in the differences in worries about what it is morality conflicts with. Thus, the Morality Critics speak of the Moral Life conflicting with, for example, "love, friendship, affection, fellow feeling, and community" (Stocker, "The Schizophrenia of Modern Ethical Theories," 461); with "the kind of personal life that many of us take to be desirable" (Nagel, *View from Nowhere*, 189); with "a healthy, well-rounded, richly developed" life which might include "reading Victorian novels, playing the oboe, or improving [one's] backhand" (Wolf, "Moral Saints," 421); with "the importance of individual character and personal relations" (Williams, "Persons, Character, and Morality," 201). These worries plainly strike a somewhat different note from Nietzsche, who speaks

---

[48] Richard Miller, *Moral Differences* (Princeton: Princeton University Press, 1992), 309.

of morality posing a threat, for example, to "the *highest power and splendor* actually possible to the type man" (GM, Preface, 6); to "the self-reliant, independent, unprejudiced men, the pillars of a *strong* civilization" (D 163); to "all that is rare, strange, privileged . . . the higher soul, the higher duty, the higher responsibility, and the abundance of creative power and masterfulness" (BGE 212); to the "men of great creativity, the really great men according to my understanding" (WP 957). Here the worry is not merely that the Moral Life will interfere with various mundane personal goods important to us all, but rather that it is incompatible with the highest forms of human excellence: it seems that the Moral Life, for Nietzsche, is not a threat to the Good Life but to the Extraordinary Life.

Yet even this difference, we might insist, is really one of degree: for, even if Nietzsche is concerned *not* with the incompatibility of the Moral Life and the Good Life but rather with the tension between the Moral Life and the *Extraordinary* Life, he still seems to join with these Morality Critics in urging that when morality would conflict with certain important nonmoral goods and considerations, morality must sometimes (perhaps for Nietzsche, every time) lose.[49]

It is *this* apparent similarity that bears most directly on the Harm Puzzle now before us. For a number of recent writers have argued—contra the Morality Critics—that morality is *not* incompatible with our various personal projects and attachments, because such projects and attachments can be accommodated within the moral point of view.[50] The utilitarian, for

---

[49] Indeed, even among Morality Critics we sometimes hear echoes of the specifically Nietzschean worry, e.g., in the famous Gauguin case, where it is supposed that the Moral Life would undermine "great creativity," or in Wolf's worry that the moral saint cannot achieve "any of a great variety of forms of personal excellence" ("Moral Saints," 426). Moreover, we have already noted that there is clearly an element of extremism running through Nietzsche's critical position; e.g., we can be sure that Nietzsche would not agree with Wolf that a critique of morality does not show "that moral value should not be an important, even the most important, kind of value we attend to in evaluating and improving ourselves and our world" (p. 438). Yet we can live (probably happily) with these differences of degree and still think that Nietzsche joins cause with the Morality Critics, quite broadly, in accepting the truth of IT and rejecting OT.

[50] See the literature cited above in n. 25. As we saw earlier, there are really two strands in the responses to the Morality Critics: what we might call "Bullet Biters" and "Accommodationists." Bullet Biters like Conly, Herman, and Baron simply "bite the bullet" on the challenge of the Morality Critics: yes, these writers concede, morality is incompatible with a certain sort of commitment to personal projects—but so much the better, the Bullet Biters claim. For the sort of ability of personal projects to override morality that the Critics envision is not appealing, admirable, or central to a person's character or integrity. By contrast, Accommodationists like Railton, Nagel, and Darwall accept the force of the Critics' challenge but claim that morality can, contrary to IT, accommodate the sorts of personal projects that the Morality Critics care about. It is the response of the Accommodationists that is analogous to the challenge posed by the Harm Puzzle. (Needless to say, the line between the two types of theory defenders is not hard and fast. See Railton's account of why "alienation is not always a bad thing" ("Alienation, Consequentialism and the Demand of Morality," 106–8, and compare with the position of the Bullet Biters.)

example, is interested in producing the greatest amount of happiness possible; if sundering people from their most basic projects and attachments
would subvert aggregate happiness, then there can be no utilitarian reason
for thinking that the right course of action.[51] Our personal projects and
attachments are sanctioned from an objective moral point of view, one that
takes into account the net effect of having us abandon them every time a
more immediate moral demand arises.

Why not think, then, that a similar response will suffice for Nietzsche's
challenge? This, of course, is just a variation on the earlier Harm Puzzle. For
if suffering will actually facilitate some individual's flourishing, then surely
morality can recommend that that person suffer. After all, a prescription to
alleviate suffering does not arise in a vacuum: presumably it reflects a concern with promoting well-being, under some construal. But if some
individuals—nascent Goethes, Nietzsches, and other artistic geniuses—
would be *better off* with a good dose of suffering, then why would morality
recommend otherwise? Nietzsche, like the Morality Critics, falls victim, it
seems, to the "objective" point of view embraced by the defenders of
morality.

Or does he? In fact, if this response does work against the Morality
Critics, it decidedly does not work against Nietzsche's critique: for
Nietzsche's point, we might say, is not about *theory* but about *culture*. That
is, Nietzsche's idea seems to be that when MPS values predominate in a
culture, they invariably affect the attitudes of all members of that culture.
If MPS values emphasize the badness of suffering and the goodness of
happiness, that will surely have an effect on how individuals with the potential for great achievements will understand, evaluate, and conduct their own
lives. If suffering is a precondition for these individuals to in fact do anything great, and if they have internalized the norm that suffering must be
alleviated and that happiness is the ultimate goal, then we run the risk that
rather than—to put it crudely—suffer and create, they will instead waste
their energies pursuing pleasure, lamenting their suffering, and seeking to
alleviate it. MPS values may not explicitly prohibit artists or other potentially "excellent" persons from ever suffering, but the risk is that a culture—
like ours—which has internalized the norms *against* suffering and *for*
pleasure will be a culture in which potential artists—and other doers of

---

[51] For doubts that this is, in fact, an adequate response, see Wolf, "Moral Saints," 428. For
related discussion of the important *political* dimension of these issues, see Railton, "Alienation,
Consequentialism and the Demands of Morality," 122–3; and Nagel, *View from Nowhere*, 206–7.
For a very different perspective on this debate, however, see the scathing critique of the Morality
Critics (including Wolf) in Catherine Wilson, "On Some Alleged Limitations to Moral Endeavor,"
Journal of Philosophy, 90 (1993), 275–89.

great things—will, *in fact*, squander themselves in self-pity and the seeking of pleasure.

In sum, for Nietzsche, the normative component of an MPS is harmful not because its specific prescriptions and proscriptions explicitly require potentially excellent persons to forgo that which allows them to flourish—that is, Nietzsche's claim is *not* that a conscientious application of the "theory" of MPS would be incompatible with the flourishing of higher men. Rather, Nietzsche's claim is that an MPS *in practice* simply does not make such fine distinctions: under a regime of MPS values—and importantly because of MPS's embrace of the idea that one morality is appropriate for all—potentially higher men will come to adopt such values as applicable to themselves as well. Thus, the normative component of an MPS is harmful because, in reality, it will have the effect of leading potentially excellent persons to value what is in fact not conducive to their flourishing and devalue what is in fact essential to it.

By contrast, recent Anglo-American Morality Critics take as their target what Wolf calls "a perfect master of a moral theory" ("Moral Saints," 435), whether that theory be consequentialist or deontological. Thus, their critique is directed against the ability of moral *theory* to accommodate the Good Life, while Nietzsche's is directed against the effects of a moral *culture*—one in which MPS norms prevail—on the Extraordinary Life. To Nietzsche's claim that a moral culture will, in practice, present obstacles to the flourishing of creative geniuses, it is simply irrelevant that a suitably "objective" moral theory would not.[52] The Morality Critics, after all, are critics of moral *theory*, and theoretical complaints invariably beget theoretical modifications to accommodate them.[53] But cultural criticism, of the sort Nietzsche mounts, requires a very different sort of response. I will consider in the final section of this paper what some of those might be.

Understand, however, that the claim here is *not* that Nietzsche could not be forced into the existing paradigms of critiques of moral *theory*—for example, as Nagel's philosopher who thinks that living well always overrides

---

[52] Of course, the theorist might object that, even if Nietzsche were right, all this would show is that our cultural practices need correction by a suitable moral theory, one that will permit nascent Nietzsches to suffer and the like. I shall postpone this worry for now and consider it, and several other objections to Nietzsche's position, in the final section of this paper.

[53] Compare Lawrence Becker's observation that defenders of morality's commitment to impartiality try to show that the "purported inadequacies [of impartiality] ... are not really attributable to a *proper theoretical commitment* to impartiality" ("Impartiality and Ethical Theory," *Ethics*, 101 (1991), 698–700, 700, emphasis added). See also Stocker: "[The phenomenon of] admirable immorality ... show[s] how immorality and defect can and must be allowed for in ethical theory" (Michael Stocker, *Plural and Conflicting Values* (Oxford: Clarendon Press, 1990), 50).

doing right.[54] My claim has been only that this was not really the heart of *Nietzsche*'s critique. Nietzsche was not interested in whether our moral theories could accommodate the Good Life or the Extraordinary Life; Nietzsche was worried whether our culture was making it impossible for anyone to live an Extraordinary Life anymore. It is one of the few themes that animated all Nietzsche's writings from start to finish. In an early essay of the mid-1870s, "Schopenhauer as Educator" (UM III), Nietzsche speaks of "the goal of culture" as "the production of genius" (6), though there he worries not primarily about the deleterious effect of morality on culture but about "the crudest and most evil forces, the egoism of the moneymakers and the military despots" (4), as well as "the greed of the state" (6). His major work of the early 1880s, *Thus Spoke Zarathustra*, begins with Zarathustra's image of a world in which all human excellence and creativity is gone, in which all that will remain is the "last man":

Alas, the time of the most despicable man is coming, he that is no longer able to despise himself. Behold, I show you the *last man*.

"What is love? What is creation? What is longing? What is a star?" thus asks the last man, and he blinks.

The earth has become small, and on it hops the last man, who makes everything small . . .

"We have invented happiness," say the last men, and they blink. They have left the regions where it was hard to live, for one needs warmth. One still loves one's neighbor and rubs against him, for one needs warmth . . .

No shepherd and one herd! Everybody wants the same, everybody is the same: whoever feels different goes voluntarily into a madhouse.

"Formerly, all the world was mad," say the most refined, and they blink.

One is clever and knows everything that has ever happened: so there is no end of derision. One still quarrels, but one is soon reconciled—else it might spoil the digestion . . .

"We have invented happiness," say the last men, and they blink. (Z, Prologue, 5)

In the last man, we encounter all the distinctive norms of MPS: the last man embraces happiness, comfort, peacefulness, neighbor love, equality. As a result, the last man can only ask, "What is creation?" thus signaling the distance between him and any type of human excellence, for, as Zarathustra says later, "the great—that is, the creating" (Z I. 12).

Finally, in his last productive year, 1888, Nietzsche speaks of Christian

---

[54] Indeed, one might pick out various points where the Morality Critics seem to echo Nietzsche. Compare Wolf: "A moral saint will have to be very, very nice. It is important that he not be offensive. The worry is that, as a result, he will have to be dull-witted or humorless or bland" ("Moral Saints," 422); cf. BGE 260: "the good human being [according to slave morality] has to be *undangerous* . . . : he is good-natured, easy to deceive, a little stupid perhaps, *un bonhomme*. Wherever slave morality becomes preponderant, language tends to bring the words 'good' and 'stupid' closer together."

morality as having "waged war unto death . . . against the *presupposition* of every elevation, of every growth of culture" (A 43), and he claims that acting in accord with what "has been called morality" "would deprive existence of its *great* character" (EH IV. 4). The distinctively Nietzschean worry, then, is that our moral *culture*—not our best moral *theory*—is ushering in the reign of the last man, of complete mediocrity and banality.

Even granting that Nietzsche's attack is ultimately a *culture critique*, rather than a theoretical critique, one might still insist that it has an important theoretical component. After all, Nietzsche does call for "*new philosophers* . . . spirits strong and original enough to provide the stimuli for opposite valuations and to revalue and invert 'eternal values'" (BGE 203). Could we not find here the real commonality of interests between Nietzsche and the Morality Critics? For aren't both "philosophers" who challenge the overridingness of moral considerations, who reconsider the *value* of letting moral considerations dominate all others?

One difference, which we have encountered several times before, is one of degree: as Nagel's appropriation of Nietzsche aptly suggests, Nietzsche's position within the debate framed by the Morality Critics is far more radical, seeming, as it does, to assign complete priority to the Good (or Extraordinary) Life over the Moral Life. Nietzsche, on this picture, really is "inverting" prior values, while the Morality Critics are, at best, calling for a slight turn away from the hegemony of the Moral Life.

Yet again, the difference cuts more deeply than this, for the *grounds* on which moral values are to be revalued are different. For Nietzsche, they are essentially empirical, growing out of his claim that in a fully moral culture no one will be able to lead an Extraordinary Life.[55] For the Morality Critics, by contrast, the claim is theoretical, namely, that even an optimal moral theory would still require its perfect adherent to forgo aspects of the Good Life. Thus, the "revaluation" envisioned by the Morality Critics—even ignoring its more modest aims—starts (and ends) within *theory*, while Nietzsche's starts from a cultural diagnosis (namely, the cause of our cultural mediocrity—of the absence of genius—is our morality) and ends with a cultural prognosis (namely, our moral culture will gradually yield a society of "last men").

---

[55] The reader may wonder in what sense Nietzsche's claims are empirical, since they are hardly the upshot of systematic investigation into, say, the psychology and etiology of genius. They are empirical, however, in the sense that Nietzsche seems to have reached these conclusions from certain sorts of observation: first, and most important, of himself and his own development (note that the theme only appears in his work in the very late 1870s, when he is about thirty-five and has already been ill for several years); second, of various historical figures and cultures with which he was acquainted through his studies and reading. As I note at the end, though, the case for his critique really requires a more sustained empirical examination.

V. NIETZSCHE'S CRITIQUE: A
CRITICAL ASSESSMENT

If the Morality Critics are right, then we have failed in our attempts to produce an ethical theory that could tell us how to live both well *and* rightly. It is decidedly not an upshot of their critique, however, that, as a matter of fact, we cannot or do not live well: if Utilitarianism, in theory, alienates us from our projects, in reality it goes without saying that it has no such effect. In the culture at large, hardly anyone knows what Utilitarianism is, let alone observes its strictures to the extremes that would lead one to worry that it "demands too much."[56] (The same might, of course, be said about deontology, as noted earlier in the discussion of Williams.) The Morality Critics have shown that the enterprise of moral theory is in a bind, unable to resolve the competing demands of the Good Life and the Moral Life; they surely haven't shown that people don't lead Good Lives.

With Nietzsche things stand differently. If the Nietzschean critique is right, then we are supposed to be confronted with something very real: our untutored morality, the morality of ordinary men and women, the morality that infuses our culture is, in fact, an obstacle to human excellence; the price of our moral culture is a culture of banality and mediocrity, one in which Zarathustra's "last men" predominate, in which "things will continue to go down, to become thinner, more good-natured, more prudent, more comfortable, more mediocre, more indifferent" (GM I. 12).

It would be neither surprising nor unreasonable for Anglo-American philosophers to express doubts about their competence to undertake or assess such a critical project: such a "philosophical" undertaking—if that is what it deserves to be called—brings to mind a very different conception of philosophy, in which reflection is manifestly not a priori and analysis is not merely "conceptual" or, in this post-Quinean world, simply the a posteriori handmaiden of the natural and social sciences. In its Nietzschean incarnation, philosophy quickly crosses the line into psychology, cultural anthropology, and social critique—territory now occupied (regrettably) almost exclusively by literary theorists.

This conception of philosophical practice, of course, has always been more common on the European continent. Indeed, it is this conception of philosophical practice that binds Nietzsche most closely to the philosophical tradition on the Continent, since he shares none of the metaphysical ambitions of the German Idealists before him and none of the phenomenological

---

[56] Compare Annette Baier's complaints about the irrelevance of moral theory, of its "construction of private fantasy moral worlds" ("Doing without Moral Theory?" 235; cf. p. 234).

scholasticism of many of those who followed.[57] It also has much to do with why the writings of Nietzsche resonate so widely in the intellectual community, while they are often thought rather suspect in the Anglo-American philosophical world.

Yet surely some doubts about the sweep of the Nietzschean criticism are warranted. I should like to conclude with four observations on this score.

1. A natural reaction the philosophical theorist might have to Nietzsche's critique was mentioned earlier: for surely, the theorist might say, what the Nietzschean critique really shows is that our cultural practices need to be *corrected* by moral theory. For if the best moral theory could, as some of the respondents to the Morality Critics have argued, accommodate the Good Life (perhaps even the Extraordinary Life), then we simply need to bring our moral culture more in line with our best moral theory. The proper response to the Nietzschean critique is not despair about morality but a healthy dose of moral philosophy.

One might wonder, of course, how realistic it is to think that our cultural practices will be reformed by the labor of philosophers. As Thomas Nagel remarked rather frankly a number of years ago, "Moral judgment and moral theory certainly apply to public questions, but they are notably ineffective."[58] If there is little reason to think that moral theory will have any effect outside the academy—certainly there is little evidence to suggest otherwise—then holding out the prospect of moral theory can hardly assuage the worries of a cultural critic.[59]

This response is not, however, Nietzsche's. Nietzsche's actual response to this challenge has a rather more sinister air, for it arises from what I will call his "Callicleanism." By this I do not mean to attribute to Nietzsche anything like Calliclean hedonism—a doctrine that many writers have rightly noted was not Nietzsche's[60]—but rather the Calliclean view of morality as a tool of the mediocre, as the means by which the inferior make "slaves of those who are naturally better" (*Gorgias*, 491e–492a), by which they try to

---

[57] Gilles Deleuze aptly calls phenomenology "our modern scholasticism" in *Nietzsche and Philosophy*, trans. H. Tomlinson (New York: Columbia University Press, 1983), 195.

[58] Nagel, *Mortal Questions*, p. xii.

[59] One might worry, though, that such a complaint will backfire against Nietzsche, for isn't he a "theorist" of sorts, hoping to affect cultural practice? The answer, I think, is that Nietzsche is an esoteric moralist, hoping to reach only a few select readers, those "predisposed and predestined for" his insights (BGE 30); thus he aims not to reform culture but to enlighten a select few to the dangers of the dominant moral culture. This is why, contrary to a large amount of recent literature, Nietzsche does not have any *political theory* or any real *politics*. I hope to address these issues, however, elsewhere.

[60] See Nehamas, *Nietzsche*, 202–3; Philippa Foot, "Nietzsche's Immoralism," *New York Review of Books*, 38 (13 June 1991), 19, repr. in *Nietzsche, Genealogy, Morality*.

"frighten [the strong] by saying that to overreach others is shameful and evil" (*Gorgias*, 483b–d). We hear this same Calliclean theme in Nietzsche's claim that "moral judgments and condemnations constitute the favorite revenge of the spiritually limited against those less limited" (BGE 219) and in his assertion that the "chief means" by which the "weak and mediocre . . . weaken and pull down the stronger" is "the moral judgment" (WP 345).[61] This Calliclean conception of morality would explain why morality would not want to except potentially higher men from its scope: it is precisely part of the aim of the proponents of morality to *harm* higher men. Reforming cultural practices with moral theory in order to permit higher types to flourish would run counter to a central purpose of morality on the Calliclean/ Nietzschean picture.

This response no doubt strikes the contemporary reader as rather odd, perhaps a bit too conspiratorial to be credible. After all, Nietzsche's claim seems to be that, *as a matter of cultural fact*, the proponents of morality aim to cut down the high—that there is, in other words, a conspiracy of the base and mediocre whose weapon is morality. Even if this image seems far-fetched as well as foreign to the central purposes of morality properly construed, Nietzsche may be right that there is a real phenomenon here, though perhaps not of conspiratorial proportions (cf. GS 359). Think, for example, of the public conflicts between the defenders of moral decency and artists. Such familiar cases might help support the Nietzschean skepticism about whether the cultural protectors of morality would really be interested in reforming morality to make room for Nietzschean creative geniuses.

I do not, however, want to push this defense of Nietzsche's Callicleanism too far. Perhaps we are better off here with the earlier response made on Nietzsche's behalf: even if moral theory *might* accommodate the Extraordinary Life, this does not seem responsive to the worry that our actual moral culture does not.

2. A second reaction one might have, however, is that the Nietzschean critique is simply hyperbolic, for surely if there is a culture of mediocrity and banality in ascendance, it is not primarily the work of morality, but perhaps of economics—for example, the free market, the leveling effects of which have been described by sociologists, historians, and philosophers. Indeed, the right model for culture critique, one might want to say, is not the "idealistic"-

---

[61] Nietzsche's polemic against Christianity in *The Antichrist* is framed in the starkest Calliclean terms, with Nietzsche describing "the cross as the mark of recognition for the most subterranean conspiracy that ever existed—against health, beauty, whatever has turned out well, courage, spirit, *graciousness* of the soul, *against life itself*" (A 62); see also WP 400: "In the history of morality a will to power finds expression, through which now the slaves and oppressed, now the ill-constituted and those who suffer from themselves, now the mediocre attempt to make those value judgments prevail that are favorable to *them*."

sounding Nietzsche described here but rather the materialist Adorno of *Minima Moralia*, who traces cultural mediocrity to its capitalist roots.

Now, while the early Nietzsche of "Schopenhauer as Educator" did, as we saw, worry about the effects of capitalism, militaristic nationalism, and proto-fascism on the cultural conditions for the production of genius, the later Nietzsche seems all too ready to lay the blame for all cultural decline at the doorstep of what I have been calling MPS.[62] Nietzsche's challenge may be a novel and important one, but no one who reads his repeated denunciations of morality can escape the feeling that he suffered from a certain explanatory tunnel vision, with the result that, in some measure, his case against morality seems overstated.

3. On further reflection, however, one might want to say something much stronger: Nietzsche's point is not just hyperbolic, but perversely backward. For surely it is the *lack* of morality in social policy and public institutions—a lack which permits widespread poverty and despair to persist generation upon generation, that allows daily economic struggle and uncertainty to define the basic character of most people's lives—that is most responsible for a lack of human flourishing. Surely in a more moral society, with a genuine commitment to social justice and human equality, there would be far more Goethes, far more creativity and admirable human achievement. As Philippa Foot has sharply put it, "How could one see the present dangers that the world is in as showing that there is too much pity and too little egoism around?"[63]

Here again, though, we must be careful in how we construe the Nietzschean point. Consider the Nietzsche who asks, "Where has the last feeling of decency and self-respect gone when even our statesmen, an otherwise quite unembarrassed type of man, anti-Christians through and through in their deeds, still call themselves Christians today and attend communion?" (A 38). Clearly this Nietzsche is under no illusions about the extent to which public actors do not act morally. Indeed, Nietzsche continues in even more explicit terms: "Every practice of every moment, every instinct, every valuation that is translated into *action* is today anti-Christian: what a *miscarriage of falseness* must modern man be, that he is *not ashamed* to be called a Christian in spite of all this!" (A 38). What, then, is going on here? If Nietzsche is not, contrary to Foot's suggestion, embracing the absurd view that there is too much pity and altruism in the world, what exactly is his critical point?

---

[62] Nietzsche also often blames "Christianity," but we must remember that for Nietzsche Christianity was simply "the most prodigal elaboration of the moral theme to which humanity has ever been subjected" (BT, Preface, 5).

[63] Foot, "Nietzsche: The Revaluation of Values," Ch. 8 in this volume, p. 220.

Nietzsche's paradigmatic worry seems to be the following: that a nascent creative genius will come to take the norms of MPS so seriously that he will fail to realize his genius. Rather than tolerate (even welcome) suffering, he will seek relief from hardship and devote himself to the pursuit of pleasure; rather than practice what Nietzsche calls "severe self-love" and attend to himself in the ways requisite for productive creative work, he will embrace the ideology of altruism and reject "self-love" as improper; rather than learn how to look down on himself, to desire to overcome his present self and become something better, he will embrace the prevailing rhetoric of equality—captured nicely in the pop psychology slogan "I'm OK, you're OK"—and thus never learn to feel the contempt for self that might lead one to strive for something more. It is not, then, that Nietzsche thinks people *practice* too much altruism—after all, it is Nietzsche who notes that egoistic actions "have hitherto been by far the most frequent actions" (D 148)—but rather that they *believe* too much in the value of altruism, equality, happiness, and the other norms of MPS. It is the prevalence of the MPS *ideology* that worries Nietzsche, for, even if there is neither much altruism nor equality in the world, there is almost universal endorsement of the *value* of altruism and equality—even, notoriously (and as Nietzsche seemed well aware), by those who are its worst enemies in practice. Nietzsche's claim is that a culture which embraces the ideology of MPS, even if it does not act in accordance with this ideology, presents the real threat to the realization of human excellence, because it teaches potential higher types to disvalue what would be most conducive to their creativity and value what is irrelevant or perhaps even hostile to it.

Nietzsche's point here is, I think, a subtle one, for surely it makes sense that individuals of great creativity and sensitivity are far more likely to take seriously the ideology of MPS than the politicians whose hypocrisy Nietzsche derides in the remark quoted earlier.[64] As Nietzsche observes at one point, "What distinguishes the higher human beings from the lower is that the former see and hear immeasurably more, and see and hear more thoughtfully" (GS 301). But it is precisely this trait of the "higher human beings" that makes them all the more susceptible to the deleterious effects of MPS: a thoughtless brute is hardly likely to worry about the morality of his acts, but neither is he likely to become a creative genius. But the higher types that Nietzsche worries about are both likely candidates for critical self-reflection in light of the norms of MPS and, at the same time, those for

---

[64] To say that they take the demands of MPS "seriously" is *not* to say that they understand them in the way a philosophical theory would; it is only to say that they are more likely to take these unsystematic and inchoate demands constitutive of morality as weighing seriously upon them.

whom such norms are most harmful. Indeed, we might say that it is precisely Nietzsche's aim to help these higher human beings "see and hear" something more, namely, that MPS values are really disadvantageous for them.

That Nietzsche's concern is with the prevalence of the MPS ideology, not the prevalence of actions in accord with MPS, and in particular with the effect of this ideology on the *self-conception* of potentially higher types is suggested in many places. In *Dawn*, Nietzsche speaks of wanting to deprive egoistic actions of "their bad conscience" (D 148). In *Beyond Good and Evil*, he observes that in order to "stand all valuations *on their head*," Christianity had to

cast suspicion on the joy in beauty, bend everything haughty . . . conquering, domineering, all the instincts characteristic of the highest and best-turned-out type of "man," into unsureness, dilemma of conscience (*Gewissens-Noth*), self-destruction. (BGE 62)

In *Twilight of the Idols*, he describes the "man" "improved" by MPS as

a caricature of man, like a miscarriage: he had become a "sinner," he was stuck in a cage, *imprisoned among all sorts of terrible concepts* (*schreckliche Begriffe*). And there he lay, sick, miserable, malevolent against himself: full of hatred against the springs of life, full of suspicion against all that was still strong and happy. (TI VII. 2, emphasis added)

In each case, we see that the thrust of the worry is that higher types will come to evaluate and think of themselves in terms of the *concepts* peculiar to MPS (and Christianity)—that they will become "imprisoned among all sorts of terrible concepts"—with the result that they will be cast into self-doubt and a destructive self-loathing, and thus never realize the excellences of which they are capable.

His general point is perhaps most strikingly put in a very Calliclean passage from *Beyond Good and Evil*:

The highest and strongest drives, when they break out passionately and drive the individual far above the average and the flats of the herd conscience, wreck the self-confidence of the community. . . . Hence just these drives are branded and slandered most. High and independent spirituality, the will to stand alone, even a powerful reason are experienced as dangers; everything that elevates an individual above the herd and intimidates the neighbor is henceforth called *evil*; and the fair, modest, conforming mentality, the *mediocrity* of desires attains moral designations and honors. (BGE 201)

"High and independent spirituality," "the will to stand alone": do these traits not call to mind many an artist, poet, and even a great philosopher or two? Yet it is these traits that MPS "brands" and "slanders," and who would be surprised if someone should abandon their independent ways with the force of morality against them? It is not, then, that there is too much pity and altruism in the world, but rather that there is too much *belief in the value* of pity, altruism, and the other norms of MPS.

4. One might want to respond on Foot's behalf, however, and insist that there is still something perverse about the Nietzschean complaint. Granted Nietzsche does not believe that most people are *actually* too altruistic and society *in practice* is too egalitarian; granted that Nietzsche's real worry is about the fact that we, as a moral culture, pay so much lip service to the value of altruism, egalitarianism, and the rest, with the resultant deleterious effects on the self-conception and development of nascent Goethes. Yet surely it is still the case that if our society *really* were more altruistic and egalitarian, more individuals would have the chance to flourish and do creative work. This is the core of the charge of perversity, and nothing said so far has exonerated Nietzsche from it.

Now, in fact, it seems that it is precisely this moral optimism common, for example, to utilitarians and Marxists—this belief that a more moral society would produce more opportunity for more people to do creative work—that Nietzsche does, indeed, want to question. Nietzsche's illiberal attitudes in this regard are apparent. He says, to take but one example, "We simply do not consider it desirable that a realm of justice and harmony (*Eintracht*) should be established on earth" (GS 377). It is bad enough for Nietzsche that MPS values have so far succeeded in saying, "stubbornly and inexorably, 'I am morality itself, and nothing besides is morality'" (BGE 202); it could only be worse on his view if more and more of our actions were really brought into accord with these values. For Nietzsche wants to urge— contrary to the moral optimists—that, in a way largely unappreciated and (perhaps) unintended, a thoroughly *moral* culture undermines the conditions under which the most splendid human creativity is possible and generates instead a society of Zarathustra's "last men."[65] If we are trained always to think of happiness and comfort and safety and the needs of others, we shall cut ourselves off from the preconditions for creative excellence on the Nietzschean picture: suffering, hardship, danger, self-concern, and the rest.

Consider a final, and I think powerful, statement of this view. Speaking of those "eloquent and profoundly scribbling slaves of the democratic taste and its 'modern ideas'" who seek to promote "the universal green-pasture happiness of the herd" and who take "suffering itself . . . for something that must be abolished" (BGE 44), Nietzsche retorts that when we look at

how the plant "man" has so far grown most vigorously to a height—we think that this has happened every time under the opposite conditions, that to this end the dangerousness of his situation must first grow to the point of enormity, his power of

---

[65] See the earlier quotations from Zarathustra's description of the last man.

invention and simulation (his "spirit") had to develop under prolonged pressure and constraint into refinement and audacity . . . We think that . . . everything evil, terrible, tyrannical in man, everything in him that is kin to beasts of prey and serpents, serves the enhancement of the species "man" as much as its opposite does. Indeed, we do not even say enough when we say only that much. (BGE 44)

Note that at the end of this passage Nietzsche hints at a role for morality as well—it is just that what morality opposes is equally important. He, of course, qualifies this by suggesting that even to concede their equal import-ance may "not even say enough": that is, perhaps there will not be much role for morality at all in the conditions under which "the plant 'man'" will grow to its greatest heights.

I want to conclude with one final observation about the nature and signifi-cance of Nietzsche's critique of morality, for Nietzsche's critique raises a difficulty that, it seems, moral theories ought to address. The difficulty is this: in practice, morality may have a tendency to undermine other sorts of goods or excellences, even when the theory does not actually require that morality do so. Note that this problem remains even if the respondents to the Morality Critics are right that moral theories, properly construed, can accommodate the Good Life and even the Extraordinary Life. For Nietzsche's challenge, recall, is pitched at the level of culture, not theory: the worry is precisely that even if the theory *would* condone or support the Extraordinary Life, the actual practice does not.[66]

We can say, then, that Nietzsche's critique raises the following general concern for any moral theory: what would the culture that embraces the moral theory *actually* look like and, in particular, would it be acceptable according to the standards of the theory itself? This would not constitute a direct criticism of the theory, but it surely constitutes a worry that any theory we might want to choose to live by should address. It might also help loosen our attachment to what Nozick aptly calls "normative sociology": "the study of what the causes of problems *ought to be*." Thus, says Nozick, "We *want* one bad thing to be caused by another [bad thing]."[67] But if Nietzsche is right, then we may have to confront the possibility that seem-ingly good things—like many of the norms of MPS—cause apparently "bad" things, like the gradual disappearance of human excellence.

Needless to say, many of Nietzsche's claims about the effects of morality are highly speculative, and they cry out for careful, empirical consideration.

---

[66] In his Calliclean moods, of course, Nietzsche believes that morality really aims to undermine the Extraordinary Life, but one might reject the Callicleanism and still think there is something to the underlying causal claim.

[67] Robert Nozick, *Anarchy, State, and Utopia* (New York: Basic Books, 1974), 247.

The Morality Critics have the advantage, at least, of conducting their critique on safer, more familiar philosophical territory. Yet it does remain striking that, more than one hundred years after Nietzsche cast down his challenge to morality, the topic still remains largely unexplored.

10

"HOW ONE BECOMES WHAT ONE IS"

ALEXANDER NEHAMAS

> People are always shouting they want to create a better future. It's not
> true. The future is an apathetic void, of no interest to anyone. The past
> is full of life, eager to irritate, provoke and insult us, tempt us to destroy
> or repaint it. The only reason people want to be masters of the future is
> to change the past.
>
> (Milan Kundera, *The Book of Laughter and Forgetting*)

Being and becoming, according to Nietzsche, are not at all related as we
commonly suppose. "Becoming," he writes, "must be explained without
recourse to final intentions. . . . Becoming does not aim at a final state, does
not flow into 'being'."[1] One of his many criticisms of philosophers
("humans have always been philosophers") is that they have turned away
from what changes and have only tried to understand what is: "But since
nothing *is*, all that was left to the philosopher as his 'world' was the imaginary."[2] His thinking is informed by his opposition to the very idea of a distinction between appearance and reality.[3] In "How the 'True World' Finally
Became a Fable," one of his most widely read passages, he concludes: "The
true world—we have abolished. What world remains? The apparent one
perhaps? But no! With the true world we have also abolished the apparent

From Alexander Nehamas, "'How One Becomes What One Is,'" *Philosophical Review*, 92 (1983),
385–417. Used by permission of the publisher, Cornell University Press. An early version of this
essay was prepared for the Chapel Hill Philosophy Colloquium in Oct. 1981. Richard Schacht's
comments on that occasion, along with those of other friends and colleagues at other institutions,
led to numerous improvements. The assistance of the readers of the *Philosophical Review* was also
very valuable.

[1] KGW viii/2. 277; WP 708. I cite KGW by division, followed by volume, followed by page
numbers. English translations in this essay are by Kaufmann or Kaufmann and Hollingdale.

[2] KGW viii/2. 252; WP 570.

[3] It does not, however, reach as far back as *The Birth of Tragedy* (BT), where Nietzsche writes
that "the contrast between this real truth of nature and the lie of culture that poses as if it were the
only reality is similar to that between the eternal core of things, the thing-in-itself, and the whole
world of appearances" (BT 19; KGW iii/1. 54–5). I am not yet convinced by the otherwise brilliant
attempt of Paul de Man to show that the book's rhetoric undermines the distinction its content
sets up; cf. *Allegories of Reading* (New Haven: Yale University Press, 1980), 79–102.

one."[4] The contrast itself is not sensible: "The apparent world and the world invented by a lie—this is the antithesis"; and the pointlessness of the antithesis implies that "no shadow of a right remains to speak here of appearance."[5]

Nietzsche does not simply attack the distinction between reality or things in themselves on the one hand and appearance or phenomena on the other. He also claims that this distinction is nothing but a projection onto the external world of our unjustified belief that the self is a substance, somehow set over and above its thoughts, desires and actions. Language, he writes,

everywhere . . . sees a doer and doing; it believes in will as *the* cause; it believes in the ego, in the ego as being, in the ego as substance, and it projects this faith in the ego-substance upon all things—only thereby does it first *create* the concept of a "thing" . . . the concept of being follows, and is a derivative of, the concept of ego.[6]

This is, to say the least, a very obscure view. Why should we suppose that a particular construction of the self precedes, and is projected onto, our construction of the external world? Nietzsche should be particularly concerned with this question since he consistently insists on the social nature of consciousness and therefore appears committed to the idea that the concepts of self and object develop in parallel to each other. In *The Gay Science*, for example, Nietzsche offers what for his time may indeed have been "the perhaps extravagant surmise . . . that consciousness has developed only under the pressure of the need for communication" and connects this development with the evolution of language.[7] In *The Will to Power*, to cite just one other instance, he writes that consciousness "is only a means of communication: it is evolved through social intercourse and with the view to the interests of social intercourse—'Intercourse' here understood to include the influences of the outer world and the reactions they compel on our side; also our effect upon the outer world".[8]

---

[4] KGW vi/3. 75; TI IV.

[5] KGW viii/3. 111; WP 461. Cf. KGW viii/3. 163; WP 567. Cp., "The antithesis of the apparent world and the true world is reduced to the antithesis 'world' and 'nothing'" (ibid.).

[6] KGW vi/3. 71; TI III. 5. Some relevant passages are KGW vii/1. 193; viii/2. 131; viii/1. 321–2; viii/2. 47–50; WP 473, 485, 519, 552.

[7] KGW v/2. 272–3. GS 374.

[8] KGW viii/2. 309–10; WP 524. It might be objected on Nietzsche's behalf that one should take into account his view that only a small part of our thinking is conscious; cf. GS 354 and KGW vi/2. 11; BGE 3. Accordingly, the objection would continue, though *consciousness* develops along with our concepts of the external world, our belief in the ego as "substance" may already be part of our unconscious, "instinctive" thinking. But Nietzsche, it seems to me, thinks of instinctive thinking and acting (which he often considers to be goals to be achieved) as modes which specifically preclude our conscious differentiation between subject and object, doer and deed; cf., for example, KGW viii/3. 119; WP 423. Such instinctive action, with its attendant identification of agent and effect, is what Zarathustra has in mind when he urges his disciples to become such "that your self be in your deed as the mother is in her child," KGW vi/1. 119; Z II. 5. The same point is suggested by the important sect. 213 of BGE; KGW vi/2. 151–2.

What concerns me on this occasion, however, is not Nietzsche's problematic "psychological derivation of the belief in things" itself. Rather, I want to focus on the close analogy he finds to hold between what is true of the world in general and what is true of the self in particular, independently of the question of which is modelled upon which. We have already seen him write that "Becoming . . . does not flow into 'being'." But if this is so, how are we to account for that most haunting of his many haunting philosophical aphorisms, the phrase "How one becomes what one is" (*Wie man wird, was man ist*), which constitutes the subtitle of *Ecce Homo*, Nietzsche's intellectual autobiography and, with ironic appropriateness, the last book he ever was to write?[9]

I

It could be, of course, that the phrase "How one becomes what one is" was simply a very clever piece of language that happened to catch (as well it might have) Nietzsche's passing fancy. But this is not true. The idea appears elsewhere in *Ecce Homo*,[10] and we can find it present in all the stages of his philosophical career. It appears as early as *Schopenhauer as Educator*, the third of Nietzsche's *Untimely Meditations*: "The man who would not belong to the mass needs only to cease being comfortable with himself; he should follow his conscience which shouts at him: 'Be yourself (*sei du selbst*); you are not really all that which you do, think, and desire now'."[11] The formulation is simplified to an aphorism in *The Gay Science*: "What does your conscience say?—You must become who you are."[12] In the same book Nietzsche claims that, in contrast to "moralists," he and the sort of people

[9] Nietzsche began writing *Ecce Homo* (EH) on his forty-fourth birthday, 15 Oct. 1888, and finished it on 4 Nov. of that year. During that time, and before his collapse in Jan. 1889, he also managed to put together *Nietzsche contra Wagner* and his *Dionysos–Dithyramben*, but both works consisted of pieces already published elsewhere and involved no new writing.

[10] KGW vi/3. 291, 317–19; EH II. 9 and EH III, UM 3. R. J. Hollingdale gives some background material in his introduction to his own translation of the work (Harmondsworth: Penguin, 1979), 14–15.

[11] KGW iii/1. 334. Quoted from Walter Kaufmann, *Nietzsche: Philosopher, Psychologist, Antichrist*, 4th edn. (Princeton: Princeton University Press, 1974), 158. Nietzsche had been fascinated by this idea since at least 1867, as a letter of his to Rohde indicates. He derived it from Pindar's Second Pythian Ode, line 73: *genoi'hoios essi mathōn*, having dropped, along with the last word, Pindar's reference to learning and knowledge, and his probable reference to the art of kingship. For a recent discussion of this crucial and difficult passage see Erich Thummer, "Die Zweite Pythische Ode Pindars," *Rheinisches Museum für Philologie*, 115 (1972), 293–307.

[12] KGW v/2. 197; GS 270. Kaufmann's translation, "You shall become the person you are," misses the imperative force of the German "*Du sollst der werden, der du bist*." One might also try to use the Biblical "Thou shalt," which is more appropriate in this context.

with whom he belongs "want to become those we are."[13] Finally, in the late works, we find Zarathustra saying of himself: "*That* is what I am through and through: reeling, reeling in, raising up, raising, a raiser, cultivator, and disciplinarian, who once counseled himself, not for nothing: Become who you are! (*werde, der du bist!*)"[14] In short, and as I shall try to show, this aphorism leads us if not to the center at least through the bulk of Nietzsche's thought.

As a consequence, in tracing its significance, we shall have to raise many more questions than we can answer. In addition, we shall be often confronted by the obstacles that commonly face such explorations of Nietzsche: on many occasions we shall find our path blocked by ideas that are at least seemingly inconsistent with our aphorism; and just as we manage to interpret them appropriately, we shall find him denying them in directions that take us even farther afield.

We have already remarked on the problem posed for our aphorism by Nietzsche's view of the relation between becoming and being. But the interpretation of the phrase "Become who you are" is also made difficult by Nietzsche's vehement conviction that the very idea of the self as subject is itself an invention, that there is no such thing as the self. As he writes, for example, in *On the Genealogy of Morals*, "there is no such substratum; there is no 'being' behind doing, effecting, becoming; 'the doer' is merely a fiction added to the deed—the deed is everything. The popular mind in fact doubles the deed; when it sees the lightning flash, it is the deed of a deed: it posits the same event first as cause and then a second time as its effect."[15] In reducing the agent self to the totality of its actions, Nietzsche is applying his doctrine of the will to power, part of which consists in a general identification of every object in the world with the sum of its effects on every other thing.[16] This immediately raises the question of how we can determine which actions to group together as belonging to one self, the question of *whose* deed is the deed that is "everything." But even before we can turn to that, we are stopped by the following passage from *The Will to Power*: "The 'spirit,' something that thinks—this conception is a second derivative of that false introspection which believes in 'thinking': first an act is imagined which simply does not occur, 'thinking,' and secondly a subject-substratum in

---

[13] KGW v/2. 243; GS 335.

[14] KGW vi/1. 293; Z IV. 1.

[15] KGW vi/2. 293; GM I. 13. This idea informs *The Twilight of the Idols*, and appears in many of the notes collected in *The Will to Power*, where it is often discussed in connection with the image of the lightning; cf. WP 481–92, 531, 548–9, 551–2, 631–4.

[16] Cf., for example, WP 553–69, most notes dating between 1885 and 1888. I have discussed this issue (though much remains to be said about it still) in "The Eternal Recurrence," Ch. 4 in this volume.

which every act of thinking, and nothing else, has its origin: that is to say, *both the deed and the doer are fictions.*"[17]

Let us leave this further twist for later consideration. What we must do now is to see Nietzsche's original reduction of each subject to a set of actions in the context of his denial of the distinction between appearance and underlying reality: "What is appearance to me now?" he asks in *The Gay Science*; "Certainly not the opposite of some essence: what could I say about any essence except to name the attributes of its appearance!"[18] For this connection immediately blocks an obvious interpretation of the aphorism.

Such an interpretation would proceed along Freudian lines. We could try to identify the self that one is and that one must become with that set of thoughts and desires which, for whatever reason, have been repressed and remain hidden and which constitute the reality of which one's current self is the appearance. Such a view would allow for the reinterpretation of one's thoughts and desires as a means to realizing who one is. To that extent, I think, it would be congenial to Nietzsche, who wrote in *The Gay Science*: "There is no trick which enables us to turn a poor virtue into a rich and overflowing one; but we can reinterpret its poverty into a necessity so that it no longer offends us when we see it and we no longer sulk at fate on its account."[19] This passage raises questions about self-deception which we must also leave aside until later. The point I want to make now is that despite this parallel, the common or "vulgar" Freudian idea that the core of one's self is always there, formed to a great extent early on in life and waiting for some sort of liberation, is incompatible not only with Nietzsche's view of the self as fiction, but also with his attitude toward the question of the discovery of truth: "'Truth' is . . . not something there, that might be found or discovered—but something that must be created and that gives a name to a process, or rather to a will to overcome that has in itself no end— introducing truth, as a *processus in infinitum*, an active determining—not a becoming conscious of something that is in itself firm and determined."[20]

---

[17] KGW viii/2. 296; WP 477. A similar point is made in connection with willing in KGW viii/2. 296; WP 668. A further complication is introduced in KGW viii/3. 286–7; WP 675.

[18] KGW v/2. 91; GS 54. The passage suggests that the distinction between appearance and reality often is motivated by an unwillingness to acknowledge the inconsistency of the object of one's inquiry.

[19] KGW v/2. 63; GS 17.

[20] KGW viii/2. 49; WP 552. Nietzsche's approach also disposes of the following objection, raised by J. P. Stern, *A Study of Nietzsche* (Cambridge: Cambridge University Press, 1979), 116. Stern quotes the statement, "Your true self . . . lies immeasurably above that which you usually take to be your self" from the first paragraph of *Schopenhauer as Educator* (KGW iii/1. 334). He then identifies the "usual" self with "the social . . . and therefore inauthentic self" and asks: "But is it not equally possible that 'your true self' may lie immeasurably below 'your usual self', and that society, its conventions and laws, may mercifully prevent its realization?" But we have seen that Nietzsche does not believe that an asocial self or a self independent of relations to other selves

In fact, Nietzsche goes so far as to write that he wants to "transform the belief 'it *is* thus and thus' into the will 'it shall become thus and thus'."[21] In general, he vastly prefers to speak of creating rather than of discovering truth, and exactly the same holds of his attitude toward the self. We have seen him praise, in *The Gay Science*, those who want to become those they are: they are, he continues, "human beings who are new, unique, incomparable, who give themselves laws, who *create* themselves." Both the hero of *Thus Spoke Zarathustra* and his disciples are constantly described as "creators"; and the book revolves around the idea of creating one's own self or (what comes to the same thing) the *Übermensch*. Goethe was one of Nietzsche's few true heroes; and Nietzsche paid him his highest compliment when he wrote of him that "he created himself."[22]

Yet, again, we have the inevitable doubling. Despite his attack on the notion that there are antecedently existing things and truths, waiting to be discovered, despite his almost inordinate emphasis on the importance of "creating," Zarathustra at one point enigmatically says, "Some souls one will never discover, unless one invents them first,"[23] and expresses the same equivocal view when he tells his disciples that "you still want to create the world before which you can kneel."[24] And though Nietzsche writes that "the axioms of logic . . . are . . . a means for us to *create* reality," it still remains the case that "rational thought is interpretation according to a scheme that we cannot throw off."[25] Making and finding, creating and discovering,

---

exists and that therefore such a self (depending on one's sympathies) should or should not be repressed. For Nietzsche, there is nothing there to be either repressed or liberated. Cf. Richard Rorty, who, in "Beyond Nietzsche and Marx," *London Review of Books*, 3, 19/2–4/3 (1981), 6, writes of "the pre-Nietzschean assumption that man has a true self which ought *not* to be repressed, something which exists *prior* to being shaped by power."

Z I. 4, "On the Despisers of the Body" (KGW vi/1. 35–7), needs to be discussed in this context. Zarathustra here distinguishes between the body, which he identifies with the self (*das Selbst*), and sense and spirit, which he identifies with consciousness (*das Ich*), that which says "I." He then argues that the body uses consciousness for its own purposes and that even those who turn against their bodies are really following the desires of their own (unconscious) selves. This appears at first sight to recall the Freudian model discussed above. But the similarity does not seem to me to go much further. For though Nietzsche, as he often does, envisages a distinction between consciousness and the unconscious, he associates a stable self precisely with these "despisers of the body": "Even in your folly and contempt . . . you serve your self . . . your self itself wants to die and turns away from life" exactly because it "is no longer capable of what it would do above all else: to *create beyond itself* . . ." (my italics). Thus the tendency of both the conscious and the unconscious self is, unless it is resisted for the many reasons that Nietzsche discusses in his later writings, to be in a continuous process of change and development.

[21] KGW viii/1. 36; WP 593. I discuss some aspects of Nietzsche's view of truth in "Immanent and Transcendent Perspectivism in Nietzsche," *Nietzsche-Studien*, 12 (1983), 473–90.

[22] KGW vi/3. 145; TI IX. 49.

[23] KGW vi/1. 47; Z I. 8.

[24] KGW vi/1. 106; Z II. 2.

[25] KGW viii/2. 53, viii/1. 108; WP 516, 522.

imposing laws and being constrained by them are involved in a complicated, almost compromising relationship.[26] It seems then that the self, even if it is to be discovered, must first be created. We are therefore faced with the question how that self can be what one is before it comes into being itself, before it is itself something that is. How could (and why should) that be one's proper self, and not some (or any) other? Why not, in particular, one's current self, which at least has over all others the advantage of existing?

Let us stop for a moment to notice that, however equivocal, Nietzsche's emphasis on the self's creation blocks another obvious interpretation of his aphorism. This interpretation would hold that to become what one is would be to actualize all the capacities for which one is inherently suited; it might be inaccurate but not positively misleading to call such an interpretation "Aristotelian."[27] Appealing to actuality and potentiality may account for some of the logical peculiarities of Nietzsche's phrase, since one (actually) is not what one (potentially) is. But this view faces two difficulties. The first is that if one actualizes one's capacities, one *has* become what one is; becoming has now ceased, it has "flowed into being" just in the sense that we have seen Nietzsche deny that this is possible. The second is that construing becoming as realizing inherent capacities makes the creation of the self be more like the uncovering of what is already there. Yet Nietzsche seems to be trying to undermine precisely the idea that there are antecedently existing possibilities grounded in the nature of things, even though (as on the view we are considering) we may not know in advance what they are. The problem therefore remains of explaining how a self that truly must be created and that does not appear in any way to exist can be considered as that which an individual is. Nietzsche's view, to which we keep returning, that becoming does not aim at a final state, constitutes yet another obstacle on our way. He holds that constant change characterizes the world at large: "If the motion of the world aimed at a final state, that state would have been reached. The sole fundamental

---

[26] This ambivalence is reflected in a number of passages of Harold Alderman's *Nietzsche's Gift* (Athens: Ohio University Press, 1977). For example, Alderman writes that "the Overman *is* the meaning of the earth ... and yet we must also *will* that he shall be that meaning ... [Zarathustra's 'Prologue'] says, in effect, both that something *is* the case and that we ought to *will* it to be so ..." (p. 26). Elsewhere, he describes the section "On the Three Metamorphoses" as "Nietzsche's statement of the conditions under which we may create—which is to say encounter—ourselves ..." (p. 35). Alderman does not discuss this problem explicitly, though at one point he writes that "to be oneself one must know one's limits; only thereby can one grow to meet—one's limits" (p. 126), which, in my opinion, places too much emphasis on the discovery-side of the distinction Nietzsche may be trying to undermine. Cf. KGW vii/2. 134; WP 495; and EH II. 9.

[27] Such an interpretation, along more individualistic lines, is implicitly accepted by Alderman in the last of the quotations in the preceding footnote.

fact, however, is that it does not aim at a final state . . ."[28] And he holds that the same is also true of each individual. In *The Gay Science*, for example, he praises brief habits, which he describes as "an inestimable means for getting to know *many* things and states."[29] Later on in the same book he uses a magnificent simile involving will and wave, expressing his faith in the inevitability (and the ultimate value) of continual change and renewal:

How greedily this wave approaches, as if it were after something! How it crawls with terrifying haste into the inmost nooks of this labyrinthine cliff! It seems that something of value, high value, must be hidden there.—And now it comes back, a little more slowly but still quite white with excitement: is it disappointed? Has it found what it looked for? Does it pretend to be disappointed?—But already another wave is approaching, still more greedily and savagely than the first, and its soul, too, seems to be full of secrets and the last to dig up treasures. Thus live waves—thus live we who will—more I shall not say.[30]

The idea of constant change is one of the central conceptions of *Thus Spoke Zarathustra*, where Nietzsche writes:

All the permanent—that is only a parable. And the poets lie too much . . . It is of time and becoming that the best parables should speak: let them be a praise and a justification of all impermanence . . . there must be much bitter dying in your life, you creators. Thus are you advocates and justifiers of all impermanence. To be the child who is newly born, the creator must also want to be the mother who gives birth . . .[31]

But if Nietzsche, as such passages suggest, advocates continual and interminable change, if, indeed, there is only becoming, what possible relation can there be between becoming and being? The most promising way to reach an answer to this question is to turn to an examination of his notion of being. Our hope will be that what Nietzsche understands by "being" may be unusual enough to avoid this apparent contradiction without, at the same time, lapsing into total eccentricity.

II

The first glimmer of an answer to the questions that have stopped us so far may appear through the final obstacle with which we have to contend. We have already seen that Nietzsche is convinced that the ego, construed as a

---

[28] KGW viii/2. 277; WP 708. This idea appears again and again in Nietzsche's notes: cf., among many others, KGW viii/2. 201; WP 639: "That the world is not striving toward a stable condition is the only thing that has been proved."

[29] KGW v/2. 215: GS 295.

[30] KGW v/2. 226; GS 310.

[31] KGW vi/1. 106–7; Z II. 2.

metaphysical abiding subject, is a fiction. But also, as by now we might expect, he does not believe in the most elementary unity of the person as agent. Paradoxically, however, I think that his shocking and obscure break-down of the assumed unity of the human personality may be the key to the solution of our problems. It may also be one of Nietzsche's great contri-butions to our understanding of the self and to our self-understanding.

Consider the breakdown first. As early as the second volume of *Human, All-Too-Human*, Nietzsche writes that the student of history is "happy, unlike the metaphysicians, to have in himself not one immortal soul but many mortal ones."[32] *The Gay Science* denies that consciousness constitutes "the unity of the organism."[33] The hypothesis that Nietzsche is merely deny-ing the abiding of the self over time, as a number of modern philosophers have done, is disproved by the following radical and, for our purposes, crucial statement from *Beyond Good and Evil*:

the belief that regards the soul as something indestructible, eternal, indivisible, as a monad, as an *atomon*: this belief ought to be expelled from science! Between ourselves, it is not at all necessary to get rid of "the soul" at the same time . . . But the way is open for new versions and refinements of the soul-hypothesis; and such conceptions as "mortal soul", and "soul as subjective multiplicity", and "soul as social structure of the drives and affects" want henceforth to have citizens' rights in science.[34]

The idea of "the subject as multiplicity" is constantly discussed in *The Will to Power* where, among others, we find the following statement:

The assumption of one single subject is perhaps unnecessary: perhaps it is just as permissible to assume a multiplicity of subjects, whose interaction and struggle is the basis of our thought and our consciousness in general? A kind of aristocracy of "cells" in which dominion resides? To be sure, an aristocracy of equals, used to ruling jointly and understanding how to command?[35]

This political metaphor for the self (which, despite Nietzsche's reputation, is at least more egalitarian than Plato's) can set us in the right direction for understanding the aphorism that concerns us. Nietzsche believes that we are not warranted in assuming *a priori* the unity of every thinking subject: unity

[32] KGW vi/3. 22; HH II. 17; my translation.
[33] KGW v/2. 57; GS 11.
[34] KGW vi/2. 21; BGE 12. In connection with our earlier discussion, it is important to notice that Nietzsche goes on to say of "the new psychologist," who accepts such hypotheses, that "precisely thereby he . . . condemns himself to *invention*—and—who knows?—perhaps to discovery."
[35] KGW vii/3. 382; WP 490. The passage continues to list as one of Nietzsche's "hypotheses" a view of "The subject as multiplicity." In WP 561 (KGW viii/1. 102) Nietzsche writes that all "unity is unity only as organization and cooperation," and opposes this conception to belief in the "thing," which, he claims, "was only invented as a foundation for the various attributes." Unity thus is achieved when the elements of a system are directed toward a common goal, as the political metaphor we are discussing would lead us to expect.

in general is an idea of which he is deeply suspicious.[36] As Zarathustra says, "Evil I call it, and misanthropic—all this teaching of the One and the Plenum and the Unmoved and the Sated and the Permanent."[37] And yet (need we by now be surprised?) it is also Zarathustra who claims that "this is all my creating and striving, that I create and carry together into One what is fragment and riddle and dreadful accident" and that what he has taught his disciples is "*my* creating and striving, to create and carry together into One what in man is fragment and riddle and dreadful accident."[38]

Nietzsche's denial of the unity of the self follows, in my opinion, from his view that the acts of thinking and desiring (to take these as representative of the rest) are indissolubly connected with their contents, which are in turn essentially connected to other thoughts, desires and actions.[39] He holds, first, that the separation of the act from its content is illegitimate: "There is no such thing as 'willing'," he writes, "but only a willing *something*: one must not remove the aim from the total condition—as epistemologists do. 'Willing' as they understand it is as little a reality as 'thinking' is: it is pure fiction."[40] It is this view, I think, which, in the face of his tremendous and ever-present emphasis on willing, also allows him to make the shockingly but only apparently incompatible statement that "there is no such thing as will."[41] His position on the nature of thinking is strictly parallel: "'Thinking', as epistemologists conceive it, simply does not occur: it is a quite arbitrary fiction, arrived at by selecting one element from the process and eliminating all the rest, an artificial arrangement for the purposes of intelligibility."[42]

The considerations underlying Nietzsche's view must have been something like the following. We tend first to isolate the content of each thought and desire from that of all others; each mental act is supposed to intend a distinct mental content, whose nature is independent of the content of all other such acts. My thought that such-and-such is the case is *there* and remains what it is whatever I may come to think in the future: though it may turn out to be false, its significance is given and determined. Having isolated the contents of our mental acts from one another, we then separate the content of each act from the act that intends it. My thinking that such-and-

---

[36] Nietzsche's attack on the concept of unity, and on other traditional concepts in western philosophy, is well documented by Eugen Fink. *Nietzsches Philosophie* (Stuttgart: Kohlhammer, 1960).

[37] KGW vi/1. 106: Z II. 2.

[38] KGW vi/1. 165, 244; Z II. 21, III. 12.

[39] Cf. "The Eternal Recurrence" (pp. 130–4 in this volume) for some comments relevant to this assertion. Cf. also KGW viii/3. 128–30, viii/1. 291; WP 584, 672.

[40] KGW viii/2. 296; WP 668.

[41] KGW viii/2. 55–6; WP 488.

[42] KGW viii/2. 296; WP 477; cf. KGW viii/3. 252–4; viii/2. 131; viii/2. 55–6; WP 479, 485, 488.

such is the case is an episode which is taken to be distinct from what it is about. Having performed those two "abstractions," we are confronted with a set of similar entities, thoughts, that we then attribute to a subject which, since it performs all these qualitatively identical acts, we can safely assume to be unified.[43]

It seems to me that it is this view that underwrites Nietzsche's conviction that the deed is a fiction and the doer, "a second derivative." He appears to believe that we are tempted to take the self, without further thought, as one because we commonly fail to take the contents of our mental acts into account. But for him each "thing" is nothing more, and nothing less, than the sum of all its effects or features. Since it is nothing more than that sum, it is not clear that conflicting sets of features are capable of generating a single thing. But since it is nothing less, when we come to the case of the self, what we must attribute to each subject (what we must use to generate it) is not simply the sum of its mental acts considered in isolation.[44] Rather, we must attribute to it the sum of its acts along with their contents: each subject is constituted not simply by the fact *that* it thinks, wants and acts but also by *what* it thinks, wants and does. And once we admit contents, we also admit conflicts. What we think, want and do is seldom, if ever, a coherent set. Our thoughts contradict one another and contrast with our desires, which are themselves inconsistent and are belied, in turn, by our actions. Thus the unity of the self, which Nietzsche identifies with this set, is seriously undermined. Its unity, he seems to believe, is to be found (if it is to be found at all) in the unity and coherence of the contents of the acts performed by an organism. It is the unity of these effects that gives rise to the unity of the self, and not the other way around.

An immediate difficulty for this view seems to be caused by the fact that Nietzsche does not distinguish clearly between unity as coherence on the one hand and unity as numerical identity on the other. For it can be argued that even if the self is not coherent in an appropriate manner, it is still a single thing; in fact, it is only because the self is a single thing that it is at all sensible to be concerned with its unity. Even the idea that we are faced with conflicting, rather than merely with disparate, sets of thoughts and desires seems to depend on the assumption that these are the thoughts and desires of a single person.

---

[43] *Akrasia* or weakness of will may still be considered as a threat to this assumption even at this point, however.

[44] Cf. KGW viii/2. 131; WP 485: "'The subject' is the fiction that many similar states in us are the effect of one substratum; but it is we who first created the 'similarity' of these states; our adjusting them and making them similar is the fact, not their similarity (—which ought rather to be denied—)."

We might think that we could avoid this difficulty if we argued that Nietzsche is in fact concerned with coherence and not with identity. But his identification of every thing with a set of effects results precisely in blurring this distinction, and prevents us from giving this answer. For since there is nothing above (or "behind") such sets of effects, it is not clear that Nietzsche can consistently hold that there is anything to the identity of each object above the unity of a set of effects. We have already seen him write that the subject is a multiplicity: but what is it that enables us to group some multiplicities together to form a subject and to distinguish them from others that constitute a different one?

At this point, the political metaphor for the self to which we have already appealed becomes important. On a very basic level, the identity that is necessary but not sufficient for the unity of the self is provided by the unity of the body. Nietzsche, we should notice, is consistent in holding that, like all unity, the unity of the body is not an absolute fact: "The evidence of the body reveals a tremendous multiplicity."[45] But this multiplicity is, in most circumstances, organized coherently: the needs and goals of the body are usually not in conflict with one another:

The body and physiology the starting point: why?—we gain the correct idea of the nature of our subject-unity, namely as regents at the head of a communality (not as "souls" or "life forces"), also of the dependence of these regents upon the ruled and of an order of rank and division of labor as the conditions that make possible the whole and its parts.[46]

Zarathustra, I think, makes the same point when he says of the body that it is "a plurality with one sense, a war and a peace, a herd and a shepherd."[47] Thus the coherence of the body's organization provides the common ground that allows conflicting mental states to be grouped together as belonging to a single subject. Particular thoughts, desires, actions, and their patterns, that is, character-traits, move the body in different directions, place it in different contexts, and can even be said to vie for its control. Dominant habits and character-traits, while they are dominant, assume the role of the subject; in terms of our metaphor, they assume the role of the leadership. It is such traits that speak with the voice of the self when they are manifested in action. Their own unity is what allows them to become the subject that, at least for a time, says "I." In the situation we are discussing, however, the leadership is not stable. Since different and often incompatible character-

---

[45] KGW viii/1. 104: WP 518.

[46] KGW vii/3. 370–1; WP 492.

[47] KGW vi/1. 35–7; Z I. 4. A similar point may be made at KGW vii/2. 280; WP 966: "In contrast to animals, man has cultivated an abundance of *contrary* drives and impulses within himself . . ."

traits coexist in one body, different patterns assume the "regent's" role at different times. Thus we identify ourselves differently over time; and though the "I" always seems to refer to the same thing, the content of what it refers to does not remain the same, and may constantly be in the process of developing, sometimes toward greater unity.

Such unity, however, which is at best something to be hoped for, certainly cannot be presupposed; phenomena like *akrasia* and self-deception, not to mention everyday inconsistency, raise serious questions about it. In a recent discussion of these phenomena, Amélie Rorty, too, finds a political metaphor for the self illuminating. She urges that we think of the self as a medieval city, with many semi-independent neighborhoods and no strong central administration. She suggests that "we can regard the agent self as a loose configuration of habits, habits of thought and perception and motivation and action, acquired at different stages, in the service of different ends."[48] The unity of the self, which thus also constitutes its identity, is not something given, but something acquired; not a beginning, but a goal. And of such unity, which is essentially a matter of degree and which comes close to constituting a regulative principle, Nietzsche is not at all suspicious. It lies behind his earlier positive comments on "the One" and he actively wants to promote it. It is precisely its absence that he deplores when he writes of his contemporaries that "with the characters of the past written all over you, and these characters in turn painted over with new characters: thus have you concealed yourselves perfectly from all interpreters of characters."[49]

Nietzsche's view, after all, bears remarkable similarities to Plato's division

---

[48] Amélie Rorty, "Self-Deception, Akrasia and Irrationality," *Social Science Information*, 19 (1980), 920. On a more abstract basis, Robert Nozick tries to account for the self as a "self-synthesizing" entity in his *Philosophical Explanations* (Cambridge, Mass.: Harvard University Press, 1981), 71–114.

[49] KGW vi/1. 149; Z II. 15, a very important section in this connection. Cf. KGW vi/2. 158; BGE 215, with its allusion to Kant: just as some planets are illuminated by many suns, and of different colors, "so we modern men are determined, thanks to the complicated mechanics of our 'starry sky', by different moralities; our actions shine alternatively in different colors, they are rarely univocal—and there are cases enough in which we perform actions *of many colors*."

The passage from *Thus Spoke Zarathustra*, with its painterly and literary vocabulary (*vollschreiben, überpinseln, Zeichendeuter*—the last word being more closely connected to the astronomical and astrological imagery of the sentence than Kaufmann's translation suggests), should be very congenial to deconstructive readers of Nietzsche, who find in his writings an insistence on the total absence of any "originary unity." A classic statement of the general position can be found in Jacques Derrida, "Structure, Sign, and Play in the Discourse of the Human Sciences," in Richard Macksey and Eugenio Donato (eds.), *The Structuralist Controversy* (Baltimore: Johns Hopkins University Press, 1970), 247–64; but the view has now become very prevalent. It is clear that Nietzsche would agree that the unity in question is not given, and that it cannot be uncovered once all the "coats of paint" are removed: nothing would remain over if that were done. But this agreement need not, and does not, prevent him from wanting to *construct* a unity out of this "motley" (*bunt*) material. I discuss such issues in relation to literary criticism in "The Postulated Author: Critical Monism as a Regulative Ideal," *Critical Inquiry*, 8 (1981), 133–49.

of the soul in the *Republic*, which also faces difficulties in locating the agent. Nietzsche, of course, envisages a much more complicated division than Plato's and does not accept Plato's view that ultimately there are three (and only three) independent sources of human motivation. In addition, Nietzsche would deny Plato's preference of reason as the dominant source: what habits and character-traits are to rule is for him an open question, which does not necessarily receive an answer dictated by moral considerations.

Now the dominant traits can completely disregard their competitors and refuse even to acknowledge their existence: this constitutes a case of self-deception. Or they can acknowledge them, try to bring them in line with their own evaluations, and fail: this constitutes a case of *akrasia*. Or again they could try and manage in some way to incorporate them, changing both their opponents and themselves in the process and thus taking one step toward the integration of the personality which, in the ideal case, constitutes the unity we are pursuing:

No subject "atoms." The sphere of a subject constantly growing or decreasing, the center of the system constantly shifting: in cases where it cannot organize the appropriate mass, it breaks into two parts. On the other hand, it can transform a weaker subject into its functionary without destroying it, and to a certain extent form a new unity with it. No "substance," rather something that in itself strives after greater strength, and that wants to "preserve" itself only indirectly (it wants to *surpass* itself—).[50]

This passage makes it clear that at least in some cases where Nietzsche speaks of mastery and power, he is concerned with mastery and power over oneself, with habits and character-traits competing for the domination of a single person. This is one of the reasons why I think that at least the primary (though not necessarily the only) object of the will to power is one's own self.[51] But more importantly, in this passage we find the suggestion that, as

---

[50] KGW viii/2. 55–6; WP 488. Cf. KGW viii/1. 320–1; WP 617.

[51] Contrast Stern, *A Study of Nietzsche*, ch. 7, esp. p. 122 with n. 1. We should remark that such a construal of the will to power, as well as the version of the eternal recurrence presented in this essay, may seem to imply that ultimately no clear distinction can be drawn between the experience of an individual (especially of a sufficiently powerful individual) and the outside world. For the world may appear to be the product of such people's will to power. Such a solipsist view is also suggested by Nietzsche when he writes, as we have already seen, that Zarathustra's disciples "want to create the world before which [they] can kneel." However, as I shall try to show below, Nietzsche also holds that the process of "surpassing" involved here can have no end: there is no such thing as the total transformation of another subject, and there are always more subjects to be (at best partially) transformed. Thus the distinction between one's experience and the world can always be in principle maintained. In addition, it is not clear that Nietzsche's specific views on the unity of the self involve a commitment to such possible solipsist consequences of the will to power. They do, however, seem to me to depend on a refusal to identify the world with something like "unconceptualized reality." The world is given to us only under a description or, as Nietzsche would prefer, an interpretation. Recent expressions of such a view can be found in, among others, Nelson

our metaphor has led us to expect, what says "I" is not the same at all times. We also see that the process of dominating (or, notice, of creating) the individual, the unity that concerns us, is a matter of incorporating more and more character-traits under a constantly expanding and, in the process, evolving rubric. It begins to appear that the distinction between being and becoming may be not quite as absolute as we originally feared.

Nietzsche often criticized the educational practices of his time. In his view, they encouraged people to want to develop in all directions instead of show-ing them how to fashion themselves, even by eliminating some beliefs and desires, into true individuals.[52] The project of becoming an individual with a unified set of features requires (a favorite term with him) hardness toward oneself: its contrary, "tolerance toward oneself, permits several convictions, and they get along with each other: they are careful, like all the rest of the world, not to compromise themselves."[53] But though Nietzsche envisages that certain character-traits may have to be eliminated if one is to achieve unity, he does not in any way consider that they are to be disowned. This is a crucial point, for it shows that the unity we are looking for is not a final stage which follows upon others, but the total organization of everything that one thinks, wants and does.

It is, in fact, one of Nietzsche's most strongly held views that everything one does is equally essential to who one is. This is another consequence of his reduction of all objects to the sum-total of their effects on the world. He believes that everything that I have ever done has been instrumental to my being who I am today. And even if today there are actions I would not ever repeat, even if there are character-traits I am grateful to have left behind, I would not have my current preferences had I not had those other preferences at an earlier time: "The most recent history of an action relates to this action: but further back lies a pre-history which covers a wider field: the individual action is at the same time a part of a much more extensive, later fact. The briefer and the more extensive processes are not separated."[54]

It begins to seem, then, that Nietzsche has in mind not a final state of

---

Goodman, "The Way the World Is," in his *Problems and Projects* (Indianapolis: Bobbs Merrill, 1972), 24–32, and Hilary Putnam, "Reflections on Goodman's *Ways of Worldmaking*," *Journal of Philosophy*, 76 (1979), 603–18, esp. 611–12.

[52] KGW vi/3. 136–7; TI IX. 41.

[53] KGW vi/3. 116: TI IX. 18. The passage continues: "How does one compromise oneself today? If one is consistent. If one proceeds in a straight line. If one is not ambiguous enough to permit five conflicting interpretations. If one is genuine." Cp. KGW vi/3. 60; TI I. 44: "The formula of my happiness: a Yes, a No, a straight line, a *goal*."

[54] KGW viii/1. 285: WP 672. Cf. KGW viii/3. 128–30; WP 584; and KGW vi/3. 54: TI I. 10: "Not to perpetrate cowardice toward one's own acts! Not to leave them in the lurch afterward! The bite of conscience is indecent!" I discuss these issues in detail in "The Eternal Recurrence" (Ch. 4 in this volume).

being which follows upon and replaces an earlier process of becoming. Rather, he is thinking of a continual process of greater integration of one's character-traits, habits and patterns of interaction with the world. This process can, in a sense, also reach backward and integrate into the personality even a discarded characteristic by showing its necessity for one's later development. The complexity of this process is exhibited in the following passage, which I will have to quote at length:

> *One thing is needful.*—To "give style" to one's character—a great and rare art! It is practiced by those who survey all the strengths and weaknesses of their nature and then fit them into an artistic plan until every one of them appears as art and reason and even weaknesses delight the eye. Here a large mass of second nature has been added: there a piece of original nature has been removed—both times through long practice and daily work at it. Here the ugly that could not be removed is concealed; there it has been reinterpreted and made sublime. Much that is vague and resisted shaping has been saved and exploited for distant views; it is meant to beckon toward the far and immeasurable. In the end, when the work is finished, it becomes evident how the constraint of a single taste governed and formed everything large and small. Whether this taste was good or bad is less important than one might suppose, if only it was a single taste![55]

Such a conception of personal unity faces a number of difficulties. Foremost among these, as we have already remarked, is the problem of self-deception. For one way to "give style" to one's character, to constrain it by a single taste, is simply to deny the existence, force, or significance of antithetical tastes and traits, and to consider only part of oneself as the whole. Nietzsche seems to me to be aware of this problem, as is shown by his distinction between the two sorts of people who have faith in themselves. Some, he writes, have it precisely because they refuse to look: "What would they behold if they could see to the bottom of themselves!"; the others have to acquire it, and are faced with it as a problem: "Everything good, fine, or great they do is first of all an argument against the skeptic inside them."[56] The possibility of self-deception is always there; unity can always be achieved simply by refusing to acknowledge an existing multiplicity.

To be accurate, however, we should not say that unity can be achieved in this way: only the feeling of unity can be secured by this process. One can think that one has completed the arduous task described by the passage we are discussing without having actually succeeded. The distinction can be made because, after all, the notions of style and of character are essentially public. Nietzsche, of course, emphasizes the importance of each individual's evaluating itself by its own standards. Nevertheless, especially since he does

---

[55] KGW v/2. 210; GS 290.

[56] KGW v/2. 207; GS 284; cf. 283; also KGW vi/1. 173–8; Z II. 21.

not believe that self-knowledge is in any way privileged, such questions are finally decided from the outside. This outside may consist of a very select public (including oneself), of an audience which perhaps does not yet exist, but the distinction between the feeling and the fact of unity is to be pressed and maintained. Zarathustra taunts the sun when he asks what its happiness would be were it not for those for whom it shines.[57] Similarly, it takes observers for the unity to be manifest and therefore there. At the end of this essay we will see that these observers may have to be readers—and qualified readers at that.

A clear sign that unity is lacking is what has been called "weakness of will," *akrasia*, the inability to act on one's preferred judgement; this is an indication that competing habits, patterns of valuation and modes of perception are at work within the same individual, if one wants to use this term at all at such a stage. Nietzsche, of course, is notorious for his attacks on the notion of the freedom of the will; but he is no less opposed, naturally, to the notion of the compelled or unfree will, which he characterizes as "mythology." "In real life," he continues, "it is only a matter of strong and weak wills."[58] Yet at the same time, as we might also by now expect, Zarathustra can mention and praise occasions "where necessity was freedom itself."[59] And in *The Twilight of the Idols* we read that "peace of soul" can be either a mind becalmed, an empty self-satisfaction, or, on the contrary, "the expression of maturity and mastery in the midst of doing, creating, working, and willing—calm breathing, *attained* 'freedom of the will'."[60]

Freedom of the will so construed is the state in which there is no internal division in a person's preference-schemes, where desire follows thought and action follows desire with no effort and no struggle, where the distinction between constraint and choice might be thought to disappear. This state, which Nietzsche of course envisages as an almost impossible ideal, is remarkably similar to the condition in which Socrates, in Plato's early dialogues, thought every single agent actually to be and which thus led him to deny the very possibility of *akrasia*. Unfortunately, I cannot pursue here the connection between this suggestive analogy of attitude and Nietzsche's deeply ambivalent feelings toward Socrates. I must return instead to the subject at hand and point out that, again, the feeling that one is in this state can be produced by self-deception and that the problems this raises cannot be avoided. But Nietzsche is clear on the extraordinary difficulty with which such states can be reached. Success can again be described in the terms

---

[57] KGW vi/1. 5; Z, Prologue, 1.
[58] KGW vi/2. 30: BGE 21: cf. KGW vi/2. 25–8, 50–1: BGE 19, 36: KGW vi/3. 88–9; TI VI. 7.
[59] KGW vi/1. 244: Z III. 12.
[60] KGW vi/3. 79: TI V. 3.

of our political metaphor: "*L'effet c'est moi:* what happens here is what happens in every well-constructed and happy commonwealth; namely, the governing class identifies itself with the success of the commonwealth."[61] What this involves is a maximization of diversity and a minimization of discord. The passage on character from *The Gay Science* suggests this point and so does the following note from *The Will to Power:* "The highest man would have the highest multiplicity of drives, in the relatively greater strength that can be endured. Indeed, where the plant 'man' shows himself strongest one finds instincts that conflict powerfully ... but are controlled."[62] It is just because of this controlled multiplicity that Goethe, who according to Nietzsche bore all the conflicting tendencies of his century within him, became his great hero: "What he wanted was totality ... he disciplined himself to wholeness, he *created* himself."[63]

This self-creation thus appears to be the creation, or imposition, of a higher-order accord among one's lower-order thoughts, desires and actions. It is the development of the ability or the willingness to accept responsibility for everything that one has done and to admit what is in fact the case, that everything that one has done actually constitutes who one is.

From one point of view, this willingness is a new character-trait, a new state of development that is reached at some time and that replaces a previous state, during which one would have been unwilling to acknowledge all one's doings as one's own. From another point of view, however, to reach such a state is not at all like what occurs when one specific character-trait replaces another, when courage replaces cowardice, or magnificence, miserliness. The self-creation Nietzsche has in mind involves the acceptance of everything one has done and, in the ideal case, its harmonization in a coherent whole. Becoming courageous involves avoiding all the cowardly sorts of actions in which one may have previously engaged and pursuing a new sort instead. Yet no specific pattern of behavior needs to be abandoned, or pursued, simply because one realizes that all one's actions are one's own. What, if anything, changes depends on what patterns or coherence already exist

---

[61] KGW vi/2. 27; BGE 19. Notice that nothing in the metaphor prevents the governing class from including all the members of the commonwealth.

[62] KGW vii/2. 289; WP 966; cf. KGW vii/2. 179–80, viii/2. 395–6; WP 259, 928.

[63] KGW vi/3. 145; TI IX. 49. Nietzsche's remarks on persons as hierarchical structures of desires and character-traits interestingly prefigure the view discussed by Harry Frankfurt in "Freedom of the Will and the Concept of a Person," *Journal of Philosophy*, 68 (1971), 5–20. Where Nietzsche does not consider that every agent has a self, Frankfurt writes (p. 11) that not every human being need be a person: only agents who have certain desires about what their will is to be are persons for him. Further, just as Nietzsche considers that freedom of the will is not something presupposed by, but attained through, agency, Frankfurt writes: "The enjoyment of freedom comes easily to some. Others must struggle to achieve it" (p. 17). Though in no way as fine-grained as his, the discussion that follows is indebted to Frankfurt.

and what new ones one might want to establish. But because further change is always possible, Nietzsche's conception of self-creation must also be contrasted to the realization, or decision, of many of us that our character has actually developed enough and that it is neither necessary nor desirable to change in any further respects. As such, it shows itself not to constitute a static episode, a final goal which, once attained, forecloses the possibility of further change and development.

For one thing, it is not clear that such an "episode" can actually occur, that it does not represent, as we have said, a regulative principle. If there were a clear sense in which our thoughts, desires, actions and their patterns could be counted, then we might be able to succeed in fitting "all" of them together. Yet how our mental acts actually fit with one another clearly has a bearing on how they are counted. And this is also suggested by Nietzsche's own view that the contents of our mental acts are indissolubly connected together. For to reinterpret a thought or an action and thus to construe it, for example, as only part of a longer, "more extensive" process, as only part of a single mental act after all, has exactly the same consequence.

More importantly, however, the fact is that as long as one is alive one always encounters unforeseen situations and one keeps performing new actions and having new thoughts and desires. The occurrence of such mental acts can always impose the need to reinterpret, to reorganize, or even to abandon earlier ones in their light. Nevertheless, the exhortation of *The Will to Power* "to revolve about oneself: no desire to become 'better' or in any way other"[64] is, I think, quite compatible with the continuous development that we have been discussing. To desire to remain oneself in this context is not so much to want one's specific character-traits to remain constant: the same passage speaks of "multiplicity of character considered and exploited as an advantage." Rather, it is to desire to appropriate and to reorganize as one's own all that one has (or at least knows to have) done and to engage in organizing it into a single unified whole. It is to be able to accept all such things, good or evil, as things one has done. It is not to cultivate stable character-traits that may make one's range of reactions predictable and, in new situations, unsurprising. Rather, it is to develop the flexibility to be able to use whatever one has done, does, or will do as elements in a constantly changing, never completed whole. Since such a whole is always in the process of incorporating new material and since the success of this incorporation may always involve the reinterpretation of older material, none of its elements need remain unchanged. Zarathustra's distrust of unity—his exhortations to avoid goals or stability—is his aversion to the stability of specific

[64] KGW viii/2. 369; WP 425; cf. KGW vi/1. 391–400: Z IV. 19.

character-traits, parallel to the praise of "brief habits" we found in *The Gay Science*. By contrast, his proud description of his own teaching as carrying "into One what in man is fragment and riddle and dreadful accident" refers to the continual, never-ending integration, and reinterpretation, of such brief habits.

The final mark of this integration, its limiting case, is provided by the test involved in the thought of the eternal recurrence. This mark is the desire to do exactly what one has already done in this life if one were to live again: "'Was *that* life?' I want to say to death," Zarathustra is made to exclaim, "'Well then! Once more!' "[65] Since Nietzsche considers the subject as the sum of its interrelated effects, the opportunity to live again would necessarily involve the exact repetition of the very same events; otherwise, there would be no reason to suppose that it was the same subject that was living again. Thus the question is not whether one would or would not do the same things again; in this matter, there is no room for choice. The question is only whether one would *want* to do the same things all over again and thus be willing to acknowledge all one's doings as one's own.[66]

III

It may finally begin to appear that becoming and being are related in a way that does not make nonsense of Nietzsche's imperative to "Become who you are." To be who one is, on the view we have been developing, is to be engaged in the constantly continuing and continually broadening process of appropriation we have been discussing, to enlarge one's capacity for responsibility for oneself which Nietzsche calls "freedom."[67] He describes as the greatest will to power the desire "to impose upon becoming the character of being" and considers the idea "that everything recurs [as] the closest

[65] KGW 1. 392; Z IV. 19. Cf. KGW vii/3. 171–2; WP 962. Gregory Vlastos has objected that, on such an interpretation of the eternal recurrence. Nietzsche is committed to the very strong view that if I were to desire my life again, I would have to want every totally insignificant thing to remain the same. But even if it is Nietzsche's theory, the objection continues, that everything I do is equally essential to who I am, surely, for example, the precise minute I happened to wake up on a particular morning could not possibly have an effect on my person. Nietzsche's point, I reply, is that one wants to repeat just those actions which *are* significant to one's being the person one is—those, in fact, are the very *actions* one wants to acknowledge as one's own. Insignificant details (unless one can interpret them so as to make them significant) make no significant difference to who one is. I discuss this point in detail in "The Eternal Recurrence" (pp. 130–1 in this volume).

[66] This point is presented and discussed in detail in "The Eternal Recurrence" (Ch. 4 in this volume).

[67] KGW vi/3. 133–4: TI IX. 38. I shall try to suggest below how some of the excessive statements of this passage can be tempered in the light of other texts.

approximation of a world of becoming to a world of being . . ."[68] And the eternal recurrence, as we have taken it, is compatible with continued development. Its significance consists in one's ability to want at some point, and in the ideal case at every point, to go through once again and "inummerable times more" what one has gone through already. Such a desire presupposes, in the limiting case, that what one has done has been assembled into a whole so unified that nothing can be subtracted without that whole's coming down along with it. Being, for Nietzsche, is that which one does not *want* to be otherwise.

What one is then, is just what one becomes. Nietzsche's aphorism is an injunction to want to become what one becomes, not to want anything about it, about oneself, to be different. To become what one is, therefore, is not to reach a specific new state—it is not, as I have tried to argue, to reach a state at all. It is to identify oneself with all of one's actions, to see that everything one does (becomes) is what one is. In the ideal case, it is also to fit all this into a *coherent* whole, and to want to be everything that one is: it is to give style to one's character; to be, if you will allow me, becoming.

The idea of giving style to one's character brings us back to Nietzsche's view in section 290 of *The Gay Science* that to have a single character ("taste") may be more important than the question whether this character is good or bad. This idea, in turn, which is quite common in Nietzsche, raises the notorious problem of his "immoralism," his virulent contempt for traditional moral virtue and his alleged praise of cruelty and of the exploitation of the "weak" by the "strong." I can only make two brief sets of comments about this very complex issue on this occasion; the second set will bring me to the concluding part of this essay.

We should notice first that despite his glorification of selfishness, Nietzsche once again is equally serious in denying the very antithesis between egoism and altruism. He dreams, in a perhaps utopian manner, of "some future, when, owing to continual adaptation, egoism will at the same time be altruism," when love and respect for others may just be love and respect for oneself: "Finally, one grasps that altruistic actions are only a species of egoistic actions—and that the degree to which one loves, spends oneself, proves the degree of individual power and personality."[69] Furthermore, the crude idea that Nietzsche's immoralism and the doctrine of the will to power are simply licenses to mindless cruelty is undermined by his

---

[68] KGW viii/1. 320; WP 617. Nietzsche also writes here: "Becoming as invention, willing, self-denial, overcoming of oneself: no subject but an action, a positing, creative, no 'causes and effects' . . . Instead of 'cause and effect' the mutual struggle of that which becomes, often with the absorption of one's opponent: the number of becoming elements not constant."

[69] KGW viii/2. 155–6; WP 786. Cf. KGW vii/2. 94–5; WP 964.

view that such cruelty, though it has certainly been practiced by people on one another and will continue to be practiced in the future, is only the coarsest expression of what he has in mind. In fact, he thinks that its net effect may be the opposite of its intent:

Every living thing reaches out as far from itself with its force as it can, and overwhelms what is weaker: thus it takes pleasure in itself. The increasing "humanizing" of this tendency consists in this, that there is an ever subtler sense of how hard it is really to incorporate another: while a crude injury done him certainly demonstrates our power over him, it at the same time estranges his will from us even more—and thus makes him less easy to subjugate.[70]

We have already seen that such "subjugation" can result in a new alliance, a new unity, even a new self.[71] Since the self is not an abiding substance, its incorporating a new entity "without destroying it" can well result in a change of both the incorporated object and the incorporating subject. Nietzsche's ominous metaphors can, in the final analysis, be applied even to the behavior of a powerful and influential teacher.

I now want to suggest that what Nietzsche says about the importance of character in itself, independently of whether it is the character of a good or a bad person, should not be dismissed out of hand. I am not sure of the proper word in this context, and I use this one with some misgivings, but it seems to me that there is something admirable in the very fact that one has character, that one has style. This does not imply that merely having character overrides all other considerations and justifies any sort of behavior: this is neither true, nor is it asserted by the passage we are discussing. But the point does introduce into our evaluation of agents a more formal quality than simply the content of their actions. It introduces, as one consideration, the question whether their actions, whatever their content, make up a personality. This seems to me a sensible consideration and one, moreover, to which we often appeal in our everyday dealings with each other.

It is not clear to me that a consistently and irredeemably vicious person does in fact have a character: the sort of agent Aristotle calls "bestial" probably does not.[72] In some way there is something inherently praiseworthy in having character or style that does prevent extreme cases of vice from being praised even in the formal sense we have discussed. Perhaps this is simply due to the fact that the viciousness of such agents totally overwhelms whatever praise we might otherwise be disposed to give them. Probably, however, the matter is more complicated. The existence of character may not be quite as independent of the quality of the actions of which it constitutes

[70] KGW vii/1. 533–4: WP 769, where its correct date should be Fall 1883.
[71] KGW viii/2. 56: WP 488: cf. nn. 14–18 above, and KGW viii/3. 165–6; WP 636.
[72] *Nicomachean Ethics*, 6. 1, 6.

the pattern: consistency may not in itself be a condition sufficient for its presence. Perhaps, to appeal to another Aristotelian idea, some sort of moderation in action (though not necessarily the exact mean necessary for virtue) may be in the long run necessary for the possession of character. Nietzsche, in any case, would attribute character to all sorts of agents and would praise them on its account even if their quality were seriously objectionable from a moral point of view.

If now we ask ourselves when it is that we feel absolutely free to admire characters who are (or who, in the nature of the case, would be if they existed) awful people, the answer is clear: we do so in the case of literature. Though we sometimes may find an actual immoral agent worthy of admiration on account of some other quality that may overshadow that agent's objectionable features, our admiration is bound to be most often mixed. The best argument for Nietzsche's view of the importance of character is provided by the great literary villains, characters like Richard III (in Shakespeare's version), Fagin, Fyodor Karamazov, Charlus. In their cases, we can place our moral scruples in the background. Our main object of concern with them becomes their overall manner of what they do, the very structure of their minds, and not primarily the contents of their actions. Here, we can admire without reservations.

Why did Nietzsche take this formalist approach to character? As a historical hypothesis, I offer the view that he developed his attitude toward character and the self in general, as he did in many other cases as well, by considering literature as his primary model and generalizing from it.[73] What is essential to literary characters is their organization: the quality of their actions is secondary. In the ideal case, absolutely everything a character does is equally essential to it; characters are supposed to be constructed so that their every feature supports and is supported by every other one. In the limiting case of the perfect character, no change is possible without corresponding changes, in order to preserve coherence, in every other feature; and the net result is, necessarily, a different character. In connection with literary characters and with the works to which they belong, the more so the better they are; taking one part away may always result in the destruction of the whole. This, we have seen, is presupposed by the thought of the eternal recurrence as a test for the ideal life. My suggestion is that Nietzsche came to hold this view at least partly because his thinking so often concerned literary models.

It could be argued that our admiration of villainous or even inconsistent

---

[73] I have given arguments to that effect both in "The Eternal Recurrence" (Ch. 4 in this volume) and in "Immanent and Transcendent Perspectivism in Nietzsche."

characters, who *can* be consistently depicted, is not directed at those characters themselves, but at the authors who have constructed them, and that
the generalization from literature to life is quite illegitimate. But we should
notice that when it comes to life, the "character" and the "author" are one
and the same, and admiring the one cannot be distinguished from admiring
the other. This is also the reason, I suspect, that though inconsistent characters *can* be admired in literature, they cannot be admired in life. In life, we
want to say, there is no room for the distinction between the creator and the
creature.[74] Thought not perhaps in the manner this objection suggested, the
parallel between literature and life is far from perfect.

Nietzsche, however, always depended on artistic and literary models for
understanding the world and this accounts, in my opinion, for some of the
most original and some of the most peculiar features of his thought. As
early as *The Birth of Tragedy* he sees Dionysus reborn in the person of
Wagner and in the new artwork by means of a process which is the exact
opposite of what he took as the dissolution of classical antiquity.[75] But as
Paul de Man has written, "Passages of this kind are valueless as arguments,
since they assume that the actual events in history are founded in formal
symmetries easy enough to achieve in pictorial, musical, or poetic fictions,
but that can never predict the occurrence of a historical event."[76] Ronald
Hayman has shown that Nietzsche, a compulsive letter-writer, preferred
what in his time still was a literary genre in its own right to conversation and
personal contact as a means of communication even with his close friends.[77]
Often enough, we find Nietzsche urging that we fashion our lives in the way
artists fashion their works: "... we should learn from artists while being
wiser than they are in other matters. For with them this subtle power [of
arranging things and of making them beautiful] usually comes to an end
where art ends and life begins; but we want to be the poets of our life—first
of all in the smallest, most everyday matters."[78] Similarly, he finds the peace
of soul which we have seen him call "attained freedom of will" primarily in
artists, who "seem to have more sensitive noses in these matters, knowing

[74] If this hypothesis is right, Nietzsche, in seeing life as a work of art written by each individual
as it goes along (an idea which can be found reflected in Sartre), can be considered as part of the
great tradition working out the metaphor of the *theatrum mundi*, and giving a secular turn to this
view of the world as a stage on which a play observed by heaven is acted out. There is some irony in
this, once again, for, as Ernest Curtius remarks, this tradition can also be traced originally to Plato
(*Laws*, 644de. 804c). See Curtius's discussion of this metaphor in his *European Literature and the
Latin Middle Ages* (Princeton: Princeton University Press, 1953; first pub. 1948), 138–44.

[75] KGW iii/1. 116–25; BT 19.

[76] Paul de Man, *Allegories of Reading*, 84.

[77] Ronald Hayman, *Nietzsche: A Critical Life* (New York: Oxford University Press, 1980), 119
et passim.

[78] KGW v/2. 218; GS 299. The analogy is also made in GS 301.

only too well that precisely when they no longer do something 'voluntarily' but do everything of necessity, their feeling of freedom, subtlety, full power, of creative placing, disposing and forming reaches its peak—in short, that necessity and 'freedom of will' then become one in them."[79]

How does then one achieve the perfect unity which we have seen Nietzsche urge throughout this essay, the unity which is primarily possessed by perfect literary characters? How does one become both a literary character who, unlike either Charlus or Alyosha Karamazov, really exists, and also that character's very author?

One way of trying to achieve this perhaps impossible goal, I think, is to write a great number of good books that exhibit great apparent inconsistency but that also can be seen as deeply continuous with one another when they are studied carefully. At the end of this enterprise, one can even write a book about those books that shows how they fit together, how a single figure emerges out of them, how even the most damaging inconsistencies are finally necessary for that figure, or character or author or person (the word almost does not matter in this context) to emerge fully through them. Earlier, Zarathustra had claimed, "What returns, what finally comes home to me, is my own self and what of myself has long been in strange lands and scattered among all things and accidents."[80] Now Nietzsche writes of his *Untimely Meditations*, three of which concern important historical figures and one, history itself: ". . . at bottom they speak only of me. . . . *Wagner in Bayreuth* is a vision of my future, while in *Schopenhauer as Educator* my innermost history, my *becoming*, is inscribed."[81] In *The Gay Science* we had read that "now something that you formerly loved . . . strikes you as an error. . . . But perhaps this error was as necessary for you then, when you were still a different person—you are always a different person—as all your present 'truth'. . . ."[82] Now Nietzsche writes of *Schopenhauer as Educator*:

Considering that in those days I practiced the scholar's craft, and perhaps *knew* something about this craft, the harsh psychology of the scholar that suddenly emerges in this essay is of some significance: it expresses the *feeling of distance*, the profound assurance about what could be my task and what could only be means, *entr'acte* and minor works. It shows my prudence that I was many things and in many places in order to be able to become one thing—to be able to attain one thing. I *had* to be a scholar, too, for some time.[83]

One way then to become one thing, one's own character, or what one is, is to write *Ecce Homo* and even to subtitle it "How One Becomes What One Is."

---

[79] KGW vi/2. 152; BGE 213.
[80] KGW vi/1. 189; Z III. 1.
[81] KGW vi/3. 318; EH III, UM 3.
[82] KGW v/2. 224–5; GS 307. Cp., among many other passages, KGW vi/2. 56–8; BGE 44.
[83] KGW vi/3. 318; EH III, UM 3.

It is to write this self-referential work, in which Nietzsche can be said to invent or perhaps to discover himself, and in which the character who speaks to us is the author who has created him and who is in turn a character created by or implicit in all the books written by the author who is writing this one.

Could this ever be a successful enterprise? No one has managed to bring literature closer to life than Nietzsche, yet the two refuse to become one, and thus his own ideal of unity may ultimately fail. Even if one insisted that more than any other philosopher Nietzsche can be identified with his texts, his texts may be all there is to him as a philosopher, but not as a person. To insist on that identification would be to do just what he so passionately argued against, to take part of him as essential and part of him as accidental. The unity he is after shows itself once more to be impossible to capture in reality. *Ecce Homo* leaves great parts of his life undiscussed and, unfortunately for him, his life did not end with it, but twelve miserable years later. To make a unified character out of all one has done, as Nietzsche wanted, would involve us in the vicious enterprise of writing our autobiographies as we lived our lives, and writing about that, and writing about writing about that. . . . And at some point, we would inevitably have to end. But, as he had written long before his own end, "Not every end is a goal. A melody's end is not its goal; nevertheless, so long as the melody has not reached its end, it also has not reached its goal. A parable."[84] This comes as close to explicating the aphorism which has occupied us and to expressing Nietzsche's attitude toward the relationship between art and the world as anything he ever wrote. But the doubt remains whether any melody, however complicated, could ever be a model a life (which is not to say a biography) can imitate.

---

[84] KGW iv/3. 280; HH III. 204; my translation.

11

THE PARADOX OF FATALISM AND SELF-CREATION IN NIETZSCHE

BRIAN LEITER

1. SELF-CREATION

I want to identify and then try to resolve a deep and troubling paradox in Nietzsche's work that threatens the core of a popular understanding of Nietzsche as the philosopher who calls for people to create themselves.[1] This paradox, as I think will become amply apparent, is striking once the texts are looked at in the right way. Yet, surprisingly, it has received almost no attention in the voluminous literature on Nietzsche.[2]

It is a commonplace about Nietzsche that he called upon people to 'create' themselves. In *The Gay Science*, he declares that 'We ... want to become those we are—human beings who are new, unique, incomparable, who give themselves laws, who create themselves.'[3] In the same work, he praises those who ' "give style" to [their] character[s]'.[4] In a later work, Nietzsche commends Goethe for having 'created himself'.[5]

Commentators working within various philosophical traditions have all emphasized this theme of self-creation. The existentialist philosopher Karl Jaspers, for example, writes in his famous study of Nietzsche that 'Creation is the highest demand; it is authentic being, the ground of all essential

---

From Brian Leiter, 'The Paradox of Fatalism and Self-Creation in Nietzsche', in C. Janaway (ed.), *Willing and Nothingness: Schopenhauer as Nietzsche's Educator* (Oxford: Oxford University Press, 1998), 217–55.

[1] Translations of Nietzsche's works, with occasional minor emendations, are by Walter Kaufmann and/or R. J. Hollingdale; in making emendations, I rely on KSA.

[2] Someone might object that there is no interest in adducing such a 'paradox', since it is (allegedly) well known that Nietzsche's corpus is full of contradictions. I can not enter here the complex debate on this issue. In reading Nietzsche, however, we should keep in mind his remark in EH: 'Alas, I am a nuance' ('The Case of Wagner', 4). Even if there are some minor contradictions in Nietzsche's sizeable corpus, it is the assumption of this essay that the sort of paradox I illustrate in what follows is so striking and significant that it requires some resolution if we are not to dismiss a central piece of Nietzsche's thought as embarrassingly incoherent.

[3] GS 335.

[4] GS 290.

[5] TI, 'Skirmishes of an Untimely Man', 19.

activity';[6] that 'Nietzsche ... never doubts that man is free and that he develops himself'; and that for Nietzsche 'freedom becomes "creation"'.[7] Under the influence of deconstruction and literary theory, more recent interpreters like Alexander Nehamas and Richard Rorty also emphasize Nietzsche's rhetoric of self-creation and claim that Nietzsche, unlike Freud, rejected the idea of an 'essential' self or an immutable human nature.[8] Rorty, for example, calls Nietzsche an 'exemplar' of what 'a self-created, autonomous, human life . . . can be like'[9] and denies (in a longer passage to which I shall return below) that Nietzsche believes that our lives have 'a predestined resting place'.[10] Rorty even rejects the idea that Nietzsche might believe, like Freud, that a person's natural endowment circumscribes the realm of possibilities available to that individual in his life. 'The idea of a fixed, unchangeable "realm of possibility" is hard to combine', says Rorty, 'with the idea [one finds in Nietzsche] that one might, by one's own efforts, enlarge that realm—not simply take one's place within a predetermined scheme, but change the scheme.'[11]

In a similar vein, Nehamas also claims that, 'Nietzsche seems intent on undermining precisely the idea that there are antecedently existing possibilities grounded in the nature of . . . people.'[12] As Nehamas notes, '*Thus Spoke Zarathustra* is constructed around the idea of creating one's own self', so that, for Nietzsche, 'the self, even if it is to be at some point discovered, must first be created'.[13] Finally, a recent book by a political theorist critical of postmodernism tells us, none the less, that Nietzsche is still the 'teacher of

---

[6] Karl Jaspers, *Nietzsche: An Introduction to the Understanding of his Philosophical Activity*, trans. C. Wallraff and F. Schmitz (South Bend, Ind.: Regnery & Gateway, 1965), 151.

[7] Ibid. 154, 140.

[8] See Alexander Nehamas, *Nietzsche: Life as Literature* (Cambridge, Mass.: Harvard University Press, 1985), chs. 5 and 6 (Ch. 10 in this volume is an earlier version of ch. 6 in Nehamas's book); Richard Rorty, *Contingency, Irony, and Solidarity* (Cambridge: Cambridge University Press, 1989), 27–8, 98–9. Rorty cites Nehamas as authority for the idea, though Nehamas, in fact, cites an earlier work of Rorty's (incorporated into *Contingency, Irony, and Solidarity*) as support for his own reading (Nehamas, *Nietzsche*, 251 n. 6)!

[9] *Contingency, Irony, and Solidarity*, p. xiv.

[10] Ibid. 99.

[11] Ibid. 108.

[12] *Nietzsche*, 175.

[13] Ibid. 174. What Nehamas and Rorty mean by 'self-creation', it bears noting, is rather odd, and would no doubt colour their response to the paradox at issue in this essay. As Nehamas explains, 'The self-creation Nietzsche has in mind involves accepting everything that we have done and, in the ideal case, blending it into a perfectly coherent whole' (*Nietzsche*, 188–9)—where that blending is effected by a certain (literary) effort at redescribing one's life in the appropriate way (hence Nehamas's startling suggestion that for Nietzsche, 'writing is also the most important part of living'; 41). For some doubts that this is Nietzsche's view, as well as more general worries about Nehamas' approach, see my 'Nietzsche and Aestheticism', *Journal of the History of Philosophy*, 30 (1992), 275–90.

self-making or self-creation', who, accordingly, promotes an 'ethics of creativity'.[14]

Commentators, then, appear to speak almost in unison:[15] Nietzsche is the philosopher of self-creation. And, as we have seen, Nietzsche indeed says things that invite precisely that interpretation.

2. FATALISM

Nietzsche the philosopher of self-creation sits uneasily, however, with a Nietzsche whom we encounter far more often in his writings: Nietzsche the fatalist. Nietzsche the fatalist holds that the basic character of each individual's life is fixed in advance in virtue of an individual's nature, that is, the largely immutable physiological and psychological facts that make the person who he is. It is striking, and no doubt important, that Nietzsche seems to endorse fatalism from the beginning of his philosophical career until the very end.

In one of his earliest works, for example, he praises Schopenhauer for his 'insight into the strict necessity of human actions' adding that we confront 'a brazen wall of fate (*des Fatums*): we *are* in prison, we can only *dream* ourselves free, not make ourselves free'.[16] In his next work, *Daybreak*, he suggests that what looks like purposive and intentional action is nothing more than the *necessary* course of events playing itself out:

perhaps there exists neither will nor purposes, and we have only imagined them. Those iron hands of necessity which shake the dice-box of chance play their game for an infinite length of time: so that there *have* to be throws which exactly resemble purposiveness and rationality of every degree. *Perhaps* our acts of will and our purposes are nothing but just such throws—and we are only too limited and too vain to comprehend our extreme limitedness: which consists in the fact that we ourselves

---

[14] Peter Berkowitz, *Nietzsche: The Ethics of an Immoralist* (Cambridge, Mass.: Harvard University Press, 1995), 149, 15. Cf. my review in *Mind*, 105 (1996), 487–91.

[15] One exception is Leslie Paul Thiele, who notes that for Nietzsche, 'The self is not so much created as unfolded' (*Friedrich Nietzsche and the Politics of the Soul* (Princeton: Princeton University Press, 1990), 215). Thiele does not, however, discuss the paradox under consideration here. Two writers who do talk explicitly about the tension between freedom and fate in Nietzsche's work are John Richardson, *Nietzsche's System* (Oxford: Oxford University Press, 1996), 207–16, and George Stack, *Nietzsche and Emerson: An Elective Affinity* (Athens: Ohio University Press, 1992), ch. 5. I find neither of their approaches to the paradox satisfactory. Richardson's solution depends too heavily on making the metaphysics of the will to power central to Nietzsche's thought, in a way that recent scholarship suggests it is not (cf. Mazzino Montinari, 'Nietzsches Nachlass von 1885 bis 1888 oder Textkritik und Wille zur Macht', in *Nietzsche Lesen* (Berlin: Walter de Gruyter, 1982), 92–119). Stack, by contrast, never resolves the paradox, claiming, instead, that 'neither Emerson nor Nietzsche ever satisfactorily resolves' it (*Nietzsche and Emerson*, 194). It is the burden of this essay to show that, at least with respect to Nietzsche, this is wrong.

[16] HH II. 33.

shake the dice-box with iron hands, that we ourselves in our most intentional actions do no more than play the game of necessity.[17]

Anticipating the later themes of *Ecce Homo* (discussed below), Nietzsche writes in *The Gay Science*: '*What does your conscience say?*—"You shall become the person you are".'[18] A few years later, in *Beyond Good and Evil*, Nietzsche observes that,

> at the bottom of us, really 'deep down,' there is, of course, something unteachable, some granite of spiritual *fatum*, of predetermined (*vorherbestimmer*) decision and answer to predetermined selected questions. Whenever a cardinal problem is at stake, there speaks an unchangeable (*unwandelbares*) 'this is I.'[19]

In his last productive year, Nietzsche writes that 'The single human being is a piece of *fatum* from the front and from the rear, one law more, one necessity more for all that is yet to come and to be.'[20] In *Nachlass* notes from the same year, he claims that 'the voluntary is absolutely lacking ... everything has been directed along certain lines from the beginning'[21] and that, not surprisingly, 'one will become only that which one is (in spite of all: that means education, instruction, milieu, chance, and accident)'.[22] His famous doctrine of '*amor fati*'—'that one wants nothing to be different, not forward, not backward, not in all eternity'[23]—takes on a new significance against the background of his fatalism: since nothing *could*, after all, have been different, the affirmative attitude towards life which Nietzsche famously commends would require, then, that we accept things the way they are.

Perhaps the starkest evidence of how deep Nietzsche's fatalism runs is that he even tells the story of his own life, in *Ecce Homo*, in fatalistic terms. This should be plain enough from the subtitle of the work: 'How One Becomes What One Is' ('Wie man wird, was man ist'). Surprisingly, interpreters like Nehamas and Rorty resist the fatalistic implications. Thus, Rorty, commenting on the subtitle, writes as follows: 'In the sense Nietzsche gave to the phrase, "who one actually is" does not mean "who one actually was all the time" but "whom one turned oneself into in the course of creating the taste by which one ended up judging oneself." The term "ended up" is, however, misleading. It suggests a predestined resting place.'[24] Rorty does not, in fact, try to ground this interpretative claim in a reading of *Ecce Homo* (he cites only Nehamas as authority!). Yet the misunderstanding of Nietzsche's point is suggested immediately by the mistranslation: one becomes *what* (*was*) one

[17] D 130.
[18] GS 270.
[19] BGE 231.
[20] TI, 'Morality as Anti-Nature', 6.
[21] WP 458.
[22] WP 334.
[23] EH, 'Why I am so Clever', 10.
[24] *Contingency, Irony, and Solidarity*, 99.

is, according to Nietzsche, not 'who' (*wer*) one is. But to speak of 'what' rather than 'who' suggests precisely the objectification of the person that one would expect from a philosopher who views persons as having immutable, determining characteristics, such that one may ask of a human being, as one may ask of a tree, '*What* is it made of essentially?'[25]

More decisive evidence that Nehamas and Rorty misunderstand Nietzsche's view comes when we consider the argument of *Ecce Homo* as a whole. This highly stylized 'autobiography' is organized around a double irony. The first concerns the real purpose of the autobiographical undertaking itself: namely, as an extended exercise in self-congratulation. But whereas the typical autobiography pursues this end while trying not to be obvious about it, Nietzsche simply declares plainly the point of the project: that is, to show 'Why I am so Wise',[26] 'Why I am so Clever',[27] and the like. This is autobiography as *unabashed* self-congratulation.

Or so it first appears—until the second irony of *Ecce Homo* becomes visible. For though Nietzsche, indeed, thinks himself wise, clever, and the author of good books, there is nothing, in fact, self-congratulatory about his answer to the question *why* he is so wise, so clever, and the rest. This is because the argument of *Ecce Homo* is imbued with the fatalism we have seen Nietzsche embraced elsewhere. Indeed, the book begins on precisely that note: 'The good fortune of my existence', says Nietzsche in the first line, 'lies in its fatality (*Verhängniss*).'[28] As a result, the answer to the apparently self-congratulatory 'why' questions is roughly this: 'It was a lucky fact of nature that I, Nietzsche, was a healthy organism, that is, the type of creature

---

[25] Nehamas's own misreading of *EH*'s subtitle is defended on different, but equally problematic, grounds. For example, commenting on the famous section 'On the Despisers of the Body' (Z 1.4), Nehamas claims that those who despise the body do so because of 'the belief that they have a stable self' (*Nietzsche*, 251 n. 6). But Zarathustra nowhere in the passage disputes the existence of a stable self; to the contrary, he equates the real self with the body, and describes how this body determines what we do even as we imagine otherwise. 'Your self [the body]', says Zarathustra, 'laughs at your ego and at its bold leaps. "What are these great leaps and flights of thought to me" it says to itself. "A detour to my end. I am the leading strings of the ego and the prompter of its concepts."' Elsewhere, Nehamas argues that the idea of an underlying, essential self is incompatible with Nietzsche's 'general denial of the idea of a reality that underlies appearance' (p. 173). Yet *this* denial is for Nietzsche a denial of the *metaphysical* distinction between the 'merely' apparent, sensible realm and a supra-sensible, unknowable reality (as drawn, for example, by Kant; cf. TI, 'How the "True World" Finally Became a Fable'); it could hardly involve a denial of the difference between superficial states (like consciousness) and the underlying, causally efficacious states (which are, in principle, knowable), like the unconscious drives or the body. For this latter distinction is plainly central to Nietzsche: for example, when he calls consciousness 'surface and skin— which, like every skin, betrays something but *conceals* even more' (BGE 33) (cf. EH, 'Why I am so Clever', 9: 'consciousness *is* a surface').

[26] EH I.

[27] EH II.

[28] EH, 'Why I am so Wise', 1.

that instinctively does the right things to facilitate its flourishing.'[29] 'I have always *instinctively* chosen the *right* means against wretched states,' declares Nietzsche.[30] As the argument of *Ecce Homo* makes explicit, this means choosing (instinctively or necessarily) the right nutrition, the right climate, the right forms of recreation, 'everything that deserves to be taken seriously in life'.[31] Nietzsche wrote such wise and clever books for the same reason the tomato plant grows tomatoes: *because it must*, because it could not have done otherwise. But there is no self-congratulation involved in simply reporting what had to be, and Nietzsche evinces none. To the contrary, as he remarks in the quotation with which the book opens: 'How could I fail to be grateful (*dankbar*) to my whole life?' This very way of putting the question, however, suggests a sharp divide between the 'life'—which runs its necessary course—and the conscious 'self' which views the life as though a spectator upon it.

Fatalistic themes recur throughout *Ecce Homo*.[32] Explaining why he returned to Rome while writing *Zarathustra*, Nietzsche comments that 'some fatality was at work'.[33] He declares that *amor fati* is the mark of 'greatness': that one does not merely 'bear what is necessary . . . but *love*[s] it'.[34] Later he remarks (not surprisingly) that '*amor fati* is my inmost nature'.[35] The depth of Nietzsche's fatalism regarding his own life becomes most apparent in a long passage from the second chapter of *Ecce Homo*. Nietzsche is here discussing his development as a philosopher, after noting that, 'To become what one is, one must not have the faintest notion *what* one is.'[36] He continues:

Meanwhile the organizing 'idea' that is destined to rule (*die zur Herrschaft berufne*) keeps growing deep down—it begins to command; slowly it leads us *back* from side roads and wrong roads; it prepares *single* qualities and fitnesses that will one day prove to be indispensable as means toward a whole—one by one, it trains all *subservient* capacities before giving any hint of the dominant task, 'goal,' 'aim,' or 'meaning.'

[29] Cf. EH, 'Why I am so Wise', 2: 'I took myself in hand, I made myself healthy again: the condition for this—every physiologist would admit that—is *that one be healthy at bottom*.'

[30] EH, 'Why I am so Wise', 2; first emphasis added.

[31] EH, 'Why I am a Destiny', 8. Cf. EH, 'Why I am so Clever', 10: 'these small things—nutrition, place, climate, recreation, the whole casuistry of selfishness—are inconceivably more important than everything one has taken to be important so far'.

[32] One might worry, though, that Nietzsche's comment about 'Accepting oneself as if fated' (EH, 'Why I am so Wise', 6) suggests that he does not really believe in fatalism: hence the 'as if'. Here Kaufmann's rendering is problematic (and probably reflects his own discomfort with finding Nietzsche to be a fatalist): for Nietzsche says simply 'wie', not 'als ob'. Thus, the phrase might have been rendered, more aptly, as 'accepting oneself as fated'—which, on Nietzsche's view, one really is!

[33] EH, 'Thus Spoke Zarathustra', 4.

[34] EH, 'Why I am so Clever', 10.

[35] EH, 'The Case of Wagner', 4.

[36] EH, 'Why I am so Clever', 9.

Considered in this way, my life is simply wonderful. For the task of a *revaluation of all values* more capacities may have been needed than have ever dwelt together in a single individual—above all, even contrary capacities that had to be kept from disturbing, destroying one another ... [Their] *higher protection* manifested itself to such a high degree that I never even suspected what was growing in me (*was in mir wächst*)—and one day all my capacities, suddenly ripe (*reif*), leaped forth (*hervorsprangen*) in their ultimate perfection.[37]

Nietzsche here views his own life as, say, an apple tree—unaware of its true nature—might view itself: although not 'suspect[ing] what was growing' in it, the tree one day finds its fruit 'suddenly ripe' and 'leap[ing] forth'.[38] We now have the answer to the book's subtitle: how one becomes what one is. The answer: by making no special effort *directed towards that end*, because one becomes what one is *necessarily*.

We may now try to state the paradox of fatalism and self-creation more precisely. According to Nietzsche the fatalist, a person's life proceeds along a fixed trajectory, fixed (as I shall explain in Section 3) by 'natural' facts about that person. Nietzsche the fatalist views a person like a plant: just as, say, the essential natural facts about a tomato plant determine its development (e.g. that it will grow tomatoes and not, say, corn), so too the essential natural facts about a person determine its development as well. Of course, the precise development of a tomato plant—whether it 'flourishes' or wilts—is affected (causally) by a host of other factors that don't constitute the 'essence' of the plant: for example, the soil in which it is planted, the amount of water it receives, and the like. So the natural facts about the tomato plant *circumscribe*, as it were, the possible trajectories, though they themselves do not uniquely determine which of these is realized. Nietzsche seems to hold the same view about persons: natural facts about a person circumscribe what that person becomes, though, within the limits set by the natural facts, the precise details of what a person becomes depend (causally) upon other factors. More formally, then, we can say that according to Nietzschean fatalism,

Natural facts about a person are *causally primary* in fixing the trajectory of that person's life.

Natural facts, in turn, are 'causally primary' with respect to some effect (i.e. some life trajectory) in so far as:

(1) they are always *necessary* for that effect; though
(2) they may not be *sufficient* for it.

---

[37] Ibid.
[38] Cf. Schopenhauer's observation that trying to use 'talk and moralizing' to 'reform' a man's 'character ... is exactly like the attempt ... by means of careful cultivation to make an oak produce apricots' (Arthur Schopenhauer, *Essay on the Freedom of the Human Will*, trans. Konstantin Kolenda (Indianapolis: Bobbs-Merrill, 1960), ch. 3, p. 54).

So, for example, natural facts (e.g. about metabolism, bone structure, body and muscle type, propensity to disease or illness) may be causally primary with respect to being a professional basketball player, in the sense that (1) to become a professional basketball player it is always *necessary* to have the right natural characteristics (height being only the most obvious), though (2) these natural characteristics are typically not *sufficient* to guarantee that one becomes a professional basketball player (e.g. not all tall, physically fit people become professional basketball players). Nietzschean fatalism is compatible, then, with the idea that factors other than natural facts about the person may still play a causal role in the trajectory of a person's life— within the limits circumscribed, of course, by the natural facts. For Nietzsche's fatalism to have any bite, of course, it must turn out that the natural facts significantly circumscribe the possible trajectories. I shall assume, with Nietzsche, that they do so, in this sense: the fundamental facts about one's *character and personality* are fixed by natural facts, and thus how one responds to differing circumstances and environments is also causally determined by natural facts. But the actual circumstances in which a person finds himself are plainly not fixed in advance by the natural facts about a person. In this sense, Nietzschean fatalism differs from the sort of fatalistic doctrine associated with Calvinism, in which *all the details* of one's life are determined in advance.

It is important here not to confuse several related concepts that may seem to be in play: what we may call classical determinism, classical fatalism, and causal essentialism.[39] Classical determinism is the view that for any event *p* at a time *t*, *p* is necessary given the totality of facts prior to *t*, together with the actual laws of nature. Classical fatalism, by contrast, is the view that whatever happens had to happen, but not in virtue of the truth of classical determinism.[40] Classical fatalism involves the notion of some sort of non-deterministic, perhaps even non-causal, *necessity*. Finally, causal essentialism is the doctrine that for any individual substance (e.g. a person or some other living organism) that substance has 'essential' properties that are causally primary with respect to the future history of that substance, i.e. they non-trivially determine the space of possible trajectories for that substance.[41] Notice that causal essentialism entails neither classical determinism nor

---

[39] The discussion that follows is indebted to Harvey Cormier, Bob Solomon and, especially, Rob Koons.

[40] Strictly speaking, classical determinism would not entail classical fatalism, since the outcomes necessitated under classical determinism are *contingent* on the past and on the laws of nature.

[41] I view talk of 'essences', as I take it Nietzsche does too, *sans* metaphysical baggage. Nietzsche can agree with Quine that 'relative to a particular inquiry, some predicates may play a more basic

fatalism. Unlike determinism, causal essentialism is compatible with there being no laws of nature. Unlike fatalism, essentialism does not entail that any particular outcome to a person's life is *necessary* (since causal essentialism only *circumscribes* trajectories, but does not necessitate any particular one).

Nietzsche's fatalism, as I read it, involves *only* causal essentialism. Nietzsche is neither a classical determinist nor a classical fatalist. That is, he holds only that there are essential natural facts about persons that significantly circumscribe the range of life trajectories that person can realize and that, as a result, make one's life 'fated', not in the classical sense, but in the sense that what we become is far more constrained, in advance, than we had ever realized.

According to Nietzsche the philosopher of self-creation, by contrast, the trajectory of a person's life is something that that person creates. Intuitively, for a person to have created himself, at least two conditions must be satisfied:

(1) The person must be the necessary, though perhaps not sufficient, cause of what he becomes ('Causal Condition').
(2) The person, in fulfilling the Causal Condition, must satisfy the requirements for autonomous or free action ('Autonomy Condition').

The Causal Condition ensures that our creator stands in the right relation to the alleged object of his creation. The Autonomy Condition ensures that, in so standing, our creator 'chooses' to contribute something independent to the production of the object, rather than simply functioning as a mere conduit for a larger causal process. If a terrorist group kidnapped and drugged me so that I would embark upon a series of criminal undertakings designed to fill the group's coffers, I would be causally responsible for the ensuing criminal acts, but I would not, presumably, satisfy the Autonomy Condition. In that case, while I might become a criminal, we should not speak of my having 'created' myself in so becoming.

We now have the paradox before us: if a person's life trajectories are determined in advance by the natural facts about himself, then how can a person really create himself, i.e. how can he make an *autonomous* causal contribution to the course of that life? The fatalism sits in tension with the Autonomy Condition that is essential to genuine self-creation.

---

role than others, or may apply more fixedly; and these may be treated as essential' (W. V. O. Quine, *Theories and Things* (Cambridge, Mass.: Harvard University Press, 1981), 120–1). See also, W. V. O. Quine, 'Natural Kinds', in *Ontological Relativity and Other Essays* (New York: Columbia University Press, 1969), 114–38. Cf. Nietzsche's reference to 'the weakness of the weak' as 'their essence (*Wesen*) . . . their sole, ineluctable, irremovable reality' (GM I. 13).

Before trying to resolve the paradox, the reader needs to be convinced, of course, that Nietzsche really is a fatalist in the precise sense with which I am concerned—a claim which, as already noted, few commentators have found plausible. In addition to the textual evidence already adduced, there remain two further reasons for taking fatalism to be at the heart of Nietzsche's view. First, the fatalism follows from a careful consideration of Nietzsche's theory of action. Nietzsche not only gives explicit voice to the doctrine of fatalism, but builds a picture of human agency that entails it. Secondly, a similarly fatalistic picture of human beings appears in the work of two of the most profound intellectual influences on mid-nineteenth-century German culture, and on Nietzsche in particular: Arthur Schopenhauer and the writers associated with the 'German Materialism' movement of the 1850s and 1860s. That Nietzsche should be a fatalist will seem far less surprising when we appreciate, as most commentators have not, the intellectual climate in which he was writing.

3. FREE WILL

If Nietzsche were a systematic philosopher, then he would have produced a fully developed theory of mind *and* action, for an account of free action—one that explains how action can satisfy the Autonomy Condition—can easily flounder at the level of the mind–body problem.[42] If, for example, the most plausible metaphysics of mind eliminates mentality, or renders mentality epiphenomenal, or reduces mentality to the physical (thus rendering it subject, perhaps, to deterministic natural laws), then it may be hard to see how we could locate an agent that satisfies the Autonomy Condition within a mind so conceived.[43] Nietzsche, however, has no worked-out theory of mind; his arguments against the Autonomy Condition all arise from his theory of action. We may locate two distinct arguments against the Autonomy Condition in Nietzsche's writings. First, Nietzsche argues that an autonomous agent would have to be *causa sui* (i.e. self-caused, or the cause of itself); but since nothing can be *causa sui*, no one could be an autonomous agent. The

---

[42] Cf. J. David Velleman, 'What Happens when Someone Acts?', *Mind*, 101 (1992), 461–81. As Velleman observes, 'Just as the mind–body problem is that of finding a mind at work amid the workings of the body, so the problem of agency is that of finding an agent at work amid the workings of the mind' (p. 469).

[43] This worry is vivid in the literature on mental causation, much of it generated by Jaegwon Kim's (to my mind, persuasive) arguments that the dominant non-reductive materialism in the philosophy of mind renders the mental epiphenomenal. For Kim's arguments, see esp. chs. 13, 14, and 17 in his *Supervenience and Mind* (Cambridge: Cambridge University Press, 1993). For an example of how the debate about epiphenomenalism is tied up with worries about autonomous agency, see Stephen Yablo, 'Mental Causation', *Philosophical Review*, 101 (1992), 245–80.

second argument grows out of Nietzsche's claim that our conscious life is essentially epiphenomenal, that what rises to the level of consciousness is simply an effect of something unconscious, or perhaps even something physical. Assuming that conscious states would have to figure in the causation of *autonomous* actions, it follows that there are no such actions, since actions are simply determined by the natural facts that determine consciousness. For reasons that will be made explicit below, I will call this the 'Naturalistic Argument'. If Nietzsche is correct in his Naturalistic Argument, this will prove fatal even to those popular attempts to reconcile free agency with deterministic processes. Moreover, as a picture of action, it will underwrite the fatalism we have seen Nietzsche give expression to in the many passages quoted already.

Before turning to an explication of these two arguments, two initial points warrant comment. Philosophers usually distinguish the problem of whether the *will* is free from the problem of whether *action* or *agency* is free.[44] In fact, of course, the problems are deeply related: a free action, for example, is often thought to be one that is caused (or 'determined') by a free will. For purposes of this essay, in any event, this is how I shall think of the issue, even if this does not do justice to the full range of possible philosophical complications.[45]

Although Nietzsche's repudiation of free will—the 'error of free will' as he calls it[46]—is well known (notwithstanding comments like Jaspers', quoted in Section 1), his reasons for rejecting it do not depend on the truth of classical determinism. From the standpoint of contemporary philosophical interests, this is a considerable virtue of Nietzsche's approach for two reasons. First, many, perhaps most, philosophers since Hume have thought free will compatible with determinism.[47] Secondly, determinism may, in fact, be false: the universe of quantum physics is often thought to be indeterministic.[48] Happily, we find in Nietzsche arguments against the

---

[44] Cf. Gary Watson, 'Free Action and Free Will', *Mind*, 96 (1987), 145–72.

[45] For some of these, see again ibid.

[46] TI, 'The Four Great Errors', 7.

[47] For doubts on this score, see Peter van Inwagen, 'The Incompatibility of Free Will and Determinism', repr. in G. Watson (ed.), *Free Will* (Oxford: Oxford University Press, 1982), 46–58, and Thomas Nagel, *The View from Nowhere* (New York: Oxford University Press, 1986), 113.

[48] This fact (if it is a fact!) still leaves us very far from having shown that the will or action is free. As Carl Ginet has aptly observed: the will is free 'only if determinism is false in certain specific ways, only if the laws of nature and the antecedent states of the world leave open all or most of the alternative actions we like to think are open to us. But that determinism is false in all those specific ways does not follow from indeterministic quantum theory' (*On Action* (Cambridge: Cambridge University Press, 1990), 94). For a different view, however, of the significance of indeterminacy, see Robert Kane, 'Two Kinds of Incompatibilism', *Philosophy and Phenomenological Research*, 50 (1989), 219–54, and also his *Free Will and Values* (Albany: State University of New York Press, 1985).

Autonomy Condition that still have force against compatibilists in a quantum world.

The Causa Sui *Argument*

According to Nietzsche, 'the concept of *causa sui* is something fundamentally absurd'.[49] If this is correct, many philosophers take it to pose a fundamental challenge to the possibility of free will. As Gary Watson explains the intuitive point: 'If the will is the product of culture and physiology, then there is no room for the idea that the agent is the author of his or her will.'[50] If all your actions arise from 'choices' (that arise from the will), but all your choices are determined by facts about your nature (say, your unconscious psyche and your physiology), then your actions appear determined not *by you*, but by facts about you. This, so the argument goes, is not sufficient for autonomous action or a free will, since what you do is determined, as it were, by what you already are.

Nietzsche seems to have drawn precisely the same conclusion:

> The *causa sui* is the best self-contradiction that has been conceived so far, it is a sort of rape and perversion of logic; but the extravagant pride of man has managed to entangle itself profoundly and frightfully with just this nonsense. The desire for 'freedom of the will' in the superlative metaphysical sense . . . the desire to bear the entire and ultimate responsibility for one's actions oneself, and to absolve God, the world, ancestors, chance, and society involves nothing less than to be precisely this *causa sui* and . . . to pull oneself up into existence by the hair, out of the swamps of nothingness.[51]

But we can not, needless to say, pull ourselves up 'out of the swamps of nothingness', and so we can not have ultimate responsibility for our actions. Our 'will' is an artefact of the facts about us, and thus can not be the source of genuinely autonomous action (the sort that would ground responsibility).

Notice that the problem is not resolved by suggesting that, even if our initial 'character' is fixed by natural facts about us, we may, later on, strive to alter this basic character through the choices we make (e.g. to undergo psychoanalysis, to 'turn over a new leaf'). For this simply pushes the requirement of a *causa sui* back one more level, yielding an infinite regress. As Galen Strawson has helpfully put the point:

---

[49] BGE 15.

[50] Watson, 'Free Action and Free Will', 164. See also Galen Strawson, 'The Impossibility of Moral Responsibility', *Philosophical Studies*, 75 (1994), 5–24. Strawson calls this *causa sui* argument the 'basic argument' against moral responsibility. Strawson also correctly attributes an earlier version of the argument to Nietzsche.

[51] BGE 21.

We may later engage in conscious and intentional shaping procedures—call them S-procedures—designed to affect and change our characters, motivational structure, and wills ... The question is then why we engage in the particular S-procedures that we do engage in, and why we engage in them in the particular way we do. The general answer is that we engage in the particular S-procedures that we do engage in, given the circumstances in which we find ourselves, because of certain features of the way we already are.[52]

If, in other words, we are not *causa sui*, then everything about our will (and, consequently, about our actions) is causally determined by something about the 'way we already are'—including those operations of will in which we attempt to alter the 'way we already are'. The result appears to be a picture of agency in which 'the person serves merely as the arena for these events: he takes no active part.'[53] This, as we shall see in Section 5, is a view Nietzsche explicitly endorses.

Many philosophers[54] have thought that the *causa sui* argument disproves something no one need believe—namely, that the will is uncaused. Free will and moral responsibility, these philosophers hold, are not only compatible with causal determination of the will, but may require it. As a result, these philosophers adopt a fairly cavalier posture towards the *causa sui* argument. As Galen Strawson has correctly observed, however, 'Belief in the kind of absolute moral responsibility [and autonomy] that [the argument] shows to be impossible has for a long time been central to the Western religious, moral and cultural tradition.'[55] Arguably, it is only certain academic philosophers who think the need to be a self-caused agent is superfluous, something that can be finessed via some adroit dialectical moves. Yet as Strawson's comment nicely brings out, the concept of 'free will' in play in the culture at large may be far more wedded to the notion of autonomous action which is rendered impossible by the argument under consideration here than the concept of 'free will' favoured by compatibilists.[56]

---

[52] 'The Impossibility of Moral Responsibility', 18.

[53] Velleman, 'What Happens when Someone Acts?', 461. In this particular passage, Velleman is concerned with the upshot of the 'standard' belief–desire story about action. But the phrase also fits the picture that emerges from the view Strawson describes and which Nietzsche also endorses.

[54] Not, however, those who embrace various libertarian theories of free will—those who think freedom of the will depends on its being outside the causal order altogether—or those (notably Roderick Chisholm) who think free will requires putting the agent, as an irreducible primitive, into the causal order. I sympathize with the dominant sentiment that libertarian, and agent causation, theories make no sense. For representative critiques, see Strawson, 'The Impossibility of Moral Responsibility', 18–20; Velleman, 'What Happens when Someone Acts?', 468–9; Watson, 'Free Action and Free Will', 161–9.

[55] 'The Impossibility of Moral Responsibility', 8.

[56] As I have argued elsewhere, Nietzsche's primary target is generally *not* the philosopher's conception of something, but rather the popular conception that informs a cultural ethos—for it is the latter that poses the threat to human flourishing with which Nietzsche is really concerned. See my 'Nietzsche and the Morality Critics', Ch. 9 in this volume, and my 'Morality in the Pejorative

The Naturalistic Argument

The *causa sui* argument just considered already presupposes a certain view of persons: namely, that each person has certain characteristics that causally determine that person's 'will'. Nietzsche's full-blown theory of action builds upon this idea. We may state Nietzsche's view, in bold outline, as follows.

According to what we may call Nietzsche's 'Doctrine of Types',

> Each person has a fixed psycho-physical constitution, which marks him or her as a particular 'type' of person. Call the relevant psycho-physical facts here 'type-facts.'

Type-facts, for Nietzsche, are either *physiological* facts about the person, or facts about the person's unconscious drives or affects. The claim, then, is that each person has certain largely immutable physiological and psychic traits, that constitute the 'type' of person he or she is.

Type-facts, for Nietzsche, are *causally primary* with respect to the course of a person's life—in the sense of 'causally primary' noted already. Type-facts are also *explanatorily primary*, in the sense that all other facts about a person (e.g. his beliefs, his actions, his life trajectory) are explicable by type-facts about the person (perhaps in conjunction with other natural facts about the circumstances or environment). This means, among other things, that a person's conscious mental states are what I will call 'kind-epiphenomenal'.[57] Consciousness is kind-epiphenomenal in the sense that conscious states are only causally effective in virtue of type-facts about the person (that is, not simply in virtue of their being conscious states). Put more simply: consciousness is not causally efficacious in its own right. While a person's conscious states may be part of the causal chain leading up to action, they play that role only in virtue of type-facts about the person. (At times, however, Nietzsche seems to embrace the more radical (and less plausible) view, that consciousness is token-epiphenomenal: i.e. that conscious states are simply *effects* of underlying type-facts about the person, and play no causal role whatsoever.)

This basic theory generates the following picture of action. We typically

---

Sense: On the Logic of Nietzsche's Critique of Morality', *British Journal for the History of Philosophy*, 3 (1995), 113–45.

[57] The distinction I have in mind is the one discussed in Brian McLaughlin, 'Type Epiphenomenalism, Type Dualism, and the Causal Priority of the Physical', *Philosophical Perspectives*, 3 (1989), 109–35, though I am substituting 'kind' for 'type', because I am already using 'type' in my notion of 'type-facts'. Roughly, the distinction is this: the book currently in the reader's hands is a *token* of a certain *type* or *kind* of book: namely, *Willing and Nothingness*. This 'kind' of book has many tokens (i.e. many copies of this book have been produced), but they are all tokens (i.e. instances) of a single 'kind'.

locate the 'will', as the seat of action, in various conscious states: for example, our beliefs and desires.[58] According to Nietzsche, however, the 'will' so conceived is nothing but the effect of type-facts about the person. This means that the real story of the genesis of an action begins with the type-facts, which explain both consciousness *and* a person's actions. Here is how Nietzsche puts it, after suggesting that the 'will' is related to, but conceptually prior to, the concepts of 'consciousness' and 'ego':

> The 'inner world' is full of phantoms . . . the will is one of them. The will no longer moves anything, hence does not explain anything either—it merely accompanies events; it can also be absent. The so-called *motive*: another error. Merely a surface phenomenon of consciousness, something alongside the deed that is more likely to cover up the antecedents of the deeds than to represent them . . . What follows from this? There are no mental (*geistigen*) causes at all.[59]

In the last line here, I take Nietzsche to mean there are no *conscious* mental causes. Indeed, in other passages, he is explicit that the target of this critique is the picture of conscious motives as adequate to account for action. As he writes in *Daybreak*, 'we are accustomed to exclude all [the] unconscious processes from the accounting and to reflect on the preparation for an act only to the extent that it is conscious',[60] a view which Nietzsche plainly regards as mistaken, both here and in the passage quoted above. Indeed, the theme of the 'ridiculous overestimation and misunderstanding of consciousness'[61] is a recurring one in Nietzsche. '[B]y far the greatest part of our spirit's activity', says Nietzsche, 'remains unconscious and unfelt.'[62] And in a *Nachlass* note of 1888, he writes: 'everything of which we become conscious is a terminal phenomenon, an end—and causes nothing'.[63] His strongest argument for the epiphenomenality of the mental is the following phenomenological argument against the *causal autonomy* of consciousness: namely, 'that a thought comes when "it" wishes, and not when "I" wish'.[64] But if that is right—as it surely is—and if actions are apparently 'caused' by thoughts (by particular beliefs and desires), then it follows that actions are not caused by our conscious mental states, but rather by whatever it is (i.e. type-facts) that determines the 'thoughts' that enter consciousness. Thus, it is the (autonomous) causal power of our conscious mental life that I take

---

[58] Cf. Velleman on the 'standard story' about action in 'What Happens when Someone Acts?'

[59] TI, 'The Four Great Errors', 3. Cf. WP 666: 'why could a "purpose" not be an epiphenomenon in the series of changes in the activating forces that bring about purposive action—a pale image sketched in consciousness beforehand that serves to orient us concerning events, even as a symptom of events, *not* as their cause?'

[60] D 129.

[61] GS 11.

[62] GS 333; cf. GS 354.

[63] WP 478.

[64] BGE 17.

Nietzsche to be attacking. Given, then, that Nietzsche claims consciousness is epiphenomenal,[65] and given our identification of the 'will' with our conscious life, Nietzsche would have us dispense with the idea of the will as causal altogether.

This latter point is significant in understanding the depth of Nietzsche's repudiation of the doctrine of free will. Compatibilists since Hume have argued that free will is compatible with the will being causally determined; all that is required for free will (and, accordingly, for free action and moral responsibility), compatibilists maintain, is that the will is causally determined *in the right sort of way*. According to the influential 'hierarchical' or 'identification' accounts—associated, most prominently, with Harry Frankfurt[66]—what is required for free will is that we *identify* with those desires that causally determine the will, that we regard these effective desires 'as our own' (in some precise sense—over which philosophers differ—though the details do not matter here). Frankfurt puts the point by describing a hierarchy of desires, in which we have second-order desires that only certain of our first-order desires should actually be effective (in generating action); our will is 'free' when these second-order desires are realized—even though, of course, the ensuing action is causally determined by a first-order desire.

After a quarter-century of philosophical debate, it should be plain that hierarchical accounts of free will have failed.[67] They all stumble over two obstacles.[68] First, these theories have no account of the *source* of our second-order desires or volitions, the ones that account for which first-order desire we 'identify' with in action. For all the hierarchical accounts tell us, our second-order desires could be causally determined in a way that is not *compatible* with free will. To put this in Nietzschean terms: since second-order desires are not, themselves, *causa sui*, they could not possibly underwrite the autonomy of the will; what second-order desires we happen to have is

---

[65] Some of the passages just quoted are, admittedly, ambiguous as between kind-epiphenomenalism and token-epiphenomenalism (the latter doctrine holding that conscious states are simply not causally effective at all, not even in virtue of underlying type-facts).

[66] See esp. chs. 2, 4, 5, and 12 in his *The Importance of What We Care About* (Cambridge: Cambridge University Press, 1988). The classic paper is, of course, 'Freedom of the Will and the Concept of a Person', *Journal of Philosophy*, 68 (1971), 5–20; repr. as ch. 2 of the above.

[67] I would not want to imply that this feature is peculiar to hierarchical accounts. Indeed, it strikes me that all philosophical defences of free will (at least the ones designed to underwrite moral responsibility) are dismal failures; the peculiarity, of course, is that the bulk of philosophical energy continues to be expended upon defending free will, rather than upon exploring the philosophical consequences of abandoning free will. For a refreshingly different suggestion along these lines, see Strawson, 'The Impossibility of Moral Responsibility', 22.

[68] For representative critiques, see Watson, 'Free Action and Free Will', 148–50; Velleman, 'What Happens when Someone Acts?', 470–3.

just a consequence of the way we already are (an effect of the type-facts). Secondly, hierarchical accounts present the spectre of an infinite regress: for even if our effective first-order desires are those picked out by certain second-order desires, the question still remains why it is one identifies with *these particular* second-order desires. What is it about these second-order desires that make them one's own? For obvious reasons, it had better not be a third-order desire that a particular second-order desire be effective *vis-à-vis* one's first-order desires! But in that case, it remains unclear how the 'identification' process even gets off the ground.

What bears noting now is that Nietzsche presents yet a *third* objection to the compatibilist account of free will. For on Nietzsche's picture of action, the sorts of desire that hierarchical accounts point to are mere epiphenomena in consciousness; the genuine causal determinants of action both lie below the surface of consciousness (in type-facts about the person) *and* are generally unknown to us. But as long as they remain unknown, then we could not possibly 'identify' with them (assuming a satisfactory account of identification were even forthcoming), and thus could not, as the hierarchical accounts would have us do, 'identify' with the *real* determinants of our action. The latter point is one Nietzsche repeatedly emphasizes. He says that 'all actions are essentially unknown' and that 'nothing . . . can be more incomplete than' a person's 'image of the totality of *drives* that constitute his being'.[69] Later, he writes that our actions 'remain impenetrable', for 'every action is unknowable'[70]—not in principle, of course, but in fact. If each action is caused by type-facts about the person—facts about that person's physiology and unconscious make-up—then it is easy to understand why our actions, for Nietzsche, would be unknowable (or certainly very hard to know). The picture that emerges is, of course, similar to Freud's (later) psychic determinism, and like Freud's it entails that the real cause of our actions may be very hard to discover.

So, for Nietzsche, each of us has an essential psychophysical constitution—a set of type-facts that make us what we are—and our actions, and even our conscious life, are all causally determined by these natural facts about us. Now plainly the language of 'type-facts' and 'causal determination by natural facts' is not Nietzsche's. None the less, this characterization of Nietzsche's view serves to throw into relief strategies of argument and analysis that simply *pervade* Nietzsche's work (even though commentators have systematically downplayed or ignored them). The following style of

[69] D 116, 119.　　　[70] GS 335.

argument, for example, is omnipresent in Nietzsche: a person's theoretical beliefs are best explained by his moral commitments; and a person's moral commitments are best explained in terms of natural facts about the type of person he is. So, for example, Nietzsche says, 'every great philosophy so far has been . . . the personal confession of its author and a kind of involuntary and unconscious memoir'. Therefore, to really grasp this philosophy, one must ask, 'at what morality does all this (does *he*) aim'?[71] But the 'morality' that a philosopher embraces simply bears 'decisive witness to *who he is*'—i.e. who he *essentially* is—that is, to the 'innermost drives of his nature'.[72] The reduction of a person's moral beliefs to psychological and physiological facts about the person—that is, the explanation of the former by the latter— is a recurring philosophical move in Nietzsche. '[M]oralities are . . . merely a sign language of the affects', he says.[73] Accepting the 'golden rule' is signifi- cant because 'it betrays *a type of man*'.[74] '[A]nswers to the questions about the *value* of existence . . . may always be considered first of all as the symp- toms of certain bodies.'[75] 'Moral judgments', he says, are 'symptoms and sign languages which betray the process of physiological prosperity or failure.'[76] '[O]ur moral judgments and evaluations . . . are only images and fantasies based on a physiological process unknown to us' so that 'it is always necessary to draw forth . . . the *physiological* phenomenon behind the moral predispositions and prejudices'.[77] A 'morality of sympathy', he claims, is 'just another expression of . . . physiological overexcitability'.[78] *Ressentiment*—and the morality that grows out of it—he claims, has an 'actual physiological cause'.[79]

Sometimes, of course, Nietzsche simply skips the reduction of 'theory' to morals, and proceeds directly to a naturalistic explanation for the theoretical belief itself. '[A]ll of the products of [a person's] thinking are bound to reflect the condition he is in'[80] is the general motto here. Philosophers like Spinoza, for example, who consider 'the instinct of self-preservation decisive . . . *had* to see it that way; for they were individuals in conditions of distress'.[81] Philosophical scepticism, he asserts, 'is the most spiritual expres- sion of a certain complex physiological condition that in ordinary language is called nervous exhaustion and sickliness'.[82] More generally, 'assuming that one is a person, one *necessarily* (*notwendig*) also has the philosophy that

[71] BGE 6.   [72] Ibid.
[73] BGE 187.   [74] WP 925.
[75] GS, Preface, 2.   [76] WP 258.
[77] D 119, 542.   [78] TI, 'Skirmishes of an Untimely Man', 37.
[79] GM I. 15.   [80] D 42.
[81] GS 349.   [82] BGE 208.

belongs to that person'.[83] He continues the theme in another preface from the following year: 'our ideas, our values, our yeas and nays, our ifs and buts, grow out of us with the necessity with which a tree bears fruit—related and each with an affinity to each, and evidence of *one* will, *one* health, *one* soil, *one* sun'.[84] In short: just as natural facts—type-facts—about a tree determine the fruit that tree necessarily bears, so too natural type-facts about a person determine the 'fruit' that person necessarily bears—that is, the ideas and values he comes to embrace. Although ahistorical interpreters like Nehamas and Paul de Man simply dismiss all this physiological and naturalistic talk as tangential to Nietzsche's 'real' concerns,[85] it should now be plain how much violence such a move does to the integrity of the texts. We shall have occasion, shortly, to see that such disregard for these themes in Nietzsche can not be sustained once one understands the intellectual climate in which Nietzsche worked. Such understanding will make clear that the foregoing remarks express a view that is not marginal, but absolutely central, to any serious understanding of persons.

Why Fatalism Follows

That the naturalistic conception of persons as constituted by certain essential psychophysical facts (type-facts) seems to lead to Nietzschean fatalism should be evident. If type-facts determine a person's 'ideas and values', then even if 'ideas and values' determine one's action and choices, these actions and choices themselves are all the necessary consequence of the underlying type-facts. The trajectory of a person's life, then, follows a necessary course, one determined by the constitutive type-facts, in interaction with the environment and circumstances. We may think ourselves 'free', we may fancy ourselves 'deliberating' and 'choosing', but this is all illusion, the mere (kind-) epiphenomena of consciousness. Type-facts run their course and we are, as it were, merely 'the arena for these events [in which we] take no active part'.[86]

Even commentators sympathetic to naturalistic themes in Nietzsche have resisted these fatalistic implications, trying to show that Nietzsche reserves, as Richard Schacht puts it, 'the possibility of a genuine and

---

[83]   GS, Preface, 2; my emphasis.

[84]   GM, Preface, 2.

[85]   See Nehamas, *Nietzsche*, 120; Paul de Man, *Allegories of Reading* (New Haven: Yale University Press, 1979), 119.

[86]   Velleman, 'What Happens when Someone Acts?', 461.

significant role for intentions in the genesis of action'.[87] In support, Schacht quotes the following passage: 'People are accustomed to consider the goal (purposes, volitions, etc.) as the *driving force* [behind actions], in keeping with a very ancient error; but it is merely the *directing* force—one has mistaken the helmsman for the steam.'[88] From this, Schacht concludes that 'it is at least possible for intention to perform a significant "directing" function where human action is concerned. And if this is so, it follows that [Nietzsche] would not have all human action thought of as determined invariably and exclusively by non-conscious forces and environmental factors.'[89]

Yet Schacht, uncharacteristically, chops the quotation from *The Gay Science* at a misleading point. For the full passage continues as follows: 'Is the "goal," the "purpose" not often enough a beautifying pretext, a self-deception of vanity after the event that does not want to acknowledge that the ship is *following* the current into which it has entered accidentally? that it "wills" to go that way *because—it must*? that it has a direction, to be sure, but no helmsman at all?' Nietzsche, then, is plainly rejecting the suggestion that intentions (goals, purposes) function like helmsmen on ships, determining the direction of the ship, although the 'steam' (the 'drives' perhaps) provide the energy. The helmsman may, out of vanity, think of himself as 'choosing' a direction, but he is simply doing what he 'must': indeed, he is altogether expendable (there may be 'no helmsman at all'). So, too, we may interpret ourselves as intentionally willing certain things, when really that 'willing' itself, like the direction we fancy ourselves to be choosing, is simply what we 'must' do, the mere necessary effect of something else. Nietzsche, then, repudiates the very possibility that Schacht embraces; that he should do so, however, is precisely what one should expect given the fatalism we have seen he embraced throughout his career.[90]

---

[87] Richard Schacht, *Nietzsche* (London: Routledge & Kegan Paul, 1983), 303.

[88] Ibid. 303; GS 360.

[89] *Nietzsche*, 303–4.

[90] I take Nietzsche in this passage to be responding, in fact, to Schopenhauer's suggestion that the 'intellect' might enjoy a steering function in action. Thus, Schopenhauer claims that 'the intellect strikes up the tune, and the will must dance to it' (Arthur Schopenhauer, *The World as Will and Representation*, trans. E. F. J. Payne, 2 vols. (New York: Dover, 1969) (WWR) ii, ch. 19, 208) and that 'the most striking figure for the relation' of will and intellect 'is that of the strong blind man carrying the sighted lame man on his shoulders' (209). See the further discussion, below, in Sect. 5.

4. NATURALISM, GERMAN MATERIALISM, SCHOPENHAUER

The robustly naturalistic Nietzsche under consideration here no doubt seems strange and unfamiliar—at least to anyone who has spent much time reading the secondary literature on Nietzsche. The 'Nietzsche' popularized by literary theorists and their philosophical sympathizers simply has nothing to say about the natural facts about persons or the causal determination of action. Much recent literature[91] has debunked this often anachronistic understanding of Nietzsche.[92] Here, I want to address briefly three immediate worries about the Nietzsche described so far—in particular, about his alleged naturalism, and his views on causation and on science. After doing so, I will turn to Schopenhauer and the German Materialists, thinkers who profoundly influenced Nietzsche, and who no doubt planted the initial ideas for both his naturalism and his fatalism.

Naturalism, Causation, Science

What does it mean for a philosopher to be a naturalist? Although the term is used loosely and in varying ways by different philosophers, I take the core of naturalism in philosophy to be a *methodological* commitment to the idea that philosophical theorizing should be continuous with, perhaps dependent upon, a posteriori empirical inquiry in the various sciences.[93] The philosophical naturalist demands 'continuity' with the sciences in one or both of

---

[91] See esp. Maudemarie Clark, *Nietzsche on Truth and Philosophy* (Cambridge: Cambridge University Press, 1990); Richardson, *Nietzsche's System*; and my 'Nietzsche and Aestheticism', and 'Perspectivism in Nietzsche's *Genealogy of Morals*', in Richard Schacht (ed.), *Nietzsche, Genealogy, Morality* (Berkeley: University of California Press, 1994), 334–57.

[92] The central anachronism (as I discuss in my 'Nietzsche and Aestheticism') is the misunderstanding of the significance of Nietzsche's talk about 'text' and 'interpretation'. For Nietzsche, the 19th-century student of philology, calling something a 'text' or some view an 'interpretation', did not mean what it would mean for a post-Derridean literary theorist today. Philology was a 'science', and a good interpretation of a text disclosed the truth about its meaning, not simply the 'play' of signifiers. See M. S. Silk and J. P. Stern, *Nietzsche on Tragedy* (Cambridge: Cambridge University Press, 1981), 11 ff. That Nietzsche, the 19th-century philologist, thought the world was a 'text' that could be 'interpreted' in no way undermines the 'hardness' of the world or the epistemic privilege of any particular 'interpretation'. To think Nietzsche's talk about 'text' and 'interpretation' connotes otherwise is to forget that Nietzsche learned the art of interpretation at the feet of Ritschl, not Paul de Man!

[93] Cf. Peter Railton, 'Naturalism and Prescriptivity', in Ellen Frankel Paul, Fred D. Miller Jr., and Jeffrey Paul (eds.), *Foundations of Moral and Political Philosophy* (Oxford: Blackwell, 1990), 156–7; Daniel Dennett, 'Foreword,' in Ruth Garrett Millikan, *Language, Thought, and Other Biological Categories* (Cambridge, Mass.: MIT Press, 1984), p. ix; Larry Laudan, 'Normative Naturalism', *Philosophy of Science*, 5 (1990), 44.

the following ways: what I will call 'results continuity' and 'methods continuity'. Results continuity requires that the claims of philosophical theories be supported, or perhaps entailed, by the results of successful sciences. Many contemporary epistemologists, for example, look to the results of psychology and cognitive science to find out how the human cognitive apparatus really works; only with that information in hand do these philosophers venture to formulate epistemic norms about how humans *ought* to form beliefs.[94]

Methods continuity, by contrast, demands only that philosophical theories emulate the 'methods' of inquiry and styles of explanation characteristic of successful sciences.[95] Historically, this has been the most important type of naturalism in philosophy, evidenced in writers from Hume to Nietzsche.[96] These latter two, for example, both construct 'speculative' theories of human nature—modelled on the most influential scientific paradigms of the day (Newtonian mechanics, in the case of Hume; physiology, as we will see, in the case of Nietzsche)—in order to account for various features of human existence and experience that do not admit of rational vindications (e.g. our belief in causation or our belief in 'free will'). Their speculative theories are 'modelled' on the sciences in the sense that, for example, they take over from science the idea that we can explain phenomena in terms of their deterministic causes, or that experience is a criterion of acceptability for philosophical theories (as it is for scientific ones).[97] Nietzsche, of course, goes further—moving into the domain of results continuity—and actually

---

[94] Cf. Alvin I. Goldman, *Epistemology and Cognition* (Cambridge, Mass.: Harvard University Press, 1986), for the classic articulation of this programme. See also Philip Kitcher, 'The Naturalists' Return', *Philosophical Review*, 101 (1992), 53–114. Goldman and Kitcher are what I call 'normative naturalists'. There is a competing paradigm for naturalizing epistemology, associated with Quine, that we might call 'replacement naturalism'. While both types of philosopher share the *methodological* commitment distinctive of naturalism—to make philosophical theorizing continuous with and dependent upon scientific theorizing—they differ as to the goal of epistemology: for the replacement naturalist, it is description or explanation; for normative naturalists, it is the traditional goal of regulating practice through the promulgation of norms or standards. Not surprisingly, normative naturalists like Goldman do not go as far as Quine in repudiating the role of a priori methods in philosophy. See the discussion in *Epistemology and Cognition*, 2–3, 6–9.

[95] Such a view does *not* presuppose the methodological *unity* of the various sciences, though, in order not to be empty, it does suppose that the methods of the sciences are not so various as to encompass simply *all* epistemic methods and strategies. I should add that the failure of philosophers to solve the so-called 'demarcation' problem—the problem of what distinguishes genuine science from pseudo-science—does not, as far as I can see, doom this understanding of naturalism, just as the 'paradox of the heap' does not doom our ability to distinguish heaps of sand from single grains, even if, in both cases, there are 'fuzzy' borderline cases.

[96] On Hume, see Barry Stroud, *Hume* (London: Routledge, 1977), ch. 1.

[97] Broadly speaking, the second of these amounts to 'empiricism', the view that all genuine knowledge must come from experience. As Quine remarks, 'empiricism . . . is a finding of natural science itself [which shows] that our information about the world comes only through impacts on our sensory receptors' (*Pursuit of Truth* (Cambridge, Mass.: Harvard University Press, 1990), 19).

appropriates the results of physiological theorizing about persons in his philosophical writing, as we shall see in a moment.

Many naturalists, however, go beyond these *methodological* commitments—commitments about how philosophy should be done—and embrace a *substantive* doctrine. 'Substantive naturalism'[98] in philosophy is either the (ontological) view that the only things that exist are *natural* or *physical* things (e.g. the doctrine of 'physicalism');[99] or the (semantic) view that a suitable philosophical analysis of any concept must show it to be amenable to empirical inquiry (e.g. the sort of view in ethics which G. E. Moore attacked with his famous naturalistic 'fallacy' argument). Although many philosophers simply equate 'naturalism' with *substantive* naturalism of one variety or another,[100] this seems to me a mistake: what distinguishes the naturalist is the eschewal of a priori inquiry as the primary philosophical method, not a particular substantive commitment. Of course, a methodological naturalist may come to think that the best philosophical account of some concept or domain will be in terms that are substantively naturalistic. But, methodologically, it should be an open question whether the best philosophical account of morality or mentality or agency must be in substantively naturalistic terms.

I take Nietzsche's basic posture to be methodologically naturalistic, like Hume's. But how, one might ask, can we understand Nietzsche as following the methodological lead of science, as searching for deterministic causes, as even being something called a 'naturalist'? Charles Taylor, for example, has correctly identified Nietzsche as the philosopher who unmasks the 'moral' and 'evaluative' motives that underlie a certain sort of *substantive* naturalism (generally reductive physicalism),[101] and thus anoints Nietzsche as an anti-naturalist philosopher. Yet Taylor fails to notice that this unmasking is, in fact, part of Nietzsche's own naturalistic strategy of *explaining* a person's theoretical commitments in terms of his moral commitments, and then explaining his moral commitments in terms of natural facts about the person.

---

[98] I take the phrase, though not the definition, from Railton, 'Naturalism and Prescriptivity', 156–7.

[99] Somewhat more broadly: only those properties picked out by the kind-predicates that figure in the explanatory laws of the sciences actually exist.

[100] For this conflation, see e.g. Philip Pettit, 'Naturalism', in J. Dancy and E. Sosa (eds.), *A Companion to Epistemology* (Oxford: Blackwell, 1992), 296–7; Stephen J. Wagner and Richard Warner, Introduction, in Wagner and Warner (eds.), *Naturalism: A Critical Appraisal* (South Bend, Ind.: University of Notre Dame Press, 1993), 1–3; David Wiggins, 'Cognitivism, Naturalism, and Normativity: A Reply to Peter Railton', in J. Haldane and C. Wright (eds.), *Reality, Representation and Projection* (Oxford: Oxford University Press, 1993), 301–13.

[101] Charles Taylor, *Human Agency and Language: Philosophical Papers I* (Cambridge: Cambridge University Press, 1985), 6, 113.

What accounts most for resistance to understanding Nietzsche as a naturalistic philosopher is precisely the false, but still widespread, image of him as an unrepentant sceptic about science (and about causation, in particular), a Rortyesque debunker of the epistemic pretences of science for the late nineteenth century. Nietzsche's own crude science-worship of the late 1870s (evident, for example, in *Human, All Too Human*) did give way briefly in the early 1880s to a quasi-Schopenhauerian scepticism about whether science could plumb the depths of reality, that is, the noumenal world. Yet Maudemarie Clark has shown that this view too gives way to a renewed appreciation of science—and a new comfort with concepts like 'causation'—as his underlying metaphysical and epistemological views evolved beyond Schopenhauer's, in particular, by repudiating the idea of a noumenal world.[102] So, for example, when Nietzsche writes that 'In the "in-itself" there is nothing of "causal connections," of "necessity" . . . there the effect does *not* follow the cause, there is no rule of "law." It is *we* alone who have devised cause . . . ',[103] he can only be understood as denigrating the epistemic integrity of 'causation' if he accepts, like Schopenhauer, the intelligibility of the idea of the world in itself, i.e. the noumenal world. But once he repudiates this metaphysical distinction (as he does explicitly in *Twilight of the Idols*, 'How the "True World" Finally Became a Fable'), then the fact that 'causation' is *our* concept makes it none the worse for purposes of philosophical theorizing: after all, what else could it be?

More generally, Nietzsche's view of science has been badly caricatured at the hands of academics and commentators who have their own—very unnineteenth-century—axes to grind with the hegemony of science. For example, in the often misunderstood third essay of the *Genealogy*—where Nietzsche attacks the *value* of truth, not its existence—Nietzsche refers to 'the domain of science' as one 'where so much that is useful remains to be done' and, regarding the 'honest workers' in science, says: 'I approve of their work.'[104] Even in the more sceptical-sounding *Beyond Good and Evil*, he comments that 'the *ideal* scholar in whom the scientific instinct, after thousands of total and semi-failures, for once blossoms and blooms to the end, is

---

[102] See Clark, *Nietzsche on Truth and Philosophy*, esp. ch. 4. See also, my 'Perspectivism in Nietzsche's *Genealogy of Morals*'.

[103] BGE 21

[104] GM III. 23. Nietzsche, of course, also says things here like: 'whoever tries . . . to place philosophy "on a strictly scientific basis," first needs to stand not only philosophy but truth itself *on its head*' (GM III. 24). But lifted out of context, this remark is highly misleading. For the real objection he is making here is his standard one: namely, that the distinctive role of the philosopher is the creation of values (from which we derive goals, purposes, etc.) (cf. BGE 207), and it is only from such values 'that science can acquire . . . a direction, a meaning, a limit' (GM III. 24). To put philosophy 'on a strictly scientific basis', then, is to imagine that it could forgo the value-creating function which *science* itself presupposes and requires.

certainly one of the most precious instruments there are; but he belongs in the hand of one more powerful [i.e. the philosopher-*qua*-creator-of-values]'.[105] Earlier, he lauds science for 'the severity of its service, its inexorability in small as in great matters . . . [and because in science] the most difficult is demanded and the best is done without praise and decorations'.[106] Indeed, this last remark gets to the real heart of Nietzsche's *methodological* naturalism: namely, its commitment to scientific *method*, rather than exclusive commitment to particular scientific paradigms. '[S]cientific *methods* . . . one must say it ten times, *are* what is essential, also what is most difficult, also what is for the longest time opposed by habits and laziness'.[107] '[T]he most valuable insights are the *methods*,' he declares, adding by way of complaint that '*All* the methods, *all* the presuppositions of our current scientific outlook, were opposed for thousands of years with the most profound contempt.'[108] 'It is not the victory of science that distinguishes our nineteenth century,' he remarks in a note of 1888, 'but the victory of scientific method over science.'[109]

The central themes of methodological naturalism are, in fact, all sounded in a famous passage from *Beyond Good and Evil*:

To translate man back into nature; to become master over the many vain and overly enthusiastic interpretations and connotations that have so far been scrawled and painted over the eternal basic text of *homo natura*; to see to it that man henceforth stands before man as even today, hardened in the discipline of science, he stands before the *rest* of nature, with intrepid Oedipus eyes and sealed Odysseus ears, deaf to the siren songs of old metaphysical bird catchers who have been piping at him all too long, 'you are more, you are higher, you are of a different origin!'—that may be a strange and insane task, but it is a *task*—who would deny that? Why did we choose this insane task? Or, putting it differently: 'why have knowledge at all?'[110]

Several things about this passage are striking. When Nietzsche calls here for man to stand 'hardened in the discipline (*Zucht*) of science'—rather than, say, 'schooled in particular substantive scientific doctrines'—he presumably has in mind precisely the discipline involved in those scientific methods we have just seen him lauding elsewhere. But it is also clear that, for Nietzsche, a commitment to the 'discipline [or method] of science' also entails a commitment to a certain sort of results continuity, namely, to the 'result' foremost in the mind of mid-nineteenth-century Germans: that

[105] BGE 207.
[106] GS 293.
[107] A 59.
[108] A 13; cf. WP 469.
[109] WP 466.
[110] BGE 230. Cf. GS 109: 'When will we complete our de-deification of nature? When may we begin to "naturalize" humanity in terms of a pure, newly discovered, newly redeemed nature?'

man is not of a 'higher ... [or] of a different origin' than the rest of nature. Indeed, if there are still any doubts about the depth of Nietzsche's naturalism, these will, I expect, be fully resolved once we recapture the intellectual *Weltanschauung* of Nietzsche's Germany. It is to this *Weltanschauung* that I now turn.

German Materialism

'Idealism', as one commentator has correctly noted, 'had ... ceased to be a real power in German thought by 1830.'[111] In its place had arisen a profoundly naturalistic world-view, well-captured by one of its leading proponents, the medical doctor Ludwig Büchner (older brother of the now better-known, proto-existentialist playwright Georg), in his 1855 best-seller *Force and Matter*:[112] 'the researches and discoveries of modern times can no longer allow us to doubt that man, with all he has and possesses, be it mental or corporeal, is a *natural product* like all other organic beings'.[113] 'Man is a product of nature', declared Büchner, 'in body and mind. Hence not merely what he is, but also what he does, wills, feels, and thinks, depends upon the same natural necessity as the whole structure of the world.'[114] So spoke the 'German Materialists' of the 1850s and after.

German Materialism had its origins in Feuerbach's works of the late 1830s and early 1840s, but it really exploded onto the cultural scene in the 1850s, under the impetus of the startling new discoveries about human beings made by the burgeoning science of physiology. In 1850 the physiologist Jacob Moleschott published two books: the scholarly *The Physiology of Nutrition* and a popular companion volume, *The Theory of Nutrition: For the People*. These were followed in 1852 by the work that made Moleschott famous, *The Cyclical Course of Life*. The year 1855 also saw the publication of two influential and polemical treatises: the physiologist Karl Vogt's *Superstition and Science* and Büchner's *Force and Matter*, the latter of which 'soon earned the reputation as the Bible of materialism', going through

---

[111] Hans Sluga, *Frege* (London: Routledge, 1980), 9. For a similar verdict from someone alive in 1830, and after, see Friedrich Lange, *The History of Materialism*, trans. E. C. Thomas (New York: Harcourt, Brace, 1925; repr. Atlantic Heights, NJ: Humanities Press, 1950), book 2, sect. 1, ch. 2, 245. Further citations to Lange will be exclusively to material from the second book.

[112] *Kraft und Stoff* appears in a serviceable, if somewhat tin-eared, translation by J. F. Collingwood (London: Trubner, 1870); my citations (with an occasional emendation) will be to this edition.

[113] Ibid., p. lxxviii.

[114] Ibid. 239.

twelve editions in seventeen years, and being translated into seventeen foreign languages.[115]

Given their tremendous impact, it is impossible that the young Nietzsche would have been unfamiliar with the materialists. A critic of materialism writing in 1856, for example, complained that, 'A new world view is settling into the minds of men. It goes about like a virus. Every young mind of the generation now living is affected by it.'[116] Moreover, we do know that Nietzsche read (with great enthusiasm) Friedrich Lange's *The History of Materialism* (originally published in 1866), viewing it at the time as 'undoubtedly the most significant philosophical work to have appeared in the last hundred years'.[117] Indeed, in a letter of February 1868, Nietzsche called Lange's book 'a real treasure-house', mentioning, among other things, Lange's discussion of the 'materialist movement of our times'[118]— including the work of Feuerbach, Büchner, Moleschott, Heinrich Czolbe, and the pioneering physiologist Herman von Helmholtz.[119] From Lange, Nietzsche would have acquired a clear picture of contemporary German Materialism, of its 'mechanical understanding of man as a mere natural creature',[120] of its view that, 'The nature of man is . . . only a special case of

---

[115] Frederick Gregory, *Scientific Materialism in Nineteenth Century Germany* (Dordrecht: Reidel, 1977), 105.

[116] Quoted ibid. 10.

[117] Ronald Hayman, *Nietzsche: A Critical Life* (New York: Oxford University Press, 1980), 82.

[118] Quoted in George Stack, *Lange and Nietzsche* (Berlin: Walter de Gruyter, 1983), 13. Stack, in my view, overstates Nietzsche's debt to Lange, and fails to note their many differences: e.g. Nietzsche was less critical of materialism than Lange, and Nietzsche plainly repudiated Lange's Kantianism (e.g. Lange's view that 'We must therefore recognize the existence of a transcendent order of things . . . '; *The History of Materialism*, sect. 3, ch. 4, 230). See also, Jörg Salaquarda, 'Nietzsche und Lange', *Nietzsche-Studien*, 7 (1978), 236–53. Stack's book does usefully demonstrate that an influence on Nietzsche can be profound (as evidenced by the views he would later express) without Nietzsche acknowledging that fact. Thus, for example, his *Nachlass* references to Büchner tend to be rather dismissive and rude. Cf. KSA vii. 596, 740. The similarities, however, between Materialist thought and Nietzsche's own turn out to be striking.

[119] See *History of Materialism*, esp. sect. 1, ch. 2; sect. 2, chs. 1 and 2; sect. 3, chs. 1, 2, and 4. Lange himself was one of a number of 'neo-Kantian' critics of Materialism who held (1) that modern physiology vindicated Kantianism by demonstrating the dependence of knowledge on the peculiarly human sensory apparatus (cf. Lange, sect. 2, ch. 1, 322, discussing the 'confirmation from the scientific side of the critical standpoint in the theory of knowledge', and sect. 3, ch. 4: 'The Physiology of the Sense-Organs and the World as Representation'); and (2) that the Materialists were naive in believing science gives us knowledge of the thing in itself rather than the merely phenomenal world (cf. sect. 3, ch. 1, 84: 'the physiology of the sense-organs has . . . produced decisive grounds for the [epistemological] refutation of Materialism'; sect. 1, ch. 2, 277 ff.; sect. 2, ch. 1, 329). At the same time, Lange's general intellectual sympathies were clearly with the Materialists as against the idealists, theologians, and others who would deny the importance of the blossoming scientific picture of the world and of human beings. Thus, for example, he remarks: 'if Materialism can be set aside only by criticism based upon the [Kantian] theory of knowledge . . . in the sphere of positive questions it is everywhere in the right . . . ' (sect. 2, ch. 1, 332).

[120] Ibid., sect. 3, ch. 4, 213.

universal physiology, as thought is only a special case in the chain of the physical processes of life.'[121]

While a reaction to Materialism did set in by the 1870s and 1880s, Nietzsche's youthful engagement with the Materialists made a profound and lasting impression on him. For example, he admits that in the late 1870s, 'A truly burning thirst took hold of me: henceforth I really pursued nothing *more* than physiology, medicine and natural sciences.'[122] This impression is evident even in his mature work of the 1880s.[123] In *Ecce Homo*, he complains of the 'blunder' that he 'became a philologist—why not at least a physician or something else that opens one's eyes?'[124] The same year, he comments that 'Descartes was the first to have dared, with admirable boldness, to understand the animal as *machina*: the whole of our physiology endeavors to prove this claim. And we are consistent enough not to except man, as Descartes still did . . . '.[125] Indeed, the importance of German Materialism to the intellectual climate of the period is evidenced by Nietzsche's repeatedly felt need to distance himself from certain Materialist doctrines that he found unpalatable. For example, the whole of chapter 6 of *Beyond Good and Evil*— 'We Scholars'[126]—is plainly a polemic against the Materialist view that 'official philosophy could be replaced with natural science', as the historian Frederick Gregory puts it.[127] In fact, when Nietzsche complains of the 'arrogant contempt for philosophy' coming from 'the lips of young natural scientists and old physicians',[128] he is almost certainly referring to Büchner—a physician—who by the mid-1880s was an old man, yet still enjoying the fame sustained by the repeated printings of his *Force and Matter*, which expressed precisely this 'arrogant contempt'.[129] (Other Materialists were 'natural scientists', notably physiologists and chemists.) Notice, however, that Nietzsche's objection in this chapter is not to science *per se*, or to the relevance of science and scientific methods to philosophy, but rather to the idea that science could dispense with the role of 'genuine philosophers' as creators of values.[130] As he says elsewhere, it is 'Around the inventors of new values

---

[121] See *History of Materialism*, sect. 1, ch. 2, 248.

[122] EH, 'Human, All Too Human', 3.

[123] Indeed, Hayman reports that Nietzsche was reading Materialist and related works as late as 1881 (*Nietzsche*, 234).

[124] EH, 'Why I am so Clever', 2.

[125] A 14.

[126] BGE 204–13.

[127] *Scientific Materialism in Nineteenth Century Germany*, 146.

[128] BGE 204.

[129] Nietzsche does concede that given the 'wretchedness of most recent philosophy'—he cites Dühring as one example—'a solid man of science *may* feel that he is of a better type and descent' (BGE 204).

[130] BGE 211.

[that] the world revolves', albeit 'invisibly' and 'inaudibly'.[131] Of course, Nietzsche is eager to utilize the information provided by 'physiologists and doctors' as to which values might contribute to 'the preservation of the greatest number' or to 'producing a stronger type',[132] but he is equally keen to resist the Materialist conceit that the creative role of philosophy might be dispensed with altogether.

Nietzsche is similarly hostile to the tendency towards *reductive* materialism evinced by many of the German Materialists, who often appeared to embrace a mind–brain identity theory[133] (as did Schopenhauer for that matter).[134] Against this view, Nietzsche made what are now familiar *phenomenological* objections (associated, for example, with Thomas Nagel and Charles Taylor) concerning the inability of reductive materialism to capture the distinctive qualitative character of experience.[135] Indeed, when he describes himself as 'the sternest opponent of all materialism'[136] he must plainly mean *reductive* materialism, since this remark comes immediately on the heels of his claim that 'When someone cannot get over a "psychological pain," that is *not* the fault of his "psyche" but, to speak crudely, more probably even that of his belly.'[137] (Natural facts may be explanatorily primary for Nietzsche— the core of Nietzsche's methodologically naturalistic commitment—but that does not entail that he embraces the substantive naturalism favoured by many of the Materialists.)

In fact, this latter passage is just one example of Nietzsche's unabashed appropriation of ideas of clear Materialist pedigree. We have seen, already, substantial evidence of his view that persons are best understood physiologically, a view clearly supported by the whole Materialist movement. He also shares with the Materialists a blanket repudiation of the idea of free will,[138] and, in fact, must be taking for granted the intellectual ascendancy of the Materialists when he quips that the 'will was firmly accepted as given' but 'Today we no longer believe a word of all this.'[139] One can surely

---

[131] Z I, 'On the Flies of the Market Place'; II, 'On the Great Events'.

[132] GM I, Remark.

[133] See the discussion in Lange, *The History of Materialism*, sect. 3, ch. 2 ('Brain and Soul'), 155–7 (incl. nn.); see also Büchner, *Force and Matter*, ch. 12 ('Brain and Soul').

[134] Cf. WWR ii, ch. 22, 272 ff.

[135] Cf. GS 373.

[136] GM III. 16.

[137] GM III. 16.

[138] Cf. Büchner, *Force and Matter*, 239–40 ('in every case free choice has only an extremely limited, if any sphere of action'); Gregory, *Scientific Materialism*, 34. The Materialists seem to have been drawn to this conclusion, however, primarily by their reductive theory of mind, which led them to the view that there is (as Thomas Nagel describes it) 'no room for agency in a world of neural impulses, chemical reactions, and bone and muscle movements' (*The View from Nowhere*, 111). Nietzsche, in fact, sometimes flirted with a similar view: e.g. 'one has a nervous system (—but no "soul"—)' (WP 229) (as did Schopenhauer, as we will see shortly).

[139] TI, 'The Four Great Errors', 3.

recognize, too, the (anachronistically) Nietzschean flavour of Büchner's claim that 'Man is subject to the same laws as plants and animals. . . . man [is] physically and mentally the product of such external influences [as "congenital physical and mental dispositions", as well as "sex, nationality, climate, soil"], and develops accordingly—certainly not that morally independent, free-willing creature as he is represented by moralists.'[140] Nietzsche plainly echoes Feuerbach's famous dictum that 'The body in its totality is my ego (*Ich*), my very essence'[141] when Zarathustra says, 'body am I entirely, and nothing else; and soul is only a word for something about the body'.[142] (Echoes of Schopenhauer are apparent here too.[143])

Perhaps most strikingly, Nietzsche's notorious speculations about the effects of nutrition, climate, and bodily fluids like bile on the thoughts and character of persons were clearly inspired by the Materialists. Moleschott's influential *Physiology of Nutrition*, for example, consisted of more than 500 pages of detailed information about the physiological and chemical aspects of food and human digestion,[144] while the popular companion volume recommended different diets for 'artisans' than for 'thinkers and scholars', in view of the differing intellectual demands made upon each.[145] In reviewing Moleschott's book, Feuerbach expressed the core idea as follows: 'If you want to improve the people then give them better food instead of declamations against sin. Man is what he eats.'[146] According to Lange, Moleschott taught that 'man is the sum of parents and nurse, of place and time, of air and weather, of sound and light, of food and dress'.[147] Büchner's work is similarly full of remarks like 'A copious secretion of bile has, as is well-known, a powerful influence on the mental disposition,'[148] as well as discussions of the effects of climate on national character types.[149] From Büchner, Nietzsche might have also learned to look for *physiological* explanations of intellectual traits or dispositions—as in Büchner's claim that 'Newton's atrophied brain caused him in old age to become interested in studying the books of Daniel and Revelation in the Bible.'[150]

With figures like Moleschott and Büchner ascendant on the intellectual

---

[140] *Force and Matter*, 243.
[141] Quoted in Gregory, *Scientific Materialism*, 30.
[142] Z I, 'On the Despisers of the Body'.
[143] Cf. WWR i, § 18, 100.
[144] Jacob Moleschott, *Physiologie der Nährungsmittel*, 2nd edn. (Giessen: Emil Roth, 1859).
[145] Jacob Moleschott, *Lehre der Nährungsmittel. Für das Volk*, 2nd edn. (Erlangen: Ferdinand Enfe, 1853), book 3, chs. 6 and 7.
[146] Quoted in Gregory, *Scientific Materialism*, 92.
[147] *The History of Materialism*, sect. 1, ch. 2, 241.
[148] *Force and Matter*, 119.
[149] Ibid. 241–2.
[150] Ibid. 111.

scene, is it any wonder, then, that we should find Nietzsche meditating on 'the moral effects of different foods' and calling for a 'philosophy of nutrition';[151] or speculating that, 'Wherever a deep discontent with existence becomes prevalent, it is the after-effects of some great dietary mistake made by a whole people over a long period of time that are coming to light';[152] or arguing that

> Whatever proceeds from the stomach, the intestines, the beating of the heart, the nerves, the bile, the semen—all those distempers, debilitations, excitations, the whole chance operation of the machine of which we still know so little!—had to be seen by a Christian such as Pascal as a moral and religious phenomenon, and he had to ask whether God or Devil, good or evil, salvation or damnation was to be discovered in them! Oh what an unhappy interpreter![153]

From the Materialist movement of Nietzsche's Germany, in short, Nietzsche would have learned to think of persons as essentially natural, bodily organisms, organisms for whom free will was an illusion, and for whom questions of physiological traits, nutrition, and climate were decisive in determining their ideas, their values, and their development. If the Materialists laid a groundwork for Nietzschean fatalism, it was, however, Schopenhauer who explicitly taught Nietzsche the relevant morals to draw.

Schopenhauer

Before the rise of German Materialism, Schopenhauer was arguing for the importance of physiology—in particular 'the physiology of the nervous system'[154]—for the 'objective' study of the human intellect and consciousness.[155] For Schopenhauer, however, consciousness is a feature of the merely phenomenal world, not a property of the thing in itself, that is, the 'will'. The details of Schopenhauer's opaque, and implausible, notion of 'will' (as the 'thing in itself') do not concern me here.[156] Nor do they concern Nietzsche. Nietzsche, as is well known, breaks with Kant and Schopenhauer in rejecting the idea of a noumenal realm. The only 'realm' for Nietzsche is the 'phenomenal'—though, as he points out, 'with [the abolition of] the true [i.e. noumenal] world we have also abolished the apparent [i.e. phenomenal]

---

[151] GS 7.
[152] GS 134.
[153] D 86. As Nietzsche put the point later, 'man's "sinfulness" is not a fact, but merely the interpretation of a fact, namely a physiological depression—the latter viewed in a religio-moral perspective that is no longer binding on us' (GM III. 16).
[154] WWR ii, ch. 22, 273.
[155] Cf. WWR ii, ch. 22, 272 ff.
[156] For a very useful and lucid overview, see Christopher Janaway, *Schopenhauer* (Oxford: Oxford University Press, 1994), esp. 28–34.

one'[157] (thus suggesting a metaphysical picture evocative of the 'middle way' between realism–Platonism and anti-realism–idealism that many contemporary philosophers have sought[158]). What is important for Nietzsche, then, in the context of his theory of action, is what Schopenhauer taught him about the self as it is found in what Schopenhauer called the 'phenomenal' world—the only world, for Nietzsche, that there is.

Certain aspects of Schopenhauer's view are familiar. Schopenhauer denied the freedom of the will in the empirical realm,[159] in virtue of the truth of determinism, which follows from 'the principle of sufficient reason', which holds that 'all necessity is the relation of consequent to ground'.[160] Since 'the principle of sufficient reason is the universal form of every phenomenon, and man in his action, like every other phenomenon, must be subordinated to it',[161] it follows that all human actions are *necessary*, i.e. causally determined. As conscious intellects, we are like 'spectators' upon our actions; while they may appear 'undetermined' to us, in reality they are completely determined, though the causes are opaque to the intellect.[162]

Schopenhauer's picture is, in fact, richer than this, and important for understanding Nietzsche. For Schopenhauer also held that each person has an 'unalterable . . . empirical character' (which, in turn, 'is the mere unfolding of the intelligible character that resides outside time', i.e. the 'will').[163] '[T]he tendency of his innermost nature and the goal he pursues in accordance therewith,' says Schopenhauer, 'these we can never change by influencing him from without, by instructing him.'[164] The necessity of one's actions, then, actually follows from the causal interaction of one's unalterable character with 'motives', that is, representations in consciousness that, for example, portray what the world contains. 'Just as everything in nature has its forces and qualities that definitely react to a definite impression, and

---

[157] TI, 'How the "True World" Finally Became a Fable'.

[158] See the discussion in my 'Perspectivism in Nietzsche's *Genealogy of Morals*'. Cf. John McDowell, 'Anti-Realism and the Epistemology of Understanding', in H. Parret and J. Bouveresse (eds.), *Meaning and Understanding* (Berlin: Walter de Gruyter, 1981) and 'Projection and Truth in Ethics', Lindley Lecture (Lawrence: University of Kansas Department of Philosophy, 1988); Hilary Putnam, *Realism with a Human Face* (Cambridge, Mass.: Harvard University Press, 1990).

[159] The exception to this generalization occurs when the merely phenomenal self 'abandons all knowledge of individual things as such', and makes contact, as it were, with the thing in itself, i.e. the will (WWR i, §55, 301; cf. §79, 404). There is, again, no reason to think that Nietzsche accepted this part of Schopenhauer's view, depending as it does on the very distinction Nietzsche repudiates.

[160] WWR i, §23, 113.

[161] Ibid.

[162] WWR i, §55, 291.

[163] WWR i, §55, 301.

[164] WWR i, §55, 294.

constitute its character,' observes Schopenhauer, 'so man also has his *character*, from which the motives call forth his actions with necessity.'[165] Since 'every individual action follows with strict necessity from the effect of the motive on the character',[166] and since the character is constant, it follows that every action we perform *had to be performed*, as though fated. Indeed, the principle of sufficient reason—which rules in the phenomenal world for Schopenhauer—entails that 'everything can be regarded as irrevocably predetermined by fate ... by means of the chain of causes'.[167] Fatalism about human action is just a particular instance of this broader thesis, as Schopenhauer makes plain: 'Just as events always come about in accordance with fate, in other words, according to the endless concatenation of causes, so do our deeds always come about according to our intelligible character.'[168] This leads Schopenhauer to the following remarkable comment on the Christian doctrine of 'predestination' according to which a man's 'life and conduct, in other words his empirical character, are only the unfolding of the intelligible character, the development of decided and unalterable tendencies already recognizable in the child. Therefore his conduct is, so to speak, fixed and settled even at his birth, and remains essentially the same to the very end. We too agree with this [doctrine]'.[169] Schopenhauer goes on to dissociate himself from some of the theological baggage associated with the Christian doctrine of predestination, but the point to note is that he endorses the key elements of its fatalistic conception of human life: it is just not God that does the determining for Schopenhauer, but rather the interaction of motive and unalterable character operating under the principle of sufficient reason (i.e. the law of cause and effect).[170]

The many resonances in Nietzsche of this Schopenhauerian view are, no doubt, apparent (see e.g. the many passages cited in Section 2). Yet Nietzsche also seems to strike some discordant notes. In several places in *Daybreak*, for example, he appears to repudiate Schopenhauer's view. For example, he writes:

One can dispose of one's drives like a gardener and, though few know it, cultivate the shoots of anger, pity, curiosity, vanity as productively and profitably as a beautiful

---

[165] WWR i, §55, 287; cf. 290, 292, 301.

[166] WWR i, §23, 113.

[167] WWR i, §55, 302.

[168] Ibid.

[169] WWR i, §55, 293.

[170] It is an interesting question—beyond the scope of this chapter, however—to what extent Schopenhauer's and Nietzsche's views were influenced by Lutheranism. For Luther's 'fatalism', see Luther, 'The Bondage of the Will', in *Luther's Works*, xxxiii: *Career of the Reformer*, ed. P. S. Watson (Philadelphia: Fortress Press, 1972), 40–1, 68–70, 176, 188–9, 194–5, 232–3. (I am grateful to Rob Koons for guidance on this subject.)

fruit tree on a trellis. . . . All this we are at liberty to do: but how many know we are at liberty to do it? Do the majority not *believe* in *themselves* as in complete *fully-developed facts*? Have the great philosophers [i.e. Schopenhauer] not put their seal on this prejudice with the doctrine of the unchangeability of character?[171]

Nietzsche voices this same theme more than once,[172] suggesting that he did not simply take over Schopenhauerian fatalism wholesale.

In fact, Schopenhauer's own view in this regard is a bit more complex. For Schopenhauer also argues that there is something called 'acquired character' which consists, essentially, in learning what one's unalterable character is really like.[173] Once we have 'acquired character', says Schopenhauer, 'we shall no longer, as novices, wait, attempt, and grope about, in order to see what we really desire and are able to do; we know this once for all, and with every choice we have only to apply general principles to particular cases, and at once reach a decision'.[174] I take Schopenhauer's idea, here, to be that once we know the facts about our character, we can (via intellect presumably) proceed in realizing our character more efficiently and effectively: to acquire character is to know our 'limits', which means we can be spared the experience of being 'often . . . driven back on to our own path by hard blows from outside',[175] when we exceed those 'limits'.

But if this is Schopenhauer's view, then it is not clear that it is really very different from Nietzsche's. For Nietzsche asks us—repeatedly in *Daybreak*— to think of ourselves as analogous to plants; and the view he opposes is simply the view that there is no work for a 'gardener' to do, whether on the roots (as in a plant) or on the drives (as in a person). Yet it appears that this is precisely Schopenhauer's view as well: the 'unalterability' of character for Schopenhauer does not, it seems, entail that there is no 'gardening' work to be done on the basic ingredients (e.g. the drives) which constitute the 'character'. As Schopenhauer writes later on, the 'will' is like 'the strong blind man carrying the sighted lame man [i.e. the intellect] on his back'.[176] This suggests, though, that there is work for the intellect to do in guiding the character—precisely what we can do when we 'acquire' character in Schopenhauer's sense. So the passages in *Daybreak* are not a repudiation of Schopenhauer's view, but a reiteration of it. We shall have to ask shortly, however, whether this modification of the doctrine can really be squared with the fatalistic picture we have seen Nietzsche—and Schopenhauer— embrace.

---

[171] D 560. [172] D 364, 382. [173] WWR i, §55, 304–5.
[174] WWR, i, §55, 305. [175] Ibid., i, §55, 304. [176] Ibid., ii, ch. 19, 209.

5. THE PARADOX RESOLVED

So far, we have only succeeded—if we have succeeded at all—in making vivid the depth of Nietzsche's fatalism, and thus in strengthening the aura of paradox about Nietzsche's work. For if, as Nietzschean fatalism holds, a person's life follows a *necessary* (i.e. causally determined) trajectory in virtue of the natural facts about a person, then in what sense can a person make an *autonomous* causal contribution to the course of that life—as Nietzsche's self-creation rhetoric would imply?

The resolution of the seeming paradox proceeds in two steps. First, we must ask more carefully about the real evidence for saying Nietzsche believed that people create themselves. Secondly, should it turn out that Nietzsche does employ 'self-creation' rhetoric, we will need to get clearer about what exactly 'creation' means for Nietzsche.

At first sight, it appears that the evidence that Nietzsche believes people create themselves is rather weak: the three passages quoted in the second paragraph of this essay[177] constitute, to my knowledge, the most explicit pieces of evidence, and, in terms of pure quantity, they are dwarfed by the fatalistic passages discussed above. Moreover, these three 'self-creation' passages are, themselves, far from being unambiguous. Nehamas, for example, notes that for Nietzsche, 'The people who "want to become those they are" are precisely "human beings who are new, unique, incomparable, who give themselves laws, who create themselves".'[178] Yet Nehamas truncates the quote precisely at the point at which it becomes troubling for his thesis that Nietzsche believes the self can be created. For Nietzsche, in the full passage, continues as follows:

To that end [of creating ourselves] we must become the best learners and discoverers of everything that is lawful and necessary in the world: we must become *physicists* in order to be able to be *creators* in this sense (*wir müssen Physiker sein, um, in jenem Sinne, Schöpfer sein zu können*)—while hitherto all valuations and ideals have been based on *ignorance* of physics. . . . Therefore: long live physics![179]

Creation 'in this sense' is, then, a very special sense indeed: for it presupposes the discovery of what is 'lawful and necessary' as revealed by physical science. The passage begins to make more sense when we recall its context: this is precisely the section, referred to earlier, in which Nietzsche claims that 'every action is unknowable', though he adds: 'our opinions, valuations, and tables of what is good certainly belong among the most powerful levers in

---

[177] GS 335, 290; TI, 'Skirmishes of an Untimely Man', 49.
[178] GS 335; Nehamas, *Nietzsche*, 174.
[179] GS 335.

the involved mechanism of our actions, but . . . in any particular case the law of their mechanism is indemonstrable (*unnachweisbar*)'. This observation leads Nietzsche immediately to the suggestion that we should create 'our own new tables of what is good', presumably with an eye to effecting the causal determination of our actions in new ways. However, we need help from science to identify the lawful patterns into which values and actions fall; even if the mechanisms are indemonstrable, science may at least reveal the patterns of value-inputs and action-outputs. So to create one's self, 'in this sense', is to accept Nietzsche's basically deterministic picture of action—as determined by subconscious causes that are hard to identify— but to use science to help identify those 'values' which figure in the causal determination of action in new, but predictable, ways.[180] If this is the right way of understanding this passage, then Nietzsche's frequent remarks else- where about 'creating' values are also evidence (as Nehamas also suggests, rightly[181]) for the claim that we may create ourselves: for values figure, caus- ally, in our actions (hence, in who we become); hence the creation of values is causally connected to the creation of ourselves.

Indeed, as I argued earlier, Nietzsche can not, it seems, sensibly hold the view that type-facts determine all aspects of a person's life, for some of what happens to a person depends on circumstances and environment, which themselves are not causally determined by type-facts. Among the factors, then, that constitute the 'circumstances' and 'environment'—and which, in turn, exert a causal influence on a person's life trajectory—are values.[182] In so far as a person creates these values, he participates in the creation of the environment which, in turn, can change the course of a person's life trajec- tory. So while type-facts may circumscribe the range of possible trajectories, it now seems that a person can 'create' his life in so far as he can create those values that (causally) determine which of the possible trajectories is in fact realized.

Yet this view, as we have seen at the end of the last section, appears to be precisely the view that both Nietzsche and Schopenhauer embrace. We can speak, for example, of the nurturing of a tomato plant as a 'creative' act, even though, of course, no amount of creative input into the process will yield an apple tree. But what we can contribute, *qua* gardener, is to shape the

---

[180] GS 290 is problematic for a somewhat different reason. Strictly, all it does is *describe* the type of person who gives style to his character; it does not suggest, or presuppose, that simply anyone *can* give such style. But a person constituted by the right type-facts could, of course, be enabled to 'give style' in the sense Nietzsche describes here.

[181] *Nietzsche*, 174.

[182] This, of course, is why Nietzsche considers it important to undertake a revaluation of values: values *do* make a causal difference.

environment in ways that will affect which of the possible trajectories—wilting, flourishing, or any of the possible stages in between—the plant will realize. So, the paradox is resolved, it seems, by simply recognizing the limited domain of creative work, while allowing for the underlying fatalism which entails only that one's possibilities are circumscribed. A place for 'self-creation' is found precisely in the conceptual space between causal essentialism (the heart of Nietzsche's fatalism) and classical determinism.

Unfortunately, this seemingly attractive solution to the paradox simply does not square with the theory of action that underlies the basic fatalistic doctrine. Recall Galen Strawson's observation that in so far as one is not a *causa sui*, then 'the particular way in which one is moved to try to change oneself . . . will be determined by how one already is'.[183] In other words, even the choice to 'create' particular values does not, in fact, satisfy the Autonomy Condition: for what values the person 'chooses' to 'create' is simply determined by the type-facts about that person—by 'how [he] already is'. So the fact that values play a causal role in a person's life trajectory only means a person can create his life *if* we can rightly speak of his having 'created' these values. But the arguments against the Autonomy Condition considered in Section 3 speak against this possibility, as much as they do against the idea of creating one's life directly (without the mediation of values). '[T]he person serves merely as the arena for these events [e.g. the "creation" of values]: he takes no active part.' This means that every time Nietzsche speaks about 'creation' it is at best a poor reflection of genuine creation; it is really a case in which only the Causal Condition, but not the Autonomy Condition, is satisfied.

Could this really be Nietzsche's view? Must we resolve the paradox, in essence, by acknowledging that by 'creation', Nietzsche really doesn't mean 'creation' in its ordinary sense? In general, such a conclusion ought not to be surprising: Nietzsche retains lots of concepts—'free will' for example[184]—in senses that are foreign to their conventional meanings. But there is an even clearer precedent for thinking that this is what happens to the concept of 'creation' in Nietzsche's work. It is to be found in a fascinating, but little-noted passage, in *Daybreak* on 'self-mastery' (*Selbst-Beherrschung*).[185] I am assuming, of course, that to speak of *mastering* oneself, just as to speak of *creating* oneself, presupposes—conventionally—that the Autonomy

---

[183] 'The Impossibility of Moral Responsibility', 7: cf. 18.

[184] See e.g. BGE 19; GM II. 2; TI, 'Skirmishes of an Untimely Man', 38.

[185] D 109. This passage, I hasten to add, is not atypical. For one thing, it squares with the theory of action already defended and documented above. But similar claims also appear in BGE 117 ('The will to overcome an affect is ultimately only the will of another, or of several, other affects') and underlie the extended discussion in GM III. 17. Note, too, that it comes from the very same work from which the earlier, seemingly anti-fatalist, passages also come.

Condition is satisfied: there must be, in ordinary parlance, an autonomous self that *does the mastering* and *does the creating*. Someone who, for example, masters his burning desire for alcohol through a medication that moderates his desire for alcohol has not, it seems, engaged in 'self-mastery': the drive has been mastered, to be sure, but it is not an autonomous *self* that did the mastering, but rather the drug.

Section 109 of *Daybreak* begins by canvassing six ways of 'combating the vehemence of a drive [or urge] (*eines Triebes*)'. What follows is Nietzsche at his most psychologically astute, as he documents six different ways of mastering a powerful urge: for example, by avoiding opportunities for gratification of the drive, thus weakening it over time; or by learning to associate painful thoughts with the drive, so that its satisfaction no longer has a positive valence.

Interesting as these observations are, the real significance of this passage lies elsewhere. For Nietzsche is also concerned here to answer the question of the 'ultimate motive' for 'self-mastery'. He explains it as follows:

that one *wants* to combat the vehemence of a drive at all, however, does not stand within our own power; nor does the choice of any particular method; nor does the success or failure of this method. What is clearly the case is that in this entire procedure our intellect is only the blind instrument of *another drive*, which is a *rival* of the drive whose vehemence is tormenting us. . . . While 'we' believe we are complaining about the vehemence of a drive, at bottom it is one drive *which is complaining about another*; that is to say: for us to become aware that we are suffering from the *vehemence* of a drive presupposes the existence of another equally vehement or even more vehement drive, and that a *struggle* is in prospect in which our intellect is going to have to take sides.

Even if the intellect must 'take sides' (*Partei nehmen*) this plainly does not mean that the intellect determines which side prevails: to the contrary, the intellect is a mere spectator upon the struggle. Thus, the fact that one masters oneself is *not* a product of autonomous choice by the person, but rather an effect of the underlying type-facts characteristic of that person: namely, which of his various drives happens to be strongest. There is, as it were, no 'self' in 'self-mastery': that is, no conscious 'self' who contributes anything to the process. 'Self-mastery' is merely an effect of the interplay of certain drives, drives over which the conscious self exercises no control (though it may, as it were, 'take sides'). David Velleman describes an account of agency in which there is, in fact, no autonomous agent as one in which 'the person merely serves as the arena for [certain] events: he takes no active part'. But I think we have now seen plainly that this is precisely Nietzsche's view. A person is an arena in which the struggle of drives is played out; how they play out determines what he believes, what he values, what he becomes. But, *qua* conscious self or 'agent', the person takes no active part in the process. Our paradox is resolved by understanding fatalism to be the dominant theme in Nietzsche's work, while his talk of 'creating' the self is merely the employment of a familiar term in an unfamiliar sense, one that actually presupposes the truth of fatalism.[186]

6. CONCLUDING REMARKS

One prominent contemporary interpreter of Nietzsche is reported to have said that he was more concerned to make Nietzsche interesting than to get him right. The consequences of such an approach are readily apparent in the Nietzsche literature. The absence, to my knowledge, of the deeply naturalistic and fatalistic Nietzsche described here is only one of many possible examples.[187] But surely the interest in 'getting Nietzsche right' is exhausted at the point that the views he *really* holds appear beyond the pale of 'reasonable' opinion. Such a worry, I fear, may have occurred to the reader of this essay. Have we really done Nietzsche any favour by showing him to believe in 'type-facts', in 'human nature', in the epiphenomenality of consciousness, in the unreality of free will, in the primacy of physiology?

My answer is unequivocally 'yes'. To recapture Nietzsche the naturalist is not only to recognize the *real*, historical Nietzsche, but to locate Nietzsche within a philosophical movement of admirable pedigree.[188] Like Hume, the great modern naturalist (whose similarities to Nietzsche have been little appreciated and discussed), Nietzsche debunks the philosophical pretension that our beliefs admit of *rational* vindications. Like Hume, Nietzsche offers in place of such failed rationalizations *explanations* for why people would hold these beliefs anyway, explanations couched in terms of a speculative theory of human nature. Like Hume, Nietzsche's speculative theory takes its cues from certain dominant scientific paradigms. Unlike Hume, Nietzsche's understanding of human nature seems both more realistic and more acute.

[186] As far as I can see, the same view should be Schopenhauer's, though he specifically disowns it. Perhaps, then, the paradox at issue here is really more dramatic in his work than in Nietzsche's.

[187] Somewhat less stringently naturalistic 'Nietzsches' are presented in Schacht, *Nietzsche* and in Ken Gemes, 'Nietzsche's Critique of Truth', Ch. 1 in this volume.

[188] The impression is, unfortunately, widespread in Nietzsche studies that the collection of sophomoric relativisms and scepticisms that go under the label 'postmodernism' is at the core of philosophy these days. But besides being bad philosophy, postmodernism is surely more of a sociological artefact of a handful of disciplines in the humanities and social sciences—philosophy largely excepted—rather than an intellectual *Zeitgeist*. As Graeme Forbes has acidly, but aptly, observed: 'It may be true that sophomoric subjectivism is running amok in some corners of the academy, but anyone to whom this represents "the wider intellectual world" is wearing very narrow blinkers indeed' (Letter to the Editor, *Lingua Franca*, 6/3 (Mar.–Apr. 1996), 79).

Nietzsche's reputation as a psychologist is well known and well deserved, but even his attempt to understand persons as fundamentally physical creatures is importantly right—in its spirit, if not its details. As one recent writer notes, 'Our culture is [currently] caught in a frenzy of biological materialism':[189] in other words, precisely the sort of *Zeitgeist* that informed Nietzsche's Germany. But whereas Nietzsche's contemporaries had generally inadequate theories of the naturalistic determinants of mind and behaviour—and thus invested too much intellectual energy on 'bile' and other false paths—we, at least, have the advantage of knowing where to look for a naturalistic understanding of persons: namely, in genetics and the neurotransmitters.[190] So even if the details of Nietzsche's naturalism are wrong, the overall project retains its scientific credibility and philosophical importance to the present day.

Notice, too, that understanding Nietzsche as naturalist does not commit us to some of the excesses characteristic of much contemporary naturalism, which envisions a world whose every feature is *reducible* to the language of physics or the machinations of computers. (Methodological naturalism, recall, does not necessarily entail a substantive view, like physicalism or the currently popular functionalism.) We can understand persons—their personalities, their values, their actions—as being *causally determined* by natural facts, while still agreeing with Nietzsche when he asks, 'Do we really want to permit existence to be degraded for us like this—reduced to a mere exercise for a calculator and an indoor diversion for mathematicians? Above all, one should not wish to divest existence of its *rich ambiguity*. . . . '[191] The naturalistic understanding of the world is surely not, as Nietzsche says, 'the only justifiable interpretation',[192] though it may very well be the one that sheds the most profound philosophical light on who we are as persons. As we have seen, this appears to be precisely Nietzsche's view. And in that respect, he was very much a philosopher of his time.

Yet, importantly, he remains a philosopher of our time as well. The 'naturalistic' turn in philosophy[193] is the most significant philosophical event of

---

[189] Peter Kramer, *Listening to Prozac* (New York, Viking, 1993), p. xiii.

[190] See e.g. many of the sources cited ibid. See also, Robert Plomin and C.S. Bergeman, 'The Nature of Nurture: Genetic Influence on "Environmental" Measures', *Behavioral and Brain Sciences*, 14 (1991), 373–427; D. T. Lykken, T. J. Bouchard Jr., M. McGue, and A. Tellegen, 'Heritability of Interests: A Twin Study', *Journal of Applied Psychology*, 78 (1993), 649–61; T. J. Bouchard Jr. *et al.*, 'Sources of Human Psychological Differences: The Minnesota Study of Twins Reared Apart', *Science*, 250 (1990), 223–8; and, for a popular account, Lawrence Wright, 'Double Mystery', *The New Yorker* (7 Aug. 1995), 45–62.

[191] GS 373.

[192] Ibid.

[193] After Rorty's 'linguistic turn'. See R. Rorty (ed.), *The Linguistic Turn* (Chicago: University of Chicago Press, 1967).

the past quarter-century. While many contemporary philosophers, committed as they are to free will and autonomous agency, are decidedly not naturalistic enough by Nietzschean lights, the philosophical climate is surely right for Nietzsche's way of addressing problems. To understand Nietzsche as a naturalist may make it possible, at last, to recognize Nietzsche as philosopher.[194]

[194] For comments on earlier drafts, I am grateful to Harvey Cormier, Kathleen Marie Higgins, Christopher Janaway, Cory Juhl, Robert C. Koons, Maurice Leiter, John Richardson, T.K. Seung, Robert C. Solomon, and Paul B. Woodruff.

12

NIETZSCHE AND GENEALOGY

RAYMOND GEUSS

In 1971 Michel Foucault published an essay on Nietzsche's conception of 'genealogy'[1] and later began to use the term 'genealogy' to describe some of his own work.[2] Foucault's writings have been remarkably influential and so it wouldn't be at all odd for someone familiar with recent developments in history and the social sciences to come to think that Nietzsche had invented a new approach to these subjects called 'genealogy', an approach then further elaborated in the work of the late Foucault. It turns out, however, to be very difficult to say exactly what this new 'genealogical' form of inquiry is and how it is distinct from other approaches (if it is). A good way to go about trying to get clarity on this issue is, I think, to look with some care at Nietzsche's original discussion of 'genealogy'.

I

Giving a 'genealogy' is for Nietzsche the exact reverse of what we might call 'tracing a pedigree'. The practice of tracing pedigrees is at least as old as the oldest Western literature. Thus Book II of the *Iliad* gives a pedigree of Agamemnon's sceptre:

> Powerful Agamemnon
> stood up holding the sceptre Hephaistos had wrought him carefully.
> Hephaistos gave it to Zeus the king, son of Kronos,
> and Zeus in turn gave it to the courier Argeiphontes,
> and lord Hermes gave it to Pelops, driver of horses,

From Raymond Geuss, 'Nietzsche and Genealogy', *European Journal of Philosophy*, 2 (1994), 275–92.

[1] M. Foucault, 'Nietzsche, la généalogie, l'histoire', in his *Hommage à Jean Hyppolite* (Paris: Presses Universitaires de France, 1971).

[2] M. Foucault, 'On the Genealogy of Ethics: An Overview of Work in Progress', in H. Dreyfus and P. Rabinow, *Michel Foucault: Beyond Structuralism and Hermeneutics*, 2nd edn. (Chicago: University of Chicago Press, 1983).

and Pelops gave it to Atreus, the shepherd of the people.
Atreus dying left it to Thyestes of the rich flocks,
and Thyestes left it in turn to Agamemnon to carry
and to be lord over many islands and over all Argos.
Leaning upon this sceptre he spoke . . .[3]

This early example exhibits the main features of what I will call a 'pedigree'. The general context is one of legitimizing or at any rate of positively valorizing some (usually contemporary) person, institution, or thing. That he has inherited such an ancestral sceptre gives Agamemnon's words an extra weight and constitutes a kind of warrant to be lord over 'Argos' and 'many islands'. The authority this sceptre gives Agamemnon—to speak anachronistically, the Greeks having notoriously had no word for 'authority'— is generally accepted by the other figures who appear in the *Iliad*. In fact that is in some sense the whole problem because, as Diomedes acidly remarks at the beginning of Book IX, although Zeus did give Agamemnon the sceptre 'he did not give you a heart, and of all power this is the greatest' (IX. 39). The only two instances we are given of explicit resistance to this authority are Achilleus and Thersites. Odysseus makes a characteristically utilitarian use of Agamemnon's sceptre to beat Thersites into submission (II. 265 ff.),[4] but Achilleus is not amenable either to the pedigree or the physical weight of the sceptre.[5]

The pedigree of the sceptre traces Agamemnon's possession of it back through a series of unbroken steps of transmission to a singular origin. For the pedigree actually to discharge its function the origin to which it recurs must be an actual source of positive value, and each of the steps in the succession must be value-preserving. So in the case of this particular pedigree it is important that one can trace the ownership of the sceptre back to Hephaistos and Zeus, the former presumably guaranteeing the quality of the workmanship, the latter the associated claim to political authority, and it is

[3] Homer, *The Iliad*, trans. Richmond Lattimore (Chicago: University of Chicago Press, 1951), book II, lines 100 ff.

[4] Note that Lattimore translates the same Greek word ('skēptron') sometimes as 'sceptre' but often as 'staff' (e.g. Homer, *Iliad*, book I, line 14; book I, line 28; book II, line 199).

[5] The treatment of Thersites in the *Iliad* is a good instance of what Nietzsche claims was a central characteristic of an aristocratic society. Thersites' criticisms of Agamemnon are virtually the same as those voiced by Achilleus (cf. *Iliad*, book II, lines 225 ff. with book I, lines 149 ff.), but whereas the Greeks (including Agamemnon) are quickly wooing Achilleus with gifts and apologies, Thersites is only beaten and laughed at (*Iliad*, book II, lines 265–77). This does seem to be a society in which the content of what is said is less important than who it is who says it.

equally important that each step in the transmission is a voluntary donation.[6]

This kind of pedigree, then, has five main characteristics:

1. In the interests of a positive valorization of some item
2. the pedigree, starting from a singular origin
3. which is an actual source of that value
4. traces an unbroken line of succession from the origin to that item
5. by a series of steps that preserve whatever value is in question.

One might think that this way of thinking (and especially characteristic 5) overlooks an important feature of pedigrees, namely that in certain cases the longer the pedigree—the further back it can be traced—the better, the greater the resultant valorization. A family that could trace its patent of nobility back to the 15th century might think that this pedigree showed it to be more noble than a family whose patent went back only to the 19th century. Two distinct thoughts run together in this. First, that what is older is better, i.e. a more genuine or more intense source of value, so that getting into contact with it is inherently desirable and it is just an accident that getting in touch with this source of value requires a large number of steps of succession. The second thought is that the increasing number of steps—the passage of time itself—enhances the prestige or value of the item in question: It isn't that the older is necessarily a better *source* of value than what is more recent, but the value increases through succession. This suggests that one should perhaps revise 5 to read:

5*. by a series of steps that preserve or enhance whatever value is in question.

---

[6] In book I Achilleus has already given a very different account of the sceptre he holds while speaking in the assembly. (Unfortunately it isn't clear whether or not this is the same one Hephaistos gave Zeus, who gave Argeiphontes . . .)

> By this sceptre which never again will bear leaf nor
> branch, now that it has left behind the cut stump in the mountains,
> nor shall it ever blossom again, since the bronze blade stripped
> bark and leafage, and now at last the sons of the Achaians
> carry it in their hand in state when they administer
> the justice of Zeus.
>
> (Homer, *Iliad*, book I, lines 234 ff.)

To say that Hephaistos 'wrought' the sceptre for Zeus presumably means that he made and inserted the gold studs or nails with which the wooden body of the sceptre was adorned—after all, Hephaistos was essentially a smith (*Iliad*, book XVIII, lines 368 ff.) not a carpenter. So Hephaistos' making of the sceptre for Zeus is perhaps not the natural origin or stopping point it may seem to be. The wood for the body of a sceptre must have come from somewhere, so perhaps there is a step in the succession before the fitting of the golden studs. The administration of the justice of Zeus requires someone to go out into the mountains to cut down an appropriate branch and strip off the bark and leafage. Cutting things down with the bronze blade, however, is just what Achilleus is good at.

'Genealogy' as practiced by Nietzsche differs from the tracing of a pedigree in all five respects. 'Genealogy' is certainly not undertaken with the intention of legitimizing any present person, practice, or institution, and won't in general have the effect of enhancing the standing of any contemporary item. As far as points 2 and 3 are concerned, genealogy doesn't characteristically discover a single origin for the object of its investigation. To take the example Nietzsche himself analyzes in greatest detail, Christian morality does not go back to a single instituting activity by a particular person or small group in ancient Palestine. The whole point of *Genealogy of Morality* is that Christian morality results from a conjunction of a number of *diverse* lines of development: the *ressentiment* of slaves directed against their masters (GM I. 1–10), a psychological connection between 'having debts' and 'suffering pain' that gets established in archaic commercial transactions (GM II. 4–6), a need people come to have to turn their aggression against themselves which results from urbanization (GM II. 16), a certain desire on the part of a priestly caste to exercise dominion over others (GM III. 16) etc.[7] The genealogy reveals Christian morality to arise from the historically contingent conjunction of a large number of such *separate* series of processes that ramify the further back one goes and present no obvious or natural single stopping place that could be designated 'the origin'.[8]

Furthermore, the further back the genealogy reaches the less likely it is to locate anything that has unequivocal, inherent 'positive' value which it could transmit 'down' the genealogical line to the present.[9] When Nietzsche writes that our world of moral concepts has an origin (*Anfang*) which 'like the origin (*Anfang*) of everything great on earth, was for a long time and thoroughly doused in blood' (GM II. 6) he is opposing the sentimental assumption that things we now value (for whatever reason) *must* have had an origin of which we would also approve.[10] Nietzsche thinks that this unquestioned assumption has tacitly guided much historiography and constitutes both an obstacle to understanding and a symptom of debility. Nietzsche, of course, is not committed to the 'world of moral concepts' that

---

[7] [Editor's note.] For abbreviations used in referring to Nietzsche's works, see Note on References above.

[8] In tracing a pedigree one is positioned, as it were, at the singular point of 'origin' and invited to look 'down' the chain of succession (from Hephaistos to Agamemnon), whereas in a genealogy one stands with Ego and looks back 'up' the lines of transmission at the seemingly unlimited and ramifying series of ancestors.

[9] At D 44 Nietzsche asserts that the closer we get to the 'origin' (*Ursprung*) of things, the less possible it is for us to evaluate what we find; our forms of evaluation simply become increasingly irrelevant. The realm of origins is the realm of radical insignificance, not of heightened meaningfulness. Oddly enough, Habermas (*Erkenntnis und Interesse* (Frankfurt am Main: Suhrkamp, 1970), 356) cites and discusses this very passage, but seems not to have recognized its implications.

[10] Cf. BGE 257.

comprises 'duty', 'guilt', 'conscience' and such things anyway, and that this world had its origins in blood and cruelty is no argument against it for him (although it might be an argument against it for those who hold the sentimental view mentioned above). Equally the violent and bloody origins of Christian morality is for Nietzsche no argument *in favour* of it.[11]

Value-preserving (or value-enhancing) transmission is perhaps a slightly more complex phenomenon than the origination of value because very different kinds of transfer might be recognized: Agamemnon's sceptre could be legitimately passed on by donation *inter vivos* or testament. However 'value-preserving transmission' is understood in a given pedigree, Nietzsche seems to go out of his way to emphasize that the history delineated in a genealogy won't generally exhibit unbroken lines of value-preserving succession, but will rather be characterized by an overwhelming contingency, and dominated by violent forms of human action based on pervasive delusions. Thus the origin of 'bad conscience' was 'not a gradual, not a voluntary transformation' nor was it 'an organic growing-over-into new conditions' but rather was 'a break, a leap, a coercion' (GM II. 17). It seems reasonable, then, to assume that a genealogy won't exhibit characteristics 4 and 5 of a pedigree.

II

I lay such great stress on the difference between tracing a pedigree and giving a genealogy because the difference seems to me often overlooked with the result that Nietzsche comes to be seen as a conscious archaizer like Ludwig Klages or Heidegger. Thus Habermas misses the distinction and ends up attributing to Nietzsche just about the exact reverse of the position he actually holds:

> Nietzsche has recourse to . . . the myth of origins . . .: the *older* is that which is *earlier* in the chain of generations, that which is nearer to the origin (*Ursprung*). The *more aboriginal* (*das Ursprünglichere*) has standing as that which ought to be more revered, that which is nobler, less corrupt, purer, in short: better. Descent (*Abstammung*) and origin (*Herkunft*) serve as the criterion of rank in both a social and a logical sense.[12]

---

[11] One might wonder whether D 44 (our forms of valuation can get less and less purchase the further back toward the 'origins' we move) is compatible with GM II. 6 (the beginnings of everything great are doused in blood). This difficulty disappears if one keeps in mind that for Nietzsche there are no absolute 'origins' or 'beginnings'; an 'origin' is a relative stopping point picked out for one or another reason, but 'behind' which there will stand a history (which one could investigate if one had some reason to do so). It is perfectly coherent to think that the period of the recent past (from three thousand to, say, five hundred years ago) was an especially nasty patch and one of particular importance for understanding how various contemporary phenomena have come to be the way they are, but also that the further back one goes the more difficult it becomes to apply our forms of valuation.

[12] J. Habermas, 'Die Verschlingung von Mythos und Aufklärung', in K.-H. Bohrer (eds.), *Mythos und Moderne* (Frankfurt am Main: Suhrkamp, 1983), 425.

Habermas is right to emphasize the importance of 'rank' and 'rank-ordering' in Nietzsche. Nietzsche is a conscious radical anti-egalitarian not just in politics[13] but also in ethics. He explicitly rejects the view that there should be one morality for everyone (BGE 198, 43, 30). In fact he even holds that it is '*immoral*' to apply the principle 'What is fair for one person, is fair for another' (BGE 221). Morality is to be subordinated to the principle of rank-ordering (BGE 221, 219, 228, 257). Habermas is wrong, however, to connect this line of argument with a purported greater nobility of that which is older or more aboriginal.

Habermas also attributes to Nietzsche a 'pragmatist theory of cognition' and a view of truth which 'reduces' it to preference.[14] I'm skeptical of this attribution; there is at any rate a clear and strong strand in Nietzsche's published works that explicitly contrasts 'what is true' and what anyone might prefer, desire or find useful. I would like now to consider some passages that exhibit this strand:

At GS 344 Nietzsche is discussing the belief he thinks constitutive of 'science', namely that truth is more important than anything else. This belief could not have arisen from a 'calculation of usefulness' because 'truth *and* untruth both continuously show themselves to be useful'.[15] If that is the case, 'usefulness' can't be the criterion by which truth is distinguished from untruth, and it becomes difficult to see how this passage would be compatible with a pragmatist theory of truth or cognition.

At BGE 39 Nietzsche claims that something might be true even though it is 'in the highest degree harmful and dangerous'; it might be a basic property of existence that full cognition of it would be fatal. I assume that the 'truth' at issue here is the metaphysical truth that human existence is at best an insignificant tissue of senseless suffering. We might not be inclined to think of this as an archetypical 'truth', but Nietzsche was.[16] Here, too, it is hard to see how one could reduce this 'truth' to any kind of preference.

At BGE 120 Nietzsche speaks of the 'philosophers of the future' (with, it

---

[13] Cf. GS 377; BGE 30, 40, 202–3, 242, 44; A 57.

[14] Habermas, 'Die Verschlingung von Mythos und Aufklärung', 421 ff.

[15] The passage actually reads: 'Whence might science then have taken its unconditional belief, its conviction, on which it rests, that truth is more important than any other thing, even than any other conviction. Precisely this conviction [i.e. that truth is more important than anything else, R.G.] could not have arisen if truth *and* untruth both had shown themselves continuously as useful, as is the case.'

[16] Nietzsche was clearly fascinated by this Romantic view that the truth about human life is literally unbearable to most humans—one finds it already in BT 3. One of the traditional functions of art for Nietzsche is to produce 'worlds of appearance' (*Schein*) which will hide the horrid truth from us and allow us to survive (cf. BT 7). The 'ascetic priest' in the third essay of GM is not only a physician and shepherd (III. 15) but also an 'artist' in feelings of guilt (III. 15): By creating an illusory 'sense' for human suffering ('You are suffering *because* you are guilty'; cf. III. 15–20) the priest seduces humans into continuing to live (III. 13).

seems to me, evident approval) and reports that they will smile if anyone says to them: 'That thought exalts me; how could it not be true?' They won't be inclined to believe that truth will be pleasing to them.

At GM I. 1 Nietzsche 'wishes' that the English psychologists who are his main opponents might be generous-spirited, courageous, and proud animals who have trained themselves 'to sacrifice all that they wish were the case to the truth'.

No one of these examples is perhaps decisive but the cumulative effect is, I think, to make one suspicious of attributing to Nietzsche any very straight-forward kind of pragmatist theory of truth or any view that directly reduces truth to mere preference. This suspicion should be reinforced by a careful reading of GM III. 24–5, where Nietzsche presents it as one of his main philosophical achievements to have called into question the value of truth (and of the will-to-truth).[17] For a pragmatist there isn't really much point in 'calling into question' the value of truth. The value of truth is obvious; after all, for the pragmatist we just *mean* by 'truth' what works, and how could that *not* have value for us?[18] Similarly if truth is just a matter of preference, the will-to-truth is unproblematic and doesn't need, one would think, any special 'justification': If 'the truth' can turn out to be something *contrary* to what I would prefer to believe, then I might ask why I should nevertheless pursue it (have a 'will-to' it) but surely I don't need some special justification to have a will-to-'what-I-prefer'. The kind of detailed and often subtle accounts Nietzsche gives of the various different ways truth (and untruth) have (or lack) values of different kinds, are pleasing to us (or not), conform to what we would wish or prefer to be the case (or not), make most sense if one assumes that Nietzsche takes truth, preference and value to be *prima facie* distinct things and does not have a philosophically reductive account which would settle the matter from the start on general grounds and make detailed investigation otiose.

From the fact that Nietzsche does not seek to 'reduce' (in the sense in which philosophers use that term) truth to preference, utility, taste etc. it does not, of course, follow that it is not of great importance to investigate the multiple way in which claims to truth are connected with various value-judgments.

Nietzsche does wish to criticize the correspondence theory of truth and the unquestioned belief in the absolute value of truth, but he does not try to

---

[17] Cf. also BGE 1.

[18] There is another version of 'pragmatism' to be found, for example in the works of Richard Rorty (cf. Rorty, *The Consequences of Pragmatism* (Minneapolis: University of Minnesota Press, 1982)) which seeks not to 'define' but dispense with a philosophical definition of truth. I adopt the view in the main text because I believe it closer to what those who attribute to Nietzsche a 'pragmatist' conception of truth (e.g. Habermas) would mean by 'pragmatism'.

substitute his own 'theory' of truth for the correspondence-theory. If one takes a basically Platonist view (to the effect that one must begin by asking and answering the question: 'What is . . . (truth)?') it will seem that there is a huge gap or blank at what ought to be the centre of Nietzsche's philosophy, and one will be strongly tempted to fill in the blank: If Nietzsche clearly attacks the correspondence view, shows no interest in coherence, and seems to present no clear alternative of his own invention, then he must tacitly hold some kind of reductivist or pragmatist view. The most fruitful way of taking Nietzsche seems to me to see him not as trying to propound his own variant theory of truth, but as formulating a new question 'How and why does the will-to-truth come about?' (and claiming that this question is more interesting than, and doesn't presuppose an antecedent answer to Plato's question 'What is truth?').

Finally it is in some sense correct, as Habermas claims, that Nietzsche wishes to 'enthrone *taste* . . . as the only organ of a "cognition" beyond true and false, good and evil'.[19] However if, as I have suggested above, the elevation of the faculty of taste is not associated with a 'reduction' of truth claims to mere claims of subjective preference, there is no reason to believe that this increased standing for taste need imply, as Habermas thinks it does, that 'contradiction and critique lose their sense'.[20] Taste may in fact be held to be more important than truth and yet it not be the case that I can reject certain statements *as untrue because* they don't appeal to me.

III

Having cleared away some of the debris blocking access to Nietzsche's texts, we can turn our attention to what he says about 'genealogy'.

Much of Nietzsche's later work is devoted to trying to give a 'genealogy' of Christianity and its associated ascetic morality, and so this genealogy of Christianity seems a reasonable place to start.

Like many other religions, 'Christianity' has a bi-partite structure: a set of antecedently existing practices, modes of behaviour, perception, and feeling which at a certain time are given an interpretation which imposes on them a meaning they did not have before[21] (GS 353). Thus in the specific case of Christianity Nietzsche distinguishes: a) a way of life or 'practice' which is

---

[19] Habermas, 'Die Verschlingung von Mythos und Aufklärung', 422.

[20] Ibid. 424.

[21] Nietzsche seems to use 'meaning' (*Bedeutung*) and 'sense' (*Sinn*) more or less interchangeably, at least in the contexts that are relevant for the discussion of 'genealogy', and so I won't try to distinguish them.

specifically associated with Jesus because he is thought to have instantiated it to a particularly high degree and in a particularly striking way, but which is in principle livable almost anywhere and at any time (A 39, WP 212)—a form of life, i.e. of instinctive practice, *not* a form of belief, which consists in the unconditional forgiveness of enemies, failure to resist evil, abstention from use of force or the moral condemnation of others, etc. (A 33, 35, 39, WP 158–63, 211–12)—from b) a particular interpretation put on that way of life (as instantiated by Jesus), i.e. a set of propositions that eventually become the content of Christian belief/faith. This interpretation is more or less 'invented' by Paul (A 42) and contains various dogmatic propositions about the existence of God, the immortality of the soul, human sinfulness and need for redemption etc. (A 39–43, WP 167–71, 175, 213). Paul did succeed in getting his reading of the 'meaning' of Jesus' life accepted but his dogmas did not fit very comfortably with the original form of practice Jesus instantiated. To be more exact, Paul's 'interpretation' represents so drastic and crude a misinterpretation of Jesus' way of life that even at a distance of 2000 years we can see that wherever the Pauline reading gets the upper hand—and it has in general *had* the upper hand for most of the period in question—it transforms 'Christianity' (as we can now call the amalgam of Jesus' form of life and Paul's interpretation of it) into what is the exact reverse of anything Jesus himself would have practiced. An essentially apolitical, pacifist, non-moralizing form of existence (cf. WP 207) is transformed into a 'Church', a hierarchically organized public institution, 'just the thing Jesus preached against' (WP 168; cf. WP 213).

Paul's interpretation of Jesus' life (which forms the core of what will eventually become 'Christian theology') is wrong in two ways. First of all it is a misunderstanding of Jesus way of life. For Paul Jesus' life and death essentially has to do with sin, guilt and redemption, but the message of Jesus life really is that there *is* no 'sin' (A 33), that the very concept of 'guilt' is 'abolished' (A 41). Second, Paul's propositional beliefs, taken by themselves (and not as a purported 'interpretation' of the meaning of Jesus' practice) are false. For Nietzsche the whole notion of 'sin' is in its origin a priestly misinterpretation of certain physiological states of debility and suffering (GM III. 16–17, III. 20) and the concept 'guilt' in the full-blown Christian sense depends on the false assumption that humans have freedom of the will and can thus decide to exercise or refrain from exercising the various powers they have (GM I. 13, D 112, BGE 18, 21, GM III. 15, 20).

Paul's hijacking of the form of life embodied by Jesus is one episode in what Nietzsche calls the 'genuine history' of Christianity (A 39), but it shows with particular clarity the bi-partite structure (of 'form of life' on the one hand and 'interpretation' on the other) which was mentioned earlier. It is important to see that Paul's (successful) attempt to take over the Christian form of life by reinterpreting it is only the first of a series of such episodes (WP 214; cf. GM II. 12–13). Each such event can be described as at the same time a new interpretation of Christianity-as-it-exists (at the given time) *and* as an attempt to take over or get mastery of that existing form of Christianity.[22] Each historically successive interpretation/*coup de main* gives the existing Christian way of life a new 'meaning'. Although Nietzsche at one point says that Paul 'annuls original Christianity' ('*das ursprüngliche Christentum*') (WP 167), this doesn't mean that Paul wishes to abolish wholesale the practices that constitute this primordial form of Christianity. Rather he wants to impress on them the stamp of a certain meaning, give them a certain direction. Nietzsche thinks that such attempts to take over/ reinterpret an existing set of practices or way of life will not in general be so fully successful that *nothing* of the original form of life remains, hence the continuing tension in post-Pauline Christianity between forms of acting, feeling, judging which still somehow eventually derive from aboriginal Christianity and Paul's theological dogmas. Equally once Paul's reading of Christian practice has given these practices a certain 'meaning' the historic- ally *next* re-interpretation will in turn find the Pauline meanings already embedded in the form of life it confronts and will be unlikely in giving a new interpretation of that form of life to be able to abolish Pauline con- cepts and interpretations altogether. Historically, then, successive layers of such 'meanings' will be, as it were, deposited (GM II. 13). There will be some gradual change in the actual practices and form of life—Pauline Chris- tianity will begin to develop a Church organization which primordial Christianity didn't have—and a rather more mercurial shift in the domi- nant 'interpretation' given to the practice, but even the dominant interpre- tation won't have been able utterly to eradicate the 'meanings' that have previously accumulated, i.e. that have been imposed upon 'Christianity' by a series of past agencies.

I write 'agencies' advisedly because although I have up to now focused on an episode in which a particular individual (Paul) reinterpreted/attempted- to-get-mastery of an existing form of life, it need not be a particular human individual (i.e. a biologically singular animal) who is the agent. According to Nietzsche, one can perfectly well speak of 'The Church' trying to get control of, and impose an interpretation on certain ways of living, feeling

---

[22] Obviously I see no reductionist implications in the claim that a certain event, such as, for example, the Protestant Reformation can be seen as at the same time an attempt to get mastery of Christian life and an attempt to reinterpret it.

and acting, such as for instance the various mendicant movements that arose at the end of the medieval period. In fact in this context Nietzsche doesn't speak of 'agencies' as I have, but of 'wills'. Nietzsche uses the term 'will' in a very flexible and expansive way to refer both to smaller and to larger entities than the will of a biologically individual human being. One can, according to Nietzsche, look at what we would normally call 'my will' as a kind of resultant of the struggle within me of various drives, impulses, and desires, and each of these can itself in some sense be called a 'will'. Similarly one can attribute a 'will' to various entities that are larger than me: The University of Cambridge can have a will, so can the UK, the European Union, etc.

The history of Christianity, then, is a history of successive attempts on the part of a variety of different 'wills' to take control of and reinterpret a complex of habits, feelings, ways of perceiving and acting, thereby imposing on this complex a 'meaning'. Although the 'meaning' imposed at any time by a successful will may in some sense be superseded by a later 'meaning' (imposed by a later will), the original meaning will in general not go out of existence altogether but will remain embedded in at least a modified form in the complex we call 'Christianity'. Part of the reason for this is that once a certain will has been able to impose its meaning on Christianity, it acquires a certain power of resistance to any further attempts on the part of *other* wills to impose their meaning on the Christian complex. Once Pauline theology has penetrated Christian practice, modified it, given it a certain direction and a particular kind of coherence, etc., any non-Pauline will which tries to impose a *new* interpretation on Christianity (as thus constituted) won't encounter, as it were, just a tabula rasa, but a set of actively structured forces, practices etc. which will be capable of active resistance to attempts to turn them into other directions, impose new functions on them etc. So each episode of 'reinterpretation' will be a struggle between a will impinging from without bent on mastery/imposition-of-a-new-meaning and a complex way of life which will resist at least by inertia and evasion and probably by more active measures.

Christianity at a given point in time will be a 'synthesis' of the various different 'meanings' imposed on it in the past and which have succeeded in remaining embedded in Christian feeling, forms of action and belief, etc. There will be nothing necessary or even particularly coherent about such a 'synthesis': What 'meanings' it will contain and how they will be related to each other will be just the result of history, and this history will be contingent in a number of ways. It will be contingent which wills encounter and try to 'interpret'/master Christianity at what times and under what circumstances, and it will be contingent how much force, energy, and success they will have in imposing their 'meaning'.[23] The history of Christianity will 'crystallize itself into a kind of unity which is difficult to dissolve, difficult to analyse, and, it must be emphasized, utterly *undefinable*' (GM II. 13).

One can't give a 'definition' of Christianity *if* one means by that an account of a purported essential meaning (or purpose or function) which is invariably characteristic of Christianity. 'Only that which has no history is definable' (GM II. 13) because anything that has a history will partake, like Christianity, in the continuing struggle between wills attempting to impose their meaning or purpose on the item in question, a struggle with constantly shifting outcomes. Instead of a 'definition' one must try to give an 'analysis' of the contingent synthesis of 'meaning' Christianity (for instance) represents. This process of disentangling the separate strands will take the form of a historical account. The reason for this seems to be that 'at an earlier stage that synthesis of "meanings" presents itself in such a way as to be more easily dissolved' (GM II. 13), the individual elements are more distinct.

The appropriate historical account is a genealogy. Starting from the present state of, say, Christianity (or of whatever else is the object of genealogical analysis), the genealogy works its way backward in time, recounting the episodes of struggle between different wills, each trying to impose its interpretation or meaning on the Christianity that existed at its time, and thereby disentangling the separate strands of meaning that have come together in a (contingent) unity in the present. Each such episode is, as it were, the branching node of a genealogical tree (see figure overleaf).

This diagram is intentionally just a sketch of Nietzsche's account, leaving out many details in order to exhibit more clearly the overall structure. At various points the branches simply end (e.g. with the 'grammatical distinction between subject and predicate' on the right toward the top) but those end-points are not absolute origins. The genealogy peters out there either because there is no more information available or because further elaboration of the genealogy at that point would lead too far afield, but in principle if information were available and there were any *reason* to continue, one could carry on with the genealogy back behind any of the points at which Nietzsche in fact stops.

This is true in particular for the end-point I have designated 'Jesus' radically non-moralizing form of life'. I said at the beginning of this discussion

---

[23] Nietzsche's view is incompatible with any 'dialectical' conception of history (at least one in the tradition of Hegel). A process can be described as 'dialectical' if it unfolds endogenously according to an inherent logic. For Nietzsche the 'wills' that come to struggle over a form of life characteristically come from *outside* that form and their encounter is contingent in that no outcome of it is more inherently 'logical' than any other. On Nietzsche as anti-dialectician, cf. G. Deleuze, *Nietzsche et la philosophie* (Paris: Presses Universitaires de France, 1962).

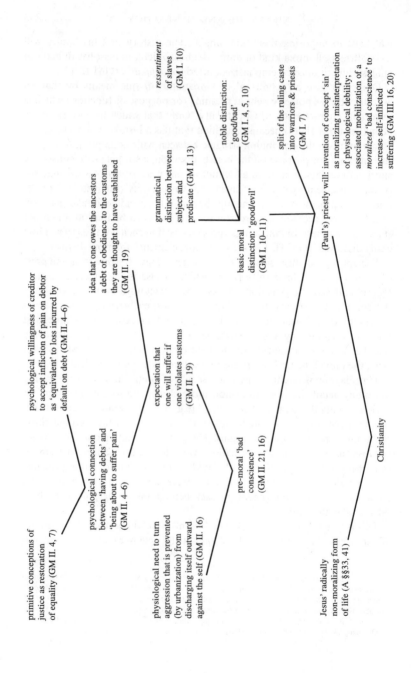

primitive conceptions of justice as restoration of equality (GM II. 4, 7)

psychological willingness of creditor to accept infliction of pain on debtor as 'equivalent' to loss incurred by default on debt (GM II. 4–6)

psychological connection between 'having debts' and 'being about to suffer pain' (GM II. 4–6)

idea that one owes the ancestors a debt of obedience to the customs they are thought to have established (GM II. 19)

ressentiment of slaves (GM I. 10)

noble distinction: 'good/bad' (GM I. 4, 5, 10)

expectation that one will suffer if one violates customs (GM II. 19)

grammatical distinction between subject and predicate (GM I. 13)

split of the ruling caste into warriors & priests (GM I. 7)

physiological need to turn aggression that is prevented (by urbanization) from discharging itself outward against the self (GM II. 16)

pre-moral 'bad conscience' (GM II. 21, 16)

basic moral distinction: 'good/evil' (GM I. 10–11)

(Paul's) priestly will: invention of concept 'sin' as moralizing misinterpretation of physiological debility; associated mobilization of a *moralized* 'bad conscience' to increase self-inflicted suffering (GM III. 16, 20)

Jesus' radically non-moralizing form of life (A §§33, 41)

Christianity

(p. 329 above) that religions for Nietzsche generally had a bipartite form: a particular way of behaving or living on the one hand and a particular interpretation of that way of living on the other. In this case, there is Jesus' way of life and Paul's interpretation of it, and only both *together* constitute what we call 'Christianity'. One might think that having thus recognized the difference between Jesus and Paul, we could now strip away the Pauline 'interpretation' and we would get back to something that was *not* thus bi-partite, not an interpretation of something, but the way of life itself, a final stopping point, an absolute origin. That one can get back to the thing itself, unvarnished and uninterpreted, is an illusion. Unless one believes in miracles, Jesus' 'practice' itself has historical antecedents which could be genealogically analyzed.[24] In addition Jesus' way of life, although it is not constituted by explicit belief in a set of propositions of the kind Paul asserts, can be itself seen as a kind of 'interpretation'. For Nietzsche, I am 'interpreting' a situation by reacting to it in a certain way. If I recoil from it, I am interpreting it as repulsive; if I draw near to it, I am taking it to be attractive; if I pass by without reacting at all, I am treating the situation as irrelevant or insignificant. This, presumably, is one of the things Nietzsche means when he claims that life itself is a process of evaluating and giving preference (BGE 9). So Jesus' form of life itself, although not characterized by explicit theological beliefs of the Pauline kind, will have the same two-part structure: It will ultimately show itself as arising from an episode in which a certain will with a certain interpretation of things tries to take over a preexisting form of living and acting (although the 'interpretation' now won't, as in the later Pauline case, be essentially a question of affirming and believing propositions, but of acting, feeling and perceiving in a certain way). I can't tell you what Nietzsche thinks this antecedently existing mode of living (which Jesus took over and reinterpreted) was, because he doesn't say, but in GM Nietzsche claims that Jesus' 'good news' of universal love was *not* the reverse of 'Jewish hatred' but grew out of it as its crowning moment (GM I. 8). It would be a mistake, I think, to interpret this as meaning that Jesus' love was not *really* love, but rather ('really') hate. It would also be a mistake to identify this transformation of hate into universal love (in the person of Jesus) with what Nietzsche calls 'the slave revolt in morality' (GM I. 7), the transformation of a valuation based on the contrast 'good/bad' into a valuation based on a contrast between 'good' and 'evil'. Paul is a central figure in the slave revolt which lies in the main line of development of modern western morality; Jesus, on the other hand, was, for Nietzsche, only very marginally

---

[24] Although I must admit that there is one passage (A 32) that might conceivably be read as incompatible with the view I present here. Nietzsche says that Jesus' 'good news' is not something he had to acquire by struggle: 'it is there, it is from the beginning . . .'

associated with the genesis of 'our' morality. *Both* arise out of the deepest
and most sublime hatred that ever was on earth, but each transforms this
hatred in a completely different direction: Paul into a form of guilt-ridden,
moralizing asceticism, and Jesus by becoming virtually a 'free spirit' *avant la
lettre*, a man incapable of negating or refuting (A 32) with no conception of
sin, guilt, or punishment (A 33). When Nietzsche sums up his campaign
against traditional morality, the formula he uses is not 'Dionysos against
Jesus' but: 'Dionysos against The Crucified' (last sentence of EH), 'The
Crucified' being of course, the name of Paul's God (Corinthians 1: 18 ff.)

IV

Alexander Nehamas is doubtless right to claim that for Nietzsche 'genealogy' is not some particular kind of method or special approach, rather it
'simply *is* history, correctly practiced'.[25] So 'Why do genealogy?' means 'Why
do history?' Nietzsche has a long early essay on the topic of the value of
history which comes to the conclusion that history, like all forms of knowledge, must be put at the service of 'life'; if thus subjected to the demands of
'life' history has genuine, if strictly limited, value. If, on the other hand,
history escapes from the 'supervision and surveillance' of 'life' and establishes itself as a scientific discipline pursued for its own sake, it becomes a
dangerous cancer which, if unchecked, can sap the vitality of the culture in
which it arises.[26]

In the *Genealogy of Morality* Nietzsche says he is trying to answer two
questions:

(1) What is the value of (our) morality? (GM, 'Preface', 3, 5, 6)
(2) What is the significance of ascetic ideals? (GM III. 1, 2, 5 etc.).

The two questions are connected for Nietzsche because our morality is an
ascetic one.

The answer to the first question is that at the moment (our) morality has
overwhelmingly negative value as a major hindrance to the enhancement of
life. The rest of the full answer to this question, though, is that in the past
(and perhaps in some special circumstances in the present, too) traditional
morality with its asceticism had the positive value of seducing inherently
weak and despairing creatures who would otherwise have been tempted to
do away with themselves into continuing to live, by giving their suffering

---

[25] A. Nehamas, *Nietzsche: Life as Literature* (Cambridge, Mass.: Harvard University Press,
1985), 246 n. 1.
[26] UM II, 'On the Use and Abuse of History'.

(which actually resulted from their own weakness) an imaginary meaning. Any meaning, though, even a fantastic metaphysical meaning based on lies and gross misapprehensions, is better than none at all (GM III. 13, 20, 28). Thus ascetic morality in the past has been a useful morality for the weak, one that allowed the maximal life-enhancement possible for *them* (given their naturally limited possibilities); it was a trick life itself used to outwit the weak and preserve itself under difficult circumstances when drastic measures were the only ones that would work.[27]

To understand the second question ('What is the significance of ascetic ideals?') and Nietzsche's answer to it, one must first recall his doctrine of 'significance' (GM II. 12–13). Things don't '*have*' significance or meaning; they are *given* it. So the question 'What is the significance of ascetic ideals?' is incomplete; the full version would have to read: 'What is the significance of ascetic ideals for . . .?' where the blank is filled in by some specification of a particular group of people or what I earlier called an 'agency'. In the third part of the *Genealogy of Morals* Nietzsche explicitly discusses this question, filling in the blank in two different ways. First: 'What is the significance of ascetic ideals for artists, philosophers, and others engaged in various creative endeavours?' The answer is that a certain asceticism is part of the natural conditions under which certain forms of creativity flourish—if one wants to paint well, one can't quite be drunk *all* the time, so some minimal forms of self-restraint can be expected to be willed by painters as preconditions of their creativity; that then will be the significance of such ideals for them (GM III. 1–9). The second form of the question is: 'What is the significance of ascetic ideals for religiously serious Christians?' The answer to this is that for Christians ascetic ideals have value in themselves—they aren't just seen as valuable because they are the natural conditions under which something *else* (for instance, creativity) will flourish. To be more exact the Christian wills ascetic ideals in order to undermine life, vitality, and the will itself; the (Christian) ascetic is a 'self-contradiction' (GM III. 13).

There is, of course, a third way to ask the question, namely 'What is the significance of ascetic ideals for Nietzsche?' That is, given Nietzsche's account of the 'meaning' of significance, how does *he* propose to get mastery of these ascetic ideals and impose upon them his own *new* function and meaning?

In one of his unpublished notes (WP 915) Nietzsche writes that he wishes to 'renaturalize asceticism' with the goal of strengthening not negating the

---

[27] The attribution of what seems to be some kind of metaphysical agency to 'life' in passages like GM III. 13 and TI, 'Morality as Counter-Nature', 5 seems to me one of Nietzsche's least inspired and most unfortunate ideas.

will. 'Strengthening the will' and 'enhancing life' seem to be more or less the same thing here, so it seems that Nietzsche's intention is to take over the traditional way of life associated with the ascetic ideal and renaturalize its asceticism in the interests of the enhancement and affirmation of life. In this context it is perhaps relevant to recall that for Nietzsche science and the will-to-truth itself are instances of the 'ascetic ideal' (GM III. 23–7, GS 344). Up to now, Nietzsche thinks, the acquisition of scientific truth has been seen as intrinsically and absolutely valuable, but this demand that we *know* as much of the truth as possible derives from a prior demand that we always *tell* the truth, never deceive others or ourselves, and this is a moral demand. It is presumably an instance of the 'ascetic ideal' because it requires that we tell the truth even when that is contrary to what we would want and what would be good for us (GM I. 1). So Nietzsche's programme of renaturalizing asceticism for the sake of enhancing life would mean, for instance, in the case of science and the pursuit of truth, taking over the various habits, modes of thinking and acting, institutions, etc. associated with science and truth-telling, detaching them from the idea that they represent any value in themselves or have any absolute standing, and transforming them in such a way that they are turned into natural conditions for the enhancement of life (and are seen to be such). The way asceticism was made to contribute concretely to the enhancement of life would then be its 'significance'.

It still isn't clear what role genealogy (or, history) can play in this process. The purpose and effect of a genealogy can't be to criticize values or valuations directly. Nietzsche asserts very clearly that nothing about the history of the emergence or development of a set of valuations could have direct bearing on its value (GS 345, WP 254)—neither can history 'support' or 'legitimize' such value-claims (as tracing a pedigree presupposes), nor can any historical account in any way undermine a form of valuation. A form of valuation has the value it has—that is, for Nietzsche, it makes the contribution it can make to enhancing or negating life—and its origin or history is a separate issue. To be sure, a genealogy *can* undermine various *beliefs* about the origins of different forms of valuation. If I have a certain form of valuation I may need to believe certain things—if I am a Christian I may need to believe certain things about the origin of Christian forms of valuation. So if those beliefs are undermined, I may feel my values undermined, too, but this is as it were *my* problem, not part of the intention of the genealogy. For Nietzsche as genealogist: '. . . the value of a prescription "Thou shalt" . . . is completely independent of . . . the opinions [people might have] about it and from the weeds of error with which it was perhaps overgrown . . .' just as the value of a medicine is independent of what the sick person *thinks* about it (GS 345).

It is a particular and idiosyncratic problem of Christianity that it culti-vates truthfulness and introspection and is a form of valuation which requires its devotees to make claims and have beliefs that won't stand up to truthful introspective scrutiny (such as that moral action arises from altru-istic sources). This means that Christianity dissolves itself (GM III. 27; GS 357) and Nietzsche's genealogy will contribute to that process. That geneal-ogy is experienced by the Christian as a form of criticism need not imply that that is how it looks from the perspective of genealogists themselves. For the Christian it may be a terrible indictment of Christianity that it requires its devotees to lie to themselves (and others). For Nietzsche it is a fact that Christianity is a tissue of lies, but this fact is of no particular evaluative significance; he has no objection to lying *per se*, but only to those forms of lying that in fact sap human vitality, turn the will against itself, denigrate life, or stunt 'the growth of the plant "man"' (BGE 44; cf. EH 'Why I am a Destiny', 7).

A genealogy of Christianity/modern morality/ascetic ideals won't *in itself* legitimize or justify Nietzsche's new positive valuation of life/will, and isn't in itself a criticism of alternative valuations. What a new form of valu-ation does, it will be recalled, is take over and reinterpret existing forms of living and acting. 'Science' in Nietzsche's wide sense of that term (which includes philology and history) is one part of our existing form of life. It has a value which is independent of its origin in the Christian ascetic ideal (because value is independent of origin, GS 345). The same is true specific-ally of the 'grey' science of history/genealogy (GM, Preface, 7), a science which makes extensive use of our 'sense for *facts*, the last and most valuable of our senses' (A 59) to discover 'what is documented, what can really be ascertained, what was really there' (GM, Preface, 7). Nietzsche's genealogy then can start from his own 'historical and philological training' (GM, Preface, 3) and has at its disposal a rich pre-existing set of sensibilities, ways of proceeding, canons of evidence, notions of what is more plausible and what less plausible (GM, Preface, 4).

Nietzsche clearly thinks he can give an historically more accurate and plausible account of the emergence and development of our Christian mor-ality from the perspective of his own new positive valuation of life than Christians themselves can from the standpoint of their own ascetic ideals. Christian truthfulness (and the apparatus of scientific history it gives rise to) will do in the Christian account of the development of our morality, leaving the field to Nietzsche's account. If Nietzsche's account is in this sense 'bet-ter' he will, he thinks, have succeeded in 'taking over' or 'gaining mastery of' a significant part of our existing form of life.

Nietzsche's genealogy of our ascetic morality doesn't yield a direct 'justification' of his positive valuation of the will and life, but the fact that he can from his perspective give a genealogy that is *more* acceptable to the grey science (on that science's own terms) than traditional accounts are, might be thought to provide a kind of indirect justification of Nietzsche's valuation. Whether or not this is the best way to think about this issue depends very much on what exactly one means by 'justification'.

Nietzsche's ability to give a genealogy of Christian morality which is historically superior to any other available certainly doesn't show that his positive valuation of life is 'true': 'Judgments, value-judgments about life, pro or contra, can in the final analysis never be true; they have value only as symptoms. . . .' (TI, 'The Problem of Socrates', 2). There are, Nietzsche thinks, no non-circular, non-contextual standards with reference to which such a value-judgment about life itself could vindicate itself. In the final analysis there is just self-affirmation (of life) or the reverse.

Nietzsche also clearly does not believe that it in any way follows from this that our whole fabric of factual discourse is simply abolished, annulled, or reduced to some kind of arbitrary play of volitions. History in the service of life can and must be *better* history than history purportedly pursued for its own sake, for the sake of the 'truth', or as an end in itself.

For Nietzsche the success of his genealogy, the fact that it is better history than alternatives, is a sign or symptom of the greater vitality of the perspective from which the genealogy was carried out. This is of great importance to Nietzsche because he judges things by the vitality they exhibit, and that the perspective which gives the highest value to life-enhancement shows itself to possess the highest vitality is for Nietzsche no tautology or triviality. It might in principle have been that a perspective devoted to the pursuit of pure science for its own sake had the greatest vitality (i.e. produced the greatest number of particular interesting hypotheses that turned out to be plausible and well-supported by the evidence, gave fruitful guidance for the organization of social life, contributed to the flourishing of the arts, etc.).

For those of us not able to adopt Nietzsche's perspective and form of valuation it would perhaps be sufficient that his genealogy gives a more plausible and well-supported account of our puzzling history than other available alternatives (if that turned out to be the case).[28]

---

[28] I have profited from helpful comments on a draft of this essay by Michael Hardimon (MIT), Michael Rosen (Lincoln College, Oxford), and Quentin Skinner (Christ's College, Cambridge).

13

NIETZSCHE, GENEALOGY, HISTORY

MICHEL FOUCAULT

I

Genealogy is gray, meticulous, and patiently documentary. It operates on a field of entangled and confused parchments, on documents that have been scratched over and recopied many times.

On this basis, it is obvious that Paul Ree[1] was wrong to follow the English tendency in describing the history of morality in terms of a linear development—in reducing its entire history and genesis to an exclusive concern for utility. He assumed that words had kept their meaning, that desires still pointed in a single direction, and that ideas retained their logic; and he ignored the fact that the world of speech and desires has known invasions, struggles, plundering, disguises, ploys. From these elements, however, genealogy retrieves an indispensable restraint: it must record the singularity of events outside of any monotonous finality; it must seek them in the most unpromising places, in what we tend to feel is without history—in sentiments, love, conscience, instincts; it must be sensitive to their recurrence, not in order to trace the gradual curve of their evolution, but to isolate the different scenes where they engaged in different roles. Finally, genealogy must define even those instances when they are absent, the moment when they remained unrealized (Plato, at Syracuse, did not become Mohammed).

Genealogy, consequently, requires patience and a knowledge of details, and it depends on a vast accumulation of source material. Its "cyclopean monuments" (GS 7) are constructed from "discreet and apparently insignificant truths and according to a rigorous method"; they cannot be the product of "large and well-meaning errors" (HH 3). In short, genealogy demands

From Michel Foucault, "Nietzsche, Genealogy, History," in P. Rabinow (ed.), *The Foucault Reader* (New York: Pantheon Books, 1984), 76–100; first pub. in D. F. Bouchard, *Language, Counter-Memory, Practice: Selected Essays and Interviews by Michel Foucault*, trans. D. F. Bouchard and S. Simon (Ithaca, NY: Cornell University Press, 1977). Used by permission of the publisher, Cornell University Press.

[1] *Ed.*: See GM, Preface, 4, 7.

relentless erudition. Genealogy does not oppose itself to history as the lofty and profound gaze of the philosopher might compare to the molelike perspective of the scholar; on the contrary, it rejects the metahistorical deployment of ideal significations and indefinite teleologies. It opposes itself to the search for "origins."

II

In Nietzsche, we find two uses of the word *Ursprung*. The first is unstressed, and it is found alternately with other terms such as *Entstehung, Herkunft, Abkunft, Geburt*. In *The Genealogy of Morals*, for example, *Entstehung* or *Ursprung* serves equally well to denote the origin of duty or guilty conscience (GM II. 6, 8); and in the discussion of logic and knowledge in *The Gay Science*, their origin is indiscriminately referred to as *Ursprung, Entstehung*, or *Herkunft* (GS 110, 111, 300).

The other use of the word is stressed. On occasion, Nietzsche places the term in opposition to another: in the first paragraph of *Human, All Too Human* the miraculous origin (*Wunderursprung*) sought by metaphysics is set against the analyses of historical philosophy, which poses questions *über Herkunft und Anfang. Ursprung* is also used in an ironic and deceptive manner. In what, for instance, do we find the original basis (*Ursprung*) of morality, a foundation sought after since Plato? "In detestable, narrow-minded conclusions. *Pudenda origo*" (D 102). Or in a related context, where should we seek the origin of religion (*Ursprung*), which Schopenhauer located in a particular metaphysical sentiment of the hereafter? It belongs, very simply, to an invention (*Erfindung*), a sleight-of-hand, an artifice (*Kunststück*), a secret formula, in the rituals of black magic, in the work of the *Schwarzkünstler*.[2]

One of the most significant texts with respect to the use of all these terms and to the variations in the use of *Ursprung* is the preface to the *Genealogy*. At the beginning of the text, its objective is defined as an examination of the origin of moral preconceptions and the term used is *Herkunft*. Then, Nietzsche proceeds by retracing his personal involvement with this question: he recalls the period when he "calligraphied" philosophy, when he questioned if God must be held responsible for the origin of evil. He now finds this question amusing and properly characterizes it as a search for *Ursprung* (he will shortly use the same term to summarize Paul Ree's activity).[3]

---

[2] GS 151, 353; also D 62; GM I. 14; TI VI. 7.
[3] Paul Ree's text was entitled *Ursprung der Moralischen Empfindungen*.

Further on, he evokes the analyses that are characteristically Nietzschean and that begin with *Human, All Too Human*. Here, he speaks of *Herkunfthypothesen*. This use of the word *Herkunft* cannot be arbitrary, since it serves to designate a number of texts, beginning with *Human, All Too Human*, which deal with the origin of morality, asceticism, justice, and punishment. And yet the word used in all these works had been *Ursprung*.[4] It would seem that at this point in the *Genealogy* Nietzsche wished to validate an opposition between *Herkunft* and *Ursprung* that did not exist ten years earlier. But immediately following the use of the two terms in a specific sense, Nietzsche reverts, in the final paragraphs of the preface, to a usage that is neutral and equivalent.[5]

Why does Nietzsche challenge the pursuit of the origin (*Ursprung*), at least on those occasions when he is truly a genealogist? First, because it is an attempt to capture the exact essence of things, their purest possibilities, and their carefully protected identities; because this search assumes the existence of immobile forms that precede the external world of accident and succession. This search is directed to "that which was already there," the image of a primordial truth fully adequate to its nature, and it necessitates the removal of every mask to ultimately disclose an original identity. However, if the genealogist refuses to extend his faith in metaphysics, if he listens to history, he finds that there is "something altogether different" behind things: not a timeless and essential secret, but the secret that they have no essence or that their essence was fabricated in a piecemeal fashion from alien forms. Examining the history of reason, he learns that it was born in an altogether "reasonable" fashion—from chance (D 123); devotion to truth and the precision of scientific methods arose from the passion of scholars, their reciprocal hatred, their fanatical and unending discussions, and their spirit of competition—the personal conflicts that slowly forged the weapons of reason (HH I. 34). Further, genealogical analysis shows that the concept of liberty is an "invention of the ruling classes" (HH III. 9) and not fundamental to man's nature or at the root of his attachment to being and truth. What is found at the historical beginning of things is not the inviolable identity of their origin; it is the dissension of other things. It is disparity.

History also teaches how to laugh at the solemnities of the origin. The lofty origin is no more than "a metaphysical extension which arises from the belief that things are most precious and essential at the moment of birth" (HH III. 3). We tend to think that this is the moment of their greatest perfection, when they emerged dazzling from the hands of a creator or in the

---

[4] In HH aphorism 92 was entitled "Ursprung der Gerechtigkeit".
[5] In the main body of GM *Ursprung* and *Herkunpt* are used interchangeably in numerous instances (GM I. 2, II. 8, 11, 12, 16, 17).

shadowless light of a first morning. The origin always precedes the Fall. It comes before the body, before the world and time; it is associated with the gods, and its story is always sung as a theogony. But historical beginnings are lowly: not in the sense of modest or discreet like the steps of a dove, but derisive and ironic, capable of undoing every infatuation. "We wished to awaken the feeling of man's sovereignty by showing his divine birth: this path is now forbidden, since a monkey stands at the entrance" (D 49). Man originated with a grimace over his future development; and Zarathustra himself is plagued by a monkey who jumps along behind him, pulling on his coattails.

The final postulate of the origin is linked to the first two in being the site of truth. From the vantage point of an absolute distance, free from the restraints of positive knowledge, the origin makes possible a field of knowledge whose function is to recover it, but always in a false recognition due to the excesses of its own speech. The origin lies at a place of inevitable loss, the point where the truth of things corresponded to a truthful discourse, the site of a fleeting articulation that discourse has obscured and finally lost. It is a new cruelty of history that compels a reversal of this relationship and the abandonment of "adolescent" quests: behind the always recent, avaricious, and measured truth, it posits the ancient proliferation of errors. It is now impossible to believe that "in the rending of the veil, truth remains truthful; we have lived long enough not to be taken in" (NCW). Truth is undoubtedly the sort of error that cannot be refuted because it was hardened into an unalterable form in the long baking process of history (GS 110, 265). Moreover, the very question of truth, the right it appropriates to refute error and oppose itself to appearance, the manner in which it developed (initially made available to the wise, then withdrawn by men of piety to an unattainable world where it was given the double role of consolation and imperative, finally rejected as a useless notion, superfluous and contradicted on all sides)—does this not form a history, the history of an error we call truth? Truth, and its original reign, has had a history within history from which we are barely emerging "in the time of the shortest shadow," when light no longer seems to flow from the depths of the sky or to arise from the first moments of the day (T1, "How the True World Finally Became a Fable").

A genealogy of values, morality, asceticism, and knowledge will never confuse itself with a quest for their "origins," will never neglect as inaccessible the vicissitudes of history. On the contrary, it will cultivate the details and accidents that accompany every beginning; it will be scrupulously attentive to their petty malice; it will await their emergence, once unmasked, as the face of the other. Wherever it is made to go, it will not be reticent—in "excavating the depths," in allowing time for these elements to escape from a labyrinth where no truth had ever detained them. The genealogist needs history to dispel the chimeras of the origin, somewhat in the manner of the pious philosopher who needs a doctor to exorcise the shadow of his soul. He must be able to recognize the events of history, its jolts, its surprises, its unsteady victories and unpalatable defeats—the basis of all beginnings, atavisms, and heredities. Similarly, he must be able to diagnose the illnesses of the body, its conditions of weakness and strength, its breakdowns and resistances, to be in a position to judge philosophical discourse. History is the concrete body of a development, with its moments of intensity, its lapses, its extended periods of feverish agitation, its fainting spells; and only a metaphysician would seek its soul in the distant ideality of the origin.

III

Entstehung and *Herkunft* are more exact than *Ursprung* in recording the true objective of genealogy; and, while they are ordinarily translated as "origin," we must attempt to reestablish their proper use.

Herkunft is the equivalent of stock or *descent*; it is the ancient affiliation to a group, sustained by the bonds of blood, tradition, or social class. The analysis of *Herkunft* often involves a consideration of race or social type.[6] But the traits it attempts to identify are not the exclusive generic characteristics of an individual, a sentiment, or an idea, which permit us to qualify them as "Greek" or "English"; rather, it seeks the subtle, singular, and subindividual marks that might possibly intersect in them to form a network that is difficult to unravel. Far from being a category of resemblance, this origin allows the sorting out of different traits: the Germans imagined that they had finally accounted for their complexity by saying they possessed a double soul; they were fooled by a simple computation, or rather, they were simply trying to master the racial disorder from which they had formed themselves (BGE 244). Where the soul pretends unification or the self fabricates a coherent identity, the genealogist sets out to study the beginning—numberless beginnings, whose faint traces and hints of color are readily seen by a historical eye. The analysis of descent permits the dissociation of the self, its recognition and displacement as an empty synthesis, in liberating a profusion of lost events.

An examination of descent also permits the discovery, under the unique aspect of a trait or a concept, of the myriad events through which—thanks to which, against which—they were formed. Genealogy does not pretend to

---

[6] For example, on race, see GS 135; BGE 200, 242, 244; GM I. 5; on social type, see GS 348–9; BGE 260.

go back in time to restore an unbroken continuity that operates beyond the dispersion of forgotten things; its duty is not to demonstrate that the past actively exists in the present, that it continues secretly to animate the present, having imposed a predetermined form on all its vicissitudes. Genealogy does not resemble the evolution of a species and does not map the destiny of a people. On the contrary, to follow the complex course of descent is to maintain passing events in their proper dispersion; it is to identify the accidents, the minute deviations—or conversely, the complete reversals—the errors, the false appraisals, and the faulty calculations that gave birth to those things that continue to exist and have value for us; it is to discover that truth or being does not lie at the root of what we know and what we are, but the exteriority of accidents (GM III. 17).[7] This is undoubtedly why every origin of morality from the moment it stops being pious—and *Herkunft* can never be—has value as a critique (TI " 'Reason' in Philosophy").

Deriving from such a source is a dangerous legacy. In numerous instances, Nietzsche associates the terms *Herkunft* and *Erbschaft*. Nevertheless, we should not be deceived into thinking that this heritage is an acquisition, a possession that grows and solidifies; rather, it is an unstable assemblage of faults, fissures, and heterogeneous layers that threaten the fragile inheritor from within or from underneath: "injustice or instability in the minds of certain men, their disorder and lack of decorum, are the final consequences of their ancestors' numberless logical inaccuracies, hasty conclusions, and superficiality" (D 247). The search for descent is not the erecting of foundations: on the contrary, it disturbs what was previously considered immobile; it fragments what was thought unified; it shows the heterogeneity of what was imagined consistent with itself. What convictions and, far more decisively, what knowledge can resist it? If a genealogical analysis of a scholar were made—of one who collects facts and carefully accounts for them—his *Herkunft* would quickly divulge the official papers of the scribe and the pleadings of the lawyer—their father (GS 348–9)—in their apparently disinterested attention, in the "pure" devotion to objectivity.

Finally, descent attaches itself to the body (GS 348–9). It inscribes itself in the nervous system, in temperament, in the digestive apparatus; it appears in faulty respiration, in improper diets, in the debilitated and prostrate bodies of those whose ancestors committed errors. Fathers have only to mistake effects for causes, believe in the reality of an "afterlife," or maintain the value of eternal truths, and the bodies of their children will suffer. Cowardice and hypocrisy, for their part, are the simple offshoots of error: not in a Socratic sense, not that evil is the result of a mistake, not because of a

---

[7] The *Abkunft* of feelings of depression.

turning away from an original truth, but because the body maintains, in life as in death, through its strength or weakness, the sanction of every truth and error, as it sustains, in an inverse manner, the origin—descent. Why did men invent the contemplative life? Why give a supreme value to this form of existence? Why maintain the absolute truth of those fictions which sustain it? "During barbarous ages . . . if the strength of an individual declined, if he felt himself tired or sick, melancholy or satiated and, as a consequence, without desire or appetite for a short time, he became relatively a better man, that is, less dangerous. His pessimistic ideas only take form as words or reflections. In this frame of mind, he either became a thinker and prophet or used his imagination to feed his superstitions" (D 42). The body—and everything that touches it: diet, climate, and soil—is the domain of the *Herkunft*. The body manifests the stigmata of past experience and also gives rise to desires, failings, and errors. These elements may join in a body where they achieve a sudden expression, but as often, their encounter is an engagement in which they efface each other, where the body becomes the pretext of their insurmountable conflict.

The body is the inscribed surface of events (traced by language and dissolved by ideas), the locus of a dissociated self (adopting the illusion of a substantial unity), and a volume in perpetual disintegration. Genealogy, as an analysis of descent, is thus situated within the articulation of the body and history. Its task is to expose a body totally imprinted by history and the process of history's destruction of the body.

IV

Entstehung designates *emergence*, the moment of arising. It stands as the principle and the singular law of an apparition. As it is wrong to search for descent in an uninterrupted continuity, we should avoid thinking of emergence as the final term of a historical development; the eye was not always intended for contemplation, and punishment has had other purposes than setting an example. These developments may appear as a culmination, but they are merely the current episodes in a series of subjugations: the eye initially responded to the requirements of hunting and warfare; and punishment has been subjected, throughout its history, to a variety of needs— revenge, excluding an aggressor, compensating a victim, creating fear. In placing present needs at the origin, the metaphysician would convince us of an obscure purpose that seeks its realization at the moment it arises. Genealogy, however, seeks to reestablish the various systems of subjection: not the anticipatory power of meaning, but the hazardous play of dominations.

Emergence is always produced through a particular stage of forces. The analysis of the *Entstehung* must delineate this interaction, the struggle these forces wage against each other or against adverse circumstances, and the attempt to avoid degeneration and regain strength by dividing these forces against themselves. It is in this sense that the emergence of a species (animal or human) and its solidification are secured "in an extended battle against conditions which are essentially and constantly unfavorable." In fact, "the species must realize itself as a species, as something—characterized by the durability, uniformity, and simplicity of its form—which can prevail in the perpetual struggle against outsiders or the uprising of those it oppresses from within." On the other hand, individual differences emerge at another stage of the relationship of forces, when the species has become victorious and when it is no longer threatened from outside. In this condition, we find a struggle "of egoisms turned against each other, each bursting forth in a splintering of forces and a general striving for the sun and for the light" (BGE 262). There are also times when force contends against itself, and not only in the intoxication of an abundance, which allows it to divide itself, but at the moment when it weakens. Force reacts against its growing lassitude and gains strength; it imposes limits, inflicts torments and mortifications; it masks these actions as a higher morality and, in exchange, regains its strength. In this manner, the ascetic ideal was born, "in the instinct of a decadent life which . . . struggles for its own existence" (GM III. 13). This also describes the movement in which the Reformation arose, precisely where the church was least corrupt (GS 148);[8] German Catholicism, in the sixteenth century, retained enough strength to turn against itself, to mortify its own body and history, and to spiritualize itself into a pure religion of conscience.

Emergence is thus the entry of forces; it is their eruption, the leap from the wings to center stage, each in its youthful strength. What Nietzsche calls the *Entstehungsherd* (GM I. 2) of the concept of goodness is not specifically the energy of the strong or the reaction of the weak, but precisely this scene where they are displayed superimposed or face-to-face. It is nothing but the space that divides them, the void through which they exchange their threatening gestures and speeches. As descent qualifies the strength or weakness of an instinct and its inscription on a body, emergence designates a place of confrontation, but not as a closed field offering the spectacle of a struggle among equals. Rather, as Nietzsche demonstrates in his analysis of good and evil, it is a "non-place," a pure distance, which indicates that the adversaries

---

[8] It is also to an anemia of the will that one must attribute the *Entstehung* of Buddhism and Christianity.

do not belong to a common space. Consequently, no one is responsible for an emergence; no one can glory in it, since it always occurs in the interstice.

In a sense, only a single drama is ever staged in this "non-place," the endlessly repeated play of dominations. The domination of certain men over others leads to the differentiation of values (BGE 260; see also GM II. 12); class domination generates the idea of liberty (HH III. 9); and the forceful appropriation of things necessary to survival and the imposition of a duration not intrinsic to them account for the origin of logic (GS 111). This relationship of domination is no more a "relationship" than the place where it occurs is a place; and, precisely for this reason, it is fixed, throughout its history, in rituals, in meticulous procedures that impose rights and obligations. It establishes marks of its power and engraves memories on things and even within bodies. It makes itself accountable for debts and gives rise to the universe of rules, which is by no means designed to temper violence, but rather to satisfy it. Following traditional beliefs, it would be false to think that total war exhausts itself in its own contradictions and ends by renouncing violence and submitting to civil laws. On the contrary, the law is a calculated and relentless pleasure, delight in the promised blood, which permits the perpetual instigation of new dominations and the staging of meticulously repeated scenes of violence. The desire for peace, the serenity of compromise, and the tacit acceptance of the law, far from representing a major moral conversion or a utilitarian calculation that gave rise to the law, are but its result and, in point of fact, its perversion: "guilt, conscience, and duty had their threshold of emergence in the right to secure obligations; and their inception, like that of any major event on earth, was saturated in blood" (GM II. 6). Humanity does not gradually progress from combat to combat until it arrives at universal reciprocity, where the rule of law finally replaces warfare; humanity installs each of its violences in a system of rules and thus proceeds from domination to domination.

The nature of these rules allows violence to be inflicted on violence and the resurgence of new forces that are sufficiently strong to dominate those in power. Rules are empty in themselves, violent and unfinalized; they are impersonal and can be bent to any purpose. The successes of history belong to those who are capable of seizing these rules, to replace those who had used them, to disguise themselves so as to pervert them, invert their meaning, and redirect them against those who had initially imposed them; controlling this complex mechanism, they will make it function so as to overcome the rulers through their own rules.

The isolation of different points of emergence does not conform to the successive configurations of an identical meaning; rather, they result from substitutions, displacements, disguised conquests, and systematic reversals.

If interpretation were the slow exposure of the meaning hidden in an origin, then only metaphysics could interpret the development of humanity. But if interpretation is the violent or surreptitious appropriation of a system of rules, which in itself has no essential meaning, in order to impose a direction, to bend it to a new will, to force its participation in a different game, and to subject it to secondary rules, then the development of humanity is a series of interpretations. The role of genealogy is to record its history: the history of morals, ideals, and metaphysical concepts, the history of the concept of liberty or of the ascetic life; as they stand for the emergence of different interpretations, they must be made to appear as events on the stage of historical process.

V

How can we define the relationship between genealogy, seen as the examination of *Herkunft* and *Entstehung*, and history in the traditional sense? We could, of course, examine Nietzsche's celebrated apostrophes against history, but we will put these aside for the moment and consider those instances when he conceives of genealogy as *wirkliche Historie*, or its more frequent characterization as historical "spirit" or "sense" (GM, Preface, 7, and I. 2; BGE 224). In fact, Nietzsche's criticism, beginning with the second of the *Untimely Meditations*, always questioned the form of history that reintroduces (and always assumes) a suprahistorical perspective: a history whose function is to compose the finally reduced diversity of time into a totality fully closed upon itself; a history that always encourages subjective recognitions and attributes a form of reconciliation to all the displacements of the past; a history whose perspective on all that precedes it implies the end of time, a completed development. The historian's history finds its support outside of time and pretends to base its judgments on an apocalyptic objectivity. This is only possible, however, because of its belief in eternal truth, the immortality of the soul, and the nature of consciousness as always identical to itself. Once the historical sense is mastered by a suprahistorical perspective, metaphysics can bend it to its own purpose, and, by aligning it to the demands of objective science, it can impose its own "Egyptianism." On the other hand, the historical sense can evade metaphysics and become a privileged instrument of genealogy if it refuses the certainty of absolutes. Given this, it corresponds to the acuity of a glance that distinguishes, separates, and disperses; that is capable of liberating divergence and marginal elements—the kind of dissociating view that is capable of decomposing itself, capable of shattering the unity of man's being through which it was thought that he could extend his sovereignty to the events of his past.

Historical meaning becomes a dimension of *wirkliche Historie* to the extent that it places within a process of development everything considered immortal in man. We believe that feelings are immutable, but every sentiment, particularly the noblest and most disinterested, has a history. We believe in the dull constancy of instinctual life and imagine that it continues to exert its force indiscriminately in the present as it did in the past. But a knowledge of history easily disintegrates this unity, depicts its wavering course, locates its moments of strength and weakness, and defines its oscillating reign. It easily seizes the slow elaboration of instincts and those movements where, in turning upon themselves, they relentlessly set about their self-destruction (GS 7). We believe, in any event, that the body obeys the exclusive laws of physiology and that it escapes the influence of history, but this too is false. The body is molded by a great many distinct regimes; it is broken down by the rhythms of work, rest, and holidays; it is poisoned by food or values, through eating habits or moral laws; it constructs resistances (GS 7). "Effective" history differs from traditional history in being without constants. Nothing in man—not even his body—is sufficiently stable to serve as the basis for self-recognition or for understanding other men. The traditional devices for constructing a comprehensive view of history and for retracing the past as a patient and continuous development must be systematically dismantled. Necessarily, we must dismiss those tendencies that encourage the consoling play of recognitions. Knowledge, even under the banner of history, does not depend on "rediscovery," and it emphatically excludes the "rediscovery of ourselves." History becomes "effective" to the degree that it introduces discontinuity into our very being—as it divides our emotions, dramatizes our instincts, multiplies our body and sets it against itself. "Effective" history deprives the self of the reassuring stability of life and nature, and it will not permit itself to be transported by a voiceless obstinacy toward a millennial ending. It will uproot its traditional foundations and relentlessly disrupt its pretended continuity. This is because knowledge is not made for understanding; it is made for cutting.

From these observations, we can grasp the particular traits of historical meaning as Nietzsche understood it—the sense which opposes *wirkliche Historie* to traditional history. The former transposes the relationship ordinarily established between the eruption of an event and necessary continuity. An entire historical tradition (theological or rationalistic) aims at dissolving the singular event into an ideal continuity—as a teleological movement or a natural process. "Effective" history, however, deals with events in terms of their most unique characteristics, their most acute manifestations. An event, consequently, is not a decision, a treaty, a reign, or a battle, but the reversal of a relationship of forces, the usurpation of power, the appropriation of a vocabulary turned against those who had once used it, a feeble domination that poisons itself as it grows lax, the entry of a masked "other." The forces operating in history are not controlled by destiny or regulative mechanisms, but respond to haphazard conflicts (GM II. 12). They do not manifest the successive forms of a primordial intention and their attraction is not that of a conclusion, for they always appear through the singular randomness of events. The inverse of the Christian world, spun entirely by a divine spider, and different from the world of the Greeks, divided between the realm of will and the great cosmic folly, the world of effective history knows only one kingdom, without providence or final cause, where there is only "the iron hand of necessity shaking the dice-box of chance" (D 130). Chance is not simply the drawing of lots, but raising the stakes in every attempt to master chance through the will to power, and giving rise to the risk of an even greater chance (GM II. 12). The world we know is not this ultimately simple configuration where events are reduced to accentuate their essential traits, their final meaning, or their initial and final value. On the contrary, it is a profusion of entangled events. If it appears as a "marvelous motley, profound and totally meaningful," this is because it began and continues its secret existence through a "host of errors and phantasms" (HH I. 16). We want historians to confirm our belief that the present rests upon profound intentions and immutable necessities. But the true historical sense confirms our existence among countless lost events, without a landmark or a point of reference.

Effective history can also invert the relationship that traditional history, in its dependence on metaphysics, establishes between proximity and distance. The latter is given to a contemplation of distances and heights: the noblest periods, the highest forms, the most abstract ideas, the purest individualities. It accomplishes this by getting as near as possible, placing itself at the foot of its mountain peaks, at the risk of adopting the famous perspective of frogs. Effective history, on the other hand, shortens its vision to those things nearest to it—the body, the nervous system, nutrition, digestion, and energies; it unearths the periods of decadence, and if it chances upon lofty epochs, it is with the suspicion—not vindictive but joyous—of finding a barbarous and shameful confusion. It has no fear of looking down, so long as it is understood that it looks from above and descends to seize the various perspectives, to disclose dispersions and differences, to leave things undisturbed in their own dimension and intensity. It reverses the surreptitious practice of historians, their pretension to examine things furthest from themselves, the groveling manner in which they approach this promising distance (like the metaphysicians who proclaim the existence of an afterlife,

situated at a distance from this world, as a promise of their reward). Effective history studies what is closest, but in an abrupt dispossession, so as to
seize it at a distance (an approach similar to that of a doctor who looks
closely, who plunges to make a diagnosis and to state its difference). Historical sense has more in common with medicine than philosophy; and it should
not surprise us that Nietzsche occasionally employs the phrase "historically
and physiologically" (TI 44) since among the philosopher's idiosyncracies is
a complete denial of the body. This includes, as well, "the absence of historical sense, a hatred for the idea of development, Egyptianism," the obstinate
"placing of conclusions at the beginning," of "making last things first" (TI,
"'Reason' in Philosophy", 1, 4). History has a more important task than to
be a handmaiden to philosophy, to recount the necessary birth of truth and
values; it should become a differential knowledge of energies and failings,
heights and degenerations, poisons and antidotes. Its task is to become a
curative science (HH III. 188).

The final trait of effective history is its affirmation of knowledge as perspective. Historians take unusual pains to erase the elements in their work
which reveal their grounding in a particular time and place, their preferences
in a controversy—the unavoidable obstacles of their passion. Nietzsche's
version of historical sense is explicit in its perspective and acknowledges its
system of injustice. Its perception is slanted, being a deliberate appraisal,
affirmation, or negation; it reaches the lingering and poisonous traces in
order to prescribe the best antidote. It is not given to a discreet effacement
before the objects it observes and does not submit itself to their processes;
nor does it seek laws, since it gives equal weight to its own sight and to
its objects. Through this historical sense, knowledge is allowed to create its
own genealogy in the act of cognition; and *wirkliche Historie* composes a
genealogy of history as the vertical projection of its position.

VI

In this context, Nietzsche links historical sense to the historian's history.
They share a beginning that is similarly impure and confused, share the same
sign in which the symptoms of sickness can be recognized as well as the seed
of an exquisite flower (GS 337). They arose simultaneously to follow their
separate ways, but our task is to trace their common genealogy.

The descent (*Herkunft*) of the historian is unequivocal: he is of humble
birth. A characteristic of history is to be without choice: it encourages thorough understanding and excludes qualitative judgments—a sensitivity to all
things without distinction, a comprehensive view excluding differences.

Nothing must escape it and, more importantly, nothing must be excluded. Historians argue that this proves their tact and discretion. After all, what right have they to impose their tastes and preferences when they seek to determine what actually occurred in the past? Their mistake is to exhibit a total lack of taste, the kind of crudeness that becomes smug in the presence of the loftiest elements and finds satisfaction in reducing them to size. The historian is insensitive to the most disgusting things; or rather, he especially enjoys those things that should be repugnant to him. His apparent serenity follows from his concerted avoidance of the exceptional and his reduction of all things to the lowest common denominator. Nothing is allowed to stand above him; and underlying his desire for total knowledge is his search for the secrets that belittle everything: "base curiosity." What is the source of history? It comes from the plebs. To whom is it addressed? To the plebs. And its discourse strongly resembles the demagogue's refrain: "No one is greater than you and anyone who presumes to get the better of you—you who are good—is evil." The historian, who functions as his double, can be heard to echo: "No past is greater than your present, and, through my meticulous erudition, I will rid you of your infatuations and transform the grandeur of history into pettiness, evil, and misfortune." The historian's ancestry goes back to Socrates.

This demagoguery, of course, must be masked. It must hide its singular malice under the cloak of universals. As the demagogue is obliged to invoke truth, laws of essences, and eternal necessity, the historian must invoke objectivity, the accuracy of facts, and the permanence of the past. The demagogue denies the body to secure the sovereignty of a timeless idea, and the historian effaces his proper individuality so that others may enter the stage and reclaim their own speech. He is divided against himself: forced to silence his preferences and overcome his distaste, to blur his own perspective and replace it with the fiction of a universal geometry, to mimic death in order to enter the kingdom of the dead, to adopt a faceless anonymity. In this world where he has conquered his individual will, he becomes a guide to the inevitable law of a superior will. Having curbed the demands of his individual will in his knowledge, he will disclose the form of an eternal will in his object of study. The objectivity of historians inverts the relationships of will and knowledge and it is, in the same stroke, a necessary belief in providence, in final causes and teleology—the beliefs that place the historian in the family of ascetics. "I can't stand these lustful eunuchs of history, all the seductions of an ascetic ideal; I can't stand these blanched tombs producing life or those tired and indifferent beings who dress up in the part of wisdom and adopt an objective point of view" (GM III. 26).

The *Entstehung* of history is found in nineteenth-century Europe: the land of interminglings and bastardy, the period of the "man-of-mixture." We have become barbarians with respect to those rare moments of high civilization: cities in ruin and enigmatic monuments are spread out before us; we stop before gaping walls; we ask what gods inhabited these empty temples. Great epochs lacked this curiosity, lacked our excessive deference; they ignored their predecessors: the classical period ignored Shakespeare. The decadence of Europe presents an immense spectacle (while stronger periods refrained from such exhibitions), and the nature of this scene is to represent a theater; lacking monuments of our own making, which properly belong to us, we live among crowded scenes. But there is more. Europeans no longer know themselves; they ignore their mixed ancestries and seek a proper role. They lack individuality. We can begin to understand the spontaneous historical bent of the nineteenth century: the anemia of its forces and those mixtures that effaced all its individual traits produced the same results as the mortifications of asceticism; its inability to create, its absence of artistic works, and its need to rely on past achievements forced it to adopt the base curiosity of plebs.

If this fully represents the genealogy of history, how could it become, in its own right, a genealogical analysis? Why did it not continue as a form of demogogic or religious knowledge? How could it change roles on the same stage? Only by being seized, dominated, and turned against its birth. And it is this movement which properly describes the specific nature of the *Entstehung*: it is not the unavoidable conclusion of a long preparation, but a scene where forces are risked in the chance of confrontations, where they emerge triumphant, where they can also be confiscated. The locus of emergence for metaphysics was surely Athenian demogoguery, the vulgar spite of Socrates and his belief in immortality, and Plato could have seized this Socratic philosophy to turn it against itself. Undoubtedly, he was often tempted to do so, but his defeat lies in its consecration. The problem was similar in the nineteenth century: to avoid doing for the popular asceticism of historians what Plato did for Socrates. This historical trait should not be founded on a philosophy of history, but dismantled, beginning with the things it produced; it is necessary to master history so as to turn it to genealogical uses, that is, strictly anti-Platonic purposes. Only then will the historical sense free itself from the demands of a suprahistorical history.

VII

The historical sense gives rise to three uses that oppose and correspond to the three Platonic modalities of history. The first is parodic, directed against reality, and opposes the theme of history as reminiscence or recognition; the second is dissociative, directed against identity, and opposes history given as continuity or representative of a tradition; the third is sacrificial, directed against truth, and opposes history as knowledge. They imply a use of history that severs its connection to memory, its metaphysical and anthropological model, and constructs a countermemory—a transformation of history into a totally different form of time.

First, the parodic and farcical use. The historian offers this confused and anonymous European, who no longer knows himself or what name he should adopt, the possibility of alternative identities, more individualized and substantial than his own. But the man with historical sense will see that this substitution is simply a disguise. Historians supplied the Revolution with Roman prototypes, romanticism with knight's armor, and the Wagnerian era was given the sword of a German hero—ephemeral props that point to our own unreality. No one kept them from venerating these religions, from going to Bayreuth to commemorate a new afterlife; they were free, as well, to be transformed into street vendors of empty identities. The new historian, the genealogist, will know what to make of this masquerade. He will not be too serious to enjoy it; on the contrary, he will push the masquerade to its limit and prepare the great carnival of time where masks are constantly reappearing. No longer the identification of our faint individuality with the solid identities of the past, but our "unrealization" through the excessive choice of identities—Frederick of Hohenstaufen, Caesar, Jesus, Dionysus, and possibly Zarathustra. Taking up these masks, revitalizing the buffoonery of history, we adopt an identity whose unreality surpasses that of God, who started the charade. "Perhaps, we can discover a realm where originality is again possible as parodists of history and buffoons of God" (BGE 223). In this, we recognize the parodic double of what the second of the *Untimely Meditations* called "monumental history": a history given to reestablishing the high points of historical development and their maintenance in a perpetual presence, given to the recovery of works, actions, and creations through the monogram of their personal essence. But in 1874, Nietzsche accused this history, one totally devoted to veneration, of barring access to the actual intensities and creations of life. The parody of his last texts serves to emphasize that "monumental history" is itself a parody. Genealogy is history in the form of a concerted carnival.

The second use of history is the systematic dissociation of identity. This is necessary because this rather weak identity, which we attempt to support and to unify under a mask, is in itself only a parody: it is plural; countless spirits dispute its possession; numerous systems intersect and compete. The study of history makes one "happy, unlike the metaphysicians, to possess in oneself not an immortal soul but many mortal ones" (HH II. 17). And in each of these souls, history will not discover a forgotten identity, eager to be reborn, but a complex system of distinct and multiple elements, unable to be mastered by the powers of synthesis: "it is a sign of superior culture to maintain, in a fully conscious way, certain phases of its evolution which lesser men pass through without thought. The initial result is that we can understand those who resemble us as completely determined systems and as representative of diverse cultures, that is to say, as necessary and capable of modification. And in return, we are able to separate the phases of our own evolution and consider them individually" (HH I. 274). The purpose of history, guided by genealogy, is not to discover the roots of our identity, but to commit itself to its dissipation. It does not seek to define our unique threshold of emergence, the homeland to which metaphysicians promise a return; it seeks to make visible all of those discontinuities that cross us. "Antiquarian history," according to the *Untimely Meditations*, pursues opposite goals. It seeks the continuities of soil, language, and urban life in which our present is rooted, and, "by cultivating in a delicate manner that which existed for all time, it tries to conserve for posterity the conditions under which we were born" (UM II. 3). This type of history was objected to in the *Meditations* because it tended to block creativity in support of the laws of fidelity. Somewhat later—and already in *Human, All Too Human*—Nietzsche reconsiders the task of the antiquarian, but with an altogether different emphasis. If genealogy in its own right gives rise to questions concerning our native land, native language, or the laws that govern us, its intention is to reveal the heterogeneous systems which, masked by the self, inhibit the formation of any form of identity.

The third use of history is the sacrifice of the subject of knowledge. In appearance, or rather, according to the mask it bears, historical consciousness is neutral, devoid of passions, and committed solely to truth. But if it examines itself and if, more generally, it interrogates the various forms of scientific consciousness in its history, it finds that all these forms and transformations are aspects of the will to knowledge: instinct, passion, the inquisitor's devotion, cruel subtlety, and malice. It discovers the violence of a position that sides against those who are happy in their ignorance, against the effective illusions by which humanity protects itself, a position that encourages the dangers of research and delights in disturbing discoveries (D 429, 432; GS 333; BGE 229–30). The historical analysis of this rancorous will to knowledge reveals that all knowledge rests upon injustice (that there is no right, not even in the act of knowing, to truth or a foundation for truth) and that the instinct for knowledge is malicious (something murderous, opposed to the happiness of mankind). Even in the greatly expanded form it assumes today, the will to knowledge does not achieve a universal truth; man is not given an exact and serene mastery of nature. On the contrary, it ceaselessly multiplies the risks, creates dangers in every area; it breaks down illusory defenses; it dissolves the unity of the subject; it releases those elements of itself that are devoted to its subversion and destruction. Knowledge does not slowly detach itself from its empirical roots, the initial needs from which it arose, to become pure speculation subject only to the demands of reason; its development is not tied to the constitution and affirmation of a free subject; rather, it creates a progressive enslavement to its instinctive violence. Where religions once demanded the sacrifice of bodies, knowledge now calls for experimentation on ourselves (D 501), calls us to the sacrifice of the subject of knowledge. "The desire for knowledge has been transformed among us into a passion which fears no sacrifice, which fears nothing but its own extinction. It may be that mankind will eventually perish from this passion for knowledge. If not through passion, then through weakness. We must be prepared to state our choice: do we wish humanity to end in fire and light or to end on the sands?" (D 501). We should now replace the two great problems of nineteenth-century philosophy, passed on by Fichte and Hegel (the reciprocal basis of truth and liberty and the possibility of absolute knowledge), with the theme that "to perish through absolute knowledge may well form a part of the basis of being" (BGE 39). This does not mean, in terms of a critical procedure, that the will to truth is limited by the intrinsic finitude of cognition, but that it loses all sense of limitations and all claim to truth in its unavoidable sacrifice of the subject of knowledge. "It may be that there remains one prodigious idea which might be made to prevail over every other aspiration, which might overcome the most victorious: the idea of humanity sacrificing itself. It seems indisputable that if this new constellation appeared on the horizon, only the desire for truth, with its enormous prerogatives, could direct and sustain such a sacrifice. For to knowledge, no sacrifice is too great. Of course, this problem has never been posed" (D 45).

The *Untimely Meditations* discussed the critical use of history: its just treatment of the past, its decisive cutting of the roots, its rejection of traditional attitudes of reverence, its liberation of man by presenting him with other origins than those in which he prefers to see himself. Nietzsche, however, reproached critical history for detaching us from every real source and for sacrificing the very movement of life to the exclusive concern for truth. Somewhat later, as we have seen, Nietzsche reconsiders this line of thought he had at first refused, but directs it to altogether different ends. It is no longer a question of judging the past in the name of a truth that only we can possess in the present, but of risking the destruction of the subject who seeks knowledge in the endless deployment of the will to knowledge.

In a sense, genealogy returns to the three modalities of history that Nietzsche recognized in 1874. It returns to them in spite of the objections that Nietzsche raised in the name of the affirmative and creative powers of life. But they are metamorphosed: the veneration of monuments becomes parody; the respect for ancient continuities becomes systematic dissociation; the critique of the injustices of the past by a truth held by men in the present becomes the destruction of the man who maintains knowledge by the injustice proper to the will to knowledge.

NOTES ON THE CONTRIBUTORS

MAUDEMARIE CLARK is George C. Carleton Jr. Professor of Philosophy at Colgate University in New York. She is the author of *Nietzsche on Truth and Philosophy* (1990), co-editor of Nietzsche's *Daybreak* (1997), and co-editor and translator of Nietzsche's *On the Genealogy of Morality* (1998).

PHILIPPA FOOT is Griffin Professor of Philosophy Emerita at the University of California, Los Angeles, and Fellow of Somerville College, Oxford. Many of her seminal papers in moral philosophy are collected in *Virtues and Vices* (1978).

MICHEL FOUCAULT (1926–84) held the Chair in the History of Systems of Thought at the Collège de France from 1969 until his death. Among his many important and influential works are *Folie et déraison: histoire de la folie à l'âge classique* (1961; trans. as *Madness and Civilization*, 1965), *Naissance de la clinique: une archéologie du régard médical* (1963; trans. as *The Birth of the Clinic*, 1973), *Les Mots et les choses: une archéologie des sciences humaines* (1966; trans. as *The Order of Things*, 1970), *L'Archéologie du savoir* (1969; trans. as *The Archaeology of Knowledge*, 1972), and *Surveiller et punir: naissance de la prison* (1975; trans. as *Discipline and Punish*, 1977).

KEN GEMES is Anniversary Lecturer in Philosophy at Birkbeck College, University of London. He has published many papers on topics in the philosophy of science, as well as on Nietzsche.

RAYMOND GEUSS is University Lecturer in Philosophy at Cambridge University. He is the author of *The Idea of a Critical Theory* (1981) and *Morality, History, and Culture* (1999), and co-editor of Nietzsche's *The Birth of Tragedy* (1999).

BRIAN LEITER is Charles I. Francis Professor of Law and Philosophy at the University of Texas at Austin. He is co-editor of Nietzsche's *Daybreak* (1997), editor of *Objectivity in Law and Morals* (2001), and author of *Nietzsche on Morality* (2002).

ALEXANDER NEHAMAS is Edmund N. Carpenter II Professor of Humanities and Professor of Comparative Literature and Philosophy at Princeton University. He is the author of *Nietzsche: Life as Literature* (1985), *The Art of Living: Socratic Reflections from Plato to Foucault* (1998), and *Virtues of*

Authenticity: Essays on Plato and Socrates (1998). He has also edited or translated several books in ancient Greek philosophy.

PETER POELLNER is Lecturer in Philosophy at the University of Warwick. He is the author of *Nietzsche and Metaphysics* (1995).

JOHN RICHARDSON is Professor of Philosophy at New York University. He is the author of *Existential Epistemology: A Heideggerian Critique of the Cartesian Project* (1986) and *Nietzsche's System* (1996).

RICHARD L. SCHACHT is Jubilee Professor of Liberal Arts and Professor of Philosophy at the University of Illinois at Urbana-Champaign. He is the author of *Alienation* (1970), *Hegel and After* (1975), *Nietzsche* (1983), *The Future of Alienation* (1994), and *Making Sense of Nietzsche* (1995). He has also edited many books, including *Nietzsche, Genealogy, Morality* (1994) and *Nietzsche's Postmoralism* (2001).

SELECTED BIBLIOGRAPHY

I. GENERAL BOOKS ON NIETZSCHE'S PHILOSOPHY

CLARK, MAUDEMARIE, *Nietzsche on Truth and Philosophy* (Cambridge: Cambridge University Press, 1990).

DELEUZE, GILLES, *Nietzsche and Philosophy*, trans. H. Tomlinson (New York: Columbia University Press, 1982). Orig. pub. 1962.

LEITER, BRIAN, *Nietzsche on Morality* (London: Routledge, 2002).

MORGAN, GEORGE, JR., *What Nietzsche Means* (Cambridge, Mass.: Harvard University Press, 1941).

NEHAMAS, ALEXANDER, *Nietzsche: Life as Literature* (Cambridge, Mass.: Harvard University Press, 1985).

POELLNER, PETER, *Nietzsche and Metaphysics* (Oxford: Clarendon Press, 1995).

RICHARDSON, JOHN, *Nietzsche's System* (Oxford: Oxford University Press, 1996).

SCHACHT, RICHARD, *Nietzsche* (London: Routledge & Kegan Paul, 1983).

II. TRUTH, PERSPECTIVISM, AND EPISTEMOLOGY

ANDERSON, R. LANIER, "Truth and Objectivity in Perspectivism," *Synthèse* 115 (1998), 1–32.

ATWELL, JOHN E., "Nietzsche's Perspectivism," *Southern Journal of Philosophy* 19 (1981), 157–170.

BITTNER, RÜDIGER, "Nietzsches Begriff der Wahrheit," *Nietzsche-Studien* 16 (1987), 70–90.

BREAZEALE, DANIEL, "Introduction," to D. Breazeale (ed.), *Philosophy and Truth: Selections from Nietzsche's Notebooks of the Early 1870s* (Atlantic Highlands, N.J.: Humanities Press, 1990). Orig. pub. 1979.

CLARK, MAUDEMARIE, "On Knowledge, Truth and Value: Nietzsche's Debt to Schopenhauer and the Development of His Empiricism," in C. Janaway (ed.), *Willing and Nothingness: Schopenhauer as Nietzsche's Educator* (Oxford: Clarendon Press, 1998).

COKER, JOHN C., "Construing Perspectivism," *International Studies in Philosophy* 34/3 (forthcoming 2002).

GERHARDT, VOLKER, "Die Perspektive des Perspektivismus," *Nietzsche-Studien* 18 (1989), 260–281.

HALES, STEVEN D. and REX WELSHON, *Nietzsche's Perspectivism* (Urbana: University of Illinois Press, 2000).

LEITER, BRIAN, "Perspectivism in Nietzsche's *Genealogy of Morals*," in R. Schacht (ed.), *Nietzsche, Genealogy, Morality* (Berkeley: University of California Press, 1994).

NOLA, ROBERT, "Nietzsche's Theory of Truth and Belief," *Philosophy & Phenomenological Research* 47 (1987), 525–562.

REGINSTER, BERNARD, "Perspectivism, Criticism, and Freedom of Spirit," *European Journal of Philosophy* 8 (2000), 40–62.

SCHACHT, RICHARD, "Nietzsche and Nihilism," repr. in R. C. Solomon (ed.),

Nietzsche: A Collection of Critical Essays (South Bend: University of Notre Dame Press, 1980). Orig. pub. 1973.

WESTPHAL, KENNETH, "Was Nietzsche a Cognitivist?" *Journal of the History of Philosophy* 22 (1984), 343–363.

—— "Nietzsche's Sting and the Possibility of Good Philology," *International Studies in Philosophy* 16/3 (1984), 71–90.

WILCOX, JOHN T., "Nietzsche Scholarship and 'the Correspondence Theory of Truth': the Danto Case," *Nietzsche-Studien* 15 (1986), 337–357.

III. ETHICS, METAETHICS, AND MORAL PSYCHOLOGY

BERGMANN, FRITHJOF, "Nietzsche's Critique of Morality," in R. C. Solomon & K. M. Higgins (eds.), *Reading Nietzsche* (New York: Oxford University Press, 1988).

BITTNER, RÜDIGER, "*Ressentiment*," in R. Schacht (ed.), *Nietzsche, Genealogy, Morality* (Berkeley: University of California Press, 1994).

CLARK, MAUDEMARIE, "Nietzsche's Immoralism and the Concept of Morality," in *Nietzsche, Genealogy, Morality, op. cit.*

—— "On the Rejection of Morality: Bernard Williams's Debt to Nietzsche," in R. Schacht (ed.), *Nietzsche's Postmoralism: Essays on Nietzsche's Prelude to Philosophy's Future* (Cambridge: Cambridge University Press, 2001).

CLARK, MAUDEMARIE and BRIAN LEITER, "Introduction," in M. Clark & B. Leiter (eds.), Friedrich Nietzsche, *Daybreak: Thoughts on the Prejudices of Morality*, trans. R. J. Hollingdale (Cambridge: Cambridge University Press, 1997).

GEUSS, RAYMOND, "Nietzsche and Morality," *European Journal of Philosophy* 5 (1997),1–20.

HUNT, LESTER, *Nietzsche and the Origin of Virtue* (London: Routledge, 1991).

—— "The Eternal Recurrence and Nietzsche's Ethic of Virtue," *International Studies in Philosophy* 25/3 (1993), 3–11.

LEITER, BRIAN, "Beyond Good and Evil," *History of Philosophy Quarterly* 10 (1993), 261–270.

—— "Morality in the Pejorative Sense: On the Logic of Nietzsche's Critique of Morality," *British Journal for the History of Philosophy* 3 (1995), 113–145.

—— "Nietzsche's Metaethics: Against the Privilege Readings," *European Journal of Philosophy* 8 (2000), 277–297.

MAY, SIMON, *Nietzsche's Ethics and his "War on Morality"* (Oxford: Clarendon Press, 1999).

MIGOTTI, MARK, "Slave Morality, Socrates, and the Bushmen: A Reading of the First Essay of *On the Genealogy of Morals*," *Philosophy & Phenomenological Research* 58 (1998), 745–779.

REGINSTER, BERNARD, "Nietzsche on *Ressentiment* and Valuation," *Philosophy & Phenomenological Research* 57 (1997), 281–305.

RISSE, MATHIAS, "The Second Treatise in *On the Genealogy of Morality*: Nietzsche on the Origin of Bad Conscience," *European Journal of Philosophy* 9 (forthcoming 2001).

WILCOX, JOHN T., *Truth and Value in Nietzsche: A Study of His Metaethics and Epistemology* (Ann Arbor: University of Michigan Press, 1974).

WILLIAMS, BERNARD, "Nietzsche's Minimalist Moral Psychology," *European Journal of Philosophy* 1 (1993), 4–14.

IV. POLITICAL PHILOSOPHY

BROBJER, THOMAS H., "The Absence of Political Ideals in Nietzsche's Writings: The Case of the Law of Manu and the Associated Caste Society," *Nietzsche-Studien* 27 (1998), 300–318.

DETWILER, BRUCE, *Nietzsche and the Politics of Aristocratic Radicalism* (Chicago: University of Chicago Press, 1990).

HUNT, LESTER, "Politics and Anti-Politics: Nietzsche's View of the State," *History of Philosophy Quarterly* 2 (1985), 453–468.

THIELE, LESLIE PAUL, *Friedrich Nietzsche and the Politics of the Soul: A Study of Heroic Individualism* (Princeton: Princeton University Press, 1990).

V. AESTHETICS

BENJAMIN, WALTER, *The Origin of German Tragic Drama*, trans. J. Osborne (London: New Left Books, 1977).

GEUSS, RAYMOND, "Introduction," in R. Geuss & R. Speirs (eds.), Friedrich Nietzsche, *The Birth of Tragedy and Other Writings*, trans. R. Speirs (Cambridge: ambridge University Press, 1999).

HIGGINS, KATHLEEN MARIE, "Nietzsche on Music," *Journal of the History of Ideas* 47 (1986), 663–672.

SCHACHT, RICHARD, "Nietzsche's Second Thoughts About Art," *The Monist* 64 (1982), 231–246.

SILK, M. S. and J. P. STERN, *Nietzsche on Tragedy* (Cambridge: Cambridge University Press, 1981).

SOLL, IVAN, "Schopenhauer, Nietzsche, and the Redemption of Life Through Art," in C. Janaway (ed.), *Willing and Nothingness: Schopenhauer as Nietzsche's Educator* (Oxford: Clarendon Press, 1998).

WHITMAN, JAMES, "Nietzsche in the Magisterial Tradition of German Classical Philology," *Journal of the History of Ideas* 47 (1986), 453–468.

YOUNG, JULIAN, *Nietzsche's Philosophy of Art* (Cambridge: Cambridge University Press, 1992).

VI. ETERNAL RECURRENCE

MAGNUS, BERND, *Nietzsche's Existential Imperative* (Bloomington: Indiana University Press, 1978).

SMALL, ROBIN, "Boscovich Contra Nietzsche," *Philosophy & Phenomenological Research* 46 (1986), 419–435.

SOLL, IVAN, "Reflections on Recurrence: A Re-Examination of Nietzsche's Doctrine, *die Ewige Wiederkehr des Gleichen*," in R. C. Solomon (ed.), *Nietzsche: A Collection of Critical Essays* (South Bend: University of Notre Dame Press, 1980). Orig. pub. 1973.

VII. WILL TO POWER

ANDERSON, R. LANIER, "Nietzsche's Will to Power as a Doctrine of the Unity of Science," *Studies in the History and Philosophy of Science* 25 (1994), 729–750.

CLARK, MAUDEMARIE, "Nietzsche's Doctrine of the Will to Power: Neither Ontological Nor Biological," *International Studies in Philosophy* 32/3 (2000), 119–135.

KAUFMANN, WALTER, "The Discovery of the Will to Power," in R. C. Solomon (ed.), *Nietzsche: A Collection of Critical Essays* (South Bend: University of Notre Dame Press, 1980). Orig. pub. 1973.

MÜLLER-LAUTER, WOLFGANG, "Nietzsches Lehre vom Willen zur Macht," *Nietzsche-Studien* 3 (1974), 1–60.

RICHARDSON, JOHN, "Clark on Will to Power," *International Studies in Philosophy* 32/3 (2000), 107–117.

—— "Nietzsche contra Darwin," *Philosophy & Phenomenological Research* (forthcoming).

VIII. GENEALOGY AND PHILOSOPHICAL METHODOLOGY

BEAM, CRAIG, "Hume and Nietzsche: Naturalists, Ethicists, Anti-Christians," *Hume Studies* 22 (1996), 299–324.

COX, CHRISTOPH, *Nietzsche: Naturalism and Interpretation* (Berkeley: University of California Press, 1998).

HIGGINS, KATHLEEN MARIE, "Nietzsche and Postmodern Subjectivity," in C. Koelb (ed.), *Nietzsche as Postmodernist: Essays Pro and Contra* (Albany: SUNY Press, 1990).

HOY, DAVID C., "Nietzsche, Hume, and the Genealogical Method," in R. Schacht (ed.), *Nietzsche, Genealogy, Morality* (Berkeley: University of California Press, 1994).

LEITER, BRIAN, "Nietzsche and Aestheticism," *Journal of the History of Philosophy* 30 (1992), 275–290.

—— "One Health, One Earth, One Sun: Nietzsche's Respect for Natural Science," *Times Literary Supplement* (Oct. 2, 1998), 30–31.

NEHAMAS, ALEXANDER, "Nietzsche, Modernity, Aestheticism," in B. Magnus & K. M. Higgins (eds.), *The Cambridge Companion to Nietzsche* (Cambridge: Cambridge University Press, 1996).

SCHACHT, RICHARD, "Nietzsche's *Gay Science*, Or, How to Naturalize Cheerfully," in R. C. Solomon & K. M. Higgins (eds.), *Reading Nietzsche* (New York: Oxford University Press, 1988).

IX. PHILOLOGICAL ISSUES

MAGNUS, BERND, "The Use and Abuse of *The Will to Power*," in R.C. Solomon & K. M. Higgins (eds.), *Reading Nietzsche* (New York: Oxford University Press, 1988).

MONTINARI, MAZZINO, *Nietzsche Lesen* (Berlin: de Gruyter, 1982).

SCHACHT, RICHARD, "Nietzsche as Colleague," *International Studies in Philosophy* 22/3 (1990), 59–66.

THATCHER, DAVID S., "*Zur Genealogie der Moral*: Some Textual Annotations," *Nietzsche-Studien* 18 (1989), 587–599.

X. BIOGRAPHIES

HAYMAN, RONALD, *Nietzsche: A Critical Life* (New York: Penguin, 1990).

JANZ, CURT P., *Friedrich Nietzsche: Biographie*, 3 volumes (Munich: Hanser, 1978).

INDEX OF NAMES

NOTE: Page numbers in **bold** refer to main sections by the commentator.

INDEX LOCORUM

BY JOEL MANN

OTHER WRITINGS BY NIETZSCHE

Grossoktavausgabe (Leipzig: Naumann, 1901).

'Philosophy in the Tragic Age of the Greeks' (PTAG)

Sämtliche Werke. Kritische Studienausgabe in 15 Bänden. (KSA)

10. 7 [77]   155
10. 7 [94]   178
11. 40 [54]   8
12. 7 [21]   21
12. 7 [48]   172

Sämtliche Werke in Zwölf Bänden, ed.
Alfred Bäumler (Stuttgart: Alfred
Kröner Verlag 1965). (SW)

X. 378   52

Werke. Kritische Gesamtausgabe.
(KGW)

V. 1. 10 [D82]   91
VII. 1. 4 [221]   115
VII. 3. 40 [53]   86
VIII. 1. 2 [77]   102
VIII. 1. 5 [10]   92
VIII. 1. 5 [12]   90, 94
VIII. 1. 5 [19]   99, 102, 106
VIII. 3. 34 [246]   89